**Fiona McConnell** is Lecturer in Human Geography and Tutorial Fellow at St Catherine's College, Oxford University. Her research interests include the everyday construction of statehood and sovereignty in cases of tenuous territoriality.

**Nick Megoran** is Lecturer in Political Geography, Newcastle University. He researches the geographies and geopolitics of post-Cold War interstate relations, especially the building of nation-states in Central Asia and the place of religion and the church in war and peace.

**Philippa Williams** is Lecturer in Human Geography, School of Geography, Queen Mary University of London. She is interested in questions of violence and non-violence, citizenship, marginalization, and the politics of development in South Asia.

# GEOGRAPHIES
## OF PEACE

Edited by
Fiona McConnell, Nick Megoran
and Philippa Williams

I.B. TAURIS
LONDON · NEW YORK

Published in 2014 by I.B.Tauris & Co Ltd
6 Salem Road, London W2 4BU
175 Fifth Avenue, New York NY 10010
www.ibtauris.com

Distributed in the United States and Canada Exclusively by Palgrave Macmillan
175 Fifth Avenue, New York NY 10010

ISBN:  978 1 78076 143 5
eISBN: 978 0 85773 492 1

A full CIP record for this book is available from the British Library
A full CIP record is available from the Library of Congress

Library of Congress Catalog Card Number: available

Typeset by Newgen Publishers, Chennai
Printed and bound by CPI Group (UK) Ltd, Croydon, CR0 4YY

*To Tenzin Tsundue, for passing on a well-travelled copy of* Hind Swaraj *and embodying non-violent activism.*

FM

*To Alan Kreider, Cathy Nobles, and Lynn Green, of the Reconciliation Walk, for teaching me how to think, do and pray peace.*

NM

*For Alexander*

PW

# Contents

# Contributors

**Ilan Alleson** is Research Associate, Centre for Voluntary Sector Studies, Ryerson University. He recently completed a PhD in the Dalla Lana School of Public Health Sciences at the University of Toronto. Email: ilan_alleson@utoronto.ca

**Simon Dalby** is CIGI Chair of the Political Economy of Climate Change at the Balsillie School of International Affairs, Waterloo, Canada. Email: sdalby@gmail.com

**Patricia Daley** is Lecturer in Human Geography, School of Geography and the Environment, Oxford University, and Tutorial Fellow at Jesus College Oxford. She teaches and researches on Africa; especially on gender-based violence, forced migration, humanitarianism and peace. She is currently writing a book entitled *Identity, Citizenship and Displacement in Eastern Africa*. Email: patricia.daley@geog.ox.ac.uk

**Jonathan Darling** is Lecturer in Human Geography, University of Manchester. His research focuses on the spatial politics of asylum and sanctuary, the role of ethics within geography, and the politics of everyday life within urban environments. He has written on issues of hospitality and asylum politics, sanctuary movements and practices and relational theories of responsibility, and is currently involved in developing a critical and prosaic approach to ideas and practices of sanctuary within the city. Email: jonathan.darling@manchester.ac.uk

**John Donaldson** is a geographer and international boundary expert. He was Senior Research Associate, International Boundaries Research Unit, Department of Geography, Durham University from 2003 to 2012, where he advised on the resolution of boundary disputes worldwide. His published research has covered river boundaries and the work of boundary commissions, particularly in Africa. He now lives and works in Auckland, New Zealand. Email: j.w.donaldson12@gmail.com

**Sara Koopman** is a Canadian Social Sciences and Humanities Research Council Postdoctoral Fellow based at Wilfrid Laurier University, Canada, and is engaged in ongoing research in Bogotá, Colombia. She is a long-time international solidarity activist, and is interested in how people from the global North can, and do, use various privileges to support efforts to improve lives in the global South, be that through development, humanitarianism, peacebuilding, or international solidarity work. She is also interested in fostering ways in which those working for change in the global North can learn from various sorts of organizing projects in the global South. She blogs at: decolonizingsolidarity. blogspot.ca. Email: sara.koopman@gmail.com

**Nicole Laliberte** is a doctoral student in the departments of Geography and Women's Studies, Pennsylvania State University. Her work explores the geopolitics of human rights, processes of militarization, and the politics of everyday life in so-called 'post-conflict' landscapes. She has taught and undertaken research in eastern and southern Africa and is currently working on her dissertation, entitled 'Embodied Geopolitics: Rescaling Rights and Responsibilities in Northern Uganda'. Email: njl148@psu.edu

**Fiona McConnell** is Lecturer in Human Geography and Tutorial Fellow at St Catherine's College, Oxford University. Her research looks at issues of sovereignty, legitimacy and state practices and she has a particular interest in the everyday construction of statehood and sovereignty in cases of tenuous territoriality. Her focus has been on exile politics and the Tibetan community in India and she has ongoing interests in the diplomacy of unrecognized states, peace and political marginality. Email: fiona.mcconnell@stcatz.ox.ac.uk

**Nick Megoran** is Lecturer in Political Geography, Newcastle University, England. He works on the political geographies of the post-Cold War world, and is particularly interested in traditions of geopolitical thought, nationalism in Central Asia, and Christianity and peace/war. Email: nick.megoran@ncl.ac.uk

**Oliver Richmond** is Research Professor at the Humanitarian and Conflict Response Institute (HCRI) and Department of Politics at the University of Manchester. He is also International Professor at the School of International Studies, Kyung Hee University, Korea. His publications include *A Post-Liberal Peace* (Routledge, 2011), *Liberal Peace Transitions* (with Jason Franks, Edinburgh University Press, 2009),

*Peace in IR* (Routledge, 2008) and *The Transformation of Peace* (Palgrave Macmillan, 2005–7). He is editor of the Palgrave book series, *Rethinking Conflict Studies*, and editor of the journal *Peacebuilding*. Email: Oliver. richmond@manchester.ac.uk

**Stuart Schoenfeld** is Chair of the Department of Sociology, Glendon College, York University, Toronto. He has published a series of articles on environmentalism and peacebuilding in the eastern Mediterranean, is the editor of *Palestinian and Israeli Environmental Narratives* and co-edits, with Itay Greenspan, the blog Environment and Climate in the Middle East: mideastenvironment.apps01.yorku.ca. Email: schoenfe@yorku.ca

**Lia Dong Shimada** is implementing the diversity strategy for the Methodist Church in Britain, and also serves as a community mediator in East London. She was awarded a PhD in geography from University College London in 2010. While conducting research on racism, paramilitarism and peacebuilding in Belfast, she worked as a Project Officer for a community regeneration charity called Groundwork Northern Ireland. Email: lshimada@alum.wellesley.edu

**Galya Sipos-Randor** is currently studying to be a registered midwife. She lives with her family in Guelph, Canada. At the Arava Institute her eyes were opened to the complex realities of the Middle East through respectful dialogue, creative conflict resolution and courageous cross-cultural cooperation. Galya is honoured to be a part of this project. Email: crossingthedivide@gmail.com

**Osama Suleiman** is a sustainability researcher and advisor at Sustainability Excellence, where he has worked on numerous projects in the region to assess sustainability at the sectoral and the organizational level. Prior to working in the field of sustainability, Osama had been with an NGO, working on transboundary projects that utilize environmental issues as a bridge to bring people at conflict in the Middle East to work together. Email: osa_suliman@yahoo.com

**Philippa Williams** is Lecturer in Human Geography, School of Geography, Queen Mary University of London. Her research spans political, developmental and economic geography, and concerns everyday life in south Asia. She has published material on citizenship practices, state–society relations, Hindu–Muslim relations in the context of violence and nonviolence, urban politics and India's Muslims. Email: p.williams@qmul.ac.uk

**Asaf Zohar** is Associate Professor and currently Founding Chair of the Masters in Sustainability Studies Program at Trent University, Ontario, Canada. He plays a leadership role in promoting and integrating sustainability into both undergraduate and graduate studies at Trent. His teaching focuses on sustainable strategic management and corporate social responsibility, in which social and environmental issues are taken as the strategic domain for economic value creation. Email: azohar@trentu.ca

# Acknowledgements

The editors are extremely grateful to David Stonestreet at I.B.Tauris for supporting this project and patiently seeing it through to publication. To all our authors we thank you for your insightful contributions, as well as your energy and patience in redrafting your chapters. The thinking for this volume has evolved through both informal discussions over the years as well as more formal academic encounters at the 2011 annual conferences of the Royal Geographical Society–Institute for British Geographers and the Association of American Geographers, and at the Newcastle 'Peace in Geography and Politics' workshop in the same year. These events have enabled us to engage with, and benefit from, the ideas of not only the authors represented here, but also of others, including Paul Routledge, Helen Wilson, Gill Valentine, Hartmut Behr, Kevin Mason and Kerry Burton. Our heartfelt thanks must extend to Colin Flint for his careful reading of earlier drafts (of the introduction and conclusion) and for his constructive feedback. Finally, as editors we have been hugely influenced by the arguments of Oliver Richmond about peace, and we are much obliged that he agreed to write the foreword.

# Foreword

*Oliver P. Richmond*

In most, if not all, disciplines there has long been a debate about whether knowledge should follow power and interest – whether this be for a good life, trade, national interest, or for humanity at large. Or should power follow knowledge as a means of providing global and local justice and emancipation? There is a fine line, if not a grey area, between both approaches to knowledge production and the interaction of peace and power. Students and scholars of peace appear to be the minority in most disciplines, and yet historically most disciplines have seen some notable examples of people who have both been famous for their formal scientific work as well as for their intellectual writings and public advocacy on peace matters (Erasmus, Kant, Gandhi, John Maynard Keynes, Albert Einstein, Bertrand Russell, and many others spring to mind). Formidable minds have turned towards the consideration of the problem of peace, along a variety of paths (more recently, in politics and international relations, development students, anthropology and philosophy, among others), producing a body of work that is often widely ignored in mainstream academia and policymaking. Yet this body of knowledge is broadly consistent in its evolution, assertions and potential. This is across time, space and culture, and disciplines. This volume, well executed and elegantly reasoned, follows in this fine, and often pioneering, tradition, which suggests multiple forms of peace, multiple dimensions, a broad range of issues and dynamics and fluidity, as well as the need for contextual and international understandings of legitimacy and authority.

The issue of space from a political perspective has long influenced world order and the exercise of power in its various forms. Space and scale, politics, order, agency, peace and power are intricately related. As with so many disciplines, geography has historically, it seems (despite some notable exceptions), followed power and its interests in the past as a 'master's tool': confirming hierarchy, bounded territories and sovereignty in its classical form (Koopman, Chapter 6). As in other disciplines, there has rarely been a consideration of, or commitment to, peace. Yet, geography has influenced more critical understandings of power, peace and order, and indeed has influenced my own work, too.[2] This critical collection of chapters interrogates such epistemic, historic–spatial power relations in order to uncover the 'eirenist' potential of geography in a range of ways: situated, transversal and transnational agency, in terms of emancipation, empathy, culture and the everyday, and via an epistemic repositioning of the 'geographies of peace'. Rich and incisive, these chapters offer a number of different significant perspectives – from critical geopolitics, peaceful geographies, cultural geographies, boundaries, emotions, agency, grass-roots activism and resistance, to contingencies, the everyday and the local/urban/ rural, the positionality of the subject in the face of hegemony, coexistence, empathy and migration. It draws on a range of sites: from Central Africa to Colombia, Tibet, Northern Ireland, India, the Middle East and ... Sheffield.

As with much critical work this volume collectively considers how the rights and needs of an ever wider population – a global constituency rather than a state or Western or northern community – have become an accepted basis for thinking about world order in a contemporary, postcolonial and increasingly unsettled world. And yet dominant understandings of both rights and needs are infused with power, and especially the positionality of the global North/West. The parochialism and selfishness of perspectives that hark back to the era of imperialism, 'trusteeship' and Westphalian forms of sovereignty, have become more clearly apparent in a world where the subaltern has begun to speak[3] and new centres of power, authority and legitimacy have appeared (or reappeared).

Cognizant of these significant ripples in established order and thought, the mobility of the current era requires new ways of thinking about geography and peace (Megoran, Chapter 11). Similarly, the thinness of the universalism, legitimacy and capacity of the liberal peace argument has become obvious to most of its post-conflict or conflict subjects, as have the failures of global capital in the world's conflict and developmental spaces. As Donaldson points out, peace is both contextual and embedded in power relations (Chapter 5), and so represents a constant reworking of agency, space, boundaries, resources, norms, identity, empathy and autonomy, as attested to by the other chapters also. Peace, if it is to be worth its name, is a complex and fluid balance. Anything else is a masquerade of interests, power and luck, and no basis for a sustainable order that history will regard kindly. The static nature of the current state, its sovereignty, and indeed the international system, attest to a conservativism loaded with both past injustices and new possibilities. Often overlooked in debates about peace is the potential of 'local agency' and in particular the persistence of everyday forms of peace even in extremely difficult contexts (as in north India and as explained by Philippa Williams, Chapter 10). Yet, it must also be recognized that such everyday attempts to develop peace are also embedded in relations with violence: so many small attempts add up to significant peace agency, however (Darling, Chapter 12).

Consequently, a 'local turn' with all of its problems and possibilities has begun to infuse dominant knowledge systems (sometimes instrumentally, and sometimes more genuinely), which attempt to reach beyond the romanticized views of local agency in peacemaking (which have historically implied that peace agency is locally absent, unobtainable, produced by 'noble savages', or can only be found locally).[4] Commensurately, the framework of 'peaceful geographies' offers a fresh conceptual perspective on both space and violence (as Laliberte points out in Chapter 3). They offer a variety of possibilities for the rearticulation of peace, in a number of ways, including the varied cultural contexts and local agencies of peace (as in Tibet: McConnell, Chapter 7). These shift the mode of analysis away from assumptions of the natural status of Western epistemologies of peace, and both problematize its assumptions and foreground a range of different ontologies, ways of viewing politics and groundings for peace.

This critical turn has so far been part anthropological, part sociological and directed at IR and political science, where most of the work on peace has recently been carried out.[5] But this is limited to uncovering everyday patterns, and so far fails to place these into a broader framework of power relations and scale (Introduction, p. 16). With this volume's contribution, its authors and their perceptive chapters engage with another missing link that has been returned to the debate and to the discourse on peace. Indeed, in some ways, putting geography at the heart of peace, and vice versa, is a homecoming. Another dimension of contextual/transnational and transversal legitimacy is within reach in a fluid, mobile world of a multitude of political struggles. Society and space, politics and power, identity, rights, equality and security are so intimately related that to speak of one without the other is to exercise discursive power in a structural or governmental framework which automatically introduces a futile separateness between the various essential components of an ecology of peace (i.e. the complex relations between and within all human societies, their environment and institutions).

It is important for the epistemological frameworks that are developed around peace to represent more widely its different ontological roots and contexts, or contested narratives of peace, as termed by the editors of this volume. The historically subaltern voice is now engaged more fully in the reconstruction of peace (the 'quiet successes' are still quiet and still successful), for which critical frameworks from geography are also necessary, partly to show how space/time and politics interact in a material and discursive manner. There can be no substantive conception of everyday peace, nor of emancipation, without this input. Neither can there be, as the editors point out in the introduction, a commitment to the study of peace without an awareness of the discursive agency that goes along with it. What is absolutely crucial is that the hegemonic power of the liberal peace and the oblique ways it has endorsed the status quo, militarism, patriarchy and inequality, is challenged fundamentally, with an eirenist goal (Daley, Chapter 4), which is exactly the approach this volume takes.

What emerges very strongly across the chapters of this volume of chapters is how important spatial practices are for the interpretation of peace: what looks like peacemaking from one position and scale is much more problematic from other perspectives – historical, institutional, state, spatial, political and economic, social, everyday, cultural and so on. This suggests the need for a far more diverse consideration of the dimensions of peace. With this volume, geography is more fully returned, as with other disciplines recently, to an *eirenist modus operandi* rather than as gathered within a framework that provides support for war, interests, domination, or instrumentalization (Introduction, p. 17). A 'pacific geopolitics' as suggested by Megoran makes this clear. We should not forget that peace and politics are intricately related, that peace may be the point of politics, and that no peace is devoid of its politics.

This volume provides another disciplinary perspective on the complex local, transnational, and transversal architectures of peace, the breadth of the issues they must engage with, and the authority and legitimacy they would need to amass. It reminds us of the key principles of many subaltern knowledge systems (for example, Ubuntu) writ large across a range of disciplines: empathy, reciprocity, inclusivity, cooperation and a shared destiny (Daley, Chapter 4). It also reminds us how easily they are ignored and coopted by elites and internationals: and therefore it emphasises the important epistemic function of academic work on peace. Increasingly across critical and interdisciplinary work, the project of a peace between states is being displaced or modified by a peace between peoples across geographies. This means it needs to be everyday, emancipatory, empathetic, involving justice and redistribution, as well as culture and identity, in a transversal and transnational, mobile, fluid and contingent but also local world, where the outmoded former geographic fixity of sovereignty and hierarchies of power can no longer be maintained. Such insights are a credit to the critical tradition of peace, and to this volume's authors and editors, and offer significant advances that we would all do well to consider across disciplines.

# Notes

1. Doreen Massey, *Space, Place, and Gender*, Cambridge University Press, 1994.
2. G. C. Spivak, 'Can the Subaltern Speak?', in C. Nelson and L. Grossberg (eds), *Marxism and the Interpretation of Culture*, Palgrave Macmillan, 1988, pp. 271–313.
3. Oliver P. Richmond, *A Post-Liberal Peace*, Routledge, 2011.
4. Oliver P. Richmond, *Peace in International Relations*, Routledge, 2008.

# Introduction: geographical approaches to peace

*Philippa Williams, Nick Megoran and Fiona McConnell*

## Why peace? Why now?

From handshakes on the White House lawn to Picasso's iconic dove of peace, from anti-war protests to religious devotees praying for peace, the images and stereotypes of peace are powerful, widespread and easily recognizable. Yet trying to offer a concise definition of peace is an altogether more complicated exercise. Not only is peace an emotive and value-laden concept, but it is also abstract, ambiguous and seemingly inextricably tied to its antithesis: war. And it is war and violence that have been so compellingly deconstructed and critiqued within critical geography in recent years. This volume is an attempt to redress that balance, and to think more expansively and critically about what 'peace' means and what 'geographies of peace' may entail.

In a 2000 retrospective, John Agnew faulted Robert Sack's 1986 groundbreaking text, *Human Territoriality*, for 'understat[ing] the violence' that occurs when people divide up the world between them.[1] David Delaney later criticized the same book for being 'rather bloodless'.[2] These statements echoed Kenneth Hewitt's 1983 lament that geographers have 'given almost no treatment' to war.[3] Three decades of scholarship have gone some considerable way to addressing these concerns by re-inserting blood, war and violence firmly into the geographical corpus. Studies of militarism, fear, geopolitics, security, biopolitics and the multiple technologies and techniques of conducting modern warfare abound across much of human geography. Geographical accounts of power can no longer be said to be 'bloodless'.

As geographers who believe that the discipline has a moral imperative to understand and contest the ways in which war is waged and violence is legitimized, we welcome this shift. However, we share a dissatisfaction with this literature. Whilst doing the important task of challenging the moral logic of war, it has failed to develop equally sophisticated theoretical engagements with, and devote sustained empirical research to, peace.

This book is a call for a re-balancing: to insist that we also pay careful attention to peace in order to conceptualize it as more than the absence or aftermath of war. The aim of the book is thus twofold. It is primarily to place peace on the agenda of a broad range of academic geographers. But its secondary aim is to demonstrate the utility of geographical analysis to an interdisciplinary community of scholars who study peace.

This is not to romanticize 'peace'. Far from it. In this book, we emphasize the importance of problematizing and conceptualizing what we mean by peace: seeing it as process not an endpoint; exploring how actors make peace in certain ways and in certain places; and stressing how practices of peace are embedded in power relations. Peace can be a yearning for a radically new and just social order, or a mechanism employed by the powerful to resist exactly such change. Peace might arise through the conscious or unconscious actions of both powerful geopolitical actors and everyday folk.

The timing of this book reflects both changing developments in global geopolitics, and a mushrooming of interest in the topic of peace amongst geographers.[4] As we are writing, NATO is preparing for a withdrawal from Afghanistan, indicating that the high point of the US–UK's so-called 'global war on terror' appears to be over, and there seems to be a shift – in rhetoric at least – from the dominance of 'war cultures' to granting more visibility to 'peace cultures'. In 2011 Philippa and Fiona in the journal *Antipode* and Nick in *Political Geography* wrote – completely independently – remarkably similar interventions making the points outlined above.[5] We received both warm receptions from people who found our arguments resonated with their own concerns, and critical engagements from scholars representing a range of perspectives who disagreed on various points. Whether for or against, the volume of interest generated persuaded us of the utility of putting together this collection to advance these discussions in dialogue with a range of colleagues from different corners of the discipline. This book is intended to take stock of this emerging field and to advance the debates that it raises.

That said, ideas do not assume importance outside of life pathways and the reasons for us coming together to edit this book at this time are also autobiographical. Philippa first approached the question of peace through her research in north India on everyday Hindu and Muslim relations. Whilst the daily reality she had witnessed more aptly resembled 'everyday peace', the plethora of literature about Indian society overwhelmingly focused on the history of violence between these two religious communities. It was clear from her research that peace was not some unproblematic, utopian endpoint – so what was it, and how might peace be interpreted? Likewise, Fiona did not start out with the aim of researching issues of peace. Rather, her work with the exile Tibetan community in India focused primarily around questions of governance and the state-like practices of the Tibetan Government-in-Exile. However, the topics of both nonviolence as a political strategy, and resistance to stereotypes of Tibetans as innately pacifist, frequently arose in her discussions with refugees and exile officials. This led her to explore how Tibetan articulations of peace have evolved and to question the relationship between violence and nonviolence in this cultural context.

Similarly, 'peace' was not a topic of Nick's research on either the life of the Danish minority of northern Germany or the place of the Uzbek minority in newly independent Kyrgyzstan. In point of fact, he explicitly refused to frame his work in terms of conflict/peace, preferring a more cultural approach. However, as the condition of the former group improved and that of the latter deteriorated, the question of what 'peace' meant in these contrasting contexts became harder to avoid. Following the 9/11 attacks and the UK–US invasions of Afghanistan and Iraq, Nick became increasingly involved in the anti-war movement in Cambridge (where we all met at that time), and also began to research very different British Christian responses to these new geopolitical scenarios. This research proved personally transformative by introducing him to the Christian peace tradition within theology. Despite his earlier efforts, 'peace' therefore became impossible to ignore as a common theme in these research interests. Thus none of us began our research careers setting out to research 'peace'. Finding that our work increasingly obliged us to think about peace, we were all disappointed to find that the geographical literature served us poorly here, and we looked to other disciplines for illumination and inspiration – chiefly international relations theory, anthropology, peace studies and theology. This book is the product of those journeys: an attempt to translate what we discovered elsewhere into a disciplinary narrative for geography.

The remainder of this introduction is structured as follows. We begin with a brief examination of critical approaches to peace in other disciplines, which frames a retrospective sketch of the genealogy of peace studies in geography. We then provide an overview of the chapters that follow, which are grouped into three sections: contesting narratives of peace; techniques of peacemaking; and practices of coexistence. The chapters are conceptually coherent in that they repeatedly return to the same set of questions: what does peace mean? How does that meaning shift through space and time? Who is peace *for*? Who produces/reproduces peace? The danger in such discussions is of losing sight of the bigger picture. Hence the chapter concludes by asking the question: what is the point of a geography of peace? We argue that the range of meanings that cohere around the word 'peace' is integral to, as Gerry Kearns put it, 'talk[ing] about what sort of home we want to make of the Earth and the ways that geographical studies direct our attention to the forces and capacities that might help or hinder making such a home'.[6] It is possible – indeed important – both to critically *conceptualize* peace, and also to be *committed* to some vision of peace.

## Critical approaches to peace in other disciplines

To enable us to think usefully about what peace means and how to study it, we first turn to the fields of international relations theory, peace studies and anthropology. Because explicit reflection on peace has been more advanced in these three fields than it has in human geography, they help us frame our consideration of how geography has thus far encountered, and engaged with, the subject of peace.

International Relations (IR) theory 'originates in the twentieth-century experience of global war and the desire to avoid subsequent wars'.[7] Although war has been its focus, the conditions necessary for peace have received a degree of attention.[8] As Oliver Richmond shows, the theoretical assumptions of the different strands of IR theory have heavily influenced what is understood by 'peace'.[9] The realist tradition of IR is based on the core proposition that the key actors in world politics are sovereign states, which act to advance their interests within an anarchic international system.[10] As such, peace is implicitly understood as bound up in the state-centric balance of power and is seen as 'limited if at all possible'.[11] The competing liberal approach remains focused on the state system, but posits the Kantian idea of a future universal peace which exists in the institutionalization of shared liberal norms – democracy, international co-operation and economic interdependence – rather than power politics. Fusing realist, liberal and other perspectives, the discourse and programme of 'liberal peace' has emerged as the dominant conceptualization of peace in IR and in the policy world. It developed from a diversification of conflict management strategies and UN peacekeeping interventions, and the co-option of broader grassroots initiatives for reconstruction and rehabilitation.[12] Premised on the assertion that armed intrastate conflicts in lower income countries pose global security threats, liberal peace is promoted through 'elitist peace negotiations and instrumental use of humanitarian and development aid'[13] and is thus intertwined with discourses and practices of liberal democracy, neoliberal development and technocratic statebuilding.

A productive area of work on peace in IR, and that which most closely informs the project we are advancing here, has emerged from critiques of liberal peace and the positing of alternative conceptualizations of peace. Pioneering this stance has been Oliver Richmond who, troubled by the normative and Western ideological underpinnings of the liberal peace paradigm,[14] argues that 'liberal forms of peacebuilding have become subservient to statebuilding',[15] that these initiatives are dominated by elite international actors and have little positive impact on local communities.[16] Arguing that peace itself is highly contested, Richmond and others have posited the idea of 'post-liberal peace'. This still connects with ideas of liberalism from IR but is a hybridized form of peacebuilding which foregrounds agency and the politics of peace, attends to the scale of the everyday and the local, and brings to the table concepts of empathy, dialogue and self-determination.[17] This fusion opens up important conceptual spaces for reconsidering peace through foregrounding the 'pluralism of peaces'[18] and the idea of peace as organic and dynamic. However, these critical IR approaches commonly fail to link the geopolitical to the everyday, and, by not sufficiently attending to 'undramatic' contexts of active peacemaking, they struggle to give requisite empirical weight to these alternatives to liberal peace.

A body of literature which has long wrestled with this challenge is peace studies. Its origins as a distinct field of inquiry go back to 1930s quantitative studies in the UK and USA on the causes and consequences of war.[19] The late 1960s and 1970s saw the broadening of studies to consider more forms of violence than simply traditional warfare, with theoretical impetus from sources such as European critical theory[20] and Latin American liberation theology.[21] Influenced by both the profusion of theoretical debate across the humanities and social sciences, and the changing challenges facing the post-Cold War world, peace studies has evolved to become an extremely wide-ranging field, as the second edition of Lester Kurtz's three volume, 2,500-page *Encyclopaedia of Violence, Peace and Conflict* demonstrates.[22]

We are influenced in particular by three recurring themes in peace studies. The first is that peace is a contested term. As Johan Galtung posited in the 1964 opening editorial to *Journal of Peace Research*, the 'absence of violence, absence of war' can be termed 'negative peace', counterposed to positive peace as 'the integration of human society'.[23] Crucially, different definitions of peace reflect different understandings of how the world works and inform different interventions in how policy should be made. Thus, as Jutila *et al.* argue, a 'critical peace research' should aim to 'show how "peace" is an essentially contested concept and how the choice of a certain understanding of peace affects the analysis made and policies chosen'.[24] A second important theme in peace studies is peace as process. As Lederach writes, 'peace is not a stage in time or a condition' but 'a dynamic social construct', and this is a theme which runs through many of the chapters in this volume.[25] Thirdly, whilst acknowledging that peace is a highly contested term, and that paths to pursue it are multiple, we recognize what Stephenson identifies in peace studies as a 'commitment to peace as a value in itself'.[26]

To augment our understanding of agency in creating and sustaining peace, we turn to anthropology. Sponsel and Gregor express discontent that conflict, aggression and violence should be dominant subjects for anthropological enquiry, whilst practices of peace are more often side-lined.[27] Nonetheless, a body of work on 'peaceful peoples' / 'peaceful societies' examines cultures which exhibit relatively low levels of overt physical aggression and violence.[28] By drawing attention to everyday empirical realities, these studies elucidate the forms of 'micro-labour' and effort that go into maintaining everyday peaceful life, which, scholars argue, is not devoid of conflict, tension and antagonism but does involve the successful prevention of violence.[29]

Anthropological studies offer us three essential perspectives that complement IR and peace studies approaches. First, detailed empirical scholarship is critical for understanding everyday social relations and the (re)production of power. Second, violence and peace are intertwined and entangled in complex ways.[30] And third, peace does not depend on wholly peaceful sociality and the successful resolution of tensions, but may also involve the suspension of tensions and/or the articulation of relations which are 'less than violent'.[31] However, although anthropology has the capacity to illuminate everyday/local processes, and to ask questions about agency, emotions and affect, it is typically less productive at drawing linkages and comparisons across scale and exploring uneven realities of power. These are issues which geography is well placed to analyse.

Taken together, IR, peace studies and anthropology have shaped our thinking on how to study peace in geography. Together they show that 'peace' is a contested term requiring careful interrogation; that it is a process not an endpoint; that its creation or pursuit is embedded in unequal power relations; that explicit research is required into its causes and conditions; and that it is valuable to interrogate the role of agency as situated in creating and sustaining peace. These disciplines also teach us that thinking critically about peace does not preclude a commitment to peace, and this is an argument we unpack in the concluding chapter. These concerns help frame the way we approach the study of peace as geographers, and, in the next section, they inform the lens we adopt to overview the history of geographical engagement with the topic of peace.

## A brief genealogy of peace in geography

Geography has a long tradition of interest in, and service to, warfare. As Yves Lacoste famously put it in the title of a pamphlet critiquing the discipline in France: '*La géographie, ça sert d'abord, à faire la guerre*' ('Geography serves, first and foremost, to wage war').[32] In the late nineteenth century and the first half of the twentieth century, geography – and the field of political geography in particular – was closely connected to, and influenced by, imperialism and competition between European powers. Geographic knowledge was employed as a tool of statecraft, and geography as a discipline was understood by many of its practitioners to be an aid to consolidating and preserving imperial power.[33] Influential thinkers such as Friedrich Ratzel, Halford Mackinder, Karl Haushofer and Nicholas Spykman framed war as a natural and normal phenomenon linked to a Darwinian competition between states.[34]

However, there is also an important, if less visible, history of engagement with issues of peace within the discipline. One surprising source is within classical geopolitics itself. As Megoran notes, Mackinder posited a 'nuanced realist conception of peace' premised on maintaining the 'status quo that protected the position of the British Empire against potential rivals'.[35] Similarly, Spykman began an essay on frontiers and international security with the statement: '[t]here will be peace after the war in which we are now engaged.'[36] In these realist accounts, peace is framed as a 'resource that could be "won" in a zero-sum competition with others',[37] and in the negative as the absence or cessation of conflict. Alternative perspectives on peace, which gesture towards more 'positive' interpretations of the concept, are also evident in the pre-Second World War era. For example, as Kearns has argued, anarchist geographers such as Peter Kropotkin and Élisée Reclus offered powerful critiques of these militarist readings of global space.[38] French geographers Jean Brunhes and Camille Vallaux outlined the role of geography in promoting interstate collaboration and stability in their 1921 book, *The Geography of History: Geography of Peace and War on Land and on Sea*.[39] British geographer Frank Horrabin made the case for socialist internationalism as a route to peace in his 1943 *Outline of Political Geography*,[40] while across the Atlantic, Wallace Atwood argued for geography's peacemaking role through fostering cross-cultural understanding.[41]

The expansion and consolidation of the discipline in the second half of the twentieth century, alongside the devastation of the Second World War, promoted a re-thinking of the concept of peace. This has continued through work which reflects critically on the nuclear stand-off of the late Cold War, the 'new wars' waged by myriad state and non-state militias and the post-9/11 'War on Terror'. As Virginie Mamadouh describes, in a valuable overview of the relationship between geographers and war, there has thus been a notable shift during the twentieth century from a war-orientated geography to a geography for peace, with the main objective for applying geographical knowledge shifting from war winning to war avoidance.[42]

The late Cold War saw some important work that would lay a foundation for future peace research in geography. Writing by Lacoste and Hewitt examined the relationship between bombing campaigns and the annihilation of place.[43] Pioneering in this regard was David Pepper and Alan Jenkins' 1985 volume, *The Geography of Peace and War*, which tackled the spatial aspects of the arms race, the influence of propaganda cartography, and different ways that geographers could engage with nuclear deterrence.[44] The next significant volume was political geographers Nurit Kliot and Stanley Waterman's 1991 book, *The Political Geography of Conflict and Peace*, which had a particular focus on geostrategic aspects of territorial conflicts in the Middle East.[45] Writing from within the tradition of quantitative research, John O'Loughlin and Herman van der Wusten argued that geography should make a contribution to 'peace science', and worked with large databases on the occurrence of conflict to investigate the spatial dimensions of war.[46]

Although work on the mapping of conflict continues,[47] this state orientated and functionalist agenda has been critiqued by critical geopolitics on the grounds that its proponents' 'unanalysed assumptions built into their concepts of peace and violence lead them to accept many of the contemporary political arrangements as a given, the starting point for analysis'.[48] Premised on a questioning of taken-for-granted understandings of the structures and practices of the interstate system, critical geopolitics has been particularly proficient at 'uncovering and explicating the circumstances and techniques whereby geopolitical reasoning constructs and reinforces divisions and thus underwrites exclusion, fear and ultimately violence'.[49] The geopolitical context of the post-9/11 'global war on terror' in particular has been a focus of attention for this field, with a series of scholars attending to the effects of new military technologies and reflecting on the 'potential for geographical technology in preventing and mitigating violence'.[50] In terms of conflict and peace specifically, and reflecting an increasing diversity of topics and approaches in recent years, Colin Flint's 2005 volume, *The Geography of War and Peace*, expanded the earlier agenda to include issues of drugs, terrorism and religion.[51]

It is striking that although each of these volumes claims to be about war *and* peace, overwhelmingly it is war that constitutes the focus of attention. We acknowledge and affirm the continuing value of these powerful critiques of violence, and we recognize that what counts as 'war scholarship' or 'peace scholarship' may be a subjective and unhelpful distinction.[52] Nevertheless, we contend that in all these publications there is both a conspicuous imbalance of chapters dealing with issues of war and peace – with the latter often constituting a handful of seemingly 'add-on' sections – and a noticeable distinction in the ways that these terms are conceptualized.[53] War and violence are dealt with in sophisticated theoretical terms, with detailed and compelling critiques of the cultures and practices of warfare, and nuanced analyses of questions of security, fear and military technology.[54] Conversely, in most cases peace is left undefined and barely conceptualized. Whilst gestured at, it is often simply assumed to be the lack of armed conflict. The implication is thus that peace exists only as a point of reference, an empty signifier defined by an absence of violence. For example, whereas a special issue of *Annals of the Association of American Geographers* on 'War and Peace' advocates the 'potential for geographers to contribute to peace',[55] the meaning of the term is not explored. Rather, the collection assumes that authors and readers alike know what peace is and know how geographers might contribute towards 'it'.

However, we argue that this relative occlusion of geographies of peace is far from a reflection of ongoing and emergent work in the discipline. The critical attention that has so fruitfully been applied to issues of war and violence *is* being applied to issues of peace, albeit not as yet under what we might identify as a coherent agenda. This ranges from re-thinking the relationship between geopolitics and peace, work on post-conflict reconstruction, diplomacy and border dispute resolution, through to research which looks at peace as situated knowledges and the idea of everyday peace.

For example, extending Gerry Kearns' concept of 'progressive geopolitics' exposing the intertwined personal and structural violences which are generated by imperialism,[56] Megoran promotes the idea of 'pacific geopolitics' as 'the study of how ways of thinking geographically about world politics can promote peaceful and mutually enriching human coexistence'.[57] Megoran grounds this approach in his own research on the transformative effects of Crusade apologies on

Christian missionaries,[58] but pacific geopolitics' agenda for a 'theoretically informed empirical research on peace'[59] potentially encompasses a range of topics from the architectures of the interstate system and international organizations, to peace movements and activism. Conventional analyses of activist peace movements are often weak on how and why they arose in particular ways and in particular places, and geographers are beginning to bring important spatial lenses to the geographical spread and transformation of organizations and their strategies, and beginning to unpack what solidarity looks like at a range of scales. This includes Guntram Herb's analysis of a 'geohistory' of peace movements,[60] Orna Blumen and Sharon Halevi's work on the Israeli Women in Black peace movement,[61] Byron Miller's research on the geography of anti-nuclear activism in the USA's Boston area,[62] and investigations by Sara Koopman and by Victoria Henderson on protective accompaniment and transnational solidarity.[63]

More broadly, geographers have for many years addressed issues which speak to the concept of peace in a variety of ways. On the one hand is scholarship which attends to peace as a state or interstate based strategy for controlling space in order to limit the potential for violence. This includes work on territorial division and the making of peaceful borders,[64] peacekeeping operations,[65] surveillance[66] and the construction of border walls as a strategy for containment.[67] On the other hand is a growing body of work which focuses on peace as the (re)production of positive relations of sociality and tolerance at different scales. For example, Emel Akçalı and Marco Antonsich, and Stuart Schoenfeld have investigated the role of environmental protection and co-operation in fostering intercommunal relations and wider peacebuilding in Cyprus and the Middle East respectively.[68] There is also a relatively small body of work on the geographies of international diplomacy[69] and spaces of conflict resolution and international mediation,[70] alongside analyses of peace processes and conflict resolution, particularly in Israel–Palestine[71] and Northern Ireland.[72]

Related to this work, geographers are increasingly turning a geographical spotlight on how the liberal peace is perceived, implemented and legitimated.[73] For example, drawing on scholarship in geography, development studies and feminist geopolitics, Jenna Loyd and Jennifer Fluri offer sophisticated critiques of US reconstruction efforts in Iraq and Afghanistan,[74] while Christine Bichsel and Kristian Stokke examine the politicized role of international development donors in peacebuilding and reordering social relations in Central Asia and Sri Lanka respectively.[75] The neoliberal agenda of liberal peace is further foregrounded and critiqued in Alex Jeffrey's work on international intervention in

Bosnia[76] and Simon Springer's analysis of the violence inherent in neo-liberal promotions of peace.[77] Another direction in which geographers are pushing this critique of liberal peace is that of teasing apart the concept of 'post-conflict' reconstruction. In a recent edited volume on this topic, Scott Kirsch and Colin Flint make a persuasive case for moving beyond the war/peace dichotomy and for examining 'the social construction of 'post-conflict' spaces as embodiments of power relations'.[78] Running through this range of work is thus a focus on the place-specific nature of war-to-peace transitions,[79] a sensitivity to the multi-scalar practices of state and non-state actors, and a linking of issues around liberal peace to questions of social justice, citizenship and the negotiation of rights. As Erinn Nicely notes, this geographical foregrounding of power relations and meaningful engagement with local grassroots perspectives offers an important alternative approach to the 'top-heavy institutional and problem-solving approach' to peacebuilding that has dominated international relations scholarship.[80]

Building upon the work of scholars in peace studies, anthropology and particularly critical IR, geography therefore has a decisive role to play in deconstructing normative assumptions about peace and in exploring peace as situated knowledges within different cultural settings. This includes problematizing the content of peace, exploring how it is understood, practised and contested within different contexts, and attending to scales not usually associated with peacekeeping or peacebuilding, in order to examine how peace is differentially constructed, materialized and interpreted. An essential component of this is a focus on the idea of everyday peace: of peace as a fragile and contingent process that is constituted through everyday relations and embodiments, which are also inextricably linked to geopolitical processes. Exemplifying this deeper understanding of peace based on 'committed and grounded research engagements'[81] are Jonathan Darling's work on the politics of hospitality towards asylum seekers in Sheffield[82] and Philippa Williams' research on everyday Hindu–Muslim relations in Varanasi, India.[83] This focus on everyday peace in turn foregrounds productive work being done within geography more generally around 'peace-ful' concepts such as tolerance, friendship, hope, reconciliation, justice, cosmopolitanism, solidarity, hospitality and empathy.[84]

## Narratives, techniques and everyday practices of peace

It is this emerging and inspiring work across human geography that serves as a launch point for this book. Our aim in bringing together eleven different takes on the geography of peace is both to highlight research that is being done in political, development, social, cultural and environmental geography in relation to peace, and to open up a series of questions that we think geographers ought to be grappling with. The chapters are grouped into three broad themes: contesting narratives of peace, techniques of peacemaking, and practices of coexistence.

The chapters in the opening section examine the theme of 'contesting narratives of peace'. They show how the idea of peace may be variously constructed and interpreted within sites and scales. The chapters share a common argument that the construction of peace is a political act that is both underpinned by, and reproduces, particular practices of power. Recognizing the hegemonic quality of peace narratives, these chapters explore some of the ways in which overarching discourses not only contrast with local realities, but may also be productively subverted and manipulated in the production of different kinds of peace. Indeed, given the shifting reality of war and new modes of violence, the need to continuously re-imagine and re-articulate peaceful geographies is shown to be paramount.

In the opening chapter of this section, Simon Dalby provides an expansive vision of the relationship between geopolitics and peace. He accepts the importance of geographers broadening their discussions of 'peace', but insists that in so doing they must grasp the changing geopolitics of violence in our world. Cold War geopolitical thinking assumed a bipolar world in danger of 'mutually assured destruction' should full-scale war break out. But 'peace' has not occurred because this threat has receded: the post-Cold War era of globalization demands more sophisticated thinking. Dalby points to quantitative studies suggesting that wars as traditionally defined are on the wane, and that violence is increasingly less regarded as a legitimate way of doing politics. However, although war may thus not be an inevitable part of the human condition, geographies of contemporary violence are more complicated. These include 'lawfare' (the use of law as power and coercion to set the rules of social and political life), resource wars, militias, and drone/robotic warfare. Similarly, violence is frequently invoked in the name of 'security' as the overarching logic of political action. Dalby argues, therefore, that a geography seriously committed to peace must link small-scale nonviolent protests to these contemporary transformations of geopolitics. Crucially, it must undercut the moral logic of violence, and continue to contest old and new cartographies of the world that make violence appear inevitable.

Shifting the scale of analysis, Nicole Laliberte draws on empirical research from post-conflict Uganda to illustrate the ways in which peaceful social landscapes may be constructed and reproduced through discourses of peace. She focuses on how a Ugandan NGO called ADO actively engages with the international language of human rights and responsibilities in order to contest local practices of inequality and violence, and thereby reconfigure social relations within different households and communities. Here, the concept of peace is linked to (local) ideas about respect and justice, which are illuminated through lived experiences and involve the active construction of peaceful emotional geographies. Importantly, the hegemonic narrative of human rights is demonstrated to be unstable and open to manipulation by an NGO that occupies a relatively marginal position outside the direct purview of the state. Yet, Laliberte is careful to highlight not just the productive agency of the NGO in vernacularizing the discourse of human rights for emancipatory ends, but also the limitations, as the NGO's work often reproduces rather than deconstructs the patriarchal structures of local society. Laliberte's chapter affords a fascinating window on how normative international discourses designed for peace are actively manipulated by actors towards constructing other peaceful geographies at different scales. The chapter highlights both the fragility of peace and the place-specific realization of peaceful emotional geographies.

Patricia Daley's chapter also engages with universal discourses of peace, but unlike Laliberte's chapter, which points to the potential for re-working such narratives for locally beneficial outcomes, Daley's is more circumspect and focuses on the incompatibility of liberal peace approaches with life in post-conflict Central Africa. Drawing on fieldwork and documentary material collected in Burundi and the Democratic Republic of Congo, Daley draws attention to the glaring contradiction between 'liberal peace', which, she argues, is based on a rational, militarized, gendered and racialized agenda, and the kind of societal transformation and healing that Central African states require. Daley outlines some of the infrastructures of liberal peace programmes and how these have been implemented before subsequently showing how and why these are limited in the context of local cultures. She demonstrates how the liberal peace agenda's emphasis on military security has further entrenched patriarchal and hyper-masculine forms of symbolic and material violence within post-conflict societies. International organizations explicitly designed to promote gender equality have, in practice, operated to promote a neoliberal rhetoric that conceives of women as 'natural' peacekeepers, rather than deconstructing the inherently uneven structures of power that perpetuate gender inequality and violence. In this post-conflict context, where the implementation of liberal peace has actually entailed persistent insecurity and gender violence, Daley concludes that in order for peace to be a truly trans-formative process, a local perspective on peace is urgently required, one that is rooted in the local political economy and sensitive to local cultures and power relations.

The second section of the book explores a remarkably varying range of what we term 'techniques of peacemaking'. These chapters widen the discussion of 'peacemaking' from the archetypical image of top-down, state-led initiatives to imperial boundary making practices, grassroots cultural identity assertion, boycotts, self-immolation, ex-paramilitary community activism, and 'protective accompaniment'. Although all these practices can be considered as 'peacemaking', they include strate-gies that either shore up or resist state power, from techniques of state-craft practised by diplomats to grassroots activism by political exiles and reformed paramilitaries. Together, these chapters move the dis-cussion of peace in geography away from romantic notions by demon-strating that peace is a contested term, is embedded in unequal power relations, and that its practices may be problematic and implicated in forms of violence.

John Donaldson's chapter opens this section, using the lens of peace to reconsider a core topic in one of geography's most enduring interests: international boundaries. A key assumption in this literature is the two-fold distinction between the *delimitation* of a boundary through bilat-eral treaty, and its subsequent *demarcation* on the landscape. Donaldson underlines that this is an imperial concept of peace, a mechanism developed to divide up newly acquired colonial territories and thereby remove potential flashpoints between imperial powers. He argues that this model of boundary making often does not work in practice, as a dispute over a poorly defined boundary may serve as the lightning rod that channels a variety of other political and social tensions within a borderland area.

Sara Koopman's chapter explores another technique of peacemak-ing, but one far removed from boundary delimitation and demarca-tion: international protective accompaniment. Accompaniment is a grassroots peacebuilding strategy that uses privilege by placing indi-viduals from Western states next to locals in the 'global South' who are under threat because of their work for peace and justice. Writing about Colombia, which has experienced periods of violent conflict over many decades since the 1940s, and is the country that hosts the larg-est number of accompaniment organizations, Koopman unpacks how accompaniment 'makes space for peace.' She investigates the every-day practices and comportment of international accompaniers. Based on interactive workshop sessions with accompaniers, she details the chains of connections and power relations that accompaniers construct and draw upon in their work on the ground. These include grassroots organizing back in the USA, to lobbying Members of the US Congress, the US embassy in Colombia, and finally the Colombian army generals who control the areas where they are seeking to operate. It is through these networks that the embodied peacemaking techniques of accompaniment are scaled up and have potentially far wider implications. As such, Koopman makes the case for thinking about space as relational, and presents accompaniment as a way of re-thinking political geography and its potential contribution to peace.

The remaining two chapters in this section consider what, at first glance, would appear to be one highly promising context in which to think about peace, and one where peace has long seemed elusive. Fiona McConnell uses the case of the exiled Tibetan community to explore how practices of peace are politicized, contested and debated. Unsettling the stereotype of Tibetan communities as quintessentially pacifist, she unpacks and problematizes the relationship between Buddhism, politics and the adoption of Gandhian ideas of *satyagraha* (the 'insistence on the truth') in relation to this case. The chapter explores three overlapping geographies of Tibetan articulations of peace, each with a different and distinct 'author'. These are the Dalai Lama's vision for 'World Peace' and master narrative of Tibet as a 'zone of peace'; the exile Tibetan government's employment of *satyagraha* in its 'Middle Way' policy *vis-à-vis* negotiations with Beijing; and finally two local forms of resistance that have become especially visible in recent years – the grassroots 'Lhakar' movement, and acts of self-immolation. McConnell argues that these various articulations of Tibetan nonviolence resonate in different ways with Gandhian principles, but at the same time their practice is distinctly Tibetan, which problematizes the meaning of nonviolence in and for Tibet. The chapter concludes by attending to the relationship between peaceful discourses and their 'messy' enactment in everyday situations, and reflects on the employment of peace as a political strategy.

Using a very different example, Lia Shimada's chapter demonstrates the contributions that cultural geographers can make to debates about geographies of peace. One of cultural geography's historic strengths has been to show how the meanings ascribed to places are contested and can change over time. Shimada demonstrates how the changing meaning of 'Eleventh night' loyalist bonfires in Northern Ireland is part of the process of peacemaking. The bonfires, which celebrate the victory of the Protestant King William III over the Catholic King James II at the Battle of the Boyne in 1690, are at the zenith of the loyalist cultural calendar. Flags of the Irish Republic are burnt on towering bonfires patrolled by masked paramilitaries firing weapons into the air. They would thus appear to be unpromising spaces in which to think about peace. However, Shimada shows how former paramilitaries are trying to use the bonfires to shift loyalist culture away from glorifying paramilitary violence to one based upon an understanding of community history and traditions.

The third and final section of the volume continues to question what peace is, who it is for and the power relations that are at its core, but it shifts the scale and focus to everyday personal relations and a range of practices around the concept of coexistence. Responding to Colin Flint's call for geographical attention to focus on 'the "quiet successes", everyday settings where humanity nurtures mutual respect and interaction',[85] and building on Galtung's concept of 'positive peace', the notion of coexistence – of living with difference and being with others – opens up important questions of how peace is crosscut by issues of contingency, agency, practice and embodiment. Each chapter in this section offers a nuanced insight into situated cases where violence and conflict is a constant memory, backdrop or threat, but where it has either been averted or is held in abeyance through everyday relations of tolerance, hospitality, friendship and conviviality. These chapters thus take conventional questions about why and how violence takes place and reverse them. Instead they ask why there was no violence here, and what relations, discourses and practices came into play to actively produce peaceful interactions. A recurrent theme in this section is the caution that peace is always articulated in power relations, and therefore should not be celebrated uncritically.

Stuart Schoenfeld, Asaf Zohar, Ilan Alleson, Osama Suleiman and Galya Sipos-Randor focus on the Arab–Israeli interface which has, for decades, been associated with protracted conflict. As the authors note, most Arab–Israeli people-to-people dialogue groups broke up with the commencement of the Palestinian Second Intifada in 2000. Bucking this trend, a number of environmental groups managed to continue their work. This chapter analyses one of them, the Arava Institute, which brings Israelis, Palestinians, Jordanians and others together to study and work on addressing transboundary environmental issues in the region. Based on narrative interviews with alumni, the authors address the question of why Arava has persisted and apparently been so successful when many other dialogue organizations have failed. The authors' main argument is that the Arava Institute's success is based on the lengths it goes to to carefully cultivate relationships. Through intentional strategies, such as shared domicile, eating together, mentoring arrangements, field trips and close attention to managing relationships, the institute works to build *empathy* between people who represent different 'sides' of intense international conflicts. The authors thus conclude that empathy, and the strategies for building it, are important aspects of peacemaking.

Again focusing on a situation which is conventionally seen as conflict-ridden, Philippa Williams turns to relations between Hindu and Muslim communities in the north Indian city of Varanasi. Based on ethnographic research in the city, Williams documents the range of responses, events and practices that were articulated following a series of bomb attacks in Varanasi in 2006. With the attacks widely perceived to be the work of Islamists, there was concern that they would spark retaliatory actions by right-wing Hindu groups. Yet intercommunity violence did not result, and a situation of 'everyday peace' was maintained. Drawing on feminist geopolitical approaches to the local and the everyday, Williams explores the critical roles that agency, claims to legitimacy, and cultural political economy play in actively reproducing everyday peace. In highlighting the importance of examining peace within situated contexts, she reconstructs the events in Varanasi from the perspectives of local residents, focusing in particular on the actions and strategic partnership of the two key local actors – a Muslim cleric (the *mufti*) and a Hindu priest (the *mahant*). The chapter thereby offers both a valuable insight into the city's social world, and captures what peace as a political process looks like. However, in cautioning against painting too rosy a picture of intercommunity harmony, the chapter concludes by outlining how the reproduction of peace can both re-inscribe marginal status as well as representing a generative and positively transformative process.

This cautionary note is echoed in Nick Megoran's chapter, which deals with one of the key issues of inquiry within human geography: that of migration. Although migration is frequently understood as a source of social tension and a threat to national security, Megoran instead examines the extent to which it can also promote peaceful coexistence. The chapter focuses on Uzbek classical singer Sherali Juraev's connections to transnational Bukharan (Central Asian) Jewish networks in Israel. Based on a detailed personal narrative, Megoran explores how Sherali's attitude to the Jewish minority in his country – one which is commonly characterized by disparagement – was transformed through a series of significant spiritual episodes that took place in Israel. These visits led Sherali to question and contest the prejudices in his own society, and come to perceive music as a mechanism for promoting understanding between different groups. Megoran uses this case to argue that examples of transformative practices can be found in surprising places, and that migration and transnationalism can be productive of more peaceful and mutually enriching human coexistence. Yet, like Williams, Megoran cautions against over-romanticizing this case, because Sherali's Israeli sponsors were also supporters of the settler movement in the occupied territories. This illustrates that peace is embedded within power relations and is not primarily to be understood as an idealized endpoint, but as a precarious and problematic process.

Jonathan Darling's chapter continues the theme of migration and develops the argument that peace should not be over-celebrated. He engages with recent work on the spatial politics of asylum, which focuses on notions of interaction as means to 'welcome' others. Based on interviews with asylum seekers in the UK city of Sheffield, the chapter describes the limits of banal moments of 'welcome' extended to asylum seekers in the city. It spotlights relations that carry with them repertoires of both welcome *and* violence. Crucially, Darling cautions against the uncritical celebration of programmes of welcome. Instead he argues that seemingly convivial encounters should be set against a context of 'domopolitics', meaning the categorizing practices through which asylum seekers are presented as a threat to the nation and are spatially contained and controlled. Premised on arguments made by Žižek and Bourdieu that violence is the imposition of power through the 'normal state of things', Darling argues that moments of violence are always present in our assumptions of peace. In thereby encouraging recognition of the impossibility of untangling relations of violence and nonviolence, Darling's chapter offers an important restraint on uncritically portraying peace as positive. Rather, it renders peace as a highly contextual and personal sense of being which is connected to notions of security and belonging and is always maintained through modes of governance and control.

## Conclusion: why geography?

The contributors to this book thus offer a rich and diverse range of analyses of peace. They engage with articulations of peaceful practices from the scale of everyday interactions to interstate conflict resolution, yet also refuse to take for granted that the claims to the production of peace are always unproblematic or even positive. Rather, the authors employ a range of theoretical and methodological tools to reveal and interrogate the power relations that underpin what peace is and in whose name it is promoted.

Our aim in bringing together these perspectives from a number of subdisciplines of human geography is not to establish a necessarily coherent agenda on the geography of peace. Instead, we believe that geographies of peace should be a deliberately broad umbrella, one under which geographers from across the discipline can gather and exchange ideas and where the concept of peace can be analysed within a range of geographical frameworks. Underpinning this is the understanding that peace is inherently spatial: that is to say, it is always shaped by the spaces through which it is produced and reproduced. We thus want a geography that is as ambitious in developing an agenda for peace as it has been at investigating the geographical correlates of violence. The concluding chapter to this volume develops this more fully by spelling out a series of questions that we believe such a geography of peace must address. These include:

- What spatial factors have facilitated the success or precipitated the failure of some peace movements or diplomatic negotiations?
- Why are some ideologies productive of violence in some places but co-operation in others?
- What can be learned from the historical geography of peace institutions, organizations, movements and ideas?
- How have some communities been better able to deal with religious, racial, cultural and class conflict than others?
- How have antagonistic geopolitical visions been overcome or rewritten?
- How have creative approaches to sharing sovereignty mitigated or transformed territorial disputes that once seemed intractable?
- Why do some nonviolent campaigns for social justice work in some places yet in others fail?

These questions arise from the chapters collected in this volume, and from them we suggest that the *concerns* and *concepts* that preoccupy geographers constitute a recognizable twofold geographical contribution to the broader, interdisciplinary study of peace. Firstly, in this book we see many cases of geographers highlighting traditional disciplinary concerns about the changing nature of borders, migration, geopolitical representations, human-environmental relations, and how ideas (such as *satyagraha* and nonviolence) change as they move from place to place. By questioning how these processes can be productive of peaceful relations, geographers can play to their disciplinary strengths and fields of expertise and offer original engagements with the topic of peace.

Secondly, the contributions to this volume demonstrate the utility of working with the key geographical concepts of place, space and scale. *Places* are differentiated bounded portions of geographic *space* in which social relations are constituted and events occur, and which are organized, related and experienced at different *scales*, from the bodily to the global. We are not arguing that geographers have a monopoly over these concepts and concerns, but we do believe that by foregrounding them geographers can make a useful contribution to the study of making, sustaining and unmaking peace. We hope that the collection of chapters we have assembled demonstrates, as Koopman argues in her chapter, that 'Peace means different things at different scales, as well as to different groups and at different times and places. Peace is not the same everywhere' (page III).

As we argue in the concluding chapter, this critical approach does not fatally undermine the value of peace as a powerful aspiration and rich resource for progressive politics. On the contrary, it is *un*critical invocations of peace that may be dangerous or problematic. Nor does an expansive consideration of peaceful concepts stretch the idea of peace as being so all-encompassing as to be virtually meaningless. As this collection demonstrates, approaching peace as we do opens up questions and research avenues that otherwise might not directly be considered. It also facilitates dialogues between different fields of geographical enquiry, and engagements with debates in other disciplines, that might otherwise not take place.

Furthermore, difficult questions about terminology should not make us forget that our discipline has a history of direct support for militarism, and that geographical ideas remain important in the creation of intellectual architectures that make violence appear inevitable and necessary. There is thus a moral obligation to critically revisit the ways in which geographers have provided justifications for violence: an obligation well served – for the time being at least – by critically exploring 'peace.' We want a geography that is as ambitious in developing an agenda for peace as it has been at investigating the geographical correlates of violence. The financial, intellectual, scientific and political resources that societies devote towards learning how to be peacemakers are paltry compared to those dedicated to preparing for – and waging – war. We thus identify the endeavour of building a geography of – and for – peace as a modest contribution to what Cortright identifies as the 'movements and ideas for peace'.[86] Geographical perspectives can make a specific contribution to this movement. For all these reasons, we think it is worth researching, writing, and teaching about peace. We hope that this volume will go some way to convincing the sceptical reader that there is indeed a place for geographies of peace.

# Notes

1. Agnew, John, 'Commentary: Classics in Human Geography Revisited'; Sack, R., 'Human territoriality', *Progress in Human Geography* 24/1 (2000), pp. 91–9.
2. Delaney, David, *Territory: A Short Introduction* (Oxford, 2005), p. 99.
3. Hewitt, Kenneth, 'Place annihilation: area bombing and the fate of urban places', *Annals of the Association of American Geographers* 73/2 (1983), pp. 257–84, p. 258.
4. See, for example, Kirsch, Scott and Flint, Colin (eds), *Reconstructing Conflict: Integrating War and Post-War Geographies* (Farnham, 2011); Inwood, Joshua and Tyner, James, 'Geography's pro-peace agenda: an unfinished project', *ACME: An International E-Journal for Critical Geographies* 10/3 (2011), pp. 442–57.
5. Williams, Philippa and McConnell, Fiona, 'Critical geographies of peace', *Antipode*, 43/4 (2011), pp. 927–31; Megoran, Nick, 'War *and* peace? An agenda for peace research and practice in geography', *Political Geography* 30/4 (2011), pp. 178–89.
6. Kearns, Gerry, 'Progressive historiography', in 'Reading Gerry Kearns' *Geopolitics and Empire: The Legacy of Halford Mackinder*', *Political Geography* 30/1 (2011), pp. 55–7.
7. Gilady, Lilach and Russett, Bruce, 'Peacemaking and conflict resolution', in W. Carlsnaes, T. Risse and B. A. Simmons (eds), *Handbook of International Relations* (London, 2002), pp. 392–409.
8. Holsti, Kalevi, *Peace and War: Armed Conflicts and International Order, 1648–1989* (Cambridge, 1991).
9. Richmond, Oliver, *Peace in International Relations* (Abingdon, 2008).
10. Waltz, Kenneth E., 'The origins of war in neorealist theory', *Journal of Interdisciplinary History* 18/4 (1988), pp. 615–28.
11. Richmond, *Peace in International Relations*, p. 9.
12. For key texts on peacebuilding see Galtung, Johan, *Peace, War and Defence: Essays in Peace Research,* vol. 2 (Copenhagen, 1975a); Boutros-Ghali, Boutros, *An Agenda for Peace,* second edition (New York, 1995). For more critical overviews see Paris, Roland, 'Peacebuilding and the limits of liberal internationalism', *International Security* 22/2 (1997); Knight, W. Andy, 'Evaluating recent trends in peacebuilding research', *International Relations of the Asia-Pacific* 3 (2003), pp. 241–64.
13. Stokke, Kristian, 'Crafting liberal peace? International peace promotion and the contextual politics of peace in Sri Lanka', *Annals of the Association of American Geographers* 99/5 (2009), pp. 932–9.
14. For critiques of the normative underpinnings of peacekeeping interventions see Higate, Paul and Henry, Marsha, *Insecure Spaces: Peacekeeping, Power and Performance in Haiti, Kosovo and Liberia* (London, 2009); Paris, 'Peacebuilding and the limits of liberal internationalism'; Enloe, Cynthia, *Maneuvers: The International Politics of Militarizing Women's Lives* (Berkeley, 2000).
15. Richmond, Oliver, 'Resistance and the post-liberal peace', *Millennium: Journal of International Studies* 38/3 (2010a), pp. 665–92.
16. Heathershaw, John, 'Seeing like the international community: how peacebuilding failed (and survived) in Tajikistan', *Journal of Intervention and State-building* 2/3 (2008), pp. 329–351.

17. Richmond, Oliver, *A Post-Liberal Peace* (London, 2011); Richmond, Oliver and Mitchell, Audra (eds), *Hybrid Forms of Peace: From Everyday Agency to Post-Liberalism* (Basingstoke, 2011).

18. Richmond, Oliver P., 'Becoming liberal, unbecoming liberalism: liberal–local hybridity via the everyday as a response to the paradoxes of liberal peacebuilding', *Journal of Intervention and Statebuilding* 3/3 (2009), pp. 324–44.

19. Stephenson, Carolyn, 'Peace studies', in L. Kurtz (ed.), *Encyclopedia of Violence, Peace and Democracy*, second edition (London, 2008), pp. 1534–48.

20. For example, Reid, Herbert and Yanarella, Ernest, 'Toward a critical theory of peace research in the United States: the search for an "intelligible core"', *Journal of Peace Research* 13/4 (1976), pp. 315–41.

21. Gutierrez, Gustavo, *A Theology of Liberation: History, Politics, and Salvation*, trans. by John Eagleson (New York, 1971).

22. Kurtz, Lester (ed.), *Encyclopedia of Violence, Peace and Conflict*, vols 1–3, second edition (London, 2008).

23. Galtung, Johan, 'What is peace research?', *Journal of Peace Research* 1/1 (1964), pp. 1–4.

24. Jutila, Matti, Pehkonen, Samu and Väyrynen, Tarja, 'Resuscitating a discipline: an agenda for critical peace research', *Millennium: Journal of International Studies* 36/3 (2008), pp. 623–40.

25. Lederach, John Paul, *Building Peace: Sustainable Reconciliation in Divided Societies* (Washington DC, 1997), p. 20.

26. Stephenson, 'Peace studies', p. 1535.

27. Sponsel, Leslie E. and Gregor, Thomas (eds), *The Anthropology of Peace and Nonviolence* (Boulder, 1994).

28. Bonta, Bruce D., 'Conflict resolution among peaceful societies: the culture of peacefulness', *Journal of Peace Research* 33/4 (1996), pp. 403–20; Fry, Douglas P., 'Maintaining society tranquility: internal and external loci of aggression control', in Sponsel and Gregor, *The Anthropology of Peace and Nonviolence*; Howell, Signe and Willis, Roy (eds), *Societies at Peace: Anthropological Perspectives* (London, 1989), pp. 133–54; Sponsel and Gregor, *The Anthropology of Peace and Nonviolence*.

29. Briggs, Jean. L., '"Why don't you kill your baby brother?" The dynamics of peace in Canadian Inuit camps', in Sponsel and Gregor, *The Anthropology of Peace and Nonviolence*, pp. 151–81.

30. Das, Veena, *Life and Words: Violence and the Descent into the Ordinary* (Berkeley, CA, 2007); Scheper-Hughes, Nancy, *Death Without Weeping: The Violence of Everyday Life in Brazil* (Berkeley, CA, 1992).

31. Bailey, Frederick G., *The Civility of Indifference: On Domesticating Ethnicity* (Ithaca, 1996); Ring, Laura, *Zenana: Everyday Peace in a Karachi Apartment Building* (Bloomington, IN, 2006).

32. Lacoste, Yves, *La géographie ça sert d'abord à faire la guerre* (Paris, 1976); Mamadouh, Virginie, 'Geography and war, geographers and peace', in Colin Flint (ed.), *The Geography of War and Peace: From Death Camps to Diplomats* (Oxford, 2005), p. 26.

33. Polelle, Mark, *Raising Carthographic Consciousness: The Social and Foreign Policy Visions of Geopolitics in the Twentieth Century* (Oxford, 1999).

34. Mamadouh, 'Geography and war, geographers and peace'.

35. Megoran, Nick, 'Violence and peace', in Klaus Dodds, M. Kuus and J. Sharp (eds), *The Ashgate Companion to Critical Geopolitics* (Farnham, 2013), pp.189–207.

36. Spykman, Nicholas, 'Frontiers, security, and international organization', *Geographical Review* 32/3 (1942), pp. 436–47.

37. Megoran, Nick, 'War *and* peace? An agenda for peace research and practice in geography', *Political Geography* 30/4 (2011), pp. 178–89.

38. Kearns, Gerry, *Geopolitics and Empire*.

39. Brunhes, Jean and Vallaux, Camille, *La géographie de l'histoire: géographie de la paix et de la guerre sur terre et sur mer* (Paris, 1921).

40. Horrabin, Frank, *An Outline of Political Geography* (Tillicoultry, 1943).

41. Atwood, Wallace, 'The increasing significance of geographic conditions in the growth of nation-states', *Annals of the Association of American Geographers* 25/1 (1935), pp. 1–16.

42. Mamadouh, 'Geography and war, geographers and peace'.

43. Lacoste, Yves, 'The geography of warfare. An illustration of geographical warfare: bombing of the dikes on the Red River, North Vietnam', in R. Peet (ed.), *Radical Geography* (London, 1977), pp. 244–61; Hewitt, 'Place annihilation'.

44. Pepper, David and Jenkins, Alan (eds), *The Geography of Peace and War* (New York, 1985). See also Kofman, Eleonore, 'Information and nuclear issues: the role of the academic', *Area* 16/2 (1984), p. 166.

45. Kliot, Nurit and Waterman, Stanley (eds), *The Political Geography of Conflict and Peace* (London, 1991).

46. O'Loughlin, John and van der Wusten, Herman, 'Geography, war and peace: notes for a contribution to a revived political geography', *Progress in Human Geography* 10/3 (1986), pp. 484–510; van der Wusten, Herman and O'Loughlin, John, 'Claiming new territory for a stable peace: how geography can contribute', *Professional Geography* 38/1 (1986), pp. 18–28.

47. O'Loughlin, John, 'The political geography of conflict: civil wars in the hegemonic shadow', in Flint, *The Geography of War and Peace*, pp.85–112; O'Loughlin, John and Raleigh, Clionadh, 'Spatial analysis of civil war violence', in K. Cox, M. Low and J. Robinson (eds), *A Handbook of Political Geography* (London, 2008), pp. 493–508.

48. Dalby, Simon, 'Critical geopolitics: discourse, difference and dissent', *Environment and Planning D: Society and Space* 9/3 (1991), pp. 261–83.

49. Megoran, Nick, 'Towards a geography of peace: pacific geopolitics and evangelical Christian Crusade apologies', *Transactions of the Institute of British Geographers* 35/3 (2010), pp. 382–98.

50. Kobayashi, Audrey, 'Geographies of peace and armed conflict: introduction', *Annals of the Association of American Geographers* 99/5 (2009), pp. 819–26. See Gregory, Derek, 'War and peace', *Transactions of the Institute of British Geographers* 35/2 (2010), pp. 154–86; Cowen, Deborah and Gilbert, Emily (eds), *War, Citizenship, Territory* (New York, 2008); Korf, Benedikt, 'Resources, violence and the telluric geographies of small wars', *Progress in Human Geography* 35/6 (2011), pp. 733–56.

51. Flint, *The Geography of War and Peace*.

52. Ross, Amy, 'Commentary: geographies of war and the putative peace', *Political Geography* 30/4 (2011), pp. 197–9.

53. For example, despite the title of Kliot and Waterman's volume, the book foregrounds war and has little to say on issues of peace. Meanwhile, Flint's volume has only four chapters ostensibly on peace – at the end of the book – compared to eleven dealing with war; and in the *Annals* special issue on 'War and peace' only Loyd's article explicitly deals with peace in a positive sense.

54. See Gregory, Derek and Pred, Allan (eds), *Violent Geographies: Fear, Terror and Political Violence* (New York, 2006); Dodds, Klaus and Ingram, Alan (eds), *Spaces of Security*

*and Insecurity: Geographies of the War on Terror* (Aldershot, 2009); Pain, Rachel and Smith, Susan J., *Fear: Critical Geopolitics and Everyday Life* (Aldershot, 2008).

55. Kobayashi, 'Geographies of peace and armed conflict', p. 821.
56. Kearns, *Geopolitics and Empire*.
57. Megoran, 'Towards a geography of peace', p. 385.
58. Megoran, 'Towards a geography of peace'.
59. Megoran, 'Towards a geography of peace', p. 385.
60. Herb, Guntram H., 'The geography of peace movements', in Flint, *The Geography of War and Peace,* pp. 347–68.
61. Blumen, Orna and Halevi, Sharon, 'Staging peace through a gendered demonstration: women in black in Haifa, Israel', *Annals of the Association of American Geographers* 99/5 (2009), pp. 977–85.
62. Miller, Byron, *Geography and Social Movements: Comparing Antinuclear Activisim in the Boston Area* (Minneapolis, 2000).
63. Koopman, Sara, 'Alter-geopolitics: other securities are happening', *Geoforum* 42/3 (2011a), pp. 274–84; Henderson, Victoria L., 'Citizenship in the line of fire: protective accompaniment, proxy citizenship, and pathways for transnational solidarity in Guatemala', *Annals of the Association of American Geographers* 99/5 (2009), pp. 969–76.
64. Newman, David, 'The geopolitics of peacemaking in Israel–Palestine', *Political Geography* 21/5 (2002), pp. 629–46.
65. Grundy-Warr, Carl, 'Towards a political geography of United Nations peacekeeping: some considerations', *Geojournal* 34/2 (1994), pp. 177–90.
66. Coaffee, Jon and Murakami Wood, David, 'Terrorism and surveillance', in T. Hall, P. Hubbard and J. R. Short (eds), *The Sage Companion to the City* (London, 2008), pp. 352–72.
67. Alatout, Samer, 'Walls as technologies of government: the double construction of geographies of peace and conflict in Israeli politics, 2002-Present', *Annals of the Association of American Geographers* 99/5 (2009), pp. 956–68.
68. Akçalı, Emel and Antonsich, Marco, '"Nature knows no boundaries": a critical reading of UNDP environmental peacemaking in Cyprus', *Annals of the Association of American Geographers* 99/5 (2009), pp. 940–7; Schoenfeld, Stuart, 'Environment and human security in the eastern Mediterranean: regional environmentalism in the reframing of Palestinian–Israeli–Jordanian relations', in P. Liotta, W. Kepner, J. Lancaster and D. Mouat (eds), *Achieving Environmental Security: Ecosystem Services and Human Welfare* (Amsterdam, 2010), pp. 113–31.
69. Henrikson, Alan K., 'The geography of diplomacy', in Flint, *The Geography of War and Peace*, pp. 369–94; van der Wusten, Herman and van Korstanje, H., 'Diplomatic networks and stable peace', in Kliot and Waterman, *The Political Geography of Conflict and Peace*.
70. van der Wusten, Herman, 'Viewpoint: new law in fresh courts', *Progress in Human Geography* 26/2 (2002), pp. 151–3; Brunn, Stanley, Nooruddin, Vaseema, and Sims, Kimberly, 'Place, culture, and peace; treaty cities and national culture in mediating contemporary international disputes', *Geojournal* 39/4 (2006), pp. 331–43.
71. Newman, 'The geopolitics of peacemaking in Israel-Palestine'; Ghazi-Walid, Falah, 'The geopolitics of "enclavisation" and the demise of a two-state solution to the Israeli–Palestinian conflict', *Third World Quarterly* 26/8 (2005), pp. 1341–72.

72. Graham, Brian and Nash, Catherine, 'A shared future: territoriality, pluralism and public policy in Northern Ireland', *Political Geography* 25/3 (2006), pp. 253–78. Guy Ben-Porat offers a revealing comparative study of Israel–Palestine and Northern Ireland: Ben-Porat, Guy, 'Grounds for peace: territoriality and conflict resolution', *Geopolitics* 10/1 (2005), pp. 147–66.

73. Le Billion, Philippe, 'Corrupting peace? Peacebuilding and post-conflict corruption', *International Peacekeeping* 15/3 (2008), pp. 344–61.

74. Loyd, Jenna M., '"A microscopic insurgent": militarization, health and critical geographies of violence', *Annals of the Association of American Geographers* 99/5 (2009), pp. 863–73; Fluri, Jennifer, '"Foreign passports only": geographies of (post) conflict work in Kabul, Afghanistan', *Annals of the Association of American Geographers* 99/5 (2009), pp. 986–94.

75. Bichsel, Christine, *Conflict Transformation in Central Asia: Irrigation Disputes in the Ferghana Valley* (London, 2009); Stokke, 'Crafting Liberal Peace?'

76. Jeffrey, Alex, 'The politics of "democratization": lessons from Bosnia and Iraq', *Review of International Political Economy* 14/3 (2007), pp. 444–66.

77. Springer, Simon, 'Violence sits in places? Cultural practice, neoliberal rationalism, and virulent imaginative geographies', *Political Geography* 30/2 (2011), pp. 90–8.

78. Flint, Colin and Kirsch, Scott, 'Conclusion', in S. Kirsch and C. Flint (eds), *Reconstructing Conflict: Integrating War and Post-War Geographies* (Farnham, 2011), pp. 315–20.

79. Flint and Kirsch, 'Conclusion', p. 315.

80. Nicely, Erinn P., Book Review: 'Out of the grassroots and into a geo-political economy of post-conflict reconstruction', *Political Geography* 28/8 (2009), pp. 508–10. See also Richmond, 'Becoming liberal', p. 338. The theoretical approaches and conceptual framings of critical human geography have begun to influence how scholars from other disciplines approach issues of peace. A prime example is Higate and Henry, *Insecure Spaces*, which, focusing on peacekeeping and peacekeepers, foregrounds concepts of space and spatiality, draws on feminist geopolitics approaches to the body and integrates non-representational theory with ethnographic methodologies.

81. Grundy-Warr, Carl, 'Commentary: pacific geographies and the politics of Buddhist peace activism', *Political Geography* 30/4 (2011), pp. 190–2.

82. Darling, Jonathan, 'A city of sanctuary: the relational re-imagining of Sheffield's asylum politics', *Transactions of the Institute of British Geographers* 35/1 (2010a), pp. 125–40; and this volume, Chapter 12.

83. Williams, P. 'Reproducing everyday peace in north India: process, politics and power', *Annals of the Association of American Geographers* 103/1 (2013): 230–250.

84. Williams and McConnell, 'Critical geographies of peace'; Megoran, 'War *and* peace?'.

85. Flint, *The Geography of War and Peace*, p. 13.

86. Cortright, David, *Peace: A History of Movements and Ideas* (Cambridge, 2008), p. 21.

# Part 1

# Contesting narratives of peace

# 2

# Peace and critical geopolitics

*Simon Dalby*

'Only the dead are safe; only the dead have seen the end of war.'

George Santayana

## Peace, war and geopolitics

This depressing epigraph, frequently erroneously attributed to Plato, notably by Ridley Scott in his cinematic rendition of *Black Hawk Down*, implies that war is a perpetual part of the human condition. It implies the futility of arguments for peace while invoking the tragedy of human organised violence that structures much of what has become called realist international relations scholarship. But the backdrop of *Black Hawk Down* was a failed humanitarian intervention in the early 1990s in Somalia, albeit one that took on imperial overtones rather quickly despite its efforts at peacemaking.[1] Two decades later, as famine and violence once again plague the region, the relationships between war and insecurity, and the failures of American counter-terrorism policies to resolve many of the country's problems, once again put the spotlight on this place. In doing so, numerous questions of geopolitics are intertwined with matters of peace, the responsibility to protect, humanitarian interventions and reinvented banditry in contemporary times. In some ways this is obviously war, but it is not a matter of great powers in direct combat with each other: the geographies of contemporary violence are altogether more complicated than the wars that Santayana implied were an inevitable part of the human condition.

This chapter suggests that a focus on war and violence has to be read against rapidly shifting global geographies and the recent general trend of reduced violence in human affairs.[2] Whether this is the promise of the liberal peace, a transitory imperial *pax*, something more fundamental in human affairs, or a temporary historical blip, remains to be seen, but substantial empirical analyses do suggest that violence is declining overall.[3] This stands in stark contrast to realist assertions of interstate war as the human condition, as well as to repeated warnings about the supposed dangers to the US-led international order of rising Asian powers. Likewise, the re-militarization of Anglo-Saxon culture since 9/11 has suggested that warring is a routine part of modern life. But it was clear to analysts by the end of the Cold War in the early 1990s that the nature of war had changed in some important ways even if contemporary imperial adventures in peripheral places look all too familiar to historians.[4] The danger of a full-scale nuclear war between the great powers has also receded, and this matters greatly in setting the context within which geographers and other scholars think about peace. Peace, all of this crucially implies, is a matter of social processes, not a final *telos* – a resolution of the tensions of human life – nor a utopia that will arrive sometime. In Christian terms the aspirational *Kingdom of God* is a work in progress. Social movements, international peacemaking operations, conflict resolution initiatives are all underway in many places despite the prevalence of combat on the front pages of the newspapers and in the lead items in television news.

If geography as a scholarly discipline is to make useful contributions to such initiatives, and support practical small-scale peace actions, too, some hard thinking is needed on the historical dimensions of geopolitics as well as contemporary transformations. Linking the practical actions of nonviolence from Tahrir Square to those of the Occupy Wall Street movement, underway as an early draft of this paper was keyboarded in 2011, requires that we think very carefully about the practices that now are designated in terms of globalization. Not all of this is novel, but the geopolitical scene is shifting in ways that need to be incorporated into new thinking within geography about war, peace, violence as well as into what the discipline might have to say about, and contribute to, nonviolence as well as to contestations of contemporary lawfare.[5]

The politics of peace plays out in this larger geopolitical context, and this chapter argues that this must not be forgotten in deliberations concerning the possible new initiatives geographers might take in thinking carefully about disciplinary contributions to peace research and practice. Critical geopolitics has long been about challenging the implicit contextualizations that structure the narratives used for war.[6] A peaceful geography has to pay attention to such contextualizations, too, if specific conflicts are to be addressed in ways that take their geographies seriously.

To make the case for thinking very carefully about the big picture when considering geographies of peace, the rest of this chapter starts briefly with nonviolence. Looking back to history, and how geopolitics has been understood in the past, the chapter then contrasts this with a discussion of contemporary geopolitical changes to make the case that in many ways we do live in new times and in circumstances where war is no longer seen as a routine legitimate part of the human condition. That being so, the latter sections of the chapter look more closely at the relationship between peace and the key term 'security', as well as at the oddity of the militarization of Anglo-American society since the events of 9/11. The chapter concludes that this is necessary if geographers are to link their aspirations for peace to careful scholarly analysis in ways that produce knowledge that is useful for practical actions and advocacy for a more peaceful world, rather than be complicit in the violence that continues to shape much of the human condition

## Nonviolence and geopolitical legitimacy

Nick Megoran in particular has suggested that geography needs to think much more carefully about peacemaking and the possibilities of nonviolence as modes of political action.[7] The key question focused on here is Megoran's pointed refusal to accept the simplistic dismissal of the efficacy of nonviolence given the obvious prevalence of violence. The point of his argument is that nonviolence is a political strategy in part to respond to violence, to initiate political actions in ways that are not hostage to the use of force. In doing so, especially in his discussion of resistance to Nazi policies in Germany during the Second World War, Megoran underlines the important points about legitimacy as part of politics, and likewise hints at the fundamental contrast between violence and nonviolence as a strategic mode of political action. Implied here is that while war may be politics by other means, to gloss the classic Clausewitzian formulation, nonviolence is politics, too.

Clausewitz was clear that political violence, and war in particular, depends on the widespread consent of those in whose name violence is used.[8] War is about combat, rivalry and violence, but it also requires at least the tacit consent of the people who pay for the weapons and who supply and provide the soldiers to do the fighting. If war is understood as being no longer an acceptable mode of political conduct then it is much more difficult to mobilize troops and pay for the extraordinarily expensive weapon systems they now use. Whether the delegitimization of violence as a mode of rule will be extended further in coming decades is one of the big questions facing peace researchers. The American reaction to 9/11 set things back, as an opportunity to respond in terms of a response to a crime and diplomacy was squandered. Nonetheless, the wider social refusal to accept repression and violence as appropriate modes of rule has interesting potential to constrain the use of military force.

The professionalization of many high-technology militaries also reduces their inclination to involve themselves in repressing social movements. Mikhail Gorbachev's refusal to use the Red Army against dissidents in Eastern Europe in the late 1980s remains emblematic of the changes to the norms of acceptable rule that have been extended in the last few generations. Much of the progress made after the Cold War was set back by the George W. Bush administration's militarization of the response to the attacks of 9/11. The norms of non-warfare between states have nonetheless held in most conflicts since, although Israel's attacks on its neighbours are an important exception. However, much violent policing by military means continues in many places, ironically justified by the supposed provision of security for neoliberal economic development.[9]

On these matters contemporary social theorists frequently look to Michel Foucault, and the argument drawn from his writings that politics is the extension of war rather than the other way round. Given the interest in biopolitics and geogovernance within geography, these matters are obviously relevant, but the connection to peace needs to be thought carefully beyond formulations that simply assume it to be the opposite of war.[10] This is especially the case given the changing modes of contemporary warfare and the advocacy of violence as an appropriate policy in present circumstances. The modes of warfare at the heart of liberalism suggest that the security of what Dillon and Reid call the 'biohuman', the liberal consuming subject, involves a violent series of practices designed to pacify the world by the elimination of political alternatives.[11] This suggests an imperial peace, a forceful imposition of a state of non-war. In George W. Bush's terms justifying the War on Terror: a long struggle to eliminate tyranny.[12] Peace is, in this geopolitical understanding, what comes after the elimination of opposition. In late 2011 such formulations dominated discussions of the death of Colonel Gaddafi in Libya. The corollary to this is precisely that eliminating such regimes, and removing the restrictions to economic activity, will facilitate their engagement in globalization and, in turn, bring prosperity to these states, which will remove their warlike and violent propensities.

In much of the recent geography literature, and in critical geopolitics in particular, the larger transformations of globalization, and in particular the changing patterns of warfare and strategic calculations, have been relatively neglected.[13] Geographers have done much work on militarization and contemporary terror and violence,[14] the military and changing notions of citizenship,[15] the use of fear in popular culture and politics,[16] and the practicalities of combat in the War on Terror.[17] But the focus on the small and immediate human scale, crucial though it is to understanding the geographies of contemporary violence and the practicalities of the functioning of security bureaucracies, frequently fails to link the practical fieldwork-based studies, or the textual analysis of popular geopolitics,[18] to the larger patterns of geopolitical transformation and to how strategic calculation works on the part of policy makers and military planners. A geography discipline seriously interested in peace needs to link the social processes on the relatively small scale, such as the nonviolent protests that Megoran highlights and the peaceful accompaniment actions that Koopman documents, to the larger geopolitical transformations of our times. This is necessary in order to make the eminently geographical point that peace activities vary widely from place to place, but now are an important part of larger contemporary geopolitical transformations.[19]

## Geopolitics and change

Geopolitics has mostly been about rivalries between great powers and their contestations of power on the large scale. These specifications of the political world focus on states and the perpetuation of threats mapped as external dangers to supposedly pacific polities. Much geopolitical discourse, particularly in what passes as a realist interpretation of great powers as the prime movers of history, specifies the world as a dangerous place where great power violence is required.[20] Geopolitical thinking is about order, and order is in part a cartographic notion. Juliet Fall emphasizes the importance of taken-for-granted boundaries as the ontological given of contemporary politics.[21] Politics is about the cartographic control of territories, as Megoran ponders regarding the first half of the twentieth century, but it is also about much more than this, despite the fascination that so many commentators have with the ideal form of the supposedly national territorial state.[22] Part of what geographers bring to the discussion of peace is a more nuanced geographical imagination than that found in so much of international studies.[23]

On the other hand, much of the discussion of peace sees war as the problem and peace as the solution. Implied in this is geopolitics as the problem: mapping dangers turns out to be itself a dangerous enterprise insofar as it facilitates the perpetuation of violence by representing other places as threats to which 'our place' is susceptible. But this only matters if this is related to the realist assumptions of the inevitability of rivalry, the eternal search for power as key to humanity's self-organization and the assumption that organized violence is the ultimate arbiter.[24] Critical geopolitics is about challenging such contextualizations and, as such, its relationships to peace would seem to be obvious, albeit, as Megoran notes, mostly by way of a focus on what Galtung calls negative peace.[25] Given the repeated reinvention of colonial tropes in contemporary Western political discourse, such critique remains an essential part of a political geography that grants peoples 'the courtesy of political geography'.[26] It remains a crucial contribution of scholarship to undercut the moral logics of violence, which so frequently rely on simplistic invocations of geographical inevitability to structure their apologetics.

Both the practical matters of recent history and the scholarly contributions by geographers do not allow simple binary distinctions of peace and war to be used as the premise of either scholarship or political practice. History and scholarship suggest, rather, that peace is what comes after war; the relationship is temporal, and peace is but one temporary stage in matters of violence related to the periodic changes in political geography. Historically, in the era of European warfare (which was coincident with the rise of modernity) peace was imposed by the victors. Much recent geographical scholarship suggests that post-conflict reconstruction is a mode of peacebuilding, literally.[27] But those of us who would challenge war as a human institution, or who think about nonviolence as a strategy for a better world, will not be satisfied with a geography that is concerned only to pick up the pieces and reconfigure them after they have been shattered by the latest round of organized violence.

The key point is that reconstruction is also sometimes a violent transformation of society, in a world where frequently neoliberal globalization is seen as the imposition of social forms that will not resist its logics. Hence peace is what victors impose, an imperial peace that may eventually be quite welcome to those who benefit from the new arrangements. Is peace, then, post-war? Perhaps it can be understood in these terms. But the corollary is the equally important point that peace is also frequently what comes before the next war. The normal human situation these days is a matter of non-war, but it is far from clear that this is more than a limited form of negative peace where security is enforced. Without demilitarization, peace is just what happens between wars.

But given this, one additional key point that geographers interested in war need to pay attention to is the matter of how peace fails, and, in turn, how conflict escalates, and how geography matters in these processes.[28] Peacekeeping is frequently about geographical separation, as the Orwellian name of "peace lines" for the huge walls through Belfast has long suggested. But there is much more geographical thinking to be done about these matters and about the scales of interactions across supposedly peaceful borders, not least where what matters most is state security and its ordering principles rather than local interactions across frontiers. This is so not least because of the marked current trend to build fences around states as the supposed solution to numerous security challenges.[29]

Putting matters into historical context also suggests that war is not what it used to be, at least not after the events of the 1940s. Negative peace is about preventing conflict; nonviolence is about political strategies to delegitimize violence, to challenge the human norms of behaviour that allow cultures of violence. It is important to link this to the issues of what are now called 'lawfare': the use of law as power and coercion to set the rules of social and political life.[30] This has been a key part of the US strategy for a long time: shaping institutions to the benefit of the US economy has been what much of international relations has been about, but the larger benefits of constraining conflict are part of the process that international law struggles to legitimize. Rules of conduct matter in the international system, and the wide-scale repudiation of the American invasion of Iraq in 2003 demonstrated this point clearly.

The United Nations has effectively made war illegal, although the number of ways round that formal restriction has been considerable. Spying, as well as military action, have become increasingly reconfigured in terms of security. The United Nations executive committee was named the Security Council not the Peace Council, and the rhetoric ever since has suggested that peace has to be conjoined with security, with the latter – not the former – being paramount. Apparently peace without security is not worth bothering about. It is peace *and* security. This suggests that war is perhaps the opposite of security, as well as the opposite of peace. But perhaps security is to be contrasted with violence instead? All of which requires careful conceptual thinking about the current geopolitical borders.

Crucial, but unremarked upon by many political geographers, is the simple fact that there is now widespread agreement that borders between states are fixed finally.[31] Demarcation disputes will continue, as will some very interesting arguments about changing coastal boundaries as sea levels rise in coming decades, but the territorial fixity assumption has changed one fundamental facet of warfare between states. Given the importance of territorial disputes historically as a cause of wars, this point is very important. So, too, is the finding that it matters greatly how these disputes are handled. Territorial disputes are more likely to lead to war if regarded as the zero-sum competition that 'realism' would have them, than if diplomacy and conflict resolution are taken seriously.[32]

The exceptions here do seem to prove the rule: Palestine and Kashmir are two flashpoints where attempts to move borders, or at least the refusal to accept their imposition, are key to continued violence. Fixing geographical borders removes one major historical cause of interstate warfare. Territorial aggrandizement is now mostly a thing of the past, as the reconstruction of Bosnia and the refusal to change antecedent boundaries illustrates, albeit very painfully. The title of Gearóid Ó Tuathail and Carl Dahlman's book is *Bosnia Remade*, not *Bosnia Removed*, and that matters in terms of how politics is now literally mapped.[33] The territorial fixity norm, and the importance of agreement on frontiers and their delimitation, tragically continues to be emphasized in the southern areas of what until recently was the singular state of Sudan.

## Resource wars

While there is optimism over the territorial covenant on both the small scale and the very large scale, the fixity of boundaries has not prevented either the violence of what Mary Kaldor called the 'new wars' after the Cold War, nor imperial adventures by the USA, the UK, Canada and other mostly English-speaking metropolitan states.[34] Indeed, looking at the macro-scale patterns of imperial power, the question is whether current Middle East warring is but the latest phase of 'Anglosphere' imperial violence.[35] Robert Fisk's subtitle to his huge book on the region is blunt in posing the matter as the conquest of the Middle East.[36]

Understanding the USA and the UK, with their various settler colonies, as extensions of an Anglosphere suggests only that the patterns of conquest and indirect but violent rule have shifted to another region of the planet: from North America in the eighteenth century to South Asia and then Africa in the nineteenth and early twentieth century. The pattern is now extended to the Middle East in the latter part of the twentieth and early twenty-first century. This shifting pattern of Anglosphere violence is the updated logic of Kevin Phillips' argument about the *Cousins' Wars* as key to the rise of British and subsequently American power.[37] Thus, focusing on the specific geographies of the War on Terror and on Anglosphere military action in South West Asia is a useful antidote to the hugely exaggerated claims of Islamic threats as a global phenomenon invoking the need for a US-led world war.[38]

Elsewhere violence has followed resources, at least to the sources of valuable ones and oil in particular.[39] Mary Kaldor's analysis of the new wars suggests both that globalization matters in terms of the patterns of connection that fuel and fund violence, and also in that the role of political violence is often about control of population and economic assets rather than a matter of territorial control.[40] Militias and gangs, as well as would-be micro-nationalists, are not the warring entities of nation states in violent competition invading each other's territories: they are more diffuse arrangements, something more analogous to medieval geographies rather than the violent interactions of discrete, clearly demarcated modern states. This is not unrelated to the imposition of the cartography of the territorial covenant, even if it has generated whole new categories of geopolitics, of ungoverned areas and peripheral regions where violence persists, and drones, interventions and mercenaries are commonplace. Peacemaking in such circumstances is far from easy, as the case of Somalia repeatedly illustrates.

Over the last few decades the potential for major power warfare seems to have lessened very considerably, the examples of great power interventions in peripheral places notwithstanding. The global economy has, of late, required much greater cooperation between political elites. The looming crises of climate change that make unilateral action less efficacious, suggest the possibilities of less confrontational assumptions as the premise in geopolitics. While resource wars get headlines, much of environmental politics is about co-operation and treaty making rather than warfare.[41] Much of the contemporary violence that grabs the attention of headline writers is matters of conflict, competition and rivalry, but it is not the classical war Clausewitz pointed to as the contest between two autonomous combatants in a struggle of wills fought until one forces the other to concede. Much of this might fit into Clausewitz's categories of small wars, but that in itself is significant if it supports the contention that great powers have given up the use of major war, if not police actions, as policy.

Over the last few decades, despite the re-militarization of American, British and much of the rest of the Anglosphere's political culture in the name of homeland security and related themes, the long-term trend in the reduction of violence seems to be holding.[42] Another serious war in South West Asia may yet upset this trend, especially if Saudi Arabia and Iran come to blows and Israel and the USA get involved. The petroleum infrastructure in the region that literally fuels globalization would, in those circumstances, be targeted, and the global economy disrupted:

such is the current Iranian mode of deterrence. If states operate in narrow self-interest in response, rather than in a collaborative way to deal with the disruptions, all sorts of confrontations are possible. Narrow notions of national security may trump broader notions of peace, never mind regional or global security. If this happens, all the dangers of escalation, as states find themselves in positions that force them to choose sides in a polarizing situation, may play out in the complex conflict-space of another war.[43]

## Peace and security

Nick Megoran conjoins peace *and* war in his response to Derek Gregory's article on 'War *and* Peace'.[44] But to think through the possible meanings of peace these days, and how geographers might make a useful contribution, it seems that it is also necessary to think about peace *and* security. To do so requires tackling the dominant practices of legitimization that constructed huge infrastructures of 'security' in the last century at the state level in terms of national security, international alliance systems, and the United Nations, as matters of global security. Security is frequently the overarching logic of political action. It justifies most things in terms of the provision of safety, but on closer inspection what is usually secured these days is the neoliberal global economy that is both transforming the planet and rendering many people very insecure in the process.

Surveillance and spying are not new, but the massive bureaucracies that now police political order in the West, justified in terms of the War on Terror now that communism has ceased to be an obviously threatening geopolitical phenomenon, are supposedly about maintaining security. Political order is being secured in all this. If that requires repression, a matter of emergency measures justified in terms of national security, then so be it. Security trumps democracy. Order is, as Hedley Bull used to remind his readers, prior to justice.[45] The major concern in terms of the infringements of the liberties of at least Western populations has been the grounds for intense legal contestations, most notably of Guantanamo Bay.[46] This emphasizes once again the importance of authority and legitimacy as key to politics, a matter of lawfare in many places, but one that is crucial to arguments for nonviolent direct action.

The militarization of responses to protests at international summit meetings in the 1990s, and since, raises the spectre of police states beyond the control of legal proceedings, but in the process challenges the legitimacy of many state practices.[47] Finding appropriate venues to argue back against the injustices of the present is precisely the genius in the slogan of 'Occupy Wall Street' and the related application of the principles of nonviolence to make the political point concerning whose side the security forces are actually on. The Egyptian military finessed the point rather well in Cairo early in 2011: maintaining control while refusing to use violence against the protestors in Tahrir Square.

The protestors in the Occupy Wall Street (and other sites around the world) movement pushed matters of gross inequality, and the consequences of the present capitalist system, squarely onto the agenda. They also spotlighted the issue of peaceful protest in contrast to the violence of police repression. At the same time, they posed the question of the real source of violence, when employees of financial institutions who make millions of dollars by derivatives trading and dubious mortgages are apparently immune from the disastrous consequences such things have for the lives of millions of people. This is now posing Johan Galtung's questions about structural violence and its geographies rather pointedly, and tying the discussion once again to what it is that is being secured if only a negative peace is considered crucial.

These issues are nearly impossible to consider without a discussion within Western states about the human security agenda. The aftermath of the Cold War brought about a much wider debate concerning security, and the needs of many impoverished peoples for the provision of basic modes of security to allow development to happen. Codified in the 1994 UN Human Development Programme report, the human security agenda subsequently became tied into the Responsibility to Protect discussion through which notions of humanitarian intervention gained fairly widespread credence in international politics.[48] Related to this is a series of arguments about warfare and intervention that frequently suggest that the only possible form of political order that is acceptable is a liberal one, populated by the 'biohuman consumer' who has to be secured if peace is to reign.[49]

More recently, human security principles have been once again brought into disrepute by the cavalier use of them as justification for the bombing campaign to force regime change in Libya in 2011. The ostensible rationale for intervention was population protection, but effectively, as was done in Bosnia and Kosovo in the 1990s, NATO provided rebels with an airforce that greatly enhanced their capabilities. Law and lawfare need to be thought together if we are to link power and order on the largest scale, but this needs to confront the relationships of peace *and* security, too.[50] This is necessary precisely because there are crucial geographies to who is secure where, and how decisions to 'intervene' *there*, are made by people *here*. Human security apparently requires interventions in some places and not in others. Nowhere in the official documents is it seriously contemplated that southern actors might 'intervene' in the metropoles to ensure the safety of southern populations in the face of climate change or other environmental dangers generated mostly in the North.[51]

Interventions are also complicated by the fact that professional militaries in Western states are increasingly a small social minority, one that frequently sees itself as under-appreciated by a civilian population that thinks violence is uncivilized. On one hand, the military has become increasingly professionalized and there is a clear understanding that it is a technically specialist social organization. On the other hand, it is also a casualty-averse organization that now usually prides itself on technical proficiency rather than whole-scale slaughter as an appropriate *modus operandi*. It is not soldiers but aerial drones that frequently claim headline attention with their attacks in Pakistan, Afghanistan, Yemen and Somalia, demonstrating how the technology of death often now undermines the warrior culture.[52] How robots are figured in the logics of contemporary warfare matters. Their peaceful possibilities need attention, too, if we are to avoid Steve Graham's nightmare worlds of militarized urbanism where elites are at war with the poor in coming decades.[53]

Simultaneously, the rapid changes in military technology have changed the nature of potential warfare between great powers and the kind of violence they unleash in peripheral regions. Nuclear weapons add a great complication to calculations of violence, and the ability of intercontinental range weapons to strike rapidly adds to the difficulty of thinking through the possible scenarios for successful military action. This technology has been key to the recent revolution in military affairs.[54] The industrial powers now need capital and technology much more than they do military manpower to make war and this, too, has changed both the incentives to use violence and the costs of doing so. Drone wars are effectively casualty avoidance exercises for those who have drones. Cyber wars – if, in fact, the general bad behaviour, espionage and hacking that so troubles contemporary security thinkers is understood as war – have neither territory nor physical combat at all.[55] Hence they simply do not meet the standard social science definitions of war as a situation involving one thousand battle casualties within a year. Is this war or something else?

Mapping all these processes requires a geographical imagination that links something along the lines of John Agnew's formulation of regimes of globalization where some rules apply, and only some boundaries apply some of the time in a very unequal global political economy, to Stuart Elden's notions of contingent sovereignty, where effectively external powers decide when the normal rules of territorial integrity do not apply and 'interventions' are justified.[56] Note that these interventions do not change frontiers. Rather, they simply suspend sovereignty until such time as the rulers judged to be no longer acceptable are replaced by more congenial figures, following which formal sovereignty is reasserted. If peacemaking is the replacement of regimes that are not enthusiastic supporters of the neoliberal order of our times, then this looks more like imperialism than anything else – however much the pacification of peripheral polities may be justified in terms of the responsibility to protect.

'Security for whom?' remains the key question, but nuancing it with the question of security precisely *where*, will undoubtedly help analysis in coming years, especially if this is linked to explicit questions of what kind of peace is being secured. Key to this is focusing on the repeated militarization of security and on the assumptions that force, rather than negotiation and larger cultures of political engagement, are the most important issues in security provision. Challenging this assumption remains a key intellectual task, although one made much easier recently for geographers by repeated empirical work that clearly suggests both that peaceful strategies work best in dealing with territorial issues,[57] and also in relation to resource and environmental matters.[58]

## Aspiration, analysis and advocacy

Thinking intelligently about peace within the discipline of geography requires us to juxtapose our aspirations for a peaceful world – one beyond war and at least the most egregious injustices of structural violence – with careful analysis of how the world is being changed, so that useful advocacy is possible. Contrary to arguments that construct a real world of politics separate from peace activism, one commonly formulated in terms of an autonomous realm of the international, the arguments from both critical international relations thinking as well as the early critical geopolitics discussions were precisely that the reasonings of politics are part of politics, and that thinking carefully about the ontological framings invoked in political discourse matter as part of the political world that constitutes the possible options for political actors.[59]

The task for scholars in present times, as so often in the past, has to be to keep aspiration, analysis and advocacy in creative tension. Wishful thinking has to be avoided at each stage. But if intellectual activity is to be useful in making a more peaceful world then naivety is no help: careful scholarly work is what is needed.[60] Analysis can channel aspiration into useful advocacy precisely by acting as an antidote to either emotional impulse or thoughtless heroic gestures. This is crucial to the task of the academic and, as such, linking academic activity directly into practical action is simply part of our trade. Teaching matters greatly here, and careful advocacy of peaceful possibilities is key to teaching critical geopolitics.

The scholarly research both on territory and war, as well as discussions of environmental degradation and its security implications, show clearly that how these issues are handled matters greatly. Confrontation is not inevitable: political initiatives toward co-operation rather than *real-politik* lead to constructive solutions. Continuing to challenge determinist arguments that argue otherwise remains an important task for geographers.[61] But the sheer scale of the human transformation of the planet, processes inadequately encapsulated in the term 'globalization', now makes this easier.[62]

Delegitimization of violence is a key part of challenging determinism. This encompasses ending death penalties, reducing physical abuse and torture, supporting Amnesty International campaigns and international solidarity in the face of suffering, as well as extending the norms of politics and the appropriate cultural modes acceptable for ruling. It is precisely the failure of the USA to live up to supposedly higher civilizational standards in Abu Graib, Guantanamo and now in the targeting of drone weapons in Pakistan and elsewhere, that undermines its legitimacy.[63] Coupled with the great lengths to which the USA has gone to render its actions legitimate, and to avoid potential problems with the International Criminal Court, matters of legality offer considerable options for activist geographers to contribute to changing societal norms away from militarism. The links to critical legal geographies need further attention too: jurisdiction matters![64]

The overall conclusion from this chapter is that geographers should never forget that politics is prior to all the other discussions, and that understanding peace in the context of particular forms of politics is not unrelated to the forms of rule and authority invoked in particular situations. The world is changing rapidly, but shaping that change is a matter of practical initiatives, and peacemaking. This simple point should never be forgotten: and neither should the opposite point: that war may happen despite good intentions. No doubt in the next few years around the centenary of the outbreak of the First World War there will be further reflections on the processes that lead to 'the guns of August' in Barbara Tuchman's famous phrase.[65] Building institutions that can negotiate and co-operate in the face of destabilizing crises events matters greatly, notwithstanding the popular animosity towards governments built up by a generation of neoliberal ideology and right-wing populist movements generously funded by those with an interest in turning states into the tools of capital.

In the face of endless neo-Malthusian fears of scarcities and disruptions to come, the possibilities of a more peaceful world remain achievable in many places. Challenging fearful cartographies, refusing the designation of difference and distance as necessarily dangerous, has long been part of the geographer's potential contribution, as in Peter Kropotkin's classic statement concerning what geography ought to be.[66] Thinking long and hard about the diffusion of military technologies and the possible ways that geographers might usefully contribute to the discussions of arms control, not least the key point about the implicit geopolitics in the supposedly technical arrangements of weapons limitation verifications, matters too.[67] Arms control needs very much more attention.

Ultimately, geopolitics is crucial in that if the dominant mappings of politics continue to specify the world in terms of territorial domains of rule in rivalry with one another, and with military force as the ultimate arbiter, then the possibilities of the use of force remain on the agenda. Realists will argue that this is inevitable. But if the pacification of international, or perhaps that should be inter-imperial, relations that the United Nations system has begun is extended, then the possibilities of what Nick Megoran calls 'pacific geopolitics' open up.[68] Now the challenge is to see new modes of rule that deal with the most important mappings of a changing globe where ecological matters require mappings of interconnection rather than emphasizing the borders of supposedly autonomous entities.[69]

Who decides the future of the planet matters greatly, but politics remains – at least, so far – a matter of *who* decides long before it is a matter of *what* gets decided. That, too, is a matter for peaceful geographers to tackle. The fate of the earth is at stake, and as a discipline with aspirations to study it as humanity's home, our attention is certainly warranted. In the circumstances of rapid global change and the potential disruptions that are coming, we now have additional compelling reasons to work towards making Santayana's dismal assertion concerning the inevitability of war a thing of the past.

# Notes

1. Dalby, Simon, 'Warrior geopolitics: *Gladiator, Black Hawk Down* and the *Kingdom of Heaven*', *Political Geography* 27/4 (2008), pp. 439–55.
2. Pinker, Steven, *The Better Angels of our Nature: Why Violence has Declined* (New York, 2011).
3. Human Security Report Project, *Human Security Report 2009/2010: The Causes of Peace and the Shrinking Costs of War* (Oxford, 2011).
4. Van Creveld, Martin, *The Transformation of War* (New York, 1991).
5. Gregory, Derek, 'The Black Flag: Guantanamo Bay and the space of exception', *Geografiska Annaler B*, 88/4 (2006), pp. 405–27.
6. Dalby, Simon, 'Recontextualising violence, power and nature: the next twenty years of critical geopolitics?', *Political Geography* 29/5 (2010), pp. 280–8.
7. Megoran, Nick, 'War *and* Peace? An agenda for peace research and practice in geography', *Political Geography* 30/4 (2011), pp. 178–89.
8. Clausewitz, Carl von, *On War* (Harmondsworth, 1968). Original: *Vom Kriege*, 1832.
9. Duffield, Mark, *Development, Security and Unending War* (Cambridge, 2007).
10. Morrissey, John, 'Liberal lawfare and biopolitics: US juridical warfare in the War on Terror', *Geopolitics* 16/2 (2011), pp. 280–305.
11. Dillon, Michael and Reid, Julian, *The Liberal Way of War: Killing to Make Life Live* (London, 2009).
12. Dalby, Simon, 'Geopolitics, the revolution in military affairs and the Bush doctrine', *International Politics* 46/2–3(2009a), pp. 234–52.
13. Dalby, Simon, 'Realism and geopolitics in the anthropocene', in K. Dodds, M. Kuus and J. Sharp (eds), *Companion to Critical Geopolitics* (Aldershot, 2012).
14. Gregory, Derek and Pred, Allan (eds), *Violent Geographies: Fear, Terror, and Political Violence* (New York, 2007).
15. Cowen, Deborah and Gilbert, Emily (eds), *War, Citizenship, Territory* (New York, 2008).
16. Ingram, Alan and Dodds, Klaus (eds), *Spaces of Security and Insecurity* (Aldershot, 2009); Pain, Rachel and Smith, Susan, *Fear: Critical Geopolitics and Everyday Life* (Aldershot, 2008).
17. Gregory, Derek, *The Colonial Present: Afghanistan, Palestine, Iraq* (Oxford, 2004).
18. Dittmer, Jason, *Popular Culture, Geopolitics and Identity* (Lanham, MD, 2010).
19. Megoran, 'War *and* Peace?'; Koopman, Sara, 'Alter-geopolitics: other securities are happening', *Geoforum* 42/3 (2011), pp. 274–84 and Koopman this volume.
20. Mearsheimer, John J., *The Tragedy of Great Power Politics* (New York, 2001).
21. Fall, Juliet, 'Artificial states? On the enduring geographical myth of natural borders', *Political Geography* 29/3 (2010), pp. 140–7.
22. Megoran, 'War *and* Peace?'
23. Dalby, Simon, 'Geographies of the international system: globalisation, empire and the anthropocene', in P. Aalto, S. Moisio, and V. Harle (eds), *International Studies: Interdisciplinary Approaches* (London, 2011a), pp. 125–48.
24. Dalby, 'Recontextualising violence, power and nature'.
25. Megoran, 'War *and* Peace?'; Galtung, Johan, 'Violence, peace, and peace research', *Journal of Peace Research*, 6/3 (1969), pp. 167–91; Galtung, Johan, 'A structural theory of imperialism', *Journal of Peace Research* 8/2 (1971), pp. 81–117.
26. Mitchell, Don and Smith, Neil, 'Comment: the courtesy of political geography', *Political Geography Quarterly* 10 (1991), pp. 338–41.

27. Kirsch, Scott and Flint, Colin (eds), *Reconstructing Conflict: Integrating War and Post-War Geographies* (Farnham, 2011).

28. Flint, Colin, Diehl, Paul, Scheffran, Juergen, Vasquez, John and Chi, Sang-hyun, 'Conceptualising conflictspace: toward a geography of relational power and embeddedness in the analysis of interstate conflict', *Annals of the Association of American Geographers* 99/5 (2009), pp. 827–35.

29. Jones, Reece, 'Border Security: 9/11 and the enclosure of civilisation', *Geographical Journal* 177/3 (2011), pp. 213–17.

30. Morrissey, 'Liberal lawfare and biopolitics'.

31. Zacher, Mark, 'The international territorial order: boundaries, the use of force and normative change', *International Organization* 55/2 (2001), pp. 215–50.

32. Vasquez, John A. and Henehan, Marie T., *Territory, War and Peace* (London, 2011).

33. Ó Tuathail, Gearóid and Dahlman, Carl, *Bosnia Remade: Ethnic Cleansing and its Reversal* (New York, 2011).

34. Kaldor, Mary, *New and Old Wars: Organized Violence in a Global Era* (Cambridge, 2006).

35. Megoran, Nick, 'Neoclassical geopolitics', *Political Geography* 29/4 (2009), pp. 1–3.

36. Fisk, Robert, *The Great War for Civilisation: The Conquest of the Middle East* (London, 2006).

37. Phillips, Kevin, *The Cousins' Wars* (New York, 1999).

38. Podhoretz, Norman, *World War IV: The Long Struggle Against Islamofascism* (New York, 2007).

39. Le Billon, Philippe and Cervantes, Alejandreo, 'Oil prices, scarcity, and geographies of war', *Annals of the Association of American Geographers* 99/5 (2009), pp. 836–44.

40. Kaldor, *New and Old Wars*.

41. Dinar, Shlomi (ed.), *Beyond Resource Wars: Scarcity, Environmental Degradation, and International Cooperation* (Cambridge, MA, 2011).

42. *Human Security Report Project: Human Security Report 2009/2010*.

43. Flint, Colin *et al.*, 'Conceptualising conflictspace', pp. 827–35.

44. Megoran, 'War *and* Peace?'; Gregory, Derek, 'War and peace', *Transactions of the Institute of British Geographers* 35/2 (2010), pp. 154–86.

45. Bull, Hedley, *The Anarchical Society: A Study of Order in World Politics* (New York, 1977).

46. Gregory, 'The Black Flag'.

47. Smith, Neil and Cowen, Deborah, 'Martial law on the streets of Toronto: G20 security and state violence', *Journal of Human Geography* 3/3 (2011), pp. 29–46.

48. Kaldor, Mary, *Human Security: Reflections on Globalization and Intervention* (Cambridge, 2007).

49. Dillon and Reid, *The Liberal Way of War*.

50. Morrissey, 'Liberal lawfare and biopolitics'.

51. Dalby, Simon, *Security and Environmental Change* (Cambridge, 2009b).

52. Singer, Peter W., *Wired for War: The Robotics Revolution and Conflict in the Twenty-First Century* (New York, 2009).

53. Graham, Stephen, *Cities Under Siege: The New Military Urbanism* (London, 2010).

54. Dalby, 'Geopolitics, the revolution in military affairs and the Bush Doctrine'.

55. Deibert, Ronald J. and Rohozinski, Rafal, 'Risking security: policies and paradoxes of cyberspace security', *International Political Sociology* 4/1 (2010), pp. 15–32.
56. Agnew, John, *Globalization and Sovereignty* (Lanham, MD, 2009a); Elden, Stuart, *Terror and Territory: The Spatial Extent of Sovereignty* (Minneapolis, 2009).
57. Vasquez and Henehan, *Territory, War and Peace.*
58. Dinar, *Beyond Resource Wars.*
59. Walker, R. B. J., *After the Globe, Before the World* (London, 2010).
60. Inwood, J. and Tyner, J., 'Geography's pro-peace agenda: an unfinished project', *ACME* 10/3 (2011), p. 445.
61. Kearns, Gerry, *Geopolitics and Empire: The Legacy of Halford Mackinder* (Oxford, 2009).
62. Dalby, 'Realism and geopolitics in the anthropocene'.
63. Gregory, 'War and peace'; Hannah, Matthew, 'Torture and the ticking bomb: the war on terrorism as a geographical imagination of power/knowledge', *Annals of the Association of American Geographers* 96/3 (2006), pp. 622–40.
64. Gregory, 'The Black Flag'.
65. Tuchman, Barbara, *The Guns of August* (New York, 1962).
66. Kropotkin, Peter, 'What geography ought to be', *The Nineteenth Century*, 18 (1885), pp. 1940–56.
67. Dalby, Simon, 'Critical geopolitics and the control of arms in the twenty-first century', *Contemporary Security Policy* 32/1 (2011b), pp. 40–56.
68. Megoran, 'Towards a geography of peace'.
69. Dalby, *Security and Environmental Change.*

# 3

# Building peaceful geographies in and through systems of violence

*Nicole Laliberte*

| | |
|---|---|
| *Iya yom kombedi.* | I am happy now. |
| *Atye ki kuc.* | I am peaceful. |
| *Ki miya woro.* | I am respected. |

These are phrases used by the women and men of ADO, a grassroots human rights organization in northern Uganda, to describe their lives.[1] Such statements are striking given that the persistence of violence in and through everyday spaces is a pivotal topic in most discussions of life in this post-conflict landscape.[2] As Williams and McConnell contend, a focus on peaceful concepts such as friendship, trust, hope and empathy can be an entry point into everyday experiences of peace.[3] It can also be a means by which to expose the co-constitution of peaceful and violent processes. By simultaneously acknowledging the continued physical, structural and cultural violence in their lives, yet choosing to focus on peaceful concepts and experiences, ADO members are actively constructing peaceful geographies in and through systems of violence.

In line with contemporary trends amongst organizations fighting violence and oppression, human rights discourses and practices are central to the work of ADO. Not only do human rights offer a normative vision of what social relations could and should look like, they also offer the promise of realizing these visions through technical practices and networks of solidarity. Human rights discourses and practices, however, are not innocent; they have been created in, and through, systems of violence. Universalist claims of human rights are implicated in multi-scalar processes that connect the particular agendas of supranational and international organizations to place-based power relations through a state-centric model. Drawing upon the experiences of ADO members, this chapter explores the limitations and opportunities of human rights as a tool for building peaceful geographies. It offers an analysis of ADO's articulation of universalist human rights claims with place-based social relations. In addition, this chapter highlights the topographies of peaceful narratives that ADO creates to express their experiences of the post-war landscape. This emotional geography highlights the importance of solidarity in creating peaceful spaces of hope and optimism.

To examine the processes through which ADO members negotiate human rights and construct peaceful geographies, I turn to postcolonial theories of agency. These theories highlight how the capacity for action is simultaneously constrained and enabled through historically specific relations of subordination.[4] Such theories of agency provide an analytic framework for examining the co-constitution of peaceful and violent geographies without directly engaging with definitional debates around the meaning of peace. This focus serves theoretical as well as empirical purposes. Theoretical definitions of peace have historically created polemics in which peace is either claimed or denied, based on simplistic definitions (e.g. the absence of war) or idealistic definitions (e.g. pure harmony and tranquillity). Whereas recent work in the geographies of peace literature seeks to avoid these polemics by complicating the idea of peace[5] and re-imagining normative constructions of peace,[6] this chapter avoids the problematic of proscriptive definitions by exploring the complex processes through which people strive to realize their individual and collective imaginings of peace. In so doing, it contributes to feminist scholarship that has demonstrated the dissonance between people's lived experiences and the binary of peace and violence.[7] Empirically, my choice to avoid definitional debates is motivated by the tendency amongst respondents to reinforce such debates when asked to speak about peace. This was true of respondents who focused on narratives of violence as well as those, such as ADO members, who described peaceful experiences. Directly engaging these definitional debates, therefore, did not provide the empirical evidence necessary to examine the differences between peaceful and violent narratives of the post-war landscape. Ultimately, this chapter contributes to the growing geographies of peace literature by answering recent calls to examine everyday practices of peace that are neither simple nor without violence.[8]

To realize this analysis, the chapter is divided into four sections. The first section briefly introduces ADO and its work within the context of northern Uganda. This empirical background is then put into conversation with postcolonial theories of agency to provide a framework for my subsequent analysis of ADO's construction of peaceful geographies. The second section initiates the application of these theories of agency through a critical analysis of human rights, a key tool ADO uses to create its peaceful geographies. The third section examines the strategies that ADO employs to create peaceful spaces in the midst of systems of violence. Finally, the fourth section turns to an emotional geographies framework to explore the motivations behind ADO members' decisions to use peaceful narratives to describe their lives.

The empirical evidence for this analysis is drawn from a year of ethnographic research beginning in July 2010. During this period, I worked closely with three organizations in northern Uganda: two professional NGOs in Gulu Town, and ADO in a rural area of Odek sub-county. The material for this chapter draws heavily from my work with ADO starting in November 2010. I conducted semi-structured interviews with approximately 60 members, collected oral histories with 27 members and was a participant-observer during mediations and group meetings. In addition, by living with ADO members, my research assistant and I were included in a wide variety of informal conversations that provided not only a nuanced perspective on the work and lives of ADO members but also the opportunity to verify interpretations of events and previous conversations.

## Background: ADO and agency

ADO was established in 2005 in the midst of a landscape characterized by violence and oppression. For more than twenty years, the civilian population of northern Uganda was caught in the middle of a low-intensity war between the Lord's Resistance Army (LRA) and the Government of Uganda. While the LRA was notorious for abducting children to fill its ranks, the government's policy of forced displacement contributed significantly to the 50,000 excess deaths per year experienced by the displaced population.[9] This prolonged violence and displacement, along with the associated dependency on humanitarian aid by the majority of the population, led to the weakening of social institutions amongst the Acholi people of northern Uganda.[10] This social disintegration was provisionally managed by governmental and humanitarian agencies, who provided governance structures within the internally displaced persons (IDP) camps throughout the region. ADO drew its members and its name from three such IDP camps: Awere, Dino and Odek. The founding members, all in leadership positions within camp governance structures and frustrated by the many needs unmet by governmental and international organizations, heeded aid agencies' calls for women to form groups in order to receive services and resources, but they did so on their own terms. They put out a call for women interested in helping their community. At the first meeting, they determined that all work for ADO would be voluntary, so that they would not be dependent on outside funding or be criticized for corruption. They then started approaching NGOs to find an organization that would support their initiatives. They ultimately connected with Human Rights Focus (HURIFO), a regional human rights organization. Subsequently, human rights became the language through which ADO sought to reduce violence and oppression within their communities.

This brief history of ADO's foundation introduces the historically specific context in which its ability to construct peaceful geographies was both constrained and enabled. The social upheaval and mass displacement associated with the war led to a destabilization of gender roles in which women were able to participate in realms of life formerly deemed masculine.[11] In some cases, such as becoming sole provider for one's family, these new roles for women were based on necessity and tended to be oppressive, while in other cases, such as leadership positions within IDP camps, these new roles were voluntary and provided opportunities for solidarity and empowerment. The mass influx of non-governmental organizations (NGOs) in the early 2000s brought with it the typical clientelism associated with aid/development agencies, yet it also brought the discourse of human rights and connected ADO to multi-scalar forms of authority. The state's neoliberal policies and relative absence from the region (save military activity) have left the population with few resources and limited access to services. This relative absence, however, has created uneven enforcement of the state's authority, effectively opening spaces for social change.

Engagements with postcolonial feminist theories of agency can illuminate how ADO members have come to negotiate these geographies of violence and opportunity. Agency, according to Asad, 'is a complex term whose senses emerge within semantic and institutional networks that define and make possible particular ways of relating to people, things and oneself'.[12] Building upon this, Mahmood argues that agency is a negotiation, 'a capacity for action that specific relations of subordination create and enable'.[13] Employing these theories of agency, I examine ADO's attempts to create peaceful geographies in and through oppressive institutions. ADO's willingness to engage with local, state-based and international institutions can at times appear to reinforce the very sources of violence and oppression it is trying to fight, but a close analysis belies the spaces of agency and change made possible through such engagements. In particular, this chapter focuses on ADO's relationship to the discourses and practices of human rights to explore the processes through which it creates peaceful geographies. In her application of the above theories to human rights discourse in Iran, Sameh argues that it is the very hybrid nature of human rights, the fact that it is constructed through the intersection of multiple historically specific discourses, which provides the opportunity for negotiation and the expression of agency.[14] In this chapter, I combine Sameh's approach to highlighting spaces of negotiation within human rights discourses with the emotional geographies of ADO members to examine how agency is employed to construct peaceful geographies.

## Human rights as relation of subordination

As a key aspect of its organizational identity, the discourses and practices of human rights structure much of ADO's work. In this section, I situate ADO's decision to adopt human rights within historically specific multi-scalar processes that made this adoption both a pragmatic and limiting choice. This analysis will provide context for the subsequent examination of ADO's efforts to construct peaceful geographies in and through its use of human rights.

In the mid-1990s, human rights discourses began to proliferate in northern Uganda and become vernacularized in the local languages. Amongst the Acholi, the Luo word *twero*, meaning authority or power, was appropriated to express this new concept. The quick spread of *twero pa dano* [rights for people or human rights] in northern Uganda was precipitated by the espousal of a 'rights-based approach' to aid/ development work in the 1990s by a wide range of actors including the United Nations, the UK's Department for International Development (DFID) and NGOs working in the global South.[15] The population of northern Uganda was a captive audience for this new policy directive given that more than 90 per cent of the Acholi population was confined to IDP camps.[16]

The rights-based approach to aid/development programming was specifically designed to increase empowerment by turning passive service recipients into active rights claimants.[17] While this is consistent with neoliberal governance policies that shift social welfare responsibility to the individual, the rights-based approach does offer possibilities for change by challenging the victim narrative so prominent within aid/development work. ADO's 84 members, for example, are predominately women running female-headed households who are struggling to put food on their tables and pay school fees for the children they are supporting. Many of them have been denied access to familial lands during resettlement, some have HIV/AIDS and only a few are literate. Instead of boxing them into the category of victim, however, the rights discourse holds the promise of empowerment through access to legal structures and universal claims.

The promise of the rights-based approach, however, is tempered by critiques demonstrating its links to hegemonic processes. Postcolonial and feminist scholars have illuminated how rights discourses can obfuscate power relations and act as a tool of empire.[18] Starting from the very foundation of rights, these scholars contend that the universality claimed in the conceptualization of rights is a buttress for particular state-centric power relations. The liberal concept of rights, for example, posits that universal subjects are the bearers of rights, yet it is only as a citizen of a particular state that one is able to access rights.[19] Furthermore, as feminists have demonstrated, citizenship is not distributed evenly, with particular types of bodies being more able to claim it than others.[20] Embodied identity is therefore central to the realization of rights, and processes of 'othering' are used to control the distribution of said rights.

In northern Uganda, the rights discourse is used by numerous actors to create and debate difference along multiple axes including ethnicity, gender, sexuality, class and age. A prime example of these processes of othering was the Government of Uganda's use of the war to justify policies that denied rights to mobility and access to livelihoods for the majority of the Acholi population. At times accused of 'social torture'[21] and genocide,[22] the role of the Government of Uganda in the war in northern Uganda is greatly debated. However, scholars and lay people alike acknowledge the legacy of ethnic rivalries produced by the British colonial era divide-and-rule practices that pitted the north (Acholiland) against the south of the country. To protest the material effects of this ethnic othering, the Acholi Religious Leaders' Peace Initiative (ARLPI) issued a report arguing that the war did not justify the mass displacement of the northern population. They used universalist human rights claims as the foundation for their argument:

The United Nations Convention on Internal Displacement prohibits displacement *'in situations of armed conflict, unless the security of the civilians involved or imperative military reasons so demand,'* and it stresses the principle that it should last no longer than absolutely required. In view of this, many wonder how the presence of hardly two hundred rebels during the last eighteen months can justify the fact of almost half a million people living in displacement in appalling conditions. [emphasis in original][23]

In this statement, ARLPI challenged the Government of Uganda's interpretation of international human rights law. The Government of Uganda, for its part, denies ethnic discrimination and claims the displacement was for the protection of the civilian population against the rebels. Reference to the Ugandan Constitution stifles this debate, as it states that rights are given to people by God, not by the government; thus they are not political.[24]

Once human rights are understood as formal and universal, as opposed to politically constructed, the ability to contest them is virtually eliminated as they are believed to be scientifically, technically or naturally derived.[25] Due to this potential for the naturalization and de-politicization of human rights, they are easily articulated with what Ferguson calls the 'anti-politics machine' of development programming.[26] According to Ferguson, aid/development institutions de-politicize complex social relations by defining problems as technical issues to be fixed by experts. By linking rights to judicial institutions based on legalistic knowledge, the negotiation of rights is distanced from the general population. Apparently stripped of agency within the technocratic institution of human rights, those seeking justice for the violation of their rights are often turned into clients who are represented by local and international NGOs in state-based systems of justice. As Neocosmos argues, this creates a paradoxical situation in which a rights discourse purportedly concerned with providing the enabling environment for freedom, within the context of liberalism in a postcolonial society, fundamentally and systematically enables its opposite – political and social disempowerment – through the hegemony of a state-centred consciousness.[27] When human rights are naturalized and de-politicized, when the struggles are obscured and when the relations between bearers of rights and protectors of rights are institutionalized, rights cease to be a site of political innovation. Human rights can therefore be seen as a tool of hegemony which simultaneously relies on claims of universality while producing regimes of difference.

However, this does not mean that human rights are inherently disempowering. As with all discourses, the meaning of human rights is not stable and exists only through place-based articulations. The goal of this chapter is to return to the possibility of rights as a means of improving people's well-being and increasing social justice while maintaining the substantial critiques outlined above. This is not a return to the idea of human rights advocacy as a *de facto* emancipatory project: rather, it is an exploration of how human rights are used to realize peaceful geographies in spite of – or perhaps even because of – their connection to hegemonic processes. In the next section, I use ADO's experiences with human rights to illustrate the co-constitution of peaceful and violent geographies. In so doing, I provide evidence for the established critique of rights outlined above while simultaneously exploring spaces of agency made possible through ADO's engagement with rights in the post-war landscape.

## Building peaceful geographies within relations of subordination

Returning now to the postcolonial feminist conception of agency as a negotiation within relations of subordination,[28] this section explores the ways in which ADO members have created peaceful geographies through the discourses and institutions of human rights. In particular, it examines ADO's role in reproducing multiple forms of authority which ultimately restrict ADO's own authority. However, it also explores how ADO has re-articulated human rights to realize its own imaginings of peaceful social relations. This section will focus on ADO's strategies as an organization whereas the next section will explore the emotional geographies that shape and are shaped by everyday peaceful experiences such as friendship and respect that have been produced in and through its human rights advocacy.

The power of the expert and the prioritization of technical knowledge in rights-based development are evident in ADO's experiences within institutions of human rights advocacy. While ADO is responsible for managing the everyday social reproduction of respect for human rights, the punitive or legal implications – along with the economic benefits – go through those with more 'expertise', such as the courts, the police or NGOs. ADO's position of authority, therefore, is based upon upholding other systems of authority. These systems reproduce the NGO's position as expert, they cede punitive authority to state structures such as the police and the court system, and they maintain popular support by reinforcing the institutions of marriage and clan leadership. ADO is not in a position to challenge these types of authority. Like others empowered through NGO activism, ADO's empowerment appears to be limited to supporting the very structures that contributed to a social landscape in which they are disempowered.[29]

However, as mentioned previously, human rights as a concept is not inherently disempowering. Like all discourses, its meaning is not stable and exists only through place-based articulations. In this section, I argue that ADO's ability to re-articulate human rights is facilitated by their very marginality. Located far from the centre of the mainstream political economies of human rights, members of ADO who draw on the language of human rights are not subject to regular discipline and surveillance by experts. The NGOs they work with only visit them once or twice a year. Taking advantage of this situation, the members of ADO carved out a space of political agency, albeit limited, through which it was able to articulate human rights within the context of its everyday experiences.

Over the past seven years, ADO has developed a practice of human rights advocacy based on a nuanced understanding of the relationship between rights and responsibilities. This approach to human rights requires constant negotiation of people's relations to one another. These relationships are determined by familial connections and professional status, as well as by readings of gender, age, health, class, ethnicity and other forms of social difference. Through this approach, rights became a discourse useful for speaking about violent and oppressive relationships between individuals. When ADO members felt that rights were being violated, they would examine the relations between people to determine responsibility. Often all people involved were held accountable for some aspect of the rights violation. For example, in one case of marital discord where the woman wanted to leave, she was told by ADO to stay and take care of her responsibilities and to respect her husband and mother-in-law. The husband was admonished for his use of alcohol and abusive ways, while the husband's mother was admonished for not supporting the young wife in her homestead. ADO sought to lay out clear expectations for all parties involved and then to hold them accountable through repeated follow-ups. ADO would visit the parties involved at random intervals to acquire updates, but it would also speak with neighbours and others aware of the situation in order to collect multiple perspectives. If things did not change, as was the case in this mediation, ADO attempted to re-articulate the social networks of rights and responsibilities in order to support those whose rights were being violated. In this case, instead of continuing to ask the husband to respect his wife's rights, ADO turned to her father. He was approached in his role of protector of his daughter and was convinced to return the bride price to the husband's family. This effectively freed the woman from her husband. If this had not happened, ADO was going to go to the clan and/or the police to enforce a little-used option within cultural marriage practices that allows a woman to leave her husband and pay back the bride price herself over time. Given the dominance of communal land tenure in the region, keeping the woman within the webs of social relations was necessary for her to maintain access to land and, with it, her livelihood.[30]

By questioning normalized social relations that perpetuate violence, ADO's work is effectively raising questions about the fixity of relational identity. The organization is constantly seeking ways to re-articulate a person's relationship to others so as to keep them connected to social networks and to improve their quality of life. ADO is using the human rights discourse to politicize social relationships and open them up to negotiation. However, it is very careful not to further jeopardize an individual's situation by removing her/him from the web of relations that is, according to ADO, responsible for protecting her/his rights. ADO's intention is not to destabilize social relations. Coming out of two decades of extreme social upheaval due to war, the goal of ADO is much the opposite: it seeks to stabilize social relations such that people respect the rights of others by fulfilling their own responsibilities. State systems are connected to these networks of relations not as abstract structures but as the individuals responsible for specific government roles, such as police officers, teachers and local councillors.

There is no question that ADO members reinforce patriarchal systems and hierarchies. For some members, this is acceptable because it was how they were raised, and they do not challenge it. For others, it is a matter of being pragmatic and manipulating the existing systems to accomplish their own goals. ADO's success is based not on reinventing these systems but on playing them against one another. If the traditional leaders said that it was a man's prerogative whether or not to beat his wife or pay school fees for a child, ADO would draw upon the conception of human rights promoted by NGOs active in the area such as HURIFO and the AVSI Foundation. These professional organizations, with their international connections and funding, tended to employ a more codified and legalistic interpretation of rights that could be used to challenge traditional social relations. Or, if the court system was proving too corrupt to judiciously handle a land dispute, ADO would call on the traditional leaders to determine a resolution. If that resolution did not address the needs of all involved, ADO would turn to HURIFO to take the case to a higher court, one slightly more disconnected from local politics. If a particular NGO was demonstrating favouritism in its distribution of resources, ADO would turn to local administrators to discipline the NGO. Through such navigations, ADO was able to challenge the assumptions of one institution (e.g. the power hierarchies of NGOs) with another (e.g. traditional gender relations) to open spaces for alternative imaginings of how life could be.

This brief examination of ADO's human rights advocacy demonstrates the multi-scalar processes through which ADO negotiates spaces of agency for itself and for the people it works with. It renegotiates social relations in intimate settings based on complex readings of identity. It plays local, national and international institutions against one another to create space for the types of social relations it desires. Moving between the public and private spaces of its communities, it strives to realize more equitable and just relations in people's everyday lives. With each of its successes, it reduces violence and increases experiences of peace, however defined by those it has helped. With each of its successes, it also increases its own sense of agency in creating more peaceful experiences in the future. After years of armed conflict, decades of political instability and lifetimes of poverty, ADO members find solace in being able to improve their own and other people's lives. This is where their sense of peace comes from. However, as discussed above, their dependence upon human rights to realize these goals is in itself a possible hindrance to their efforts due to its tie to structural forms of violence.

## Articulating peaceful geographies

While the previous analysis demonstrates *how* ADO and its members were able to re-articulate human rights to reduce some forms of violence in their communities, it does not explain *why* they constructed peaceful narratives to describe their lives. ADO members could just as easily have focused on the systems of violence that continued to shape their lives. To address this question, I turn to the recent literature on emotional geographies. Analyses of emotional geographies – be they of hope, fear, or other emotional experiences – can contribute to the study of processes of peace due to their implicit focus on agency.[31] Building upon Pain's argument that emotional geographies have the potential to connect 'political processes and everyday emotional topographies in a less hierarchical, more enabling relationship,'[32] this section examines the peaceful and hopeful emotional geographies of ADO members in relation to their human rights advocacy.

ADO's choice to focus on the articulation of peaceful geographies was remarkably different from the tendency amongst most people and organizations in northern Uganda to focus on the persistence of violence in the post-war landscape. In many cases, claims of peace were political moves to prioritize one type of violence over another, in order to access political and economic resources. For example, there was a documented gap between governmental claims of peace following the LRA movement out of northern Uganda in 2006 and the claims of civilians who argued that the structural violence of economic and political disenfranchisement was part of the war and therefore its continuation indicated that peace had not yet been achieved.[33] In this case, the government was able to gain geopolitical clout for having ended the war while civilians were trying to access international funds and attention which had shifted to newer and more 'trendy' humanitarian emergencies.[34]

The importance of refuting claims of peace was particularly evident within the professional human rights and peace NGOs in Gulu Town. Aware of their reliance on external funding, these organizations purposefully looked for new sites of violence in order to justify their funding applications. To claim peace, in other words, would be to undermine their existence. Local organizations often expressed frustration with funding agencies' priorities and the subsequent removal of resources from the region because it was now considered 'at peace'. Such tensions between local organizations and funding agencies about the definitions of peace belie the fact that there is a political economy to narratives of peace as they become articulated through institutions of post-war development.

Far from the centre of these political economies of peace, ADO's articulation of peaceful narratives serves the opposite purpose: it justifies its existence as a group. As an organization of volunteers, it motivates itself through the assertion that it can and has made a difference. If they were not successful at creating peaceful relationships, ADO members would lose their *raison d'être* personally and within their communities. It is therefore necessary for the continuation of the group that ADO members regularly remind themselves, and the people around them, about their successes. Towards this end, they frequently perform peaceful narratives through oral histories of past cases and assertions that life is getting better.

Given that the guns of war have been silent in northern Uganda for the past five years, it may not seem unreasonable to claim that things are getting better. As the life histories of ADO members make apparent, however, the war was just one in a series of violent episodes in their lives. Poverty, denial of education, forced marriages, domestic violence and the violent deaths of loved ones were repeated themes. While the war may have dominated the stories of the young men in the group, it was just another example of the difficulty of life for many of the women and older men. ADO's goal of fostering peaceful relations was not about ending the war but, rather, about addressing systems of violence of which the war was only one manifestation.

Within this landscape of complex social relations and multiple systems of violence, the geography of peaceful experiences for ADO members is not confined by a heuristic divide between public and private spaces. The negotiation of social relations towards peaceful ends occurred regularly with close friends and family, as well as with strangers and officials. For most members, however, the story began with themselves. As a middle-aged female ADO member commented:

> I used to be wild. I wouldn't give time to my husband. When he started a fight, I would just fight back. Since being in ADO, my approach to violence is different; I have learned how to avoid confrontation. I know that it is better to talk to my husband later than to jump into the fray and fight back. I also used to beat my children, but now I understand children's rights. I am grateful that I joined ADO, it has changed my life.

For this woman and many like her, being in ADO meant taking responsibility for her own actions and role in creating violence. Avoiding confrontation did not mean submission. It was a strategic move to confront her husband when she was most likely to receive a positive response – when he was sober and in a good mood. Such strategies did not challenge patriarchal assumptions directly, but made her life easier and often led to improved domestic relations in which she had more freedom.

These strategies did not ensure the reduction of violence, as was evident in two separate instances during the period of my fieldwork in which female ADO members had to be hospitalized after incidents of domestic violence. These cases made real the threat that existing violence could escalate and new violence could present itself at any time. ADO's peaceful geographies, therefore, were not created by an absence of violence but by a feeling that the violence could be managed. Individuals felt they had the support structures and the agency to manoeuvre in, and through, life's challenges. In the cases of the two hospitalized women, both were relocated to live with other family members. One decided to stay with her brother in town and to try to make a new life there. The other eventually decided to move back in with her husband. She saw it as the lesser of two evils; she decided it would be better to be in her husband's home and near her ADO friends than disrespected by her brother's family. She was able to reframe this violent experience and incorporate it into her peaceful geography, her reading of her surroundings as non-oppressive, by focusing on the fact that she made the decision herself to return.

There is a complex relationship between the public and private spaces of ADO's interventions. As the years have passed, ADO has gained a public reputation for being a dependable peacebuilder within the community. It is given space to speak in local government meetings as well as clan gatherings. In many cases, individual ADO members have gained this reputation due to their ability to model nonviolent conflict resolution within their own households as evidenced in the earlier quote about the female member who learned how to avoid confrontation at home. Similarly, success in public forums enhanced ADO members' freedom and mobility as their partners and family members accepted the importance of community activities that took them away from household responsibilities. As the cases of domestic violence above indicate, however, this does not always translate into respect and nonviolence in private spaces. Nor does it indicate that they are always effective in public spaces. The further they get from the communities of Awere, Dino and Odek, the less their voices are respected. However, the experiences they have gained by working together on public and private expressions of violence have given them the confidence to address new situations as they arise.

The experiences of ADO members support Wright's contention that 'there is no immediate and easy state of hopefulness and agency. Rather, it is generated through practice.'[35] For ADO, the initial imaginings of collective action were realized by individuals who had previously practised exercising their agency; the founders had individually been camp leaders, run successful businesses or had left abusive relationships. In comparison, many of those who subsequently joined the group had previously felt disempowered, and ADO offered them the opportunity to practise realizing their agency through action and solidarity. Amito's experience is a representative example of how individuals found empowerment and realized their agency through ADO.[36] The following excerpt from my field notes summarizes a conversation I had with Amito while visiting her home:

When Amito signed up for ADO, her life was falling apart. Her husband had left her and she was alone with four children, living in the camps and barely surviving. She was depressed, and said that if ADO hadn't come into her life, she probably would have killed herself through AIDS. She didn't know how to manage and was about to give up. But then someone told her that they were taking names for a women's group, so she went and signed up. And then they got a training, and she started to understand the importance of human rights. She started understanding her responsibilities to ensure the rights of her children. And with the help and support of other ADO members, she started to feel that she could do it, that she could support these children. She has now gotten this land [where her house was located] and no one disputes it because they know she knows her rights and can defend it. She has even taken in additional children, knowing that she can find a way to support them.

It is Amito's agency, her ability to purposefully negotiate social relations, which underlies her pride in her ability to protect her own rights and those of her children. When new challenges arrived, such as an unplanned pregnancy, she turned to ADO for support and solidarity. In group spaces, she was able to express her fear and frustration about the pregnancy without having her agency or ability to handle the situation questioned. Rather, other members helped her give voice to the ways she could manage the situation. Experiences such as these support Wright's claim that hope (as an expression of agency) 'draws on connection and on the work of creating and recreating solidarities through the very act of living'.[37]

In addition to a sense of agency in shaping their domestic lives, ADO members highlighted specific knowledges and technical skills which improved their lives and expanded their peaceful geographies. These ranged from understanding property rights to mediation training and literacy. Some members spoke about conquering a fear of public speaking and gaining the confidence to travel long distances and move through unknown cities. Collectively, these skills and experiences reinforced a feeling of empowerment that strengthened the peaceful emotional landscapes that the men and women of ADO described in their lives. The only concerns voiced as a collective focused on the logistics of continuing their work – for example, the need for an office, better transportation and new uniforms. ADO members kept the attention on what had been done and could be done instead of focusing on what was wrong. By doing so, ADO members highlighted their abilities to bring peaceful social relations to a wide range of intimate and public spaces.

Through an analysis of ADO's peaceful geographies, this chapter contributes to the nascent literature on the geographies of hope and optimism, which seek to understand how people move forward in the face of violence, dispossession and despair.[38] In northern Uganda, claims of peace are tempered by fear of the rebels returning, trauma from war experiences, the inability to meet basic needs, the escalation of violent land conflicts and the Government's military interventions in neighbouring countries. The sense of insecurity fostered by such concerns has the potential to undermine peaceful readings of the social and political landscape. Yet members of ADO persist in their use of peaceful concepts, such as respect, trust, friendship and happiness, to describe their lives. They speak about being strong, gaining confidence and self-esteem, learning to be patient, and making solid and positive decisions.

They use phrases that emphasize living well and having peace in the heart and the home. As I have demonstrated, these peaceful readings of their social landscapes did not come easily: they required effort, practice and solidarity. These readings required the determination to find spaces of agency in and through the relations of subordination in which ADO members were immersed.

## Conclusion

This chapter has used the discourses and practices of human rights to frame an analysis of the everyday practices of building peaceful geographies in northern Uganda. This frame is particularly salient in contemporary debates about peace, as human rights are used as both a measure and a tool for realizing less violent and less oppressive social relations. Universal claims for human rights are not based on what is, but on normative imaginings of what should be. As such, they offer a medium through which peaceful geographies can be imagined and debated. The institutionalization of human rights, however, significantly limits the ways in which human rights can be practised and imaginaries realized. As this chapter has demonstrated, the limitations and opportunities of human rights as a tool for building peaceful geographies can be illuminated through an analysis of everyday expressions of agency by those seeking to create social change.

By attending to the apparent contradictions in the experiences of ADO members – peaceful experiences in the midst of systems of violence – the pragmatic strategies used to improve the lives of ADO members and their communities become apparent. These strategies are not forms of resistance in a revolutionary sense. They are not even a direct re-working of a particular institution. Rather, these strategies are a creative interplay between institutions in which ideological elements and territorial forms of authority can be re-articulated to create spaces of hope and possibility. These are not innocent or naive expressions of peaceful experiences: there is a clear understanding of their complex intersections with systems of violence. By using embodied social relations as a site of negotiation, ADO members offer place-based re-articulations of multi-scalar processes as they affect people's everyday lives. This strategy, of course, has significant limitations. Working in and through multiple relations of subordination, ADO's efforts do not address underlying structural sources of inequality and violence. Similarly, its work often reinforces one axis of oppression while trying to undermine another. However, ADO's repeated articulation of peaceful narratives reminds those of us interested in peace that we cannot dismiss pragmatic strategies as a means of reducing violence.

The unique attributes of the post-war landscape of northern Uganda certainly play into the politics of peace and the construction of peaceful narratives in this case study, but the analyses of agency and emotional geographies within this analysis are not tied to a post-war context. Rather, such analyses offer a means by which to investigate agency as it is realized through the creation of peaceful geographies in relation to a wide range of violences. In addition, as this chapter demonstrates, the focus on agencies that construct peaceful landscapes in and through hegemonic processes and relations of subordination, highlights the importance of collective action and solidarity in creating spaces of agency and experiencing these spaces as peaceful and hopeful. These emotional topographies belie the contingent nature of hegemonic processes and open possibilities for realizing peaceful geographies in and through systems of violence.

## Acknowledgements

I wish to thank Lakor Lakony and the women and men of ADO for their significant contributions to this project. I would also like to thank those who read earlier drafts of this chapter and gave significant feedback, including the editors of this volume, Dr Lorraine Dowler and the Feminist Geographers' Writing Group at Pennsylvania State University. Finally, this research would not have been possible without financial support from the National Science Foundation, Society of Woman Geographers, and the Africana Research Center at Pennsylvania State University.

## Notes

1. These phrases are drawn from my ethnographic research with ADO members.
2. SPRING, 'Unpacking the "P" in PRDP', *Conflict and Recovery*, Briefing Report #7 (Gulu, 2010).
3. Williams, Philippa and McConnell, Fiona, 'Critical geographies of peace', *Antipode* 43/4 (2011), pp. 927–31.
4. Mahmood, Saba, *Politics of Piety* (Princeton, 2005).
5. Koopman, Sara, 'Let's take peace to pieces', *Political Geography* 30/4 (2011b), pp. 193–4.
6. Megoran, Nick, 'War *and* Peace? An agenda for peace research and practice in geography', *Political Geography* 30/4 (2011), pp. 178–89.

7. For example, Giles, Wenona and Hyndman, Jennifer (eds), *Sites of Violence: Gender and Conflict Zones* (Berkeley, 2004); Fluri, Jennifer L., 'Bodies, bombs and barricades: geographies of conflict and civilian (in)security', *Transactions of the Institute of British Geographers* 36/2 (2011), pp. 280–96; Loyd, Jenna M., '"Peace is our only shelter": questioning domesticities of militarization and white privilege', *Antipode* 43/3 (2011), pp. 845–73.

8. Koopman, 'Let's take peace to pieces'; Williams and McConnell, 'Critical geographies of peace'.

9. World Health Organization, *Health and Mortality Survey among Internally Displaced Persons* (Geneva, 2005).

10. Annan, Jeannie and Brier, Moriah, 'The risk of return: intimate partner violence in northern Uganda's armed conflict', *Social Science & Medicine* 70/1 (2010), pp. 152–9; van Acker, Frank, 'Uganda and the Lord's Resistance Army: the new order no one ordered', *African Affairs* 103/412 (2004), pp. 335–57; El-Bushra Judy and Ibrahim, M. G. Saul, *Cycles of Violence: Gender Relations and Armed Conflict* (Nairobi, 2005).

11. El-Bushra and Ibrahim, *Cycles of Violence*.

12. Asad, Talal, *Formations of the Secular: Christianity, Islam, Modernity* (Stanford, CA, 2003), p. 78.

13. Mahmood, *Politics of Piety*, p. 18.

14. Sameh, Catherine, 'Discourses of equality, rights and Islam in the One Million Signatures Campaign in Iran', in Dana Collins, Sylvanna Falcon, Sharmila Lodhia and Molly Talcott (eds), *New Directions in Feminism and Human Rights* (London, 2011).

15. Institute of Development Studies, 'Developing rights', *IDS Bulletin*, Special Edition 36/1 (2005).

16. Internal Displacement Monitoring Centre, *Focus Shifts to Securing Durable Solutions for IDPs: A Profile of the Internal Displacement Situation* (Geneva, 2008).

17. Cornwall, Andrea and Nyamu-Musembi, Celestine, 'Putting the "rights-based approach" to development into perspective', *Third World Quarterly* 25/8 (2004), pp. 1415–37.

18. For example, Chatterjee, Partha, *The Politics of the Governed: Reflections on Popular Politics in Most of the World* (New York, 2004); Neocosmos, Michael, 'Can human rights culture enable emancipation? Clearing the theoretical ground for the renewal of a critical sociology', *South African Review of Sociology* 37/2 (2006), pp. 356–79.

19. Mamdani, Mahmood, 'Democratic theory and democratic struggles', in E. Chole and J. Ibrahim (eds), *Democratisation Processes in Africa: Problems and Prospects* (Dakar, 1995).

20. For example, Yuval-Davis, Nira, *Gender & Nation* (Thousand Oaks, CA., 1997).

21. Dolan, Chris, *Social Torture: The Case of Northern Uganda, 1986–2006, Human Rights in Context, 4* (New York, 2009).

22. Whitmore, Todd, 'Genocide or just another 'casualty of war'?', *Practical Matters* (2010). Retrieved 18 March 2011 from http://www.practicalmattersjournal.org/issue/3/analyzing-matters/genocide-or-just-another-casualty-of-war.

23. Acholi Religious Leaders Peace Initiative, *Let My People Go: The Forgotten Plight of the People in the Displaced Camps in Acholi* (Gulu, 2001), p. 26.

24. *Constitution of the Republic of Uganda* (1995), Article 20, 1.

25. Shivji, Issa, *The Concept of Human Rights in Africa* (London, 1989).

26. Ferguson, James, *The Anti-politics Machine: 'Development', Depoliticization and Bureaucratic Power in Lesotho* (Cambridge, 1990).
27. Neocosmos, 'Can human rights culture enable emancipation?', p. 366.
28. Mahmood, *Politics of Piety*.
29. Nagar, Richa and Lock Swarr, Amanda, 'Organizing from the margins: grappling with "empowerment" in India and South Africa', in L. Nelson and J. Seager (eds), *A Companion to Feminist Geography* (Oxford, 2005).
30. This insight was originally drawn from ethnographic observations of active ADO cases as well as a review of five years of archived case logs. Focus group conversations with ADO members in December 2011 confirmed these findings.
31. Crawford (2000) and Ling (2000) in Rachel Pain, 'Globalized fear? Towards an emotional geopolitics', *Progress in Human Geography* 33/4 (2009), pp. 466–86.
32. Pain, 'Globalized fear?', p. 466.
33. SPRING, 'Unpacking the "P" in PRDP'.
34. Personal interview with United Nations representative (4 April 2011).
35. Wright, Susan, 'Practising hope: learning from social movement strategies in the Philippines', in R. Pain and S. Smith (eds), *Fear: Critical Geopolitics and Everyday Life* (Burlington, VT, 2008), p. 227.
36. Pseudonyms have been used for individual ADO members.
37. Wright, 'Practising hope', p. 224.
38. See Sparke, Matthew, 'Geopolitical fears, geoeconomic hopes, and the responsibilities of geography', *Annals of the Association of American Geographers* 97/2 (2007), pp. 338–49; Wright, 'Practising hope'.

# 4

# Unearthing the local: hegemony and peace discourses in Central Africa

*Patricia Daley*

## Introduction

This chapter is concerned with how an ostensibly Western construction of peace has acquired hegemonic authority in the global sphere, and the implications of this for non-Western experiences of peace. I argue that when transposed to the African context, this hegemonic peace promotes norms and practices that are counter to local notions of peace, contributing to persistent insecurity after peace agreements have been signed and peacebuilding is instituted. Critics of post-conflict interventions in post-Cold War Africa highlight the failure of the universalized liberal peace to de-militarize areas affected by civil wars and to effect transformative and emancipatory changes to the lives of the impoverished masses. Policy makers have responded to critics by incorporating the local into the 'liberal peace' agenda through engagement with non-governmental organizations (NGOs) and resurrecting traditional justice institutions. Such additions leave the 'liberal peace' largely intact, unchallenged in its hegemony, and assured by a nexus of donors, peace industry professionals and state elites.

Our understanding of peace and how it can be achieved varies with our position in relation to structures of power, both socially and spatially. In the West, feminist critics have highlighted the gendered biases of the liberal peace.[1] In the non-Western world, its appropriateness remains under-theorized and little space has been given to exploring the content of a local, contextualized, everyday peace, in the light of scholarly recognition of the situatedness of knowledge and that, as Williams and McConnell note, peaceful co-existence depends on a range of 'everyday acts and practices', and on processes operating 'in distinct situated contexts'.[2]

According to Emmanuel Hansen, 'the perspective which a group brings to the peace problematic depends on its history and material conditions as well as the position of the group within the power structure of national or international systems'.[3] Hansen, in making a case for an African perspective on peace during the Cold War, argues that peace and security in mainstream Euro-American thought is minimalist and based on fear and mutual distrust. Such thinking became globalized through colonialism and became institutionalized in the global structures of governance that emerged after the Second World War. It was supported and tolerated by many, as modernity held out the promise of the 'liberation of human beings from physical want' – the question is whether such freedom is perceived by those with power as socially and globally inclusive. Recognition of global power differentials has led to calls for a feminist geopolitics[4] which, Hyndman argues, should take into consideration an 'embodied political vision': in essence an 'analytic and politics that is contingent upon context, place and time'.[5] Such a stance enables questioning of the dominant geopolitical narrative and may reveal how ordinary non-Western people challenge the imaginative geographies of themselves as others and create spaces of peace, as Megoran concludes, 'out of the most unlikely political geographical rock faces'.[6]

Central African states provide a space to study the limitations of externally derived liberal peace and the necessity of articulating a progressive conceptualization of peace that is localised, feminist and culturally contextual. Wars and genocidal violence in the Democratic Republic of Congo (DRC), Burundi and Rwanda[7] during the last decade of the twentieth century were followed by internationally and regionally sponsored peace negotiations and peace and ceasefire agreements.[8] Since the beginning of the twenty-first century, these states have been undergoing internationally assisted post-conflict reconstruction. However, civilians remain vulnerable to rebel and state-sponsored direct violence, including sexual violence, and extreme material deprivation.

The main proposition of this chapter is that the failure of the post-Cold War liberal peace in Central Africa can be attributed to its attempt to universalize the cultural values of modernity and neoliberalism, whilst being bolstered by Western military superiority and geopolitical interests. It is through such processes that local cultures of peace are marginalized. This chapter is organized around four sections. First, I argue that the liberal peace in the African context privileges top-down political, economic and technical reforms rather than transformation. Second, that it leads to the further embedding of militarism and patriarchy in African societies. The liberal peace is shown to prioritize a violent, masculine form of militarism which sits incongruously with its simultaneous concern for gender equality. For example, UN Resolution 1325 encourages the integration of women into peacemaking and peacebuilding without fundamentally challenging patriarchal structures.[9] Third, the liberal peace fails to understand local life and cultures, and discounts the pre-colonial experience. When the 'local' is integrated into the liberal peace, the emphasis is on resurrecting patriarchal 'traditional' justice structures, such as the 'Council of Wise Men' (*bashingantahe* in Burundi or *Gacaca* in Rwanda), which, even in their modern form, contradict the liberal peace policy of gender equity and run counter to local 'established societal practices'.[10] Nevertheless, this is not an argument for a singular African perspective on peace, because of the continent's diverse local histories and cultures. In the final section, I consider what the content of a locally situated peace might look like, drawing on debates in African peace scholarship and feminist activism that seek to articulate an African feminist perspective of peace that is simultaneously contextual and emancipatory.

Theoretically, this chapter draws on Gramscian notions of hegemony to articulate the dominance of the liberal peace discourse in the region; Foucauldian concepts of biopolitics as a form of governance that relies on hierarchies of human beings; and Hill Collins' use of the concept of intersectionality as an analytical tool to show how oppressions, in this case structural, racial and gendered, work together to produce injustice in particular locales.[11] I argue that with its roots in Western modernity, the hegemonic liberal peace, based on a rational, militarized, gendered and racialized conceptualization, runs counter to the societal transformation and healing that African societies crave. Here, I utilize the African concept of *ubuntu* to explore the potentialities for localized and collectivized approaches to peace.

Evidence for this chapter is derived from multiple sources: partly from fieldwork in Burundi in 2006, involving interviews with local key informants, representatives from UN agencies and local and international NGOs; and, since then, analysis of human rights reports, media sources for Burundi and the DRC, and reviews of scholarly articles.

## Unpacking the liberal peace: the roots of its hegemony in Africa

Drawing from the scholarship of Duffield and Kaldor, the term 'liberal peace' defines the emergence of a perspective on peaceful co-existence that separates territory/state from civil society, that interprets state militarism as security, and that is differentiated hierarchically in its global reach.[12] While the liberal peace is seen as resulting from the emergence of discursive liberal governance in the late modern period, at its core are ideologies and values that have deep historical roots – both colonial and modern. Of relevance here are three aspects of the liberal peace that are at odds with an African understanding of peace: its privileging of the territorial security of the state above that of the well-being of citizens; its embodied gendered dimension of national security and militarism; and the ways in which its global expansion is interconnected with imperialism and the racialized 'other'.

The historical roots of the liberal peace originate in the experience of warfare in Europe and the emergence of the nation-state ideal in the seventeenth century.[13] Classical European scholarship, such as that represented by Max Weber, which maintains that wars are fought by states and civil wars result from the loss of state monopoly of violence, has dominated modernist thinking about peace.[14] At the global scale, Steans notes that 'hegemonic states dominate international institutions and, in this way, "manage" international security, [assuming that] the security of one state is closely, inextricably even, linked with the security of other states'.[15] This model was universalized with the establishment of the United Nations (UN) and its key institution – the Security Council – and has a central role in shaping the global peace architecture. Western states are supported by an intellectual and popular culture that produces and maintains imaginative geographies about other spaces and peoples that legitimizes their actions. Since the Second World War, the UN has established international norms governing the promotion of peace and security, which frame the peace discourse of policy makers, scholars and activists. Gramsci's concept of hegemony partly explains the universalizing of Western elites' concept of peace.[16] Hegemony does not arise purely from the use of physical power, but from the ability to impose your worldview onto others less powerful. Following Gramsci, I propose that the Western professional peace industry has been able to insert its understanding of 'social life' into the liberal peace because of the 'prestige' and 'confidence' that it 'enjoy(s) in the world'.[17] Such meta-narratives, concerning peace and security, have been applied and adopted in particular ways within Africa.

Since the 1960s, neo-realists have equated national security in Africa with state militarism and territoriality. Africans have accepted the liberal peace because of the material resources that the West can bring forth to stop warfare and facilitate reconstruction. Peace processes have been driven largely by Western aid donors whose investments are shaped by their geopolitical and economic interests. During the Cold War, proxy wars helped to maintain the peace in Europe and North America. Western states' perception of threats to global peace varies historically: throughout the Cold War it was communist expansionism and nuclear proliferation; then, after 11 September 2001, amorphous groups that can be labelled 'terrorists' and 'rogue states'. Since the start of the War on Terror, the USA has perceived its security as being dependent on greater intervention in Africa, leading to the further militarization of African states under the United States Trans-Sahel Initiative and Africa Command.[18]

Securing the physical territory of the state against the material well-being of its citizens produces a dichotomy that Johan Galtung terms 'negative' and 'positive' peace.[19] The former refers to the ending of direct violence (physical combat), whilst the latter refers to a more holistic state of being, in which those conditions that may lead to the break-down of society and the pursuance of war (structural violence) are erad-icated. The international framing of peace for Africa has not implied the absence of direct and structural violence. International peacemak-ing in Central Africa is mired with failures to even promote negative peace. International interventions, such as in Katanga, Congo (1960) and Rwanda (1994), have fallen short of putting in place the mechanisms needed to prevent either the escalation of violence or to promote posi-tive peace. In the case of Rwanda, while supporting the Arusha Peace Agreement with Security Council Resolution 868 of 29 September 1993 and the despatch of 2,700 peacekeepers, the UN mission lacked the mandate to intervene in the 1994 genocide and its number was reduced to 270 at a critical moment when it could have saved lives.[20] Almost ten years later, in DRC and Burundi, UN peacekeepers were neither able to avert the killing of 1,000 people in Ituri, DRC (April 2003) and the massacre of 152 refugees in Gatumba, Burundi (August 2004) nor to prevent the persistence of human rights violations in these states, including the scale of sexual violence in the Eastern DRC.[21]

Galtung's influential peace/violence dichotomy remains essentially a liberal interpretation and has been criticized for its lack of attention to gender inequalities as a form of violence – a factor which pre-disposes a society to war.[22] Feminist scholarship has demonstrated the intercon-nectedness of militarism, national security and patriarchy in the modern state.[23] Militarism is reliant on the promotion of hypermasculinity – a stereotypical form of masculine behaviour and attributes with exag-gerated characteristics, such as aggression and the ability to perpetu-ate extreme violence.[24] Such forms of masculinity are central to state instability and outbreaks of violence.[25] Recent policies to incorporate women into militaries and to gender sensitize peacekeepers have not resulted in any significant shift in ideology.[26]

With the potential for violence against the female body, women have become stereotyped as being symbolic of the nation and in need of protection.[27] However, such vulnerability is not extended to all women, who are differentiated hierarchically by class, race, ethnicity and age. Hill Collins' concept of intersectionality becomes a useful analytical tool to understand how gender intersects with race and class in particular spaces of oppression.[28] Also useful is Foucault's concept of 'biopolitics', which he refers to as a set of processes by which the modern state attempts to regulate human life. This centres on the construction of the people as population, producing a rational, measurable and hierarchical category. For Foucault, modern racism (dating from the nineteenth century) became a 'technique of power' that depicts other races as threats to the population. It acts as the ultimate 'mechanism that allows biopower (sovereignty over death and regulation of life) to work', so that 'in a normalizing society, race or racism is the precondition that makes killing acceptable'.[29] Central to the nation-state ideal is the emphasis on racial and cultural homogeneity as prerequisites for a peaceful and stable society. This places discriminatory practices at the ideological core of the modern state. Though racism is considered abhorrent in international arenas, racial hierarchy underlies how people in different geographical spaces are represented and treated, even in the context of peacekeeping.[30] In Western popular discourse, Africa has become a space where normal rules do not apply and people are de-humanized. Roméo Dallaire, the UN military general in charge of the peacekeepers in Rwanda during the genocide, was told that 'the lives of 800,000 Rwandans were only worth risking the lives of ten American troops'.[31]

European biopolitical conceptualizations of peace entered Central Africa during the period of colonial conquest when colonial militaries were established for pacification and the subjugation of people to foreign rule. 'Pacification' was often constituted as a violent act whereby, through force, the foreign power could instil fear as a means of domination, a tactic which sometimes involved the destruction of whole communities.[32] For many Africans, the externally imposed peace that came with pacification meant the loss of control over territory and subjection to violence of genocidal proportions and other de-humanizing practices, justified by colonial biopolitics, which institutionalized racial and ethnic differences within the colonial state.

Nationalists seeking to forge modern nation-states in post-independence Africa discounted difference, especially ethnicity, representing it as a hindrance to modernization. Consequently, political and social mechanisms to deal with diversity in modern African states are under-developed theoretically.[33] This vacuum has led to the perpetuation of models of the state, even under the liberal peace, that rest upon supposedly normative practices of discrimination and inherent instability, which in Central Africa contributed to genocide against those Africans constructed as 'non-indigenous'.

Realist solutions to the failings of the liberal peace vary from more intense and protracted military intervention and exercising a trustee-ship role over the 'non-liberal others', to co-opting local elite institutions. For Richmond, localising peace should mean moving beyond elite interests and penetrating the everyday lives of ordinary people to produce a liberal-local hybrid – a 'post-liberal peace' – that combines the benefits of the liberal peace with attention to 'cultures, societies and identities'.[34] However, the ontological shift that is needed in order to tap into the peaceful energies in African society, lies outside the framework of Western conceptualizations of modernity, rationality, governance and security. In contrast, I suggest that a feminist critique, with its focus on intersectionality, allows some exploration of a peaceful world beyond militarism, masculinism and racial 'othering'.

## Limitations of the liberal peace in Central Africa

The central contention here is that the liberal peace is antithetical to the promotion of positive peace in Central Africa. Its implementation is done in a formulaic, technocratic and managerial fashion, often focusing on top-down interventions which tend to be either reform or palliative in nature. Two aspects stand out: its privileging of political and economic reforms – rather than transformation – at the level of the state, and its role in further embedding militarism and patriarchy within post-conflict societies.

Theories of late twentieth-century African wars are informed by a biopolitical discourse that interprets them as 'new' and 'non-ideological' – the consequence of innate flaws in African societies.[35] Rather than see such wars as the consequence of capitalist modernity, such interpretations re-traditionalize wars by representing them as essentially tribal, often arising from age-old enmities or entrenched inequalities based on ethnicity, race or religion. Even when interpretations attempt to avoid ethnic reductionism, they nevertheless commonly resort to simplistic arguments about the greed of ethnic elites or 'warlords' who seek to capture state resources for private gain.[36]

A popular post-Cold War liberal peace solution to the problem of multi-ethnicity and other forms of difference in Africa is powersharing.[37] Here, the institutions of governance are divided between political parties, ethnic elites and rebel movements as a precursor to liberal state-building. In practice, elites and rebels prefer to negotiate themselves into power-sharing deals rather than commit themselves to the electorate. Power sharing does not lead to any radical changes in the nature of the state, and often encourages 'insurgent violence'.[38] In the DRC and Burundi, power sharing favoured those with military might. It led to an intensification of the fighting, especially against civilians, which was used as a bargaining tool in peace and ceasefire negotiations. Crucially, though liberal, state-building at the national level tends to ignore local competition and conflicts, leaving them unresolved.[39] Such conflicts, such as access to land and power struggles between local elites, remain as stumbling blocks to peace in the post-conflict phase.

At the national level, post-conflict reconstruction provides the opportunity to introduce reforms that entrench neoliberal economic policies, which are presented as strategies to counter corruption. In Burundi, the privatization of state economic concerns did not reduce corruption but led to key public resources being captured by political elites or external actors. In effect, the liberal peace has not altered the neo-patrimonial character of the state. Structural violence remains, as the masses are expected to suffer wage freezes, public sector retrenchment and 'accumulation by dispossession'.[40]

The discursive character of liberal peace interventions means that whilst economic liberalization at the state level promoted the self-maximising individual, humanitarian agencies focused on socially engineering peace among rural communities by instituting intra-ethnic cooperation into development projects, though without much success.[41] Failure can be attributed to a marked absence of knowledge about how the various ethnic groups co-existed peacefully prior to colonial rule or how people negotiate cross-ethnic alliances, friendships, marriages, and carry out economic transactions below the level of the state.

The key limitation of the liberal peace in Central Africa is its emphasis on strengthening territorial state power by privileging its military arm. This embeds a militarized and patriarchal vision of the state that may not resonate with local cultures of peace. Consequently, state military expenditure has often surpassed social expenditure, even under post-conflict reconstruction situations. Post-war Burundi's military expenditure in 2008 amounted to 3.7 per cent of Gross Domestic Product – the highest in the economic union of the East African Community.[42] Militarism is evident not just in the continued power of the coercive arms of the state, such as the Burundi secret services, but also in the widespread use of weaponry to settle minor disputes and the involvement of military peacekeepers in the sexual abuse of local women.[43]

## Embedding militarism

A crucial limitation of the liberal peace in Africa is its failure to de-militarize former conflict zones. Security Sector Reform (SSR) is a universal policy component of the liberal peace that involves the restructuring of the national security apparatus. This includes the demobilizing of rebel armies and militias, integrating them into the national army and security services, and rehabilitating them into society through the provision of economic incentives. In Central Africa, this multi-million dollar process was controlled by the World Bank, which subcontracted to UN agencies and private military companies. A key component of SSR is the Disarmament, Demobilization and Rehabilitation (DDR) programme, the experience of which, in Burundi and DRC, indicates that the policy was seriously flawed in terms of delivering even sustainable negative peace. A consideration of the continued militarism and the prevalence of gender-based violence, in particular sexual violence, in these societies, can illustrate DDR's inherent weakness.

Despite the implementation of programmes orientated towards peace, the infrastructures of violence were reproduced in four significant ways. First, rebel armies used DDR as an opportunity to augment their numbers – some purely on paper. This was especially the case in Burundi, where numbers were inflated and recruitment continued after peace agreements were signed. Second, militias cached their weapons rather than surrendered them to the authorities. Burundi rebels CNDD/FDD (Conseil National pour la Défense de la Démocratie/ Forces pour la Défense de la Démocratie; National Council for Defence and Democracy / Forces for Defence and Democracy) and Palipehutu / FNL (Parti pour la Libération du Peuple Hutu / Forces Nationales de Libération; Party for the Liberation of the Hutu People / National Forces for Liberation) brought only a fraction of their arsenal to the demobilization sites. This facilitated the return to the 'bush' of the FNL leadership, and rebel skirmishes during and after the 2010 elections. Thirdly, the agreement that allowed senior rebel leaders to retain their rank when they were integrated into the national army meant that those leaders who were responsible for gross crimes against humanity were empowered militarily under peace. In the DRC, these former rebel officers were formally able to retain control over the spaces they had previously terrorized through the continuation of direct violence, now sanctioned by the state. Here, the failure to incorporate situated knowledge in DDR increased the people's vulnerability to direct violence. Finally, cash payments were given to former fighters, at the same time as benefits to citizens were reduced, through the introduction of cost-recovery in essential services, such as hospitals and schools. This signals the importance of military values within the new, post-conflict society, underpinned by patriarchy and a violent form of hegemonic masculinity. In 2006, Burundi's heads of police and intelligence were the generals from the rebel armies, where they were not guided by any formal code of conduct. The UN representative in charge of human rights pointed to the 'military and elected officials' abuse of local people' and remarked: 'because they are elected they feel that they have the authority to do what they like'.[44]

One outcome of this militarized peace in Central Africa is the prevalence of gender-based violence (GBV) long after conflict has ended and peacebuilding has started. This is due partly to the persistence of rebel activity, especially amongst those groups that were excluded from or were formed after the peace process started. In Burundi, the evidence indicates that GBV, especially rape, was even more widespread in the post-war context than it was before and during the war.[45] Reported cases of rape rose dramatically after the peace agreement, with most of the perpetrators being community members known to the victims. The NGO *Ligue Iteka*, saw cases rise from 983 in 2003 to 1,791 in 2005. Another NGO, *Nturengaho*, reported 93 cases in 2003 and 446 cases in 2004, some 40 per cent of which were committed by armed personnel. *Centre Seruka* – a rape crisis centre – received 1,119 cases between September 2003 and 2004.[46] Burundi human rights organizations attribute this to the demobilization of young men from the army and the rebel forces.

The scale of sexual violence in Central Africa has led to a flurry of international attention, manifested in outrage in the international media and numerous scoping reports by human rights groups and aid agencies.[47] This enormous level of interest has drawn attention to the plight of women and men who have been subjected to extreme forms of abuse. However, the failure to contextualize rape, beyond its representation as 'a weapon of war' among tribal peoples, prevents due consideration of its expansion under a liberal peace framework that promotes militarism and hypermasculinity.

As Pratt and Richter Devore note, the liberal peace intervention to protect women is through providing 'technocratic, legalistic gender mainstreaming and humanitarian relief'.[48] In the case of GBV, this involves immediate and palliative health care for the victims, which is, no doubt, of critical importance. The other main focus is on the legislative space, holding leaders to account at the International Criminal Tribunal for Rwanda (ICTR)[49] and reforming the laws of the country concerned so that perpetrators of sexual violence can be punished.

Nowrojee criticizes the ICTR for not taking sexual violence seriously, and for conducting investigations that de-humanize, demean and marginalize the victims, with excessive interrogations and no post-trial support.[50] Such interventions leave the structural causes of wars unexamined.

Even though the liberal peace at the national level is antithetical to women's welfare, its advocates nevertheless champion women's rights at the international and regional level, where gender is articulated as a legitimate and non-political field of action. At the turn of the twenty-first century, international discourse altered to incorporate women as agents of peace and to mainstream principles of gender equality into international peacekeeping and peacebuilding.[51] This new policy framework is reflected in the UN Security Council Resolution 1325 (2000), which recognizes the specific experiences of women during wartime, and advocates a role for women in peacekeeping. Resolution 1325 urges states to end impunity and to prosecute those responsible for sexual violence and other forms of violence against women and girls. UN agencies were able proactively to support local women's organizations mobilizing for peace in Burundi and in the Congo.[52] However, according to recent research, Resolution 1325 forces women's organizations at the UN to refrain from critiquing militarism and masculinity and, instead, to adopt the hegemonic neoliberal discourse, which constructs women as enterprising and efficient peacemakers.[53] Olonisakin and Okech draw attention to the inconsistency between the male-dominated security narratives, which simultaneously privilege sovereignty and territory within international discourse, and the proposals for gender equality in peacekeeping and peacebuilding.[54] They call for total transformation of the security and governance architecture, if women's rights are to be realized.

## Towards an African conceptualization of peace

So far, I have argued that the liberal peace in Central Africa has failed to recognize the lived material experiences of Africans, and local political and cultural dynamics, at the expense of realizing sustainable peace. The continued presence of structural violence and the proxy wars fought on the African continent informed Hansen's call for Africans to reject a position on peace where it is understood as the peace of Europe and North America and to replace it with an 'African perspective', that is concerned not merely with 'the resolution of conflicts [but with] the transformation of the extant social systems at both national and international levels'.[55] Hansen argues for a perspective on peace that 'makes it possible for the majority of the people on this planet to enjoy physical security, a modicum of material prosperity, the satisfaction of the basic needs of human existence, emotional well-being, political efficacy and psychic harmony'.[56] Linking the liberal peace with the increasingly hollow concept of 'human security' appears to meet this demand theoretically. However, the continued assumption that universal human well-being can be achieved within the extant social system, despite evidence to the contrary, serves to limit its transformative potential. Similarly, while there is much of value in the modern concept of universal rights, for neo-realists such rights continue to be underpinned by notions of differential human worth, which are reinforced by unequal power relations in the global order. The questions now are: can Africans continue to rely on frameworks that do not reflect their histories, cultures and everyday realities and that are non-participatory? and what would an African perspective on peace look like?

Under neo-liberal governance, peace is promoted by a multiplicity of actors: the UN, Western governments and their militaries, international and African-based NGOs, private military contractors, multinational corporations and Africa's political elites. Most ascribe themselves the mantle of mediators, acting on behalf of the people, who are depicted as disenfranchised victims. These actors do not necessarily share a common understanding of the complex dynamics of violence and they often seek to champion particular individuals or groups, and even enter the process for their own vested interests.[57] To ensure locally appropriate blueprints for post-war societies, the African body politic has to be incorporated into the peace process in its locally contingent and culturally diverse forms.

Within Africa, cultural differences and local histories of state formation and colonial legacies make a monolithic African perspective on peace unworkable.[58] However, one can start with the commonalities exposed by the limits of the liberal peace. A locally contingent peace needs to unpack the gendered dynamics of war and peace, and open up to the everyday lived experiences of people with respect to conflict resolution and peaceful co-existence in different geographical and cultural contexts. An African understanding of peace therefore necessitates considering how societies were organized prior to modernity and what constitutes social healing prior to contemporary religious practices and justice systems. Attention to African traditional cultures allows for, as Osei-Hwedie and Abu-Nimer note, a new approach 'associated with and promoted by diversity' and which 'emphasises open-mindedness, continuous learning and mutual acceptance'.[59]

All African societies had mechanisms for resolving conflict, and for punishing those who transgressed the rules and norms of the society. Some of these punitive measures would now be considered barbaric, especially when they result in death through torture, and when viewed uncritically. However, these justice systems tended to be representative of the community, especially in acephalous societies, and in some monarchical systems they were separated from the monarchy. Pre-colonial African justice systems were largely participatory and maintained the social order and the health of the social body.[60] The denigration of indigenous justice systems as 'backward', along with attempts to control them by successive colonial and postcolonial states, has led to a mixed picture of resistance and resilience in some localities and in others de-legitimization among the people.[61]

Many Africans can identify indigenous notions of peace in the philosophical tradition known as *ubuntu* (I am because we are) in Southern Africa and as *utu* and *umunthu* in East and Central Africa, whilst other variations exist across the continent. *Ubuntu* exists in strong contrast to the individualism of modernity. It refers to the concept of a common humanity – that the essence of being human is dependent on the individual being part of a community.[62] Murithi identifies *ubuntu*'s key principles: empathy, reciprocity, inclusivity, 'cooperation in efforts to resolve common problems' and 'a sense of a shared destiny between people'.[63] The epistemological basis for *ubuntu* was undermined by the arrival of colonial modernity and its vision of progress. Africans were encouraged or forced to discount their understandings of what it means to be humans, to live together harmoniously, and how to protect themselves in times of individual and group insecurity. Under the principles of *ubuntu*, Murithi notes, 'a law-breaking individual thus transforms his or her group into a law-breaking group'.[64] Therefore, perpetrators of violence, in order for themselves and their kin-group to be re-admitted into their community, have to go through a process of confessing responsibility or guilt, requesting forgiveness from the victim and his/her kin-group (who is encouraged to show mercy), and paying compensation before the families are reconciled and harmony is restored to the community. Unless such processes have taken place, kin-groups are stigmatized and communities fracture. What is central to these systems is thus communal accountability and participation.

The Truth and Reconciliation Commission (TRC) in South Africa, devised by Archbishop Desmond Tutu as a means of forgiveness and healing for the fractured and traumatized post-Apartheid society, drew on traditional African concepts of *ubuntu*. The success of the TRC was hailed as a model that could be adopted elsewhere in Africa. However, in

South Africa, *ubuntu* has been subject to criticism, especially by the left, as it appears to have been co-opted by neoliberal forces.[65] And the TRC has also been criticized for not considering the difficulties women experience in using such public fora to recall their abuses; and its non-contextualized application elsewhere on the continent ignores the complexities of local dynamics.[66] In Burundi, where many of those who would be culpable for crimes against humanity are incorporated into the ruling and main opposition parties, the prospect of them developing a mechanism that would expose their own criminality is limited. Hence, the government's foot-dragging, agenda change, and the constraining of the power of the TRC proposed in the peace agreement, as the state response to donor pressure. Even if implemented, this top-down imposition of reconciliation will fail to reunite and heal those affected. Macdonald proposes the wresting of *ubuntu* from neoliberal forces and reviving a 'more radical *ubuntu* discourse' by sticking to its ideals of collective action. He states: 'to be true to *ubuntu* ideals collective process is as important as its collective product'.[67] Therefore, *ubuntu* offers a more fitting alternative to the individualism of neoliberalism, since it largely reflects the pre-modern, as well as the everyday, practices of peace among many African communities.

The collapse of the modern justice systems during late twentieth-century wars, along with the scale of the violence, has compelled proponents of the liberal peace to encourage a return to traditional systems of justice, such as the *bashingantahe* of Burundi and the *Gacaca* courts of Rwanda. As Ingelaere notes, the basic principles of these traditional institutions are the establishment of accountability and fostering reconciliation at the local scale.[68] However, despite the potential benefits of using African value systems in contemporary justice mechanisms, it would be naive to assume that one could fully replicate such justice systems within the modern context, or that they would be representative, especially if their restitution and the form they adopt are determined by the state and funded by aid donors. These 'modern' traditional systems tend to reflect the patriarchal nature of the national state, uphold the priorities of the political elite rather than those of the people, and are less effective in resolving conflicts for women and, according to Thomson, 'may exacerbate local power dynamics and social and political inequalities'. [69]

African people's attitudes to the militarized body are in stark contrast to the assumptions made by Western peace experts: that, given monetary payments, soldiers can be rehabilitated into their local communities. Recent research highlights the social abhorrence to the militarized body that pervades certain cultures in Africa. In northern

Uganda, DRC and Burundi, known association with rebels makes one an outcast in the society.[70] Former soldiers continue to be feared and, in turn, terrorize communities, using gender-based violence as a strategy for re-establishing the power associated with the hypermasculinity of wartime. The stigmatization of soldiers and rebels who are known to have committed acts of atrocity is found in many local communities and signifies a rejection of militarist ideology; yet post-conflict reconstruction enhances ex-combatants' material and physical power in peacetime. This stigmatization can be destructive because it extends to all those who have been implicated in acts of extreme violence, whether bush wives, child soldiers or rape victims. However, an examination of the healing processes would allow for greater African agency in effecting peace at a local level. This should be concomitant with understanding how nonviolent forms of masculinity are performed within these societies.

Finally, the content of an African feminist perspective has to be different from the non-emancipatory women-centred activities of the liberal peace. So far, African women's campaigns for greater participation in peace processes have tended to perpetuate essentialist notions of women as natural peacemakers. As Diop claims, the assumption is that 'women are better equipped than men to prevent or resolve conflicts' because they 'are excessively affected by war and should be playing a fundamental role in reconciliation, reconstruction and rehabilitation',[71] thereby implying that women possess some innate suitability for peace negotiations.

Africa's regional organizations, under pressure from women's NGOs, Western donors and institutions, have adopted protocols to address gender issues in peace and security. One example is Article 10 (1) of the African Union's Protocol to the African Charter on Human and Peoples' Rights on the Rights of Women, which stipulates that 'all women have the right to a peaceful existence and the right to participate in the promotion and maintenance of peace'.[72] Other regional organizations, such as Southern African Development Community and the Economic Community of West African States, have also produced their own protocols. However, such legislation, though enlightening, has not been localised and, where the national state is structured around patriarchy and militarism, attention to gender issues beyond women's numerical representation in government, remains limited. African feminist scholars have criticized the disempowering role of elite women who have been co-opted into militarized institutions.[73] Olonisakin and Okech call for a reform of African women's organizations in order to prevent the mobilization of gender identities (mothers, sisters, and wives) by the masculinized states, elite women and humanitarian actors.[74]

By not paying attention to local cultures of difference, measures towards gender equality in the liberal peace run the risk of essentializing African women. For example, Burundian women had diverse war experiences, based on ethnicity, class, location (urban or rural) and association with state or rebel (bush wives or fighters) forces. Equally, their interpretation of peace is also differentiated. Blanchard's suggestion that 'the identification of women with peace be balanced by recognition of the participation, support and inspiration women have given to war making', requires detailed consideration.[75] Despite the popularity of the discourse on African women as victims in wartime, there is widespread evidence to suggest that some women participated in genocide and sexual violence against other women. African Rights documents how Hutu women in Rwanda identified people to be killed. They contend that educated women, who held government positions, bore 'a special responsibility for the breadth and depth of women's participation in the killings'.[76] Women parliamentarians, councillors and mayors were willing to order the killing of Tutsi girls and the Tutsi children of Hutu women married to Tutsi men.

Women were also able to take on very proactive roles as fighters and community leaders. In the DRC, Peuchguirbal shows how 'war provided Congolese women with opportunities as well as burdens. They took up leadership positions and revived local networks. They were not mere victims as they fought for their survival.'[77] In the absence of men, war can liberate women from the patriarchal straitjacket. Wars expose the false dichotomy between the public and the private, and force women and their interests into the spotlight. Essentially, the view of African women in the liberal peace as universal victims runs counter to local realities.

An African feminist perspective on peace demands recognition of class and cultural differences between African women across the continent, whilst asserting that peace requires a dismantling of the patriarchal state, but, at the same time, noting how oppressions of race, gender and place intersect at the global level to disempower African men and women together. First and foremost, this means being critical about those cultural traditions that deny women's agency. African feminist scholars have started to revisit the past to examine gender relations in pre-colonial matriarchal societies, in order to understand 'the role a matriarchal moral philosophy' might play in constructing locally appropriate [gender equality] in contemporary African politics and society'.[78] The goal is a more grounded, non-hierarchical and emancipatory vision of peace for women and men.

## Conclusion

In Central Africa, the liberal peace has delivered neither positive nor sustainable negative peace. From its origins in the Euro-American political experience the liberal peace has become globally hegemonic, and has remained so because of its intersection with the geopolitical interests of Western states and neoliberal capitalism. On top of its geographic specificity, its embodiment of a gendered and militarist conceptualization of national security make it increasingly less appropriate for non-Western societies, where peace requires far-reaching emancipatory politics. The major limitations of the liberal peace as implemented in the Central African region is its emphasis on a militarized interpretation of national security with its negative implications for the well-being of citizens, especially under conditions where the institutions of governance, and the material conditions of life, are weak and impoverished respectively. Peace and de-militarization necessitate concomitant transformation in the socio-economic system, new forms of state/society relationships and alternative forms of masculinity. These must be based on an acceptance of diversity and a recognition of how the intersections between race, ethnicity and gender at the local, national and global levels shape policy responses.

Unearthing alternative geographies of peace requires challenging the structural inequalities and the racialized and gendered discourses that are embedded in contemporary framings of the hegemonic liberal peace. It requires an ontological and epistemological shift in our understanding of the social body and more contextualized and critical research that at the outset privileges local experiences of peaceful co-existence. So far, local mechanisms for peace have been co-opted and re-shaped by state elites and the external peace industry. Progressive scholars need to push for greater engagement of local communities in a collective framing of the peace process from the bottom-up. A localized and gender sensitive peace has the capacity to fashion a post-war society that gives prominence to the well-being of all African peoples and challenges the de-humanizing conditions that Africans have been socialized into accepting as the norm. Here, recognizing and drawing on the contribution of African feminists is an essential prerequisite for peace.

## Notes

1. Steans, Jill, *Gender and International Relations: An Introduction* (New Brunswick, NJ, 1998); Enloe, Cynthia, 'Demilitarization – or more of the same? Feminist questions to ask in the postwar moment', in C. Cockburn and D. Zarkov (eds), *The Post-war Moment: Militaries, Masculinities and International Peacekeeping* (London, 2002), pp. 927–31.

2. Williams, Philippa and McConnell, Fiona, 'Critical geographies of peace' *Antipode* 43/4 (2011), p. 928.

3. Hansen, Emmanuel (ed.), *Africa: Perspectives on Peace and Development* (London, 1987), p. 1.

4. Dalby, Simon, 'Gender and critical geopolitics: reading security discourse in the new world disorder', *Environment and Planning D: Society and Space* 12/5 (1994), pp. 595–612; Hyndman, Jennifer, 'Beyond either/or: a feminist analysis of September 11th', *ACME* 2/1 (2003), pp. 1–13.

5. Hyndman, 'Beyond either/or', pp. 1, 3.

6. Megoran, Nick, 'War *and* Peace? An agenda for research and practice in geography', *Political Geography* 30/4 (2011), pp. 178–89.

7. Daley, Patricia, *Gender and Genocide: The Search for Spaces of Peace in Central Africa* (Oxford, 2008); Lemarchand, Rene, *The Dynamics of Violence in Central Africa* (Philadelphia, 2009).

8. Burundi's Arusha peace and reconciliation agreement was signed in 2000 after almost three years of negotiation. DRC's Lusaka peace agreement was signed in 1999. In both countries, the peace agreements were followed by numerous ceasefire agreements with various rebel groups. Two successive democratic elections have been held in these countries.

9. Gibbing, Sheri Lynn, 'No angry women at the United Nations: political dreams and the cultural politics of United Nations Security Council Resolution 1325', *International Feminist Journal of Politics* 13/4 (2011), pp. 522–38.

10. Ingelaere, Bert, 'Does the truth pass across the fire without burning? Locating the short circuit in Rwanda's Gacaca courts', *Journal of Modern African Studies*, 47/4 (2009), pp. 507–28.

11. Hill Collins, Patricia, *Black Feminist Thought: Knowledge, Consciousness and the Politics of Empowerment* (Perspectives on Gender) (London, 2000), p. 18.

12. Duffield, Mark, *Global Governance and the New Wars: The Merging of Development and Security* (London, 2001); Kaldor, Mary, *New and Old Wars: Organized Violence in a Global Era* (Cambridge, 2001).

13. Kaldor, *New and Old Wars*.

14. Weber, Max, *Economy and Society* (Berkeley, 1978).

15. Steans, Jill, *Gender and International Relations*, p. 107.

16. Gramsci, Antonio, *Prison Notebooks* (Bodmin and Kings Lynn, 2007).

17. Gramsci, *Prison Notebooks*, p. 12.

18. Keenan, Jeremy, 'Terror in the Sahara: the implications of US imperialism for North and West Africa', *Review of African Political Economy* 31/101 (2004), pp. 475–96.

19. Galtung, Johan, 'Violence, peace and peace research', *Journal of Peace Research* 6/3 (1969), pp. 167–91.

20. Melvern, Linda R., *A People Betrayed: The Role of the West in Rwanda's Genocide* (London, 2000).

21. See UN Security Council, *Regarding the Events that Occurred at Gatumba*, S/2004/821 (http://www.un.org/Docs/sc/unsc_presandsg_letters04.html, 2004), and International Crisis Group, *Maintaining Momentum in the Congo: The Ituri Problem* (Nairobi/Brussels, 2004).

22. Confortini, Catia C., 'Galtung, violence, and gender: the case for a peace studies/feminist alliance', *Peace & Change* 31/3 (2006), pp. 333–67; Hudson, Heidi, 'Peacebuilding through a gender lens and challenges of implementation in Rwanda and Cote d'Ivoire', *Security Studies* 18/2 (2009), pp. 287–318.

23. Enloe, Cynthia, *Maneuvers: The International Politics of Militarizing Women's Lives* (Berkeley and Los Angeles, 2000); Steans, *Gender and International Relations*; Yuval-Davis, Nira, *Gender and Nation* (London, 1997).

24. Messerschmidt, James W., *Masculinities and Crime: Critique and Reconceptualization of Theory* (Lanham, MD, 1993).

25. Daley, *Gender and Genocide*; Hudson, 'Peacebuilding through a gender lens'.

26. Enloe, 'Demilitarization – or more of the same? Feminist questions to ask in the postwar moment', in Cynthia Cockburn and Dubravka Zarkov (eds), *The Postwar Moment: Militaries, Masculinities and International Peacekeeping* (London, 2002); Simić, Olivera, 'Does the presence of women really matter? Towards combating male sexual violence in peacekeeping operations', *International Peacekeeping* 17/2 (2010), pp. 188–99; Hudson, 'Peacebuilding through a gender lens'.

27. Yuval-Davis, *Gender and Nation*.

28. Hill Collins, *Black Feminist Thought*.

29. Foucault, Michel, *Society Must Be Defended* (London, 2004), pp. 253–6.

30. Fluri, Jennifer, '"Foreign-passports only": geographies of (post) conflict work in Kabul, Afghanistan', *Annals of the Association of American Geographers* 99/5 (2009), pp. 986–94.

31. Dallaire, Romeo, *Shake Hands with the Devil: The Failure of Humanity in Rwanda* (London, 2004), p. 522.

32. Crowder, Michael, 'Whose dream was it anyway? Twenty-five years of African independence', *African Affairs* 86/342 (1987), pp. 7–24.

33. The nationalist leaders, Julius Nyerere and Kwame Nkrumah, who experimented with methods of social tolerance and nation-building in multiethnic and multicultural states, were criticized by the West for their socialist policies, despite their success at forging national unity.

34. Richmond, Oliver, 'Becoming liberal, unbecoming liberalism: liberal–local hybridity via the everyday as a response to the paradoxes of liberal peace building', *Journal of Intervention and State Building* 3/3 (2009), pp. 324–44.

35. Kaldor, *New and Old Wars*.

36. Collier, Paul and Hoeffler, Anke, 'Greed and grievance in civil war', *Oxford Economic Papers* 56 (2004), pp. 563–95.

37. Tull, David M. and Mehler, Andreas, 'The hidden cost of power sharing: reproducing insurgent violence in Africa', *African Affairs* 104/416 (2005), pp. 375–98; Mehler, Andreas, 'Peace and power sharing in Africa: not so obvious a relationship', *African Affairs* 108/432 (2009), pp. 453–73.

38. Tull and Mehler, 'The hidden cost of power sharing'.

39. Eriksen, Stein S., 'The liberal peace is neither: peace building, state building and the reproduction of conflict in the Democratic Republic of Congo', *International Peacekeeping* 16/5 (2009), pp. 652–66; Austerre, Séverine, 'Hobbes and the Congo: frames, local violence and international intervention', *International Organization* 63/Spring (2009), pp. 248–80.

40. Harvey, David, *The New Imperialism* (Oxford, 2003), Chapter 4, and Daley, *Gender and Genocide,* for a discussion with respect to Burundi.

41. Vervisch, Thomas, 'The solidarity chain: post-conflict reconstruction and social capital building on three Burundian hillsides', *Journal of Eastern African Studies* 5/1 (2011), pp. 24–41.

42. Oluoch, Fred, 'Burundi's "smallest" military budget highest as fraction of GDP in region', *The East African*, 12 April 2010.

43. Clayton, Jonathan and Bone, James, 'Sex scandal in Congo threatens to engulf UN's peacekeepers', *The Times*, 23 December 2004. Retrieved 6 October 2011 from http://www.timesonline.co.uk/tol/news/world/article405213.ece; Simić, 'Does the presence of women really matter?'.

44. Interview conducted with head of the human rights section of the UN mission in Burundi (ONUB), June 2006.

45. The increase in the number of reported rapes could also have been attributed to better data gathering exercises in the post-war period, as donors allocated resources to tackle GBV, and it was accepted that because of the stigma associated with rape, under-reporting was widespread and the scale of sexual violence was far greater.

46. Data collected from Ligue Iteka, *Déclaration de la Ligue ITEKA: Violence dans certaines localités du Burundi I* (Bujumbura, 2005). Retrieved December 2005 from http://www.ligue-iteka.africa-web.org/, and during interviews with representatives of *Ligue Iteka, Médecins sans Frontières*, Nturengaho and Centre Seruka, June 2006.

47. See, for example, *Réseau des Femmes pour un Développement Associatif* (RFDA), *Réseau des Femmes pour la Défense des Droits et la Paix* (RFDDP) and International Alert (IA), *Women's Bodies as a Battleground: Sexual Violence Against Women and Girls During the War in the Democratic Republic of Congo, South Kivu (1996–2003)* (London, 2005), and Eriksson-Baaz Maria and Stern, Maria, *The Complexity of Violence: A Critical Analysis of Sexual Violence in the DRC* (Uppsala, 2010).

48. Pratt, Nicola and Richter-Devore, Sophie, 'Critically examining UNSCR 1325 on Women, Peace and Security', *International Feminist Journal of Politics* 13/4 (2011), pp. 498–9.

49. ICTR, based in Arusha Tanzania, was established by the United Nations Security Council resolution 955 of 8 November 1994 and resolution 977 of 22 February 1995 to perpetrators of the 1994 Rwandan genocide.

50. Nowrojee, Binaifer, 'Your justice is too slow: will the ICCTR fail Rwanda's rape victims?' (Geneva, 2005).

51. Olonisakin, Funmi and Okech, Awino, *Women and Security Governance in Africa* (Cape Town, Dakar, Nairobi and Oxford, 2011).

52. Burke, Enid de Silva, Klot, Jennifer and Bunting, Ikaweba, *Engendering Peace: Reflections on the Burundi Peace Process* (Nairobi, 2001); Puechguirbal, Nadine, 'Women and war in the Democratic Republic of Congo', *Signs: Journal of Women in Culture and Society* 28/4 (2003), pp. 1271–81.

53. Gibbing, '"No angry women at the United Nations"'; Pratt and Richter-Devore, 'Critically examining UNSCR', pp. 489–503.

54. Olonisakin and Okech, *Women and Security Governance in Africa*; Pratt and Richter-Devore, 'Critically examining UNSCR 1325', pp. 498–9.

55. Hansen, *Africa: Perspectives on Peace and Development.*

56. Hansen, *Africa: Perspectives on Peace and Development*, p. 1.

57. Daley, *Gender and Genocide.*

58. Hudson, 'Peacebuilding through a gender lens'.

59. Osei-Hwedie, Bertha Z. and Abu-Nimer, Mohammed, 'Editorial: Enhancing the positive contributions of African culture', *Peacebuilding and Development* 4/3 (2009), pp. 1–5.
60. Diop, Cheikh Anta, *Precolonial Black Africa: A Comparative Study of the Political and Social Systems of Europe and Black Africa, from Antiquity to the Formation of Modern States* (London, 1987) and *The Cultural Unity of Black Africa: the Domains of Matriarchy & Patriarchy in Classical Antiquity* (London, 1989).
61. Herbst, Jeffrey, *States and Power in Africa* (Princeton, NJ, 2000).
62. Ramose, Mogobe B., 'The philosophy of *Ubuntu* and *Ubuntu* as a philosophy', in P. H. Coetzee and A. P. J. Roux (eds), *Philosophy from Africa*, second edition (Cape Town, 2002), pp. 230–8.
63. Murithi, Tim, 'An African perspective on peace building: *Ubuntu* lessons in reconciliation', *International Review of Education* 55 (2009), pp. 221–33.
64. Murithi, 'An African perspective on peace building', p. 227.
65. MacDonald, David, 'Ubuntu bashing: the marketisation of "African values" in South Africa', *Review of African Political Economy* 37/124 (2010), pp. 139–52.
66. Ross, Fiona, *Bearing Witness: Women and the Truth and Reconciliation Commission in South Africa* (London, 2003); Borer, Tristan Anne, 'Gendered war and gendered peace: truth commissions and post-conflict violence: lessons from South Africa', *Violence Against Women* 15 (2009), pp. 1169–93.
67. MacDonald, 'Ubuntu bashing', p. 149.
68. Ingelaere, 'Does the truth pass?'.
69. Thomson, Susan, 'The darker side of transitional justice: the power dynamics behind Rwanda's Gacaca courts', *Africa* 81/3 (2011), pp. 373–90.
70. Eriksson-Baaz and Stern, *The Complexity of Violence*; Wilhelm-Solomon, Matthew, *Displacing AIDS: Therapeutic Transitions in Northern Uganda* (Oxford, 2011).
71. Diop, Bineta, 'Engendering the peace process in Africa: women at the negotiating table', *Refugee Survey Quarterly* 21 (2002), pp. 142–54.
72. The Protocol to the African Charter on Human and Peoples' Rights on the Rights of Women was adopted by the second summit of the African Union on 11 July 2003 in Maputo, Mozambique. It came into force in October 2005 after it was ratified by the 15th member state.
73. For example, the UN Commission on the Status of Women and the OAU co-sponsored the organization of the 'First Summit of First Ladies for Peace and Humanitarian Issues', held in Abuja, Nigeria, 5–7 May 1997.
74. Olonisakin and Okech, *Women and Security*.
75. Blanchard, Erica M., 'Gender, international relations, and the development of feminist security theory', *Signs: Journal of Women in Culture and Society* 28/4 (2003), pp. 1289–1312.
76. African Rights, *Not So Innocent: When Women Become Killers* (London, 1995), p. 2.
77. Puechguirbal, Nadine, 'Women and war', p. 1274.
78. Amadiume, Ifi, *Reinventing Africa: Matriarchy, Religion, and Culture* (London, 1997), p. 157.

# Part 2

# Techniques of peacemaking

## 5

# Re-thinking international boundary practices: moving away from the 'edge'

*John Donaldson*

## Exposing delimitation and demarcation to critique

In his seminal history of French territorial boundaries, Peter Sahlins revealed that by 1775 the French Ministry of Foreign Affairs had assumed responsibility for defining territorial boundaries from the War Ministry.[1] A seemingly unremarkable shift in eighteenth-century French bureaucracy, this can be seen to represent a paradigm shift in the resolution of boundary disputes that continues to reverberate today. Boundary studies began to move away from a more militaristic view of boundaries that conceived of them as the limits of imperial conquest or as *de facto* armistice lines concluded at the close of battle. Instead, the practices of defining boundaries became activities conducted between two recognized, neighbouring politico-territorial entities through diplomatic dialogue and established procedures. Sahlins notes that this bureaucratic change was representative of a more introspective shift in French politics of the mid-eighteenth century that was best conveyed by the comments of the Marquis d'Argenson, Foreign Minister under Louis XV, who stated in 1765: 'It is time to start governing, after spending so much time acquiring what to govern.'[2]

The (notionally) peaceful definition of territorial boundaries through diplomatic agreement reached a climax in the imperial expansion of the late nineteenth century, where such practice was heralded as being essential to prevent the much feared inter-imperial conflicts of competing claims for vast areas of Africa and Asia. Fixing the linear limits of sovereignty through 'civilized' diplomatic practices was also an integral part of the European state model of territorial governance being imposed through liberalized notions of imperialism. Within this specific geopolitical situation at the end of the nineteenth and start of the twentieth century, a procedural rubric developed to define those boundaries: the boundary-making processes of delimitation and demarcation.

European geographers of the early twentieth century were instrumental in developing these practices, largely from the experiences of imperial surveyors such as Henry MacMahon and Thomas Holdich, as well as international legal scholars including Paul de la Pradelle and Vittoroio Adami.[3] From this work, the rubric was most famously outlined by the geographer Stephen Jones in 1945 and more recently by the political geographer Victor Prescott and jurist Gillian Triggs.[4] The distillation of these practices through this literature, particularly up to 1945, has sought to define a systematic procedure for defining boundaries that are least likely to cause dispute and provoke inter-state conflict, by eliminating any ambiguity that might leave room for overlapping jurisdictional claims.

In recent decades, much of the discourse in political geography concerning international boundaries has expanded into notions of bordering practices that emphasize the actual exercise of state control. This rich development has broadened the intellectual scope of border studies to encompass a wide range of interdisciplinary scholarship that embraces geographic multiplicity[5] and, in particular, challenges the current strategies of border securitization.[6] In so doing, contemporary political geography, and border studies more specifically, have shifted away from practices related to definition of the boundary line itself. Within this shift, the tendency has been to confine the practices of delimitation and demarcation under the subdiscipline moniker of 'traditional boundary studies', rather than subjecting the practices themselves to direct critique.

Julian Minghi suggests that there has been a tendency for traditional boundary studies to gravitate towards inter-state conflict and the prevention thereof.[7] This concentration on just one level of political conflict and dialogue, succumbs to the notion of states as individual homogeneous actors; falling squarely into John Agnew's 'territorial trap'.[8] In his call for a new theory on borders, David Newman suggests that:

> Any attempt, therefore, to create a methodological and conceptual framework for the understanding of boundaries must be concerned with the process of 'bordering' rather than simply with the means through which physical lines of separation are delimited and demarcated.[9]

Conceiving delimitation and demarcation as 'practical' or 'technical' procedures has made it difficult to subject them to the critiques of border studies which 'embraces the theoretical away from the empirical'.[10] As Nick Megoran has suggested, traditional boundary studies have tended to be 'staunchly empirical, and bereft of any serious engagement with politically informed theory'.[11] Dennis Rumley and Julian Minghi agree, stating that

> one of the limitations of previous research is that it has tended to be overly descriptive and classificatory, preferring to pursue a conceptually narrow approach which has been primarily concerned with physical artefacts (for example, boundary markers).[12]

Within the empiricism of traditional boundary studies, the terms 'delimitation' and 'demarcation' themselves have tended to be used as binary descriptors of individual boundaries, rather than as practices that can be problematized: boundary $x$ was delimited in year $y$, boundary $x$ is or is not demarcated.[13] This is not to say there have not been critiques of the delimitation and demarcation rubric itself, most notably by Stephen Jones (ironically) and Ladis Kristof in 1959, as well as some early work by Victor Prescott.[14] However, these critiques have failed to supplant delimitation and demarcation as the standard model accepted by state actors for the resolution of boundary disputes.[15]

Disputes over the definition of territorial boundaries continue to cause conflict and violence on a variety of social and political scales, including (but not exclusively) the very real risk of violent engagement between state actors. My concern in this chapter is largely not with major territorial conflicts involving disputed historic or ethno-territorial claims to large regions and populations, although these certainly involve elements of boundary definition. Instead, the focus here is on the seemingly minor disputes concerning the ambiguous definition of specific boundaries which has led to overlapping claims and served as the catalyst for conflict and violence at a variety of scales. In many (if not the majority) of cases, a dispute over boundary definition simply serves as the lightning rod that channels a variety of other political and social tensions within a borderland area. For example, while poor marking of the Kenya-Ethiopia boundary played a role in the recent violence around the northern shoreline of Lake Turkana, it was the underlying tensions between local groups, particularly in relation to transboundary grazing, water rights and food scarcity, that fuelled local violence.[16] Similarly, although often described as a boundary conflict, the devastating war between Eritrea and Ethiopia from 1998 to 2000 must be set within the general political tension following Eritrea's independence in 1994, and the personal animosity between the two heads of state.[17] A local disagreement over the ambiguous position of the boundary round the small border town of Badme simply served as the fuse.

These types of positional boundary dispute expose the limitations of the delimitation–demarcation model as a mechanism for conflict resolution. However, government actors continue to turn to this rubric despite the fact that it was developed for a very specific geopolitical situation and with a very specific – negative – concept of peace. This chapter will suggest that the existing delimitation-demarcation rubric, as interpreted and applied particularly within international law, is insufficient to address the wider range of conflicts raised at varying socio-political levels that are often caged under the aegis of 'boundary dispute'. It will first examine the geopolitical conditions in which the delimitation and demarcation procedures took form, placing them firmly within what has been referred to as the 'negative peace': being based on imperial practices, deeply embedded in the liberal ideals of the post-1918 world and framed in the immediacy of post-conflict settlement. The chapter will then reveal how the rubric has been accepted by states in practice, specifically within international judicial settlement which is an increasingly popular route for resolving inter-state boundary disputes.[18] Three recent situations will illustrate how boundary disputes fail to be 'resolved' simply through a legally binding settlement. While the resolution of disputes through legal means is preferable to resolution through violence, it will be argued that this particular avenue continues to accentuate the contested nature of territorial claims and exposes the limitations of the delimitation–demarcation rubric.

This critical reassessment of the delimitation–demarcation rubric will be informed by two intertwined conceptual shifts that will permeate this discussion. The first relates to the operation of time in boundary making, whereby re-thinking delimitation–demarcation should encourage a shift from conceptualizing a boundary as the product of a finite system within the immediacy of conflict settlement, towards a more organic conception of the boundary as possessing an ongoing life-cycle of peacebuilding within the borderland context. This draws on the insistence in peace studies for 'peace' to be conceived not simply as the negation of conflict, but the cultivation of sustainable, long-term peaceful practices and relations.[19] Contemporary thought and practice all too commonly assume that 'peace' results when delimitation has been agreed and demarcation executed: this chapter contributes towards the development of a geography of peace by problematizing this traditional rubric. Closely woven into this conceptual shift in defining boundaries is an attempt to change the ways in which territory and maritime space under national jurisdiction are conceived by political actors at varying scales as spaces of rights towards seeing them as spaces of responsibility. While such a shift has been examined in relation to the notion of state sovereignty,[20] the focus here on the delimitation–demarcation processes relates more closely to notions of territory and its continued capacity to provoke conflict. It is hoped that a critical reassessment of the traditional rubric will help to encourage a shift in the concept of international boundaries away from the secretive and precarious 'razor's-edge' imaginary, towards an approach that addresses them as normal, ongoing responsibilities of governance; banal administrative issues rather than *casus belli*.*

## A system of boundary production in geopolitical context

Given the nature of inter-state conflict in the geopolitical situation of the late nineteenth and early twentieth centuries, as well as his core political position within the British Empire, it is understandable why Lord Curzon famously postulated in 1907 that frontiers were the 'razor's edge on which hang suspended the issues of war or peace, of life and death to nations'.[21] Within the imperial epoch leading up to 1914, not only were fixed, linear and agreed territorial boundaries designed to prevent conflict between neighbouring imperial powers by eliminating overlapping territorial claims, but boundaries conceived in such a way were also an integral part of the civilizing mission of European imperialism; bringing peace to non-European populations whose constant warfare was largely blamed on the instability of their territorial limits.[22] Geographers of the early twentieth century such as Albert Brigham suggested that the 'evolution' of fixed linear boundaries from more zonal concepts of frontiers was a clear indication of political advancement.[23] Lauding the benefits of boundaries in uncompromising modernist language, Curzon argued that

> the more scientific character of which (the frontier or boundary), particularly where it rests upon treaty stipulations, and is sanctified by International Law, is undoubtedly a preventive of misunderstanding, a check to territorial cupidity, and an agency of peace.[24]

From a legal perspective Malcolm Shaw suggests that the imperial division of Africa especially stood at 'the high point of the exclusivity concept of the State in international law as fostered by nineteenth century positivism'.[25] This was dominated by:

> the view that the organised tribes of peoples of non-European lands had no sovereign right over their territories and thus no sovereign title by means of effective occupation. The inhabitants, therefore,

were merely factually and not legally in occupation of the territory, which could be treated as *terra nullius* and acquired by any State in accordance with the requirements of international law.[26]

Woodrow Wilson's comments in his 1919 book, *The State: Elements of Historic and Practical Politics*:

How is it possible, for instance, for the modern mind to conceive a distinctly travelling [*sic*] political organisation, a State without territorial boundaries or the need of them, composed of persons, but associated with no fixed or certain habitat?[27]

The particular imaginary of boundaries, derived from imperial practices, was an essential component of being a peaceful and 'civilized' state and was then integrated into what Oliver Richmond has examined as the conflict resolution approach towards 'the liberal peace'.[28] Also writing in 1919 following conclusion of the First World War, Brigham wrote:

If victory had rested with the enemy, we well know on what principles boundaries would have been drawn. Victory being where it is, just and rational boundaries, we may safely hope, will safeguard peace in our time.[29]

The terms 'delimitation' and 'demarcation' were first used by McMahon in his 1897 article describing his efforts to define the boundaries of Afghanistan.[30] From this introduction, they became commonly accepted as describing the legally binding verbal or cartographic description of a boundary (delimitation) and the physical marking of a boundary on the ground (demarcation). Although Holdich argued in 1916 that demarcation was the 'crux of all boundary-making',[31] the two practices eventually were inextricably linked in a formula that gives temporal precedence to delimitation:

Delimitation + Demarcation = Boundary

Even the phrase 'boundary-making', introduced by Holdich in 1916, is caged in the language of modernity, viewing a boundary as a product of a system of production. It can be seen as an operation borne out of a point in the production of space identified by Lefebvre to be

expressly industrial in nature – a space in which reproducibility, repetition and the reproduction of social relationships are deliberately given precedence over works, over natural reproduction, over nature itself, over natural time.[32]

By using a systematic procedure for the definition of boundaries, the limits of sovereign territory could be removed from the vagaries and complications of the natural and human landscapes. The boundary product could be permanently fixed in time to ensure acceptance by neighbouring sovereign powers and prevent future conflict by eliminating overlapping claims.

The ordering of delimitation before demarcation is a methodology that was perfectly suited to the pre-eminent role played by maps in imperial negotiations and post-conflict peace arrangements of the early twentieth century. Maps allowed diplomats to negotiate, define and agree boundaries when far removed from the actual border landscapes. Critique of the relationship between cartography and imperialism has been prevalent within contemporary critical geopolitical and historical geography[33] and Jeremy Crampton has looked specifically at the role played by maps in the Paris Peace conference as the American party attempted to rearrange the ethnicities of Europe to prevent future conflict.[34] Within the 'peace conference' scenario, the small scale 'cartographic gaze'[35] also lent itself to using territory itself as a method of reward and punishment, as best illustrated by the treaties following the 1919–20 Paris Peace Conference. Italy was rewarded by the victorious powers with boundary adjustments following the territorial dissolution of the Austro-Hungarian Empire,[36] while Germany had its boundary with France famously adjusted and was stripped of all its colonial territories in Africa.[37]

The delimitation–demarcation methodology was a key component of the post-1918 territorial arrangement in Europe as boundary commissions were dispatched to implement the newly delimited boundaries in particular parts of Europe so as to prevent future conflict. It was understood by the treaty negotiators at the Paris Peace Conference that there would be local discrepancies when it came to boundary demarcation, which is why relevant governments were mandated to assist boundary commissions by supplying all relevant data about border localities.[38] While these treaties anticipated some local adjustments to boundaries on the ground by the boundary commissions, the treaties themselves had already provided a legally binding delimitation of boundaries. Such a situation, which continues to be faced by boundary commissions today, leads immediately to tension between the boundary defined in the treaties and the realities of the local border landscapes. What imagined line takes precedence, and how much flexibility do commissions have to adjust the delimited line in local contexts?

As Neil Smith has argued, Isaiah Bowman, Geographer to the US State Department, was an instrumental part of Wilson's negotiating team at the Paris Peace Conference.[39] Alison Williams and I explored the link between Isaiah Bowman and his successor S. Whittemore Boggs in relation to boundary-making methodologies.[40] In particular, we suggest that Bowman's experience at the Paris Peace Conference was likely a key inspiration for Boggs' initiative in 1945 to have Stephen Jones produce a handbook on boundary-making in preparation for what was expected to be a similar peace conference at the conclusion of the Second World War. While the foreseen 1945 Paris Peace Conference (arguably) never took place, Jones' well known handbook remains remarkably influential in advising state practice on boundary practices, and particularly in the resolution of international boundary disputes through international law.

## Boundary dispute resolution not peacebuilding

There is sound legal logic to this systematic approach giving delimitation priority over demarcation, since the intention is to prevent state actors from claiming territory based simply on a *de facto* situation on the ground. Such a scenario would effectively validate the use of force in the creation of territorial sovereignty, a contagion at the heart of inter-state warfare in the first half of the twentieth century. This was intended to be eradicated under Wilsonian principles of liberal peace on which the later model of the United Nations was based.[41] Being reflective of both imperial boundary practices and the peace conference model of the early twentieth century, this systematic methodology of legal delimitation preceding physical demarcation is also conducive to resolving boundary disputes through international adjudication or arbitration.

The Permanent Court of Arbitration (PCA), which continues to act as a registry and forum for international arbitration, was established in 1899. Curzon remarked in 1907 that the creation of the PCA was one of the key 'evidences of progress' in the resolution of international boundary disputes.[42] As part of peace initiatives in the post-1918 period alongside the creation of the League of Nations was the establishment of the Permanent Court of International Justice (PCIJ) in 1920. A standing court, as opposed to the previous method of using temporary tribunals or arbitrators, the PCIJ was intended to provide an available and respected forum for the resolution of international disputes, including boundary and territorial disputes. Much like the League of Nations, the PCIJ became largely inept in the Second World War and was officially dissolved in 1946.[43] Just as the PCIJ had been an integral part of the Covenant of the League of Nations (Article 14), its successor the International Court of Justice (ICJ) was constituted on 24 October 1945 with a statute that was annexed to, and an integral part of, the Charter of the United Nations.

Although not a standing court, the original PCA remains active as the registrar for *ad hoc* arbitrations, and alongside the ICJ they have been the pre-eminent mechanisms for seeking binding legal settlement to land and maritime boundary disputes since 1945. Indeed, the average number of land and maritime boundary cases submitted to the ICJ or binding arbitration per five-year period has jumped from just two or three in the early 1950s, to some five or six in the last decade (see Figure 1).

There are many factors that may have affected this trend, including the independence of many former colonial territories largely from the 1960s, as well as the introduction of the 1982 UN Convention on the Law of the Sea, which allowed coastal and island states to claim expansive maritime zones, creating many new potential maritime boundaries worldwide. Likewise it is difficult to prove if this quantitative data indicate that governments are now more likely to resolve a boundary dispute through binding adjudication or arbitration. However, the growing prevalence of this form of dispute resolution does raise some concerns.

While settlement of a dispute through binding legal means is certainly preferable to resolution through violence, it remains a forum that involves a strong degree of contestation. Feuding governments

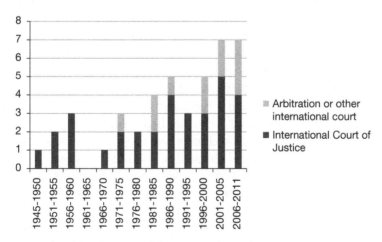

Figure 1    Number of territorial, land or maritime boundary cases submitted to binding third-party adjudication and arbitration

are now using threats of 'legal action' in more combative diplomatic rhetoric in relation to boundary disputes. President Morales of Bolivia has frequently indicated that his government will take Chile to Court (read: ICJ) to regain territorial access to the Pacific Ocean.[44] Officials in both Kenya and Uganda have frequently threatened to take the dispute over the tiny island of Migingo in Lake Victoria to the ICJ for arbitration.[45] At the height of the tension over Migingo in April 2009, angry Kenyans in the Kibera slum of Nairobi tore up sections of the railway linking Uganda with the Kenyan port of Mombasa.[46] The Slovenian government has threatened to veto Croatia's bid to accede to the European Union until their ongoing land and maritime boundary dispute is resolved through adjudication or arbitration.[47] This type of rhetoric from political leaders, hurling the diplomatic gauntlet of 'see you in court', continues to imbue boundary and territorial issues with accentuated political sensitivity.

If judicial settlement continues to grow in popularity with feuding governments, there is the possibility that it will emerge as the involuntary or default response to any issues (legal or otherwise) relating to boundaries and territory. Just in 2010–11, two boundary disputes have led to states appealing to the ICJ for emergency provisional measures alongside requests for judgments or interpretations. Provisional measures are requests intended to force one state to halt immediately some kind of activity that may be affecting the possible resolution of a dispute. Alongside a request to clarify delimitation of their river boundary, Costa Rica appealed to the ICJ in November 2010 for provisional measures to stop Nicaraguan works that were held to be attempts to divert the San Juan river (and hence the boundary) into a new channel.[48] In a clear tit-for-tat, Nicaragua then submitted a separate case to the ICJ in December 2011 claiming that Costa Rica was causing irreparable damage to the San Juan river by constructing a road along its bank.[49] In May 2011, Cambodia requested the ICJ to interpret its 1962 decision concerning the boundary around the Temple of Preah Vihear (see below) and sought provisional measures to exclude all Thai military forces from the disputed area.[50] Despite being 'urgent' requests, the ICJ took more than two months to indicate provisional measures between Cambodia and Thailand, and almost four months between Costa Rica and Nicaragua. Nevertheless, this type of appeal for emergency intervention further indicates a growing reliance on the resolution of disputes through international judicial means.

Having an international court or tribunal resolve a boundary dispute provides both governments with a degree of political cover, in that if the decision does not go their way, at least they will have been seen by their populations as having exhausted all peaceful means of settlement. The blame for a poorly received decision can then be directed at the court or tribunal. However, this places a great deal of political as well as legal responsibility on international courts and tribunals that are limited in their capacity to settle a dispute. The jurisdiction of a court or tribunal, and the question posed to it, must be agreed (either directly or indirectly) by the two disputant state governments. This means that a government which does not wish to have a dispute taken to adjudication or arbitration can simply choose not to. Jurisdiction can be compulsory, but both states must have to have consented, directly or indirectly to that jurisdiction.[51] In addition, international courts and tribunals are only mandated to answer the questions posed to them by the disputant states, which are 'legal' in nature. In this regard, the decision of a court or tribunal may resolve whatever question was posed by the parties, but it may not address the actual problems that may underlay the dispute. It also has a tendency to fix the boundary as it stands at the moment when a dispute is perceived to be resolved.

## When is a boundary dispute resolved?

While state leaders, diplomats and international lawyers congratulate themselves for seeing boundary or territorial disputes peacefully 'resolved' through the binding decision of a court or tribunal, this settlement is confined to delimitation based on legal evidence. The relationship between the boundary and the lived physical and human border landscape negotiated through demarcation, is further reinforced as being a subsequent practice. Yet in reality judicial delimitation is just the start of much more complex negotiations as the decision comes to be applied on the ground. Outside the high-profile nature of an international court case, implementing a decision may be less of a priority, and far more politically sensitive domestically, to the neighbouring governments. After brief border skirmishes in the mid-1970s, and a more significant conflict in 1985, Burkina Faso and Mali had the disputed sections of their boundary delimited by the ICJ in 1986.[52] Some of the initial difficulties implementing this decision were reviewed in 2002 by Tim Daniel[53] and demarcation itself did not take place until a German-funded project in 2008, more than two decades after the boundary had been legally delimited.[54] Similarly, it was a decade after the 1992 ICJ judgment delimitation that the leaders of El Salvador and Honduras committed to demarcating their boundary, which was officially completed in 2004.[55]

Even some international legal scholars admit that boundary adjudication may actually create more problems for state actors than it solves: 'a judgment or an award may prove to be less of a source of comfort and more a basis for new or continuing conflict'.[56] In 1962, the ICJ ruled that the disputed Temple of Preah Vihear was situated within Cambodian rather than Thai territory, but it had not been asked by the two parties to define the boundary around the temple.[57] Perched at the edge of a steep escarpment, the most accessible route to the temple of Preah Vihear is through Thailand. In 2008, under objections from Thailand, Cambodia submitted the temple to UNESCO for World Heritage status, which was awarded. This prompted a tense military stand-off around the temple complex and eventually led to exchanges of fire leading to several deaths and the displacement of surrounding villages. Overtures to resolve the dispute through the Association of South East Asian Nations (ASEAN) were rejected, and eventually Cambodia sent the dispute back to the ICJ in May 2011 for interpretation of the original judgment. While the dispute over sovereignty to the temple may have been settled in 1962, the lack of engagement with the realities of the situation on the ground left the boundary dispute open to be used again as a catalyst for violence.

After a long and complex case, in October 2002 the ICJ gave its judgment delimiting numerous disputed sections of the land and maritime boundary between Cameroon and Nigeria.[58] Most controversially, the court placed the disputed Bakassi peninsula within Cameroonian territory, based largely on colonial delimitation instruments and subsequent mapping, even though the population of Bakassi had been administered for many years as part of Nigeria. The Nigerian government initially rejected the 2002 judgment after significant public backlash, and it was only after the presidents of the two states penned the Greentree Agreement four years later in 2006 that both sides committed to implementing the court's delimitation based on a phased withdrawal of Nigerian administration in Bakassi.[59] Even then, as the two parties have come to demarcate the adjudged boundary through the UN-monitored Mixed Commission, innumerable ambiguities have arisen in interpreting the delimited boundary on the ground.[60] Luckily these minor disputes have been resolved largely by representatives within the Mixed Commission, who have built a strong level of trust and co-operation. However, the more politically sensitive issue of the displacement of residents of Bakassi being resettled in Nigeria (as most have chosen) has been plagued by problems, including questions over land rights, voter registration and replacement housing.[61]

In a similar situation, problems continue in the El Salvador–Honduras borderlands, as a result of the 1992 land boundary decision of the ICJ.[62] It has already been noted that demarcation was completed in 2004, and the boundary notionally 'produced'. However, the decision placed some 12,000 Salvadoran citizens on the Honduran side of the boundary and 3,000 Hondurans on the Salvadoran side.[63] Faced with numerous legal problems as a result of these 'misplaced' populations, the two governments agreed a convention in 1998 that effectively guaranteed pre-existent property rights and addressed issues of citizenship.[64] This agreement even required the Honduran government to revise its constitution in order to allow borderland residents to hold dual citizenship. However, even as recently as March 2011, reports have indicated that the Salvadoran population now in Honduras still lacked adequate administrative support from the Honduran government.[65] As with the Bakassi situation, these issues of borderland populations and the resulting administrative problems created by the delimitation were of subsidiary importance to the legal settlement of the boundary dispute.

These three situations illustrate how the notional resolution of a boundary dispute at legal delimitation fixes a moment of peace seemingly without foresight into the long-term application of the decision in the reality of the borderland environment. During the legal proceedings, state governments will commit significant resources to proving their respective cases and acquiring as much of the disputed territory or maritime space as possible. However, once a judgment is rendered, and a boundary legally delimited, engagement with the human and physical borderland environment becomes less urgent and is left to the subsequent process of demarcation. Contrasted with the urgency of delimitation in settling a boundary dispute, the three situations noted above suggest that implementing the responsibilities of administration (such as housing and services) over affected border populations has been much less of a priority to the state actors involved.

## Conclusion

Rather than proposing a specific, alternative model to supplant the delimitation–demarcation rubric, my intention in this chapter has been to distance the methodologies for defining international boundaries away from the limitations of a mechanistic approach. Development of the delimitation and demarcation rubric has been shown to be deeply entwined within the liberal concept of negative peace, being 'the absence of armed conflict and the development of good diplomatic relations between states and in the inter-state system'.[66] Like the peace conference scenario, resolution of a boundary dispute through the standard delimitation and demarcation equation has been shown to be inherently reactive to conflict rather than actively preventing it, as well as remaining confined to a limited number of political actors.

While the main architects of the rubric – Holdich and Jones – were adamant that delimitation should be informed by comprehensive knowledge of the border landscape,[67] the growing reliance by state actors on resolving boundary disputes through adjudication/arbitration places continued primacy on delimitation over demarcation. This privileged place of legal delimitation has also been accentuated within the postcolonial context, whereby many boundaries were left suspended in vague and ambiguous delimitation treaties or administrative acts, often never being identified or adjusted to the realities on the ground. Concentration on legal delimitation restricts definition of the boundary line to a specific moment in time, with the accompanying limitations of geographic knowledge at that particular moment. The use of remotely sensed imagery and high quality mapping may have improved geographic information available at the delimitation stage from the small-scale imperial maps of the early twentieth century, but it remains subject to critiques of the cartographic gaze, detached from the mobile lived environment of the borderland area and limited to an image of space at one moment in time. In addition, reliance on the apparent accuracy of seemingly hyper-accurate imagery can make demarcation less subjective and much more of a technical application of the *a priori*, legally defined abstraction that falls back to the systematic notions of boundary as product. This trend is readily apparent from the decision of the Eritrea-Ethiopia Boundary Commission which, albeit under significant intransigence from both states, elected to 'virtually' demarcate the boundary on a series of high-quality, large-scale maps.[68] Thus a conception of 'peace' assumed by treaty-makers may not necessarily produce the desired 'peace' on the ground. This illustrates one of the major contentions of this volume: that peace is contextual and embedded in power relations. It is necessary to ask: 'Who is peace *for*?'

In examining what he terms as the 'mesoscale' tendencies of territorial legitimacies with boundary conflicts, Alexander Murphy indicates that

> the regimes of territorial legitimation are grounded in particular understandings of state entitlement to a certain piece of the Earth's surface, and that sense of entitlement, in turn, is rooted in what a state is imagined to be.[69]

Resolution of the boundary dispute through adjudication/arbitration returns to the traditional 'game' mentality of zero-sum result, with the notion of territory and maritime space under national jurisdiction as de-contextualized and homogeneous planes. The victor assumes more territory or maritime space while the loser has its space 'amputated', to invoke a term used by Prosper Weil to describe the delimitation of maritime boundaries.[70] While (hopefully) removed from the physical violence of warfare, the contested atmosphere of the courtroom continues to imbue boundary disputes with the 'glamour' associated with critiques of masculine political geography and continues to restrict the actors involved.[71] Within this contested atmosphere, the perceived 'value' territory and maritime areas become spaces of rights; rights that can be real or imagined.

This is not to downplay the utility of the boundary concept in the prevention of disputes arising from overlapping claims to rights over land or maritime space at a variety of political scales. Any erosion of the conceptual construct would require much deeper examination of the political significance of sovereignty and territory that is well beyond the scope of this chapter. However, this critical reassessment of the delimitation-demarcation rubric suggests that there needs to be a recognition that boundary disputes are not single events to be resolved through the finite production of a boundary, no matter how clearly defined it may be. The existence of a boundary line itself is the defining element for borderland areas, informing the ongoing social, political and economic practices that are unique to these areas on both sides of the line.

Likewise, in order to fulfil its role in preventing disputes, definition of the boundary should not be restricted to the top political strata, continuing to frame knowledge of the boundary as part of a finite diplomatic game where information must be kept secret from an opponent so as to avoid 'losing'. Instead, boundary definition should be part of the ongoing responsibilities for ensuring everyday peace within borderland areas that engages a variety of actors. Contemporary political geography, and border studies, need to re-engage with these practices that have been left abandoned on the shelf of 'traditional boundary studies'. Bringing theoretical insight based on empirical examples of state control, such an engagement can help further break down the delimitation + demarcation equation by looking at multi-scalar practices. Hopefully, such a move towards building peace initiatives outside the limitations of the liberal and negative peace, will approach boundaries not as the precarious 'razor's edge' but as part of routine responsibilities for mediating a peaceful society.

# Notes

\*   The Latin phrase *casus belli* refers to a legitimate or just cause for war. Its modern application, particularly in relation to the early development of modern international law, is traced back most familiarly to the influential 1625 work of Hugo Grotius, *De Jure Belli ac Pacis* (*On the Rights of War and Peace*).

1.  Sahlins, Peter, 'Natural frontiers revisited: France's boundaries since the seventeenth century', *American Historical Review* 95/5 (1990), pp. 1423–51, p. 1438.

2.  Sahlins, 'Natural frontiers revisited', p. 1437.

3.  McMahon, A. Henry, 'The southern borderlands of Afghanistan', *Geographical Journal* 9/4 (1897), pp. 393–415; Holdich, Thomas, *Political Frontiers and Boundary Making* (London, 1916); Hills, E. H., 'The geography of international frontiers', *Geographical Journal* 28/2 (1906), pp. 145–55; Adami, Vittorio (trans. T. T. Behrens), *National Frontiers in Relation to International Law* (London, 1927); de la Pradelle, Paul G., *La Frontière: Étude de Droit International* (Paris, 1928). Although de la Pradelle used slightly different terminology, his sequence of 'preparation, decision, execution' is effectively the same systematic boundary-making model as delimitation-demarcation.

4.  From Jones's work, Prescott and Triggs include the stage of territorial allocation prior to delimitation and demarcation, although it could be argued that the processes of allocation and delimitation are effectively the same. Jones, Stephen B., *Boundary-Making: A Handbook for Statesmen, Treaty Editors and Boundary Commissioners* (Washington, DC, 1945); Prescott, Victor and Triggs, Gillian D., *International Frontiers and Boundaries: Law, Politics and Geography* (Leiden, 2008).

5.  Newman, David, 'Conflict at the interface: the impact of boundaries and borders on contemporary ethnonational conflict', in C. Flint (ed.), *The Geographies of War and Peace: From Death Camps to Diplomats* (Oxford, 2005), p. 321.

6.  See especially Vaughan-Williams, Nick, *Border Politics: The Limits of Sovereign Power* (Edinburgh, 2009).

7.  Minghi, Julian, 'From conflict to harmony in border landscapes', in J. Minghi and D. Lumley (eds), *The Geography of Border Landscapes* (London, 1991).

8.  Agnew, John, 'The territorial trap: geographical assumptions of international relations theory', *Review of International Political Economy* 1/1 (1994), pp. 53–80.

9.  Newman, David, 'From the international to the local in the study and representation of boundaries: Theoretical and methodological comments', in H. N. Nicol and I. Townsend-Gault (eds), *Holding the Line: Border in a Globalized World* (Vancouver, 2005), p. 400.

10. Newman, David and Paasi, Anssi, 'Fences and neighbours in the postmodern world: boundary narratives in political geography', *Progress in Human Geography* 22/2 (1998), pp. 186–207, p. 189; van Houtum, Henk, Kramsch, Olivier and Zierhofer, Wolfgang (eds), *B/ordering Space* (Aldershot, 2005), p. 4.

11. Megoran, Nick, 'Review essay: international boundaries and geopolitics: two different lectures, two different worlds?', *Political Geography* 22/7 (2003), pp. 789–96, p. 794.

12. Minghi, Julian and Lumley, Dennis, 'Introduction: The border landscape concept', in Minghi and Lumley, *The Geography of Border Landscapes*, p. 3.

13. Especially in encyclopedic or regional boundary studies, such as: Biger, Gideon (ed.), *The Encyclopaedia of International Boundaries* (New York, 1995); Brownlie, Ian, *African Boundaries: A Legal and Diplomatic Encyclopaedia* (London, 1979),

Prescott, John Victor, *Map of Mainland Asia by Treaty* (Carlton, 1975a) and Hertslett, Edward, *Map of Europe by Treaty* (London, 1891).

14. Jones, Stephen B., 'Boundary concepts in the setting of place and time', *Annals of the Association of American Geographers* 49/3–1 (1959), pp. 241–55; Kristof, Ladis, 'The nature of frontiers and boundaries', *Annals of the Association of American Geographers* 49/3–1 (1959), pp. 269–82; Prescott, John Victor, *Political Frontiers and Boundaries* (London, 1975b).

15. Donaldson, John and Williams, Alison, 'Delimitation and demarcation: analysing the legacy of Stephen B. Jones' Boundary-Making', *Geopolitics* 13/4 (2008), pp. 676–701.

16. Donaldson, John, 'Concern mounts over Ethiopia dam project while border tensions with Kenya are addressed', *Boundary News*, International Boundaries Research Unit, 16 August 2011.

17. Jacquin-Berdal, Dominique and Plaut, Martin (eds), *Unfinished Business: Eritrea and Ethiopia at War* (Trenton, NJ, 2004).

18. This includes binding settlement by a standing international court such as the International Court of Justice or International Tribunal for the Law of the Sea (known as adjudication), or by an *ad hoc* tribunal set up to resolve a specific dispute (known as arbitration). Merrills, John G., *International Dispute Settlement*, second edition (Cambridge, 1991).

19. Galtung, Johan, *Peace by Peaceful Means: Peace, Conflict, Development and Civilization* (Oslo and London, 1996); Megoran, Nick, 'War *and* peace? An agenda for peace research and practice in geography' *Political Geography* 30/4 (2011), pp. 178–89; Williams, Philippa and McConnell, Fiona, 'Critical geographies of peace', *Antipode* 43/4 (2011), pp. 1–5.

20. Inayatullah, Naeem and Blaney, David L., 'Realizing sovereignty', *Review of International Studies* 21/1 (1995), pp. 3–20.

21. Curzon, George N., *Frontiers: The Romanes Lectures 1907* (Oxford, 1908).

22. Curzon, *Frontiers*.

23. Brigham, Albert P., 'Principles in the determination of boundaries', *Geographical Review* 7/4 (1919), pp. 201–19.

24. Curzon, *Frontiers*, p. 48.

25. Shaw, Malcolm, *Title to Territory in Africa: International Legal Issues* (Oxford, 1986), p. 32.

26. Shaw, *Title to Territory in Africa*, p. 32. Shaw actually challenges this popularized notion, suggesting that contrary to a strict interpretation of the results of the 1885 Berlin Conference, the imperial powers did not acquire title to territory initially in Africa through effective occupation. Rather, the original acquisition of title was largely through arrangements reached with local political rulers. Of course the legality of many of these arrangements is highly dubious, as examined in: McEwen, Alec, *International Boundaries of East Africa* (Oxford, 1971), pp. 12–16.

27. Wilson, Woodrow, *The State: Elements of Historical and Practical Politics* (London, 1919), p. 7.

28. Richmond, Oliver, *Peace in International Relations* (Abingdon, 2008) and Richmond, Oliver, 'A genealogy of peace and conflict theory', in O. Richmond (ed.), *Peacebuilding: Critical Developments and Approaches* (Basingstoke, 2010b).

29. Brigham, 'Principles in the determination of boundaries', p. 203.

30. McMahon, 'The southern borderlands of Afghanistan'.

31. Holdich, *Political Frontiers and Boundary Making*, p. 179.
32. Lefebvre, Henri, *The Production of Space*, trans. by D. Nicholson-Smith (Oxford, 1991), p. 120.
33. Especially Pickles, John, *A History of Spaces: Cartographic Reason, Mapping and the Geo-coded World* (London, 2004); Ó Tuathail, Gerard, *Critical Geopolitics* (London, 1996); Edney, Matthew, *Mapping an Empire: The Geographical Construction of British India 1765–1843* (Chicago and London, 1997); Wood, Denis, *The Power of Maps* (New York, 1992).
34. Crampton, Jeremy, 'The cartographic calculation of space: race mapping and the Balkans at the Paris Peace Conference of 1919', *Social and Cultural Geography* 7/5 (2006), pp. 731–52.
35. Pickles, *A History of Spaces*, pp. 80–1.
36. This was prefaced by the secret 1915 *Treaty of London* in which the Triple Entente (Great Britain, France and Russia) promised Italy boundary and territorial provisions in return for its leaving the Triple Alliance. See Reeves, Jesse, 'Treaty of Rapallo', *American Journal of International Law* 15/2 (1921), pp. 252–5.
37. 1919 *Treaty of Peace between the Allied and Associated Powers and Germany (Treaty of Versailles)*.
38. See especially the provisions for a boundary commission in Articles 5 and 7 of the 1923 *Treaty of Lausanne*, which defined several adjusted boundaries of the Ottoman Empire, and Articles 29–32 in the 1919 *Treaty of Saint-Germaine-en-Lye* for boundaries of the dissolved Austrian Empire.
39. Smith, Neil, *American Empire: Roosevelt's Geographer and the Prelude to Globalization* (Berkley, 2003).
40. Donaldson and Williams, 'Delimitation and demarcation'.
41. See especially the preamble to the Covenant of the League of Nations and the pledge by the High Contracting Parties 'to achieve international peace and security...by the maintenance of justice and a scrupulous respect for all treaty obligations in the dealings of organised peoples with one another'. See also the Preamble of *The Charter of the United Nations* and the well known territorial integrity principle of Article 2(4).
42. Curzon, *Frontiers*, p. 53.
43. Hudson, Manley, 'The succession of the International Court of Justice to the Permanent Court of International Justice', *American Journal of International Law* 53/3 (1957), pp. 569–73.
44. Gilmour, Ann, 'Bolivia to take Chile to court over sea access', *IHS Global Insight Ltd*, 24 March 2011.
45. Olita, Reuben, 'International Court to decide on Migingo', *New Vision (Kampala)/All Africa Global Media*, 20 April 2009; WangYaNan, 'Kenya says to take disputed islands to Hague', *Xinhua News Agency*, 31 May 2011.
46. Olita, Reuben, 'Kenyan youth block railway', *New Vision (Kampala/All Africa Global Media*, 27 April 2009; 'Kenyan youth destroy railway line over island row with Uganda', *BBC Monitoring Africa*, 25 April 2009.
47. *Arbitration Agreement between the Government of the Republic of Slovenia and the Government of the Republic of Croatia*, 4 November 2009.
48. International Court of Justice, 'Costa Rica institutes proceedings against Nicaragua and requests to indicate provisional measures', Press Release No. 2010/38, 19 November 2010.

49. International Court of Justice, 'Nicaragua institutes proceedings against Costa Rica with regard to "violations of Nicaraguan sovereignty and major environmental damages to its territory"', Press Release No. 2011/40, 22 December 2011.

50. International Court of Justice, 'Cambodia files an application requesting interpretation of the judgment rendered by the Court on 15 June 1962 in the case concerning the Temple of Preah Vihear (Cambodia v. Thailand) and also asks for the urgent indication of provisional measures', Press Release No. 2011/14, 2 May 2011.

51. Merrills, *International Dispute Settlement*, p. 112.

52. International Court of Justice, 'Frontier dispute (Burkina Faso/Mali) judgment of 22 December 1986', *ICJ Reports* (1986), pp. 554–651.

53. Daniel, Tim, 'After judgment day', in C. Schofield, D. Newman, A. Drysdale and J. A. Brown (eds), *The Razor's Edge: International Boundaries and Political Geography* (London, 2002).

54. Coulibaly, Issa, 'Démarcation des frontières africaines post-conflit: L'expérience de la démarcation de la frontière Mali-Burkina', in J. Donaldson (ed.), *Boundary Delimitation and Demarcation: An African Union Border Programme Practical Handbook* (Addis Ababa, 2010).

55. Speech to the Nation delivered by the President of the Republic of El Salvador, Francisco Flores, 10 September 2002. Forwarded to the Organization of American States (OAS), 11 September 2002. Retrieved 16 November 2011 from http://www.oas.org/sap/peacefund/hondurasandelsalvador/.

56. Kaikobad, Kaiyan, *Interpretation and Revision of International Boundary Decisions* (Cambridge, 2007), p. 5.

57. International Court of Justice (ICJ), 'Case concerning the Temple of Preah Vihear (Cambodia v. Thailand), judgment of 15 June 1962', *ICJ Reports* (1962), pp. 6–38.

58. International Court of Justice (ICJ), 'Land and maritime boundary between Cameroon and Nigeria (Cameroon v. Nigeria with Equatorial Guinea intervening), judgment of 10 October 2002', *ICJ Reports* (2002), pp. 301–458.

59. *Agreement between the Republic of Cameroon and the Federal Republic of Nigeria Concerning the Modalities of Withdrawal and Transfer of Authority in the Bakassi Peninsula*, 12 June 2006; See also UN Cameroon–Nigeria Mixed Commission, part of UN Office for West Africa (UNOWA). Retrieved 19 August 2012, from http://unowa.unmissions.org/Default.aspx?tabid=804. See also Asiwaju, Anthony I. (ed.), *Peaceful Resolution of African Boundary Conflicts: The Bakassi Peninsula Settlement* (Imeko Ogun State-Nigeria, 2007).

60. Toure, Ai and Isa, Sani, 'Post conflict demarcation of African boundaries: The Cameroon-Nigeria experience', in J. Donaldson, (ed.), *Boundary Delimitation and Demarcation*.

61. See especially Agba, A. M. Ogaboh, Akpanudoedehe, J. J. and Ushie, E. M., 'Socio-economic and cultural impacts of resettlement on Bakassi people of Cross River State, Nigeria' *(CS Canada) Studies in Sociology of Science* 1/2 (2010), pp. 50–62.

62. International Court of Justice (ICJ), 'Land, island and maritime frontier dispute (El Salvador/Honduras: Nicaragua intervening), judgment of 11 September 1992', *General List*, No. 75, pp. 350–618. Again for initial problems implementing the decision see Daniel, 'After judgment day'.

63. Ayala, Edgardo, 'El Salvador: forgotten people of the border pact', *Inter Press Service/Global Information Network*, 29 March 2011.

64. 'Decreto 95–99, 11 June 1999', *La Gaceta: Diario Oficial de la Republica de Honduras*, Num. 28.905 (1999).

65. Ayala, 'El Salvador: forgotten people of the border pact'.

66. Megoran, 'War *and* Peace?', p. 182.

67. Holdich, *Political Frontiers and Boundary Making*, p. 179 and Jones, *Boundary-Making*.

68. Donaldson and Williams, 'Delimitation and demarcation'.

69. Murphy, Alex, 'National claims to territory in the modern state system: geographical considerations,' *Geopolitics* 7/2 (2003) pp. 193–214, p. 204.

70. Weil, Prosper, *The Law of Maritime Delimitation – Reflections* (Cambridge, 1989), p. 5.

71. Megoran, 'War *and* Peace?', p. 187.

# 6

# Making space for peace: international protective accompaniment in Colombia

*Sara Koopman*

The discipline of geography is a 'master's tool' that has long been used to make war. Nevertheless, I want to use it to 'dismantle the master's house'.[1] I believe that geography can help to build peace because peace is inherently spatial. I do not simply mean that peace is a matter of territory, but that it is made through space – space as a doing. Peace is shaped by the space in which it is made, as it too shapes that space. It makes a difference if peace is made through a network, a hierarchy or in closed rooms. If we imagine peace as something delivered by men sitting in suits in a negotiation room, we may not see a role for ourselves to play. If we imagine space as simply a container, this also shapes what we imagine we can do to, and in, it. Peace will always be shaped by the spaces through which it is made. Theories about spatiality may seem obscure, but they can actually make on the ground peace work more effective. As such, the discipline of geography can contribute to peace, and I want to re-imagine what geography can be, and do, by focusing on grassroots peacemaking practices.

This is a chapter about a type of peacework known as international protective accompaniment, and how it works spatially. In conflict zones some bodies are more likely to be attacked than others. Certain outsiders, for example, tend to be left alone by armed actors. Accompaniment is a grassroots peacebuilding strategy that uses privilege by putting internationals who are less at risk – literally – next to locals who are under threat because of their work for peace and justice. Sometimes international accompaniers are called 'unarmed bodyguards'.[2]

This strategy was started in the early 1980s by US solidarity activists in Central America. Since then, thousands of human rights workers, grassroots organizations, and communities have been protected by accompaniers. Today there are 24 organizations doing international accompaniment in 12 countries.[3] There may be only a few hundred accompaniers around the world, but their actions are no 'little thing', but rather part of a broader shift to engage in what I understand as 'alter-geopolitics'.[4] Most accompaniers are from the USA, Canada and Western Europe, and most serve in Latin America. Colombia, with thirteen groups, is far and away the country with the largest number of accompaniment organizations.

Ironically, accompaniers use the reality that their lives 'count' more in the current geopolitical system, to try to build a world where everyone's life is respected, and everyone 'counts'. International accompaniers are less likely to be attacked because, in a sense, their passports make their lives 'worth more' than the lives of locals. Accompaniment is generally done to protect human rights activists who are threatened by state and para-state actors, who themselves often receive support from the USA, and sometimes from Canada and European states.

There is a dramatic case from Colombia of a death squad coming in the night when Peace Brigades International (PBI) was there. It was in Barrancabermeja, on 23 December 1997, and two PBI accompaniers were spending the night in the home of Colombian human rights worker Mario Calixto because he had received serious threats.[5] Two armed men came to the door that night, saying they were going to kill Mario. When the accompaniers stepped forward and said 'we are internationals and we are here with him,' the armed men left. However, scenarios like this are extremely rare. The aim of accompaniment is to ensure that armed actors will already know that the accompaniers are present, and so will not even knock on the door. But, as Mahony puts it, we have no way of knowing how many times they choose not to knock on the door.[6] I would add that we have no way of knowing *why* they chose not to knock.

In this chapter I do not look at *whether* accompaniment works, because there is no way to know fully if a Colombian who received a death threat was then not attacked because of an accompanier's presence or because of a myriad other factors. Given that those accompanied regularly say that they believe they are alive because of accompaniment, and that more and more Colombian groups request international accompaniment – far more than currently receive it – I assume that it generally does work, at least in Colombia. Instead this chapter is about *how* accompaniment works, how it 'makes space for peace', to use the PBI slogan.

I begin the chapter with the peace part of this equation and discuss various meanings of peace, in general and in Colombia, particularly amongst accompaniers and the groups that they accompany. Understanding peacework in Colombia requires some sense of the war there, so I then turn to how struggles over land and US involvement shape the conflict. These are not necessarily the two most important factors of the conflict, but they are key to understanding how international accompaniment works. I then describe what the typical work of an accompanier looks like in this context, before turning to how accompaniers themselves described and diagrammed how accompaniment works in my conversations with them. I then present my own understanding of how accompaniment works spatially to make peace, and conclude by arguing how geographers can contribute to struggles for peace.

## Thinking of peace in the plural

Defining peace is anything but simple. Peace for some means pacification, the peace of the graveyard. For others it means free reign for corporations. Foucault argues that war is the motor of institutions and order, that war is inside peace.[7] But peace, too, exists inside war. The two are intertwined, and we cannot understand one without the other. If ever there was a clear line between war and peace, it is all the more blurred, Gregory argues, by what he calls 'late modern war', which has no clearly defined beginning or end in time or space.[8] This is very much the case in Colombia. War is not simply about control of territory, but ever more about control of people and resources and their circulation.

The increasingly hegemonic understanding of peace amongst elites is of a 'liberal peace': that (neo)liberal democracies will not go to war against one another.[9] This is closely linked to the idea that (capitalist) 'development' will bring peace. Paradoxically though, as Higate and Henry argue, rushed 'political and economic liberalization has been destabilizing in war shattered states'.[10] Not defining peace makes it susceptible to this misuse.

Peace means different things at different scales, as well as to different groups and at different times and places. Peace is not the same everywhere any more than war is. When peace is portrayed as a mythical singular it can become so abstract as to appear always out of reach, an unachievable ideal. Or it can become so unspecified that it is open to manipulation by politicians and attached to violent situations of pacification. Instead I find it more useful to think of peace as located and spatial, as practical and material and, as such, as necessarily plural. I suggest we take peace to pieces.[11]

## Understandings of peace in Colombia

I understand the current war in Colombia to have begun in the 1940s and 1950s, a period that is called simply *'la violencia'*, which included napalm bombing attacks by the Colombian armed forces on groups of organized *campesinos* (small farmers). Some argue that the current war began with the official 1967 founding of the FARC[12] guerrillas by those who had escaped the state's bombing of the town of Marquetalia.[13] The other armed actor in this war, the paramilitaries, was also established in the 1960s, by the Colombian army at the urging of the USA,[14] though it was not until the 1980s that paramilitary violence rose dramatically. There is no clear count of the number of dead and disappeared in this war, but it is far more than in Guatemala, Argentina, or any other war in the Americas in this century.

The violence increased in the 1990s, and in the late 1990s many marches and symbolic unofficial votes for peace were held across the country. These began with a vote organized by UNICEF and held by, and for, children at 'voting booth' stands set up across the country.[15] For these votes peace was not defined: the ballots simply offered a choice between war and peace. Colombian human rights activists argued that rights and justice were lost in these unspecified calls for 'peace'.[16] Others argue that these votes created the pressure for then president Pastrana to open negotiations with the FARC in 1998, though these broke off in 2002.[17]

The debate in Colombia about the utility of those votes for peace can be understood as turning on different understandings of peace as either negative or positive. These terms have been used in various ways since the early nineteenth century.[18] Martin Luther King, in his letter from a Birmingham gaol in 1963, defined negative peace as 'the absence of tension' and positive peace as 'the presence of justice'.[19] In peace studies these terms are widely associated with Johan Galtung, who in 1964 argued that negative peace was the absence of *direct violence*, i.e. bodily harm, and that positive peace was the absence of *structural violence*, i.e. social structures with life-shortening consequences. Thirty years later Galtung added a third type of violence, *cultural violence*, which he defined as the ideas used to legitimize both direct and structural violence. In Galtung's triangle, structural violence leads to cultural violence leads to direct violence. Negative peace is the absence of direct violence (though not the absence of all conflict, as is sometimes imagined). Positive peace, he now argues, is the absence of both structural and cultural violence.[20] Ironically, though, even in Galtung's definition of positive peace, peace is being defined by what it is not rather than by, as King defined it, the presence of justice or life-affirming values and structures.

When conceived as negative peace, the term 'peace' is often used in Colombia (as elsewhere) in ways that end up supporting militarism. For example, in February 2008 a huge march for peace was held in cities across Colombia and across the world that were widely called the 'Facebook march'. As the name suggests, the march was initiated on Facebook by individuals not affiliated to any group, though it was then widely promoted by the major media. In this march everyone wore white and many carried classic peace symbols like the dove, though many more carried, or even wore, the Colombian flag. Yet rather than saying 'No more war', the message on most T-shirts, in the colours of the Colombian flag, said 'No more kidnapping, no more FARC'. Some worried that these marches would be used to justify *more* war (i.e., peace as victory), and particularly militarized rescues of hostages. The FARC guerrillas had promised to kill their hostages in such a senario.

A different vision of peace and how to build it was taken to the streets a month later by MOVICE, the Movement of Victims of State Crimes. In this march many wore black and the mood was mournful, with thousands carrying large photographs of the dead and disappeared (see Figure 1). This second set of marches emphasized the lack of justice in Colombia, and can be understood as promoting a variety of different visions of a positive peace. Many of the organizations that are protected by international accompaniers in Colombia were present in the latter march in Bogotá. I would not characterize these groups as members of a 'peace' movement, but rather as active in the broader 'justice and human rights' movement in Colombia, a movement that can be understood as working for a more positive peace, against both physical and structural violence. However, many of these groups avoid the term 'peace' all together, feeling it has been so misused in Colombia to support war as to be a bankrupt concept.

Figure 1   MOVICE march, 6 March 2008 (photo by author)

Part of that larger movement for justice in Colombia are groups of *campesinos* (small farmers) who resist being pushed off their land by violence, or sometimes go back to land which was stolen from them, and who ask the armed actors simply to stay out of their communities. International accompaniment, by organizations such as Peace Brigades International, Fellowship of Reconciliation, and Christian Peacemaker Teams, has been crucial for making this resistance possible. These communities at first called themselves 'peace communities', but now many have started using other terms such as 'humanitarian zone' or 'community for dignity and life'. The community most emblematic of this movement, San José, still calls itself a 'peace community'.[21] Each of these communities has their own understanding of what peace with justice means in their context. Clearly, for all it means being able to stay on their land, but for the peace community of San José, for example, not allowing alcohol in the community is a key part of peace for them, something certainly not all communities resisting displacement agree with. This no alcohol rule is also something that some international accompaniers in San José have struggled with, and it begs the question of how accompaniers understand 'peace'.

I did my research with international accompaniers in Colombia through a collaborative theorizing process, which included a series of workshops. I opened the workshops by asking the accompaniers to draw a free-association mind map, starting with the term 'peace' placed in the middle of a piece of paper. After a couple of minutes I asked them to pass their sheet to the right, and then to continue free-associating off the chains on the sheet they had received. I then had the accompaniers pass these to the right one more time and then asked them to read out the things on the sheet they now had in their hand, as a way of opening a discussion.[22] Most of the mind maps had lines with words like 'death' and 'killing', and most also had the words 'justice' or 'rights' on them.

After some discussion I presented the idea of categorizing peace as either positive or negative. Most accompaniers had not heard of these terms, but were used to the distinction between peace as simply the ending of the armed conflict versus peace as social justice. Accompaniers widely agreed that the groups they accompanied were working for various visions of a positive peace, depending on their contexts and priorities. In some groups there was some debate as to whether they, as accompaniers, understood themselves also to be working for some version of a positive peace, or whether they were simply supporting Colombians in *their* work for peace. A few understood accompaniers as working for a negative peace, as a prerequisite for Colombians to then be able to work for a positive peace.

## Struggles over land in Colombia

Understanding peacemaking in Colombia requires a basic understanding of the nature of the ongoing war there, one of the oldest internal wars in the world, which has left far more dead than any other conflict in the Americas. What is most fought over in the Colombian conflict is control over land. The numbers of people violently expelled from their lands (largely by paramilitaries) increased dramatically in the 1980s and has continued to grow. From the mid-1980s through to 2009 around one in ten people in Colombia had to flee their homes, communities and land. Over four million people in total were internally displaced.[23] More than 80 per cent of those were displaced after 2000 (when the Colombian army's 'Plan Colombia' began), and 98 per cent were displaced from rural areas, which is to say it is the rural poor whose land is being taken.[24]

By the 1980s, land distribution in Colombia was already one of the most unequal in the world, and it has continued to get worse. From the colonial period through to today political conflicts have turned around control over land for economic activities.[25] Colombia started exporting coffee in 1870 and bananas in 1900, and barbed wire made its first appearance around that time, expanding and enclosing ranch lands. LeGrande argues that these activities pushed more people to the 'frontiers', starting a long running cycle where poor settlers (*colonos*) would clear and cultivate the land, but were followed a decade or so later by men with resources who used various methods to push them off their small plots (which they often had no legal title to) and consolidate these plots into larger private properties.[26] This cycle of displacement has been repeated again and again over the years as 'frontier' land has taken on new value when 'new' commercial crops emerge, or other natural resources are found or become more valuable.

Though this process started around 1900, by 1950 more than half of Colombia was still a 'frontier zone', and the areas most disputed between armed actors have continued to be these zones.[27] These cycles have varied by region, but LeGrande argues that in general terms in the 1970s the new crop was marijuana, in the 1980s and 1990s it was coca leaf for cocaine, and in the 2000s it was oil palm for biodiesel.[28] In the late 1980s there were significant new discoveries of oil and coal and the former in particular have continued.[29] In the last few years, as the price of gold has taken off, so too have gold mines.[30] In broad strokes this is an ongoing cycle of accumulation through dispossession.[31] This is a development model that is made possible by, and relies on, violence.[32]

These land grabs have aggravated an already extremely unequal division of wealth in Colombia. In 2009 the UNDP ranked Colombia as the sixth most unequal country in the world.[33] Land concentration is striking: 1 per cent of the population now owns 52 per cent of the land.[34] Displacement is not a side-effect of the armed conflict: rather, the conflict turns around the theft of land and resources. Yet many *campesinos* are resisting displacement, as well as returning to their stolen lands. These acts are particularly spatial forms of resistance that can be more easily supported through the physical presence of accompaniers than, say, a hunger strike. It is largely these communities, and/or the human rights groups that support them, that are protected by international accompaniers. Accompaniers' ability to deter attacks is also shaped by the 'special role' of the USA in Colombia.

## US involvement in the Colombian conflict

In the last eleven years the Colombian Government has received far more US military aid than any other country in the Americas. US military aid to Colombia was drastically increased in 2000 when Congress approved funding for 'Plan Colombia', which came to more than six billion dollars between 2000 and 2010.[35] The US role in the conflict in Colombia is not only geopolitical but also geoeconomic. The neoliberal program pushed by the USA and US-led international financial institutions has aggravated the Colombian conflict. Neoliberal policies were first widely adopted in Colombia in the late 1980s.[36] Tariff barriers went from 83 per cent in 1985 to 6.7 per cent by 1992, which had a huge impact on the agricultural sector and opened the door for drug barons to push their way onto land.[37] As unemployment skyrocketed in certain parts of the country,[38] many turned to the drug trade, the paramilitary or the guerrillas, which were often the only employers in remote areas.

It is no coincidence that the US–Colombia Free Trade Agreement (FTA) was put forward along with the military 'Plan Colombia'. The FTA offers special concessions and protections for US corporate investment and opens access to key resources. But as cheap corn and other US products flood the Colombian market it will put many more Colombian *campesinos* out of work. The FTA was signed in late 2006, but only approved by the US Congress in October 2011. Colombia is thus not as much a case of neoliberalism creating havoc that is then contained with repression, as it is one of violence creating havoc that neoliberal 'development' takes advantage of.

Access to, and control of, resources is tied to control of land. Colombia has a wealth of reserves of untapped oil, natural gas, gold and coal, as well as emeralds, uranium, hardwoods and ample fresh water, which is used in particular to grow bananas, sugar cane, oil palm, cattle and roses.[39] Colombia is a major Latin American exporter of oil to the USA,[40] but perhaps more importantly it also has large untapped future oil reserves, many of which are thought to be located in what has traditionally been territory controlled by the FARC guerrillas.[41]

Though two organizations were providing international accompaniment in Colombia in the 1990s, it was when US involvement in the Colombian conflict increased drastically in 2000 that a wave of international organizations came to offer accompaniment. These were led by US-based groups, though other European groups later followed. Accompaniers came because of the military aid in several senses. The increased militarization was leading to more violent land grabs, displacement and other human rights abuses. Some accompaniment organizations were inspired by a sense of responsibility to work on the ground and support those struggling against military abuses funded by their tax dollars. However, the increase in US aid is also important for understanding the workings of accompaniment because, ironically, it offers accompaniers leverage through the use of a US passport that is now even more powerful in Colombia.

## Using 'passport privilege' for peace

So, in this context, how do accompaniers use a passport to 'make space for peace' in Colombia? Accompaniers talk of going on 'accompaniments'. The peace community of San José is at the northern end of the Andes, near the border with Panama. Going on an accompaniment there can mean a six hours hike farther up the mountains with three community leaders who are going to speak with members of one of the hamlets of the community, or it can mean sitting next to a community member on the back of a truck on the hour long ride into town and going through several military checkpoints. The paramilitary checkpoints tend to disappear when an accompanier is present. Accompaniers usually go on these trips in pairs, wearing uniforms and, if they are hiking in the mountains, with a satellite phone and sometimes carrying a white flag.

I talked with accompaniers about what they did with their bodies and these props to shape the space on these trips. They agreed on the importance of walking with confidence, standing straight and looking vigilant rather than slouching or looking distracted (which can be difficult during long meetings in hot weather!). They also agreed on the importance of very obviously speaking in English (or Swedish, etc.) as a way of performing the passport privilege they are leveraging. One Latina accompanier from the USA whose citizenship was regularly questioned said that if she had no one to speak English with at a checkpoint, she would make a phone call in English, even a fake one.

Accompaniers disagreed on where they should stand (or sit, or walk) in relation to the person or persons they accompanied. For example, some accompaniers choose to sit in the circle of a meeting of those they are accompanying, some just outside and some far outside. Some listen, whereas others make a point of reading or doing other things to show that they are not listening. Different groups do accompaniment differently and disagree on best or even standard practices. In this case there is no clear equivalent to Butler's example of 'wearing pink' to explain gender performativity, though most accompaniers would argue for at the minimum 'wearing a uniform' to be read as an accompanier.[42]

Ideally, each time before they head out on an accompaniment, most accompaniers do a safety analysis of the current situation in that area. If it is high risk some groups fax a letter to the Colombian general in the area letting them know they will be coming through. They carry a copy of that letter to show at checkpoints, and often they have the mobile phone number of the general to call if there is a problem. Accompaniers get that number by meeting with the general. Often they get that meeting by having the US embassy call the general and, if necessary, they get the US embassy to make that call by having a member of the US Congress call the embassy and ask them to do that. They get the member of Congress to make that call by getting their constituents to call them, and they get constituents to make those calls by sending letters, action alerts, speaking tours and generally through grassroots organizing in the USA. The more calls and letters accompaniers can generate from the USA, the more protection they can provide in Colombia. A lot of the practices and performances of accompaniers on the ground in Colombia – like vest uniforms with multiple languages on them (see Figure 2) – are aimed at reminding armed actors of the power of that chain of connections behind them.

Before heading out on an accompaniment, ideally accompaniers consider not only where they are going, what the situation has been like there and what type of action they are accompanying, but also how long it has been since they activated a chain like that described above and how strong the response was. However, I found that some accompaniers skimp on analysing and strengthening these chains and get seduced into thinking that their bodies alone provide protection, particularly if their bodies easily stand out as different, as the two accompaniers do in Figure 2.[43]

Figure 2    March by the *Ruta Pacifica de Mujeres* (Women's Peaceful Way)
with Peace Brigades accompanier and Christian Peacemaker teams accompanier
(photo by author)

## Imagining the makings of space(s) for peace(s)

I had many informal conversations with accompaniers serving in
Colombia, both one-to-one and in small groups, about how they understood accompaniment to work. These built towards eight more formal
group workshops I held with six different accompaniment organizations, with a total of 35 participants. Most of these organizations regularly held training workshops, so I shaped my methods to their format.
Early in the workshops I asked participants to diagram, in small groups,
the relationship between space and society (see Figure 3). Given the
context of displacement in Colombia, it is not surprising that many
depicted parts of society as struggling for, and over, space. Many were
then confused as to how to include and to diagram the relationship
between what they often referred to as physical space and what they
described, variously, as emotional space, moral space, economic space,
legal space, political space and space for democracy, space for development and space for organizing. I then asked them to put accompaniers in their diagrams in a way that showed what they were doing in
relation to space and, again, this was difficult for many. Though the

Figure 3   Diagram of relationships between society and space,
drawn at workshop with Peace Brigades in Bogotá,
19 February 2009

PBI slogan is 'Making space for peace' none of them used that phrase. They described themselves, in their diagrams, as: opening space, widening space, giving space, extending their 'safe space' to another, and connecting different spaces. One group showed themselves 'squeezing hegemonic space' but also getting into its cracks and widening them.

Most of their diagrams relied on an imaginary of space as fixed, as something that remains the same but that there is more or less of. The accompaniers tended to imagine space as a container for society (space as abstract) rather than imagining society and space each shaping each other (space as relational). Seeing space as abstract works well to explain certain things, like who owns what property, but I suggest that it is not the best frame for understanding how accompaniment works, nor for thinking about how to do it more effectively. Rather, accompaniment can be best understood as part of the constant creation of space, by all of us, in and through interaction. In the workshops, I offered an explanation of how geographers understand space as relational and we discussed how that might be useful for understanding the accompaniers' daily work.[44] For example, space is shaped by accompaniers through their practice of wearing a uniform, the production of carrying a white flag on a hike, or the performance at a military checkpoint of showing the notification letter that was faxed to the general the day before.[45] Of course, space is shaped not just by the accompaniers but also by the practices, productions and performances of space by other actors, notably the Colombians they are accompanying and the armed actors that are threatening them. Relational space is thus both a product of social relations (both physical *and* mental, emotional, political, etc.) and at the same time shapes those relations.

However, space is not only shaped by things humans do and make. That there is a river running through San José also shapes the space there. But a river will not always shape space in the same way: it depends on how society sees, understands and uses the river. People might be afraid to cross the river, they might use it for irrigation or use it for travel; each of these interactions shapes how the river shapes the space. Some socio-spatial relations are so naturalized that we no longer see them. Some are so sedimented that they seem permanent. But everything changes; even the river may move or dry up.

Space is also shaped by memory, emotion and morality, as much as by material things. The space of the river in the peace community of San José is shaped by its being where community leader Luis Eduardo Guerra and his family were killed and the pieces of their bodies were found. This is not some 'non-real' space in the mind – it absolutely shapes understandings of, and thus practices around and interactions with, the material world that may seem more 'real'.[46] Memories can shape how people respond to the space (such as the annual pilgrimages made to the site where Luis Eduardo was killed, and praying at the altar that was built there), and these, in turn, shape the space again. Except that, again, it is not a neat process of space shaping society and then society shaping space in some linear order. Rather, both things are happening at once.

Space is not, however, infinitely changeable.[47] Certain aspects of space recur and are more sedimented (for example, the river will not dry up overnight unless a dam is put in). 'Space is a performance of power and we are all its performers', writes Rose.[48] An accompanier changes the configuration of power in the space, particularly by networking to power in and from other spaces (and times – both past and future). Space is not simply a reflection of social relations: it produces relations of power. Soja calls this relationship the socio-spatial dialectic.[49]

An accompanier can never know all of the ways space will be shaped, say, tomorrow on the trip she has been asked to make to accompany a leader of the community down to town. But in deciding whether to go she can predict that the space will be shaped not only by rains that have made the river hard to cross, but also by stories that have been running on the local radio station saying that the peace community works with the guerrillas, and by there being a new driver on the *chiva* (the jeep public transit). Her conversation last week with the general will also play a role, and how long it has been since she met with embassy staff, or flooded them with emails. Having a complex understanding of the ways in which space is relational and constantly being created will help her decide not only *if* but also *how* to do the accompaniment: for example, which uniform to wear, whether to carry a satellite phone openly, and if it is worth taking photographs at the checkpoint. Most accompaniers in Colombia are regularly doing some of this analysis, but the priority placed on doing so, and accompaniers' ability to analyse the subtleties of these situations, would be improved if they understood and talked about these components as together creating and shaping space. That is, if they recognized space as relational rather than seeing space as simply *either* material or political, or as something they are trying to clear away or make 'more' of.

## Using chains for peace

In discussing how accompaniment works only a few accompaniers emphasized the chain of connections they use, for example, to pressure a member of Congress to get a meeting at the embassy and have them call the local general. They also had a hard time showing this in their visualizations of how accompaniment works. Those accompaniers who did describe these connections did not call it a 'chain'. In using the term I am drawing on Galtung's theory of how 'the chain of nonviolence' works. Galtung argues that nonviolence

> works better the shorter the social distance. More particularly, when the other party has been totally dehumanized in the mind of the oppressor, civil disobedience may be seen only as one more instance of queer, strange behaviour, uncivilized rather than civil in its disobedience... It is when one's own people... start reacting the same way, non-violently,... that chords of responsiveness are being touched... The long-term approach would be struggle against the sources of dehumanization, bridging all gaps within and between societies. But the short-term approach would be to mobilize the in-between groups, have them act out their political conscience and consciousness on behalf of those too far down and away to have an

effective voice. And then build social and human ties to solidify that political cooperation, in both directions, with the oppressors and with the oppressed.[50]

Martin and Varney argue that although Galtung presents this as a psychological chain, it can also be seen as a communication chain, where intermediaries can communicate more directly, be that because of language, meaning systems, or other reasons.[51] As they see it, '[t]he chain gets around power inequalities by utilizing a series of links, each of which is closer to power equality than the direct connection between resisters and their opponents'.[52] As Clark puts it:

> when an oppressed community cannot directly influence power-holders in a situation, they begin link-by-link to construct a chain of nonviolence by approaching those people they can reach, planning that each link will in turn connect with others until the chain extends to people closer to the power structures and even to decision-makers themselves.[53]

Clark cites Summy's argument that this is useful when a power holder is not directly dependent on the co-operation of the subject population, and so the chain connects with those on whom the power holder does depend.[54] In the case of Colombia, the general depends on US military aid, that aid depends on votes from US Congress, the member of Congress depends on votes from their constituency, and one of those constituents just got an email from, say, someone they go to church with whose niece is in Colombia serving as an accompanier. If this chain happens enough times, the accompanier may eventually be able to call the general directly when a threat happens, and without mentioning the chain the general will know that this kind of pressure can be generated.

Accompaniment is not based on one chain of relationships but many such chains. These chains move closer to centres of power, and people on one end of the chain will have more access to resources than those on the other end. However, these connections do not happen just in moments of crisis. Rather, these chains are built up over time. Church basements across North America play a key role, as they are regularly the site of talks by accompaniers and the accompanied that make it more likely that people will understand and care when they receive an 'action alert' email or letter. This sort of groundwork has been done for years by the Solidarity movement in North America, which has built a culture of connection to struggles across Latin America, as well as national policies, paradigms and institutions that they can draw on (like Congressional subcommittees). The work of accompaniment may seem dramatic – 'putting bodies on the line', getting ambassadors to call generals – but it relies, through these chains, on more ordinary actions elsewhere, from a church dinner to an email or a phone call.

New information and communication technologies have made these chains longer, wider, denser and easier to access. The Solidarity movement in the 1980s relied on faxes but now software allows for 'quick click' action widgets to be circulated as a Facebook status update. Social media on the internet make it much easier to take many more steps along the chains in the web – to find, say, someone who goes to church with a staff person from the Congresswoman's office. In addition, the dramatically lower cost and smaller size of not only cellular but also satellite phones makes it possible for accompaniers to go into areas with little or no cell phone coverage, like the mountains around San José, and still be able to call out and reach that network. Likewise, the lower cost of airfares has made accompaniment more possible, as well as the delegations and speaking tours that create the networks it relies on. Video recording, editing and subtitling are all now dramatically cheaper and more accessible, and accompaniers are increasingly using short online videos to build and strengthen links on these chains.[55]

My hope is that if accompaniers both think of space as relational and emphasize how they use chains of connection to 'make space', this can improve their conjunctural analyses and strategizing. For example, many accompaniers choose not to take photographs of or video armed actors because they do not want to anger the actor in that moment. Yet recognizing the importance of mobilizing those chains, and the power of images to do so, in some cases the short-term anger may be outweighed by the pressure that could be brought to bear on that actor with the use of such a photograph. Accompaniers can also be more conscious of reminding others of their chains of connection through their daily practices, productions and performances of space. Arguments that space is relational may seem like obscure geographical theory, but imagining space this way, and peace as spatial, can actually make both this and other types of peace work more effective.

I attempt to diagram how accompaniment uses these chains in Figure 4, though there is a good deal of complexity that is not captured in it. Inside 'US decision makers', for example, there can be a big difference, most notably between Congress, the State Department and the Embassy, and there are, of course, different offices within each of these. A key part of strategizing by accompaniers is figuring out who inside which of these entities to pressure, and who can then pressure whom.

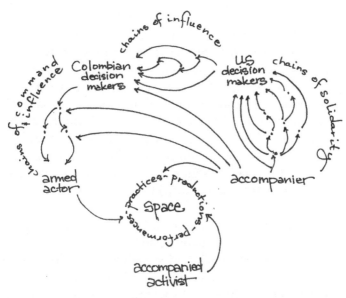

Figure 4    Author's diagram of how accompaniment works spatially

## Geography of and for peace

That the USA is so heavily involved in the Colombian conflict means that when accompaniers generate a call to a Colombian general from the US embassy it has far more impact than a call from the Bolivian embassy. In so doing, accompaniers leverage and even influence dominant geopolitics. But what may have more impact in the long term is how accompaniment is itself engaging in an alternative form of geopolitics. It is the ongoing work of building new and different connections between people in the USA and Colombia, and the global North and South more generally, that will ultimately wear away at the very privileges accompaniers use to do this work by slowly changing the political, economic and social systems that make some lives worth more than others. One way to understand this work is as an alternative way of doing geopolitics, or alter-geopolitics.[56]

Accompaniers may protect a relatively small number of activists, but those systemic changes they are a part of are far from small. It is my hope that accompaniment can have a bigger impact if I as an academic learn from, contribute to, and share the work they are doing. Much as Gibson-Graham's focus on alternative economic practices has been a way to re-imagine what economic geography can be and do,[57] I see focusing on alternative peacemaking efforts such as accompaniment as a way of re-imagining political geography and how it can contribute to peace.

'Making space for peace' is the slogan of Peace Brigades. It can be understood as an explanation of what accompaniment does and how it works. Yet it can be interpreted in very different ways. It means something quite different if one imagines space as abstract and peace as a (neo)liberal peace than if you see space as relational and peace as multiple, positive and always in the making. Even the 'making' in the slogan can be interpreted either as clearing away death threats (space as abstract) or as using different practices, productions and performances of space to reference chains of connection. The latter 'makes' relational space, in a shared struggle to shape space again and again such that it allows for ever more full and dignified lives – that is, for more positive peace(s).

Peace is not a static thing, nor an endpoint, but a socio-spatial relation that is always made and made again.[58] Peace(s) are shaped by the spaces and times through which they are made, as they too shape those spaces. Peace is always situated – it is made in some *way* but also some-*where* for some *people*.[59] Much can be learned from different discussions about what peace means in different places and spaces, and the ways people there are working to build it. Haraway argues that it is because knowledge is always situated that we need to enter into non-innocent conversations that open us to understanding and alliances with oth-ers.[60] Likewise, it is because peace(s) are situated that it is so important to draw connections across them to build more just peace(s). I want to learn from, as Williams and McConnell put it, situated knowledges of peace. They call for geographers to research more 'sites and scales to show how peace is differentially constructed, materialised and inter-preted through space and time'.[61] Geography's contribution to peace can be not only to see the various pieces of positive peace, but to put those peace(s) together and connect the different experiences and experiments in peacemaking around the world. Let us 'make space for peace' in the discipline of geography.

## Acknowledgements

*Tujay-chay* to Fiona McConnell for such thoughtful and careful edit-ing, and to Fiona, Philippa and Nick for all of the work they have put in to this issue and to promoting the study of peace in geography in general. *Mil gracias* to all the accompaniers who thought this through with me, and in particular my fabulous housemate Suzanna Collerd. This chapter is based on my dissertation, which is much stronger for the support of my committee: Pilar Riaño, Philippe LeBillon, Gerry

Pratt, and particularly my adviser, Derek Gregory. This research was made possible in part by funding from the Canadian Social Sciences and Humanities Research Council and the American Association of University Women.

## Notes

1. Audre Lorde famously argued that 'the master's tools will never dismantle the master's house'. I believe that sometimes they can, but should always be held with careful awareness of their potential toxicity. Lorde, Audre, *Sister Outsider: Essays and Speeches* (Darlinghurst, 2007).

2. Mahony, Liam and Eguren, Enrique, *Unarmed Bodyguards: International Accompaniment for the Protection of Human Rights* (West Hartford, CN, 1997). Most protective accompaniers reject the term 'human shield'. The media use of this term for accompaniers is a conflation and confusion because the term is also and more commonly used to refer to those who have not chosen this role, i.e. civilians used by armed actors as a buffer. Aside from the question of choice, the term 'shield' also implies accompaniers are standing in front of the accompanied rather than walking beside them, as companions.

3. Colombia, Guatemala, Honduras, Nicaragua, Mexico, First Nations territory in North America, Palestine, Kurdistan (Iraq), Mindanao (Philippines), Sri Lanka, Nepal, Sudan.

4. Thrift, Nigel, 'It's the little things,' in K. Dodds and D. Atkinson (eds), *Geopolitical Traditions: A Century of Geopolitical Thought* (London, 2000), pp. 380–7; Koopman, Sara, 'Alter-geopolitics: other securities are happening', *Geoforum* 42/3 (2011a), pp. 274–84.

5. Ripper, Velcrow, *In the Company of Fear*, 48-minute self-released video documentary (Vancouver, 1999).

6. 'Peaceful strategies for protecting human rights defenders', *Peace Talks* (25 June 2010), radio programme available at www.goodradioshows.org.

7. Foucault, Michel, *Society Must Be Defended: Lectures at the Collège de France, 1975–1976* (New York, 2003), p. 50. 'Law is not pacification, for beneath the law war continues to rage in all the mechanisms of power, even in the most regular. War is the motor behind institutions and order. In the smallest of its cogs, peace is waging a secret war.'

8. By 'late modern war' Gregory is referring to both what are called 'new wars' (over there) and the Revolution in Military Affairs (over here). For an analysis of the relationship between these two and the changing dynamics of war, see Gregory, Derek, 'War and peace', *Transactions of the Institute of British Geographers* 35/2 (2010), pp. 154–86.

9. Campbell, Susanna, Chandler, David and Sabaratnam, Meera (eds), *The Liberal Peace? The Problems and Practices of Peacebuilding* (London, 2011).

10. Higate, Paul and Henry, Marsha, *Insecure Spaces: Peacekeeping in Liberia, Kosovo and Haiti* (London, 2009), p. 12.

11. Koopman, Sara, 'Let's take peace to pieces', *Political Geography* 30/4 (2011b), pp. 193–4.

12. *Fuerzas Armadas Revolucionarias de Colombia,* the Revolutionary Armed Forces of Colombia.

13. For a review of different analyses of violence in Colombia see González, Fernán, Bolívar, Ingrid Johanna and Vázquez, Teófilo, *Violencia política en Colombia: de la nación fragmentada a la construcción del estado* (Bogotá, Colombia, 2003). In English see Richani, Nazih, *Systems of Violence: The Political Economy of War and Peace in Colombia* (Albany, NY, 2002); Hylton, Forrest, *Evil Hour in Colombia* (New York, 2006); Bouvier, Virginia Marie, *Colombia: Building Peace in a Time of War* (Washington, DC, 2009); Bergquist, Charles, Peñaranda, Ricardo and Sánchez, Gonzalo, *Violence in Colombia, 1990–2000: Waging War and Negotiating Peace* (Lanham, MD, 2001).

14. Grandin, Greg, *Empire's Workshop: Latin America, the United States, and the Rise of the New Imperialism* (New York, 2007), pp. 96–8.

15. Tate, Winifred, *Counting the Dead: The Culture and Politics of Human Rights Activism in Colombia* (Berkeley, CA, 2007), p. 69.

16. For more on the history of these divisions see Isacson, Adam and Rojas Rodriguez, Jorge, 'Origins, evolution and lessons of the Colombian peace movement', in V. Bouvier (ed.) *Colombia: Building Peace in a Time of War* (Washington, DC, 2009), pp. 19–38; García Durán, Mauricio, *Movimiento por la paz en Colombia. 1978–2003* (Bogotá, Colombia, 2006); García Durán, Mauricio 'Colombia - nonviolent movement for peace and international solidarity', in H. Clark (ed.) *People Power: Unarmed Resistance and Global Solidarity* (London, 2009), pp. 64–75.

17. Tate, *Counting the Dead*, p. 70.

18. Thanks to Sam Diener for pointing out in response to my inquiry on the Peace and Justice Studies Association listserve that the first use of the term 'positive peace' in the corpus of American English online at googlebooks.byu.edu is in 1810 in a sermon by Edward Cooper.

19. King, Martin Luther (Jr), *A Testament of Hope: The Essential Writings and Speeches of Martin Luther King, Jr* (San Francisco, 1991).

20. Galtung, Johan, *Peace by Peaceful Means: Peace and Conflict, Development and Civilization* (Thousand Oaks, CA, 1996).

21. I describe the history of San José in more detail in Koopman, 'Alter-geopolitics', pp. 278–9.

22. This is a method I learned from Linda Tuhiwai Smith in her Decolonizing Methodology seminar at the University of British Columbia in 2005.

23. CODHES, 'CODHES: Consultoría para los Derechos Humanos y el Desplazamiento,' *CODHES* (no date), retrieved 8 February 2011, from www.codhes.org

24. Most are internally displaced, which is to say that they flee to another part of Colombia. However, some with more resources flee to other countries, primarily across the border to Ecuador, and next to formal asylum in Canada. Arango, Diana and Romoser, Annalise *Closer to Home: A Critical Analysis of Colombia's Proposed Land Law* (Baltimore, MD and Bogotá, Colombia, 2011), Retrieved February 26, 2011 from www.usofficeoncolombia.org

25. Oslender, Ulrich, 'Violence in development: the logic of forced displacement on Colombia's Pacific coast', *Development in Practice* 17/6 (2007), pp. 752–64.

26. LeGrand, Catherine, 'The Colombian crisis in historical perspective', *Canadian Journal of Latin American and Caribbean Studies* 28/55–6 (2003), p. 3.

27. González, Bolívar and Vázquez, *Violencia política en Colombia*, pp. 260–5, 315–18.

28. Given the difficulty of getting crops to market across the mountains on the few roads, which frequently wash out under heavy rains, crops that are light and of high value have often been the only viable option in remote areas.

29. LeGrand, Catherine, 'The roots and evolution of conflict in Colombia', presented at Colombia, the Conflicts and Beyond (Vancouver, Canada, 19 April 2009). US citizens are the major consumers of all of these commodities.

30. Walsh, Heather, 'Gold eclipses cocaine as rebels tap Colombian mining wealth', *San Francisco Chronicle* (14 October 2011).

31. Harvey argues for using this term rather than Marx's 'primitive' or 'original' accumulation since it is ongoing. See his chapter explaining this concept in Harvey, David, *The New Imperialism* (New York, 2005), pp. 137–82. In that book, however, Harvey does not emphasize the role of violence in carrying out acts of dispossession. Instead, he writes of how the dispossession will create resistance that will then be met with repression, p. 208.

32. Oslender, 'Violence in development'; Oslender, Ulrich, 'Another history of violence: the production of "geographies of terror" in Colombia's Pacific coast region,' *Latin American Perspectives* 35/5 (2008), pp. 77–102.

33. After Angola, Haiti, Botswana, Comoros and Namibia. Castaneda, Sebastian, 'Land, Colombia's natural resource curse', *Colombia Reports* (28 October 2009). Retrieved 20 December 2011 from colombiareports.com/opinion/117-cantonese-arepas/6609-land-colombias-natural-resource-curse.html.

34. Colombia's GINI coefficient for land is 0.85. The GINI coefficient for land is a measure of land concentration. It ranges between 0 and 1, where 0 is total equality. UNDP, *Informe Nacional de Desarrollo Humano 2011: Colombia rural, razones por la esperanza* (Bogotá, Colombia, 2011). Retrieved 20 December 2011 from pnudcolombia.org/indh2011/razones por la esperanza\\io{} (Bogot\\uco\\u225{}, Colombia, 2011.

35. Obama has reduced military aid only slightly. CIP, the Center for International Policy, LAWGEF, the Latin America Working Group Education Fund, and WOLA, the Washington Office on Latin America, *Just the Facts: a Civilian's Guide to US Defense and Security Assistance to Latin America and the Caribbean* (no date). Retrieved 11 October 2010 at justf.org.

36. Murillo, Mario, *Colombia and the United States: War, Unrest, and Destabilization* (New York, 2003), p. 132.

37. Ballvé, Teo, 'Everyday state formation: territory, decentralization, and the narco land-grab in Colombia', *Environment and Planning D: Society and Space* 30/4 (2012), pp. 603–22.

38. Not well captured in national statistics, but these did register a nearly 20 per cent official unemployment rate in 2000. DANE, *DANE - Departamento Administrativo Nacional de Estadística* (no date). Retrieved 3 July 2011 from www.dane.gov.co

39. Palm oil is used for commercial cooking and soaps, but its recent surge in growth is due to its increasing use for biofuel. Colombia has become the largest producer of oil palm in the Americas and the fourth largest in the world. Colombia is the second largest exporter of fresh flowers in the world after Holland, and almost all the roses sold in the US are from Colombia. Justice for Colombia, *About Colombia* (no date), retrieved 21 October 2010 from hwww.justiceforcolombia.org/about-colombia/.

40. Behind Mexico and Venezuela, but exports from those two countries are dropping whereas Colombia's have been rising. Alexander's Gas and Oil Connections, 'Overview of Latin American oil exports to the USA' (27 April 2008), retrieved October 17, 2011 from www.gasandoil.com/news/n_america/3cd816c5a3d1696189f fb00a4a4b10f7.

41. Hylton, *Evil Hour in Colombia*, p. 102; Walker, Michael, 'Oil and US policy toward Colombia', *Colombia Journal* (7 January 2008). Retrieved 17 October 2011 from colombiajournal.org/oil-and-us-policy-toward-colombia.htm

42. Butler, Judith, *Bodies That Matter: On the Discursive Limits of Sex* (New York, 1993).

43. Whiteness does indeed play a role in accompaniment, but in complicated ways, and it is not all that is at work. Koopman, Sara, 'Making Space for Peace: International Protective Accompaniment in Colombia (2007–2009)', dissertation (Vancouver, Canada, 2012).

44. My explanation was primarily based on the arguments in Lefebvre, Henri, *The Production of Space* (Oxford, 1991); Gregory, Derek, *Geographical Imaginations* (Oxford, 1994); Harvey, David, 'Space as a keyword', in D. Gregory and N. Castree (eds), *David Harvey: A Critical Reader* (Oxford, 2006), pp. 270–98.

45. 'Practices, productions and performances of space' was the framework for a seminar I took with Derek Gregory in 2005 that has continued to shape my understanding of how we make space together.

46. Rose, Gillian, 'Performing space', in D. Massey, J. Allen, and P. Sarre (eds), *Human Geography Today* (Cambridge, 1999), pp. 247–59.

47. Rose, 'Performing space', p. 248.

48. Rose, 'Performing space', p. 249.

49. Soja, Edward, 'The socio-spatial dialectic', *Annals of the Association of American Geographers* 70/2 (1980), pp. 207–25. The other way of framing this is that 'social life is both space-forming and space-contingent', Soja, Edward, 'The spatiality of social life: towards a transformative retheorisation', in D. Gregory and J. Urry (eds), *Social Relations and Spatial Structures* (New York, 1985).

50. Galtung, Johan, 'Principles of nonviolent action: the great chain of nonviolence hypothesis', in *Nonviolence and Israel/Palestine* (Honolulu, 1989), pp. 19–20, 32.

51. Martin, Brian and Varney, Wendy, 'Nonviolence and communication', *Journal of Peace Research* 40/2 (2003), pp. 213–32.

52. Martin and Varney, 'Nonviolence and communication', p. 229.

53. Clark, Howard, *People Power: Unarmed Resistance and Global Solidarity* (London, 2009), p. 215.

54. Clark, *People Power*, p. 216.

55. Many of these are posted on my blog: decolonizingsolidarity.blogspot.ca.

56. Koopman, 'Alter-geopolitics'.

57. Gibson-Graham, J. K., 'Diverse economies: performative practices for "other worlds"', *Progress in Human Geography* 32/5 (2008), pp. 613–32.

58. Agnew, John, 'Killing for cause? Geographies of war and peace', *Annals of the Association of American Geographers* 99/5 (2009b), pp. 1054–9.

59. Williams, Philippa and McConnell, Fiona, 'Critical geographies of peace', *Antipode* 43/4 (2011), pp. 927–31.

60. Haraway, Donna, 'The promises of monsters', in L. Grossberg, C. Nelson, and P. Treichler (eds), *Cultural Studies* (London, 1992).

61. Williams and McConnell, 'Critical geographies of peace', p. 929.

# 7

# Contextualizing and politicizing peace: geographies of Tibetan *satyagraha*

*Fiona McConnell*

'Tibet is a land where people are naturally gentle, slow to anger and mostly compassionate, and where religion and moral culture abound.'

Samdhong Rinpoche[1]

The case of Tibet appears, at first glance, to epitomize issues of peace. Mention 'Tibet' and a series of stereotypical images comes to mind: a mountainous Shangri-la; smiling maroon-robed monks; and the figure of the Dalai Lama, who is so often seen to personify Buddhist values of compassion, tolerance and universal responsibility. The myth of Tibet as an essentialized space of nonviolence, and of Tibetans as embodying pacifism, is a powerful rhetoric that has been promoted by both Western commentators and by (exile) Tibetans.[2] It effectively positions the Tibetan nation, people and freedom movement in important moral hierarchies: Tibet as utopia, as virtuous, as victim.[3] However, this is also a set of representations and discourses that works to silence violent pasts and presents, has internal contradictions, and is contested – and at times resisted – within the Tibetan community. This chapter seeks to unpack, contextualize and problematize this rhetorical association between Tibet and peace. It does so both to provide a more nuanced insight into this case and to offer a geographical lens on three issues often overlooked within extant literature on peace: the seriousness of culturally contextualizing what is understood by peace and how it is (mis)interpreted in different sites and at different scales; the role of agency and 'authors' of distinctive narratives of peace; and how peace can be framed as a political strategy.

My way in to such issues is to examine how the principle of *ahimsa* – 'to do no harm' – and Gandhi's philosophy of *satyagraha* – 'insistence on the truth' are employed, enacted and re-worked by Tibetans and their exile leaders at a range of scales. As Boulding notes,

a feature of nonviolence in the twentieth century, for which we owe a great deal to Gandhi, is the movement of...'informal and unorganized nonviolence' onto 'formal and organized nonviolence' as a political tool.[4]

This chapter explores how Tibetan actors – from religious and political leaders in exile to non-elite Tibetans in Tibet – have brought Gandhian ideas into dialogue with Buddhist values in a politically strategic promotion of nonviolence. However, decisions to conduct the Tibetan struggle by peaceful means do not go uncontested. From veteran resistance fighters attempting to reconcile their Buddhist principles with their commitment to the struggle, to cases of 'unto-death' hunger strikes in Delhi and the recent series of self-immolations in Tibet creating a new realm of consternation over self-sacrifice and violence, the 'tension between violence and nonviolence is one that…[Tibetans] navigate with care'.[5]

In exploring such tensions, I will first sketch out the context of this case in terms of connections between Tibetan Buddhism, politics and the adoption of Gandhian ideas of *satyagraha* as influenced by the community's exile in India. Attention then turns to three overlapping geographies of Tibetan articulations of peace, each with a different and distinct 'author'. First, in terms of the global scale, I examine the Fourteenth Dalai Lama's visions for 'World Peace' and masternarratives of Tibet as a 'zone of peace and *ahimsa*' and exemplum of soft power. Shifting to the national scale and the role of the former exile Kalon Tripa (Tibetan Prime Minister), Professor Samdhong Rinpoche, attention will turn to the exile government's 'Middle Way' approach to seeking a solution to the future of the homeland, and its employment of *satyagraha* as an ideology underpinning governing in exile. Thirdly, in focusing on the scale of the local and the everyday, the self-immolations in Tibet and a new grassroots protest movement known as 'Lhakar' will be discussed in terms of their interpretations of nonviolence and the extent to which they constitute Tibetan articulations of *satyagraha*. The chapter concludes by unpacking the relationship between peaceful discourses and their 'messy' enactment in everyday situations, and reflects on the employment of peace as a political strategy.

### Setting the scene: when Buddhism, politics and Gandhian philosophies meet

As Mark Kurlansky asserts, 'while there is often a moral argument for nonviolence, the core of the belief is political: that nonviolence is more effective than violence'.[6] There is thus an inherent power within nonviolence, and this is a quality which most religions, including Buddhism, have actively promoted. However, with the notable exception of Carl Grundy-Warr's work on the politics of Buddhist peace activism in Burma,[7] Buddhism has been overlooked both in geographical analyses of peace and in explorations of the intersections of religion and geopolitics.[8] Indeed, more generally, secular peace philosophies ranging from liberal internationalism to feminism and anarchism have dominated policy and scholarly debates around peace in recent years.[9] This chapter moves against this trend by bringing Buddhism, peace and politics directly into dialogue. By foregrounding the importance of context, and of authors of different narratives of peace, this approach speaks both to calls to 'localize geopolitics'[10] and to contextualize peace.[11]

The aim of unpacking Tibetan articulations of peace resonates with important recent work which has been documenting Tibet's violent past. As Carole McGranahan notes, 'Tibetan history is full of wars and battles, of local skirmishes and major disputes with neighbouring polities',[12] and these are not events confined to an ancient past. The most notable recent case of violence is the armed resistance offered by thousands of Tibetans against the Chinese from the mid-1950s until 1974.[13] This was centred around a guerrilla army led by Tibetans from the eastern provinces, who had covert support from the exile Tibetan leadership and the governments of India, Nepal, and the USA, including, controversially, the Central Intelligence Agency (CIA). However, this period of Tibetans taking up arms against the Chinese is both often overlooked by Western commentators seeking a sanitized version of Tibetan history, and actively brushed under the carpet by the exile leadership, who strive to sustain a national narrative of Buddhist pacifism. Such adherence to an official policy of nonviolence has, McGranahan persuasively argues, led to an arresting of these violent histories. They are

> delayed until a time in the future when it will be deemed appropriate to tell them and other histories are told in its place, histories focused primarily on the Dalai Lama's diplomatic and nonviolent efforts to regain Tibet.[14]

As such, despite this relatively recent armed resistance, despite Tibetans continuing to serve in a special unit within the Indian military,[15] and despite incidents of Tibetan violence in the protests that swept across the plateau in 2008, the official policy of the Dalai Lama and the Tibetan Government-in-Exile (TGiE) has, since 1987, been one of strict nonviolence. In tracing the origins of such a resolute promotion of nonviolence, the obvious place to begin is with Buddhism.

Buddhist values and political policies are deeply intertwined in the Tibetan case, to the extent that the political philosophy of Tibet is *chos srid gnyis ladan,* or 'religion and politics combined'.[16] Buddhism was first brought to Tibet in the seventh century by King Songtsen Gampo and, under the following Tibetan kings, it became established as the state religion.[17] Between the seventeenth century and 1959, the Dalai Lamas – a lineage of religious leaders of the Gelug school of Tibetan Buddhism – were both the religious and political leaders of Tibet and headed the Lhasa-based Tibetan government.[18] Whilst this intertwining of Buddhism and politics has been deliberately teased apart in exile by the Dalai Lama, including his decision to retire from political life in March 2011, Buddhist values still remain central to Tibetan political decisions, policies and identities.[19]

On the one hand, it is important to recognize that, despite Western romanticism, Buddhist societies are not necessarily nonviolent, nor is Buddhism itself a nonviolent religion.[20] Not only were there Buddhist soldiers in sixth century China but the fifth Dalai Lama turned to military force to protect his government in the mid-seventeenth century,[21] and in the twentieth century we have seen religious wars in Sri Lanka and armed monks in southern Thailand.[22] However, on the other hand, the current Dalai Lama's interpretation of Buddhism does promote a strict adherence to nonviolent principles. He interprets Buddhist thought as consisting of two principles: that all phenomena are interdependent; and that all beings should lead a nonviolent and non-harming way of life. Central to how such principles are translated into policy stances and brought into the political arena is the exile leadership's engagement with and adoption of the political philosophy of Mahatma Gandhi.

With the majority of the exile Tibetan population, its government, monasteries, NGOs and the Dalai Lama himself based in India since 1959, this host state has had a profoundly important influence on exile Tibetan politics. As the Dalai Lama put it in a recent address at the University of Mumbai: 'Non-violence and religious harmony are the two treasures of India. I feel people should learn religious harmony and non-violence from India.'[23] Moreover, with the arrival of the first wave of Tibetan refugees into India coinciding with its early years of independence, it was 'inevitable that the lessons of the Indian struggle for independence [were] going to have an impact on those working to liberate Tibet'.[24] With a shared conviction of the intertwining of religion and politics, it was the philosophy of Gandhi and his political application of ideas of nonviolence to national struggle which resonated with the exiled Tibetan leadership.[25] Gandhi's texts were translated into

Tibetan in the 1970s and his philosophies were made a cornerstone of exile school curricula.[26] In public talks the Dalai Lama frequently pays homage to Gandhi's legacy; and Samdhong Rinpoche, who served as Kalon Tripa from 2001 to 2011, has stated:

> we must learn, we must read this great book [*Hind Swaraj*]... wherever 'India' and 'British' are mentioned or used in this book, if you substitute them by 'Tibet' and 'China,' the whole book is entirely relevant to the Tibetan issue.... After reading Gandhi's many works particularly 'Hind Swaraj', my understanding of Buddhism and Non-Violence has immensely widened and became practical in every word.[27]

*Satyagraha* is the concept from Gandhi's work that the exile Tibetan leadership has adopted and promoted with most enthusiasm. Taken from two Sanskrit words, *satya* meaning truth and *agraha* meaning firm-grasping, *satyagraha* can be interpreted as meaning 'insistence on truth', although Gandhi often defined it as 'truth-force'.[28] Asserting that terms such as 'pacifism' or 'nonviolence' did 'not fully convey the essential spirit of his philosophy of action',[29] Gandhi set out three principles as core to the practice of *satyagraha*: truth, *ahimsa* – the active refusal to do harm – and self-suffering.

As Jane Ardley has argued, whilst the exile Tibetan religious and political leadership claim to adhere to Gandhian principles of *satyagraha*, Tibetan interpretations of nonviolence also depart from them in important ways.[30] For a start, Gandhi's methods were developed within and drew upon traditional Hindu religious philosophy, which opens up the question of the extent to which it is applicable outside its cultural context. Whilst the exile leadership's theorization of *satyagraha* is similarly rooted in spirituality, the different religious context of its production brings with it important interpretive and operational differences over the nature of the self and of violence. These include the extent to which violence can ever be justified in the context of a national struggle, the role of self-sacrifice, and the (lack of) existence of mutual respect between the *satyagrahi* and his opponent. The sections which follow examine how these tensions play out at different scales.

## 'World peace', soft power and the geopolitics of ahimsa

In turning to the first of these three geographies of Tibetan *satyagraha* we need to 'think big', both historically and geographically. During a period of imperial invasions and alliances across Central Asia, the

Tibetan Yarlung kings and the Chinese Tang Dynasty negotiated a series of peace treaties. One of them, signed in 821/823 AD, was inscribed in Tibetan and Chinese on three stone pillars: one in front of the Chinese Kengshi Palace in Chang'an, one on the border at Gugu Meru, and one outside the Jokhang Temple in the Tibetan capital Lhasa, which remains standing today.[31] Its declaration includes the following:

> With great compassion, making no distinction between outer and inner in sheltering all with kindness, they have agreed in their counsel on a great purpose of lasting good.... Both Tibet and China shall keep the country and frontiers of which they are now in possession.... Tibetans shall be happy in Tibet and Chinese shall be happy in China.[32]

Not only has this pillar become a crucial political and aspirational symbol of the exile Tibetan struggle for their homeland, but one 'reincarnation' of the pillar is particularly striking. It stands 3 metres high at the entrance to the 'Tibetan Peace Garden' in the grounds of the Imperial War Museum in London, and has a 'message of world peace' from the Dalai Lama engraved on each of its sides in Tibetan, Chinese, English and Hindi.[33] Extending the ninth-century pillar's message of peaceful coexistence from the regional context of Tibet and China to the world as a whole at the turn of the twenty-first century, the engraving includes the following text:

> We human beings are passing through a crucial period in our development. Conflicts and mistrust have plagued the past century, which has brought immeasurable human suffering and environmental destruction. It is in the interests of all of us on this planet that we make a joint effort to turn the next century into an era of peace and harmony. May this peace garden become a monument to the courage of the Tibetan people and their commitment to peace.

With its stress on the contemporary necessity of a commitment to non-violence, this message is one of a series of public pronouncements and ritual ceremonies performed by the Dalai Lama which develop a discourse of 'world peace'. This is a discourse which in many ways defines the Dalai Lama's position as an important moral voice in the international community[34] and forms a key component of Tibetan soft power.[35] As a number of scholars have noted, the myth of Tibet as a spiritual and physical Shangri-la is often interpreted as a superior 'other' to negative aspects of Western culture, including violence. As a form of 'reverse orientalism',[36] such positive framing has been politicized by the exile elite since the 1980s. Tibetan culture has been promoted as a repository of ancient wisdom needed to solve international issues[37] and 'Tibet' has been actively constructed as a transnational symbol of soft power based on discourses of peace, human rights and environmental protection.[38] Aimed specifically at a Western audience, the promotion of such soft power resources has conferred the Tibetan cause with certain legitimacy in the international community.

Central to this is the rhetorical and literal placing of the territory of Tibet within discourses of peace. In his speeches to countless audiences and world leaders across the globe, the Dalai Lama has increasingly focused on the concept of Tibet as a 'Zone of Peace'.[39] Such a vision was scripted in a literal sense a few years later in the *Guidelines on Future Tibet's Constitution*, a blueprint for the future role and governmental structure of Tibet produced by the TGiE in 1992 which states that:

> The Tibetan polity should be founded on spiritual values and must uphold the interests of Tibet, its neighbouring countries and the world at large. Based on the principles of Ahimsa, and aimed at making Tibet a zone of peace, it should uphold ideals of freedom, social welfare, democracy, cooperation and environmental protection.... Tibet shall be a zone of peace based upon the principles of non-violence, compassion and protection of the natural environment. Tibet will remain non-aligned in the international communities and will not resort to war for any reason.[40]

Two key tropes underpin these distinctly geographical imaginaries of peace: the uniqueness of Tibet, and the concept of interconnectedness as drawn from Buddhist philosophy. As noted above, assertions as to the uniquely spiritual, environmentalist and pacifist culture of Tibet have been fostered by exile Tibetan religious and political leaders, and provide the important moral underpinning for the Dalai Lama's internationalizing of nonviolence.[41] Buddhist concepts of interconnectedness and integration are also brought into play to make this scalar jump from Tibet as a *regional* zone of peace to its role as an actor in the promotion of *world* peace. As former Prime Minister, Professor Samdhong Rinpoche, expressed it in an interview with *The Pioneer*: 'it has to be realised that the future of Tibet is inseparably linked with the future of the world as a whole. The future of Tibet should be viewed from this integrated perspective.'[42]

This promotion of compassion in geopolitics, and the notion of Tibet as a buffer zone between the Asian giants of India and China, have been interpreted as somewhat naive, utopian and idealistic. However, as Martin Mills argues, such readings fail to recognize the geographical imaginations being invoked and the historical significance of these ideas within pre-1959 Tibetan systems of theocratic statecraft.[43] Given the vast territorial size of the Tibetan plateau, the governing authority of the Lhasa-based Tibetan Government was limited, and was compensated by ritualized loyalty and systems of religious authority.[44] In contrast to realist interpretations of peace as the absence of sovereign violence often at the level of a territorially-bounded nation-state (see the introduction chapter of this volume), the invoking of 'world peace' in Tibetan political thought reflects less bounded understandings of sovereignty and statehood. As such, this rhetoric of 'world peace' should be seen as promoting a vision of Tibet as an imagined community that 'combines partially overlapping vectors of Tibetanness' and 'projects peace to the surrounding Asian region'.[45] Moreover, such discourses of 'world peace' can also be read as a broader alternative 'master-narrative' to the increasingly dominant narratives of militarism and territorial integrity that have come 'to legitimate killing, making violence and exploitation appear "natural" and "taken-for-granted"'.[46] It thus might go some way to emulating Megoran's notion of 'pacific geopolitics': geographical thinking about world politics that promotes 'peaceful and mutually enriching human coexistence'.[47]

Tracing the historical, cultural and political contexts of such discursive representations of peace is therefore revealing; but what is notably missing in the 'world peace' vision is any relationship with individual Tibetans, let alone acknowledgement of their agency. For, if we are to ask who this vision of peace is 'for',[48] then the answer would seem to be primarily liberal western governments from whom the exile leadership are seeking legitimacy and support and, to a lesser extent, the host state India in whose interests the wider geopolitical framing is promoted. Moreover, if 'world peace' and Tibet as a 'buffer zone' both hark back to a peaceful past and forward to peaceful futures, what is to be made of the present? The following section starts to address these issues.

## Satyagraha and 'Middle Way' politics

Turning from the global scale to that of the nation, and from utopian visions to more pragmatic policies, the adherence to a stance of peace also forms the basis both of the TGiE's position vis-à-vis the political future of Tibet, and its mode of governing in exile. After sending four fact-finding expeditions to Tibet and envoys to two rounds of exploratory talks with the Chinese leadership in Beijing, in September 1987 the Dalai Lama presented his 'Five Point Peace Plan for Tibet' to the US Congressional Human Rights Caucus. Nine months later, His Holiness announced his 'Framework for Sino-Tibetan Negotiations' in Strasbourg whereby he formally renounced his government's previous demands for independence and formally launched his 'Middle Way approach'. Premised on the Buddhist description of seeking a path of moderation and wisdom between the extremes of self-discipline and self-indulgence, the transposition of the 'Middle Way approach' into politics represents a framework in which China would accede to *genuine* Tibetan autonomy within Tibet without compromising China's territorial integrity or security.[49] It thereby seeks a path between the 'political extremes' of independence from China and remaining under the present situation. This policy of compromise over confrontation remains the exile government's official policy to this day. As the current Kalon Tripa, Lobsang Sangay, recently stated:

Guided by his [the Dalai Lama's] wisdom, my administration will continue the Middle Way policy.... This remains the best opportunity for a durable solution for both the Tibetan and Chinese peoples. We believe in a peaceful resolution for Tibet, which means a peaceful process and peaceful dialogue. We stand ready to negotiate with the Chinese government anytime, anywhere.[50]

Gandhian influence is also strong within the Middle Way policy, in particular its focus on autonomy, which is framed both as paralleling Gandhi's choice of 'self-rule: Swaraj' over 'independence' and as an aspect of truth and thus as a form of *satyagraha*: 'We perceive that to remain in association with China with full self-rule for the entire Tibetan nation is an aspect of truth, and we pursue it.'[51] However, whilst certainly grounded in Buddhist values of coexistence and mutual co-operation, as well as the moral principles of the exiled political and religious leaders, the Middle Way approach is also a pragmatic political strategy. With its small population size, lack of military force, and an 'adversary' as vast and internationally dominant as China, the Tibetans arguably lack other feasible options to bring to the table. This is not to say that this strategy of dialogue and compromise cedes all power and authority to China. Rather, reflecting the fact that power is inherent within a stance of nonviolence, this is a strategy premised on moral authority and claims to international legitimacy.

Apparent from the citations referenced here, whilst the Dalai Lama has been the instigator and primary promoter of the Middle Way policy, it has been the former Kalon Tripa, Samdhong Rinpoche, who has articulated these ideas in explicitly Gandhian terms. Indeed, as Garfield asserts, Rinpoche has, in recent years, been 'the world's foremost theoretical exponent and practical advocate of a specifically Gandhian approach to nonviolence, both as a doctrine of political action and as a personal religious practice'.[52] In 1995, Samdhong Rinpoche, then Chairman of the Tibetan Parliament-in-Exile, published what is ostensibly a Tibetan *satyagraha* manifesto, which sets out a Gandhian programme of 'nonviolent demonstration of truth, love and compassion and would include civil disobedience, non-cooperation and boycotts'.[53] This proposed a concise plan for 'a Truth Movement... a Satyagraha Movement... to restore Tibet's freedom through the nonviolent path of peace'.[54] Like Gandhi blaming Indians for the situation they faced in British ruled India, Samdhong Rinpoche asserts that:

> Tibet lost its freedom due to the blunders of the Tibetan people, and it is only due to the blunders of the Tibetan people that China has been able to maintain its illegal occupation Tibet [*sic*] ... the only way to rid ourselves of these problems is to rely uniquely on a path of nonviolence, which will stand in opposition to our previous violence.[55]

The idea of Tibetans practising *satyagraha en masse* inside Tibet has, until recently (see below), been seen as idealistic and impractical given the odds against them.[56] However, Rinpoche also sought to implement *satyagraha* policies in a more material way within the exile administration. This has included exile Tibetan democracy being based on ideas of co-operation rather than competition,[57] the promotion of 'insistence on truth' within the TGiE by requesting that civil servants do not infringe Indian law,[58] and the resolution of disputes with host communities through dialogue, displays of communal unity and active building of community relations.[59]

However, both the Middle Way policy and this implementation of *satyagraha* as a mode of governing have come under significant criticism. There has been persistent questioning of this strategy from cohorts within the diaspora who disagree with the Dalai Lama's request for a Tibetan political status less than independence and who are increasingly frustrated with the lack of political progress. Both the Five Point Peace Plan and the Strasbourg Proposal were rejected by the Chinese leadership in 1990 and, despite eight rounds of Sino-Tibetan dialogue since 2002, no tangible agreements have been reached.[60] Perceiving the Middle Way policy as obstructing the nationalist freedom struggle, some Tibetans call instead for *rangzen* – or full Tibetan independence.[61]

There are also frustrations with what is perceived to be a more general policy agenda premised on pacifism, with the strict adherence to a policy of nonviolence seen as shutting down other political strategies both in terms of the future of the homeland, and in dealing with issues in exile. As a former official of the Tibetan Youth Congress put it to me:

> I think as people we are guinea pigs of high morals – who else is asked to sacrifice everything, to give up all we have fought for in order for 'world peace'! We are seen as non-violent people but this is a myth.... We have never been true to ourselves, we are always acting a role and generations to come will look back and say that we gave up, that we should have fought for Tibet while we could.[62]

Such resistance to the representation of Tibetans as a passive, non-violent people continues, but changes are also afoot. The election of Western-educated Lobsang Sangay as Kalon Tripa in 2011 may not have seen any shift away from the Middle Way policy, but strict adherence to *satyagraha* policies appears to be weakening. However, crucially, it is not in exile but in Tibet itself that key shifts in Tibetan interpretations of nonviolence are emerging and new geographies of Tibetan 'peace' are being created.

### The 'Lhakar' movement and self-immolation protests in Tibet

There have been two main phases of resistance to Chinese rule in Tibet: 'armed resistance from the mid-1950s to the mid-1970s, and nonviolent [clergy-led] protest from the late 1980s to the present'.[63] The latter has, until 2008, taken a visible form of resistance in terms of street demonstrations.[64] However, since Beijing put the streets under lockdown, to deter such protests after the widespread uprising in spring 2008, Tibetans have adapted other forms of resistance. Two new and divergent modes of protest have emerged recently: a series of self-immolations, and a grassroots cultural movement known as 'Lhakar'. Rather than discursive pronouncements from spiritual and political leaders, it is individual Tibetans in Tibet who are the 'authors' of these new articulations of nonviolent protest, and both movements raise important issues regarding the form and geographies of Tibetan peaceful resistance and its relation to Buddhist and Gandhian values.

The so-called 'Lhakar' movement can be traced to a series of incidents around the awarding of the Congressional Gold Award to the

Dalai Lama in 2007. Communications were received in Dharamsala from a group of individuals from eastern Tibet, detailing a series of cultural practices that were to be observed on Wednesdays, and announcing that this be known as 'Lhakar' or 'White Wednesday' in reference to the Dalai Lama's soul day.[65] The movement has since evolved into both a series of initiatives promoting Tibetan language, culture and identity, and a range of non-co-operation tactics, including boycotting Chinese institutions and businesses. As such, a growing number of Tibetans across Tibet are, every Wednesday, reclaiming and embracing their Tibetan identity and making a political statement by wearing traditional clothes, speaking Tibetan, eating in Tibetan restaurants and buying from Tibetan owned shops. In addition, Tibetans in the diaspora are increasingly mirroring Lhakar activities in their own communities[66] and Lobsang Sangay has also publically promoted the movement.[67]

Whilst in many ways these activities and practices are nothing new – Tibetans have long taken pride in their language, culture and identity – the labelling of such activities as 'Lhakar' and the now global spread of this movement is both novel and important. With it being difficult to criminalize or prevent an individual for speaking a particular language, wearing an item of clothing or eating certain food, the largely individual and quotidian activities of Lhakar form a subtle yet powerful alternative form of protest. Interestingly, the form that Lhakar is taking in many ways echoes the type of *satyagraha* movement that Samdhong Rinpoche was calling for in his 1995 manifesto. Not only are Rinpoche's suggested 'types of *satyagraha*' – such as boycotting Chinese stores and not purchasing or selling items produced by the Chinese government – being enacted through Lhakar, but there is also a gradual scaling up from individual to collective actions as he calls for in Section IX of the manifesto. Though the scale of the Lhakar movement is, by its very nature, difficult to measure, there are reports of monks in Sershul monastery seeking to protect their mother tongue by fining each other a yuan for every Chinese word they use, and villagers in Markham province blockading the only road to a mining site that was poisoning the local water supply.[68] Interestingly, it has been cohorts within the Tibetan diaspora who have been critical of Samdhong Rimpoche's articulation of *satyagraha* in the past for being too passive, who are now framing Lhakar as active. As one Tibet activist put it recently:

Fifty years after Chinese troops marched into Lhasa, Tibetans are marching in Gandhi's footsteps, demonstrating not only courage but also a deeper understanding of strategic nonviolence as they fight for fundamental rights in small, winnable battles.... Half a century after

Gandhi died, his satyagraha is reborn in Tibet. This time its name is Lhakar.[69]

Echoing the scale jumping – from Tibet as a regional zone of peace to discourses of world peace – here the politics of the everyday are being refracted through a geopolitical lens. However, the likening of Lhakar to Gandhi's non-co-operation struggles in India has not gone uncontested. There is certainly no evidence that Lhakar is in any way a response to Samdhong Rinpoche's manifesto, and the labelling of Lhakar as a '*satyagraha*' movement was challenged by a number of Tibetan commentators I spoke to in Dharamsala, both on the grounds that the term would mean little to those who initiated it, and that it brought cultural and political baggage which was potentially problematic to the broader cause.[70] A more 'technical' disjuncture might also be the lack of mutual respect between the *satyagrahi* (Tibetans taking part in Lhakar) and their opponent (the Chinese authorities), which is central to Gandhi's thesis on *satyagraha*. Perhaps Lhakar is better seen as dynamic, innovative and a distinctly Tibetan movement.

If Lhakar demonstrates both the parallels and limitations of *satyagraha* as a model for Tibetan protest, then the other form of resistance emerging from Tibet stretches Tibetan interpretations of Gandhian ideas even further, and raises a series of difficult questions. At the time of writing, fifty Tibetans – mostly young monks and nuns – have, since March 2011, set themselves on fire in protest at repressive Chinese policies. At least forty-two of these individuals have died, and the status and whereabouts of the others is currently unknown.[71] The majority of these cases has taken place in Tibetan areas of Sichuan province, where Chinese authorities have been restricting religious freedom by forcing monks to participate in 'patriotic education sessions' and to renounce the Dalai Lama.[72] Beijing has responded to the self-immolations by increasing troop numbers in the areas in question and accusing the Dalai Lama of inciting this form of protest to generate instability within China. Meanwhile, both the Dalai Lama and the TGiE have issued statements saying that while they do not encourage or support self-immolation as a form of protest, they stand in solidarity with those sacrificing their lives and call on the 'international community to urge Beijing to open a dialogue on its policies in Tibet'.[73]

Whilst there are historical references to self-immolation as a Buddhist devotional practice,[74] there has only been one other recorded Tibetan self-immolation, that of Thupten Ngodup in India thirteen years previously.[75] The context of this act is important and revealing. In 1998 the Tibetan Youth Congress (TYC) launched the ultimate

Gandhian campaign in the heart of Delhi: an 'unto death' hunger strike aimed at drawing international attention to the Tibetan cause. Though admiring the determination of the six hunger strikers, the Dalai Lama considered the act of deliberate self-harm as a form of violence unacceptable under the values of Tibetan Buddhism.[76] In response, the then TYC President, Tseten Norbu, publically asked, 'How can it be that what was peaceful and nonviolent action when Gandhi did it becomes violent when the TYC does it?'[77] After forty-eight days, the hunger strike was forcibly ended by the Indian police. In protest, former monk and solider, Thupten Ngodup, set himself alight and died of his burns. Reflecting broader differences of opinion within the exile community, the TYC, not the TGiE, have honoured Thupten Ngodup as a martyr to the Tibetan cause and annually mark the anniversary of his death.[78]

The recent series of acts of Tibetan self-sacrifice has provoked soul-searching within the Tibetan community. They raise questions which are at the core of Tibetan understandings and articulations of peace: is taking one's own life a form of violence, and thus unacceptable? Does the fact that these individuals are harming no one else mean that their acts are nonviolent and can therefore be respected and honoured? If self-suffering and self-sacrifice are essential parts of Gandhian *satyagraha*, then to what extent do Tibetan interpretations of *satyagraha* deviate from Gandhi's own beliefs about what nonviolence entails and includes? The fact that these questions remain unresolved and the source of much consternation and debate, is in itself significant. Tibetans have long been 'handicapped by the myth of Shangri-la, the external view of Tibet as a forbidden, yet desirable land in which lives a peaceful, happy, nonviolent people who will save the world'.[79] In very different ways, the Lhakar movement and the series of self-immolations are challenging these stereotypes. Contradictions and complexities have been exposed, Tibetan agency is now more visible, new 'authors' of Tibetan narratives of peace are asserting themselves, and debates about the nature of peace are being played out in public.

## Conclusion: contextualizing and politicizing peace

Tibet is an unusual case in which issues of peace have, in recent times, been prioritized over issues of violence; where military pasts have been silenced and peaceful visions promoted. This discussion of Tibetan conceptions of peace, at a range of scales and from a range of 'authors', has sought to tease out what is meant by peace in this context. It has sought to ask: 'what is meant by peace, how is it understood within different contexts, who is peace for, and in whose image is it (re)produced?'[80] Far from the images of Tibet as a pacifist paradise inhabited by a quintessentially nonviolent people, Tibetan forms of peace are articulated, practised and prescribed in very specific socio-cultural contexts. Indeed, this chapter has foregrounded the impor-tance of context to unpacking what is meant by peace. From the Dalai Lama's visions of world peace emerging from pre-1959 Tibetan state-craft, to the influence of the host state on exile Tibetan politics in the form of Gandhian ideas of *satyagraha*, to the emergence of Lhakar as a reaction to current Chinese policies in Tibet, the context in which ideas, discourses and practices of peace emerge is of fundamental importance. However, none of these interpretations goes uncontested. Each definition of nonviolence is up for grabs, and varies according to scale: from world visions to everyday actions, from regional geopolitics to the body. These complex and intertwined geographies of Tibetan peace demonstrate the need to explore peace as situated knowledges within distinct social and cultural settings, and to be attuned to the spa-tialities through which peace is represented, practised and contested.

We might also push the term context into the post-structuralist realm and argue that a series of texts is key to the constructions – and contestations – of Tibetan articulations of peace.[81] These range from the Dalai Lama's *Strasbourg Proposal* to the TGiE's *Guidelines on Future Tibet's Constitution*, from Samdhong Rinpoche's *satyagraha* manifesto to the *Lhakar Pledge*. Underpinning many of these discursive explorations of peace and peaceful resistance is another text: Gandhi's *Hind Swaraj*. In charting how Gandhian ideas of *satyagraha* have been adopted and re-worked in the Tibetan case – how they have been translated on the ground and are being re-worked and at times resisted by this community – this chapter has foregrounded peace as a set of processes and practices that are situated and are constituted through their active reproduction. The relationship between peaceful discourses and their 'messy' enact-ment in everyday situations has been exposed to reveal a complex and often contradictory set of narratives, discourses and practices around issues of peace and nonviolence. Charting the similarities and differences between Gandhian and Tibetan interpretations of *satyagraha* has opened up fruitful lines of inquiry into the contested spectrum of violence and nonviolence, the extent to which ideas around peace can travel, the nego-tiations involved when different readings of peace come into contact, and the relationship between religion and politics *vis-à-vis* this case.

Indeed, fundamental to why peace becomes differentially inter-preted and contested in the Tibetan case is the framing of nonviolence as an explicitly political philosophy *and* as a strategic mode of political action.[82] *Satyagraha* is framed as both a personal philosophy and a mode of governing. The Middle Way policy is both a political ideology rooted in Buddhist principles, and a political strategy for the future of the homeland. On the one hand, this conflating of nonviolence strategies and political policies has proved to be somewhat problematic. The resolute promotion of nonviolence by the TGiE over past decades makes a (re)turn to violence politically very difficult, and thus arguably closes down political options. Some even go as far as to argue that the singular focus on nonviolence has 'turned the Tibetan struggle from a political one to a cultural one... such that multiple global actors position Tibetans as occupying the "moral high ground" while not taking them seriously as political actors'.[83] However, on the other hand, from the positioning of Tibet within the master narrative of 'world peace', to the 'soft power principles' which underpin the Middle Way approach and the non-co-operation tactics of Lhakar, nonviolence emerges as a strategically important and impressively flexible form of politics. Ranging from everyday practices to narratives of 'pacific geopolitics', nonviolence can be seen as both a pragmatic strategy in a situation where the tools of hard power are unavailable and a key ideological framework from which international legitimacy can be sought.

## Acknowledgements

This chapter is partly based on research funded by an Economic and Social Research Council (ESRC) PhD studentship and University of London Central Research Fund grant, and additional fieldwork funding from Trinity College, Cambridge. The author would like to thank Philippa Williams for her thoughtful and constructive comments and the many Tibetans in India who generously shared their time and thoughts. An earlier version of this chapter was presented at a session on 'Geographies of Everyday Peace' at the RGS-IBG Annual Conference 2011.

## Notes

1. Rinpoche, Samdhong, 'Satyagraha: truth-insistence', *World Tibet News* (1995). Retrieved 4 April 2007 from http://tibet.ca/en/newsroom/wtn/archive/old?y=1995 &m=8&p=11_1.
2. Huber, Toni, 'Green Tibetans: a brief social history', in F. J. Korom (ed.), *Tibetan Culture in the Diaspora*. Papers presented at a panel of the 7th International Seminar of Tibetan Studies, Fraz, 1995 (Vienna, 1997).

3.  See Hess, Julia M, *Immigrant Ambassadors: Citizenship and Belonging in the Tibetan Diaspora* (Stanford, 2009).

4.  Boulding, Kenneth E., 'Nonviolence and power in the twentieth century', in S. Zunes, L. R. Kurtz and S. B. Asher (eds), *Nonviolent Social Movements: A Geographical Perspective* (Oxford, 1999), p. 15.

5.  McGranahan, Carole, *Arrested Histories: Tibet, the CIA and Memories of a Forgotten War* (Durham NC, 2010), p. 187.

6.  Kurlansky, Mark, *Non-violence: The History of a Dangerous Idea* (London, 2007), p. 7.

7.  Grundy-Warr, Carl, 'Commentary: Pacific geographies and the politics of Buddhist peace activism', *Political Geography* 30/4 (2011), pp. 190–2.

8.  McConnell, Fiona, 'The geopolitics of Buddhist reincarnation: contested futures of Tibetan leadership', *Area* 45/2 (2013), pp. 162–169.

9.  Herb, Guntram (2005), 'The geography of peace movements', in C. Flint (ed.), *The Geography of War and Peace: From Death Camps to Diplomats* (Oxford, 2005); Richmond, Oliver, *A Post-Liberal Peace* (London, 2011). For an important exception within geography see Megoran, Nick, 'Towards a geography of peace: pacific geopolitics and evangelical Christian Crusade apologies', *Transactions of the Institute of British Geographers* 35/3 (2010), pp. 382–98, which examines Christian ideas of peace.

10. Ó Tuathail, Gearóid, 'Localizing geopolitics: disaggregating violence and return in conflict regions', *Political Geography* 29/5 (2010), pp. 256–65.

11. Grundy-Warr, 'Pacific geographies and the politics of Buddhist peace activism'; Williams, Philippa, 'Reproducing everyday peace in north India: process, politics, and power', *Annals of the Association of American Geographers* 105/1 (2013), pp. 230–250.

12. McGranahan, *Arrested Histories,* p. 186.

13. Dunham, Mikel, *Buddha's Warriors: The Story of the CIA-backed Tibetan Freedom Fighters, the Chinese Invasion, and the Ultimate Fall of Tibet* (Los Angeles, 2004); Knaus, John K., *Orphans of the Cold War: America and the Tibetan Struggle for Survival* (New York, 2000).

14. McGranahan, *Arrested Histories*, p. 2.

15. The 'Special Frontier Force', also known as 'Establishment 22', was established in the early 1960s under the supervision of the Intelligence Bureau and is predominantly composed of exile Tibetans. See Arpi, Claude, *India and her Neighbourhood: a French Observer's Views* (New Delhi, 2005).

16. Shakabpa, Tsepon W. D., *Tibet: A Political History* (New Haven, 1967).

17. Whilst Tibet was, and is, an overwhelmingly Buddhist society, there is a small Tibetan Muslim population, now predominantly in exile. Based mainly in Kashmir, this community receives some welfare support from TGiE but is largely independent. See Siddiqui, Ataullah, 'Muslims of Tibet', *Tibet Journal* 16/4 (1991), pp. 71–85.

18. See Kolås, Ashild, 'Tibetan nationalism: the politics of religion', *Journal of Peace Research* 33/1 (1996), pp. 51–66.

19. McConnell, 'The geopolitics of Buddhist reincarnation'.

20. Jerryson, Michael and Juergensmeyer, Mark (eds), *Buddhist Warfare* (Oxford, 2010).

21. Sperling, Elliot, '"Orientalism" and aspects of violence in the Tibetan tradition', in T. Dodin and H. Räther (eds), *Imagining Tibet: Perceptions, Projections, and Fantasies* (Somerville, MA, 2001).

22. Jerryson and Juergensmeyer, *Buddhist Warfare*.

23. Dalai Lama, 'Ancient wisdom, modern thought' (18 February 2011). Retrieved 30 October 2011 from http://www.dalailama.com/webcasts/post/170-ancient-wisdom-modern-thought.

24. Ardley, Jane, *The Tibetan Independence Movement: Political, Religious and Gandhian Perspectives* (London, 2002), p. 119.

25. It is important to note that it was not a wholesale embracing of Gandhian ideas as soon as the Tibetan elite arrived in India in 1959, but rather a gradual and at times contradictory engagement (see Sperling, '"Orientalism" and aspects of violence in the Tibetan tradition').

26. See Stoddard, Heather, 'Tibetan publications and national identity', in R. Barnett (ed.), *Resistance and Reform in Tibet* (Bloomington, 1994). Indeed, *Hind Swaraj* was a text that travelled more generally, translations, through the impetus it gave to a diverse range of socio-political movements, and the foundational role it plays in conflict resolution studies. See Parel, Anthony J., *Gandhi: Hind Swaraj and Other Writings* (Cambridge, 1997).

27. Rinpoche, Samdhong, 'Speech on Hind Swaraj, DIIR, Dharamsala' (19 August 2002). Retrieved 4 April 2007 from http://www.friendsoftibet.org/sofar/himachal/20020819-hind_swaraj-rinpoche_talk.htm.

28. Parel, *Gandhi*.

29. Norbu, Jamyang, 'Non-violence and non-action: some Gandhian truths about the Tibetan peace movement', *Tibetan Review* 32/9 (1997), pp. 151–60, p. 151.

30. Ardley, *The Tibetan Independence Movement*.

31. Shakabpa, Tsepon W. D., *One Hundred Thousand Moons: An Advanced Political History of Tibet,* Volume 1 (Leiden, 2010), p. 153.

32. Richardson, Hugh E., 'The Sino-Tibetan Treaty Inscription of A.D. 821/23 at Lhasa', *JRAS* 3 (1978), p. 153.

33. For analysis of a 'peace garden' in a different context, and linked more explicitly to ideas of 'locational harmony', see Brunn, Stanley and Munski, Douglas, 'The iternational peace garden: a case study in locational harmony', *Boundary and Security Bulletin* 7 (1999), pp. 67–74.

34. Ritual ceremonies which explicitly promote the idea of World Peace include the Kalachakra Initiations for World Peace, the construction of a series of world peace stupas, and large-scale prayers for peace at key Buddhist pilgrimage sides. See Mills, Martin, 'This circle of kings: modern Tibetan visions of world peace', in P. Wynn Kirby (ed.), *Boundless Worlds: An Anthropological Approach to Movement* (Oxford, 2009).

35. Huber, 'Green Tibetans'; Magnusson, Jan, 'A myth of Tibet: reverse orientalism and soft power', in P. C. Klieger (ed.), *Tibet, Self, and the Tibetan Diaspora: Voices of Difference* (Leiden, 2002).

36. Abu-Lughod, Janet, 'Going beyond global babble', in A. King (ed.), *Culture, Globalization and the World-System* (London, 1991).

37. Huber, 'Green Tibetans'.

38. See Nye, Joseph S., *Soft Power: The Means to Success in World Politics* (New York, 2004).

39. Mills, 'This circle of kings'.

40. Shiromany, A. A. (ed.), *The Political Philosophy of HH the XIV Dalai Lama: Selected Speeches and Writings* (New Delhi, 1998), p. 283.

41. Adams, Vincanne, 'Suffering the winds of Lhasa: politicised bodies, human rights, cultural difference and humanism in Tibet', *Medical Anthropology Quarterly* 12/1 (1998), pp. 74–102; Huber, 'Green Tibetans'.

42. The Pioneer, 'Do and die: Prof. S. Rinpoche proposes a programme for launching Tibetan Satyagraha', *The Pioneer* (26 November 1996). Retrieved 30 March 2010 from http://w3.iac.net/-moonweb/Tibetan/News/TibetNews1.html.

43. The circle of kings
44. Samuel, Geoffrey, 'Tibet as a stateless society and some Islamic parallels', *Journal of Asian Studies* 41/2 (1982), pp. 215–29; Samuel, Geoffrey, *Civilized Shamans: Buddhism in Tibetan Societies* (Washington DC, 1993).
45. Mills, 'This circle of kings', p. 112.
46. Inwood, Joshua and Tyner, James, 'Geography's pro-peace agenda: an unfinished project', *ACME* 10/3 (2011), pp. 442–57.
47. Megoran, 'Towards a geography of peace'.
48. Williams, Philippa and McConnell, Fiona, 'Critical geographies of peace', *Antipode* 43/4 (2011), pp. 927–31.
49. Lafitte, Gabriel, 'Tibetan futures: imagining collective destinies', *Futures* 31/2 (1999), pp. 155–69.
50. Testimony before the Tom Lantos Human Rights Commission in Washington DC in November.
51. Rinpoche, Samdhong, 'Satyagraha: speech delivered at 4th International Conference of Tibet Support Groups, Prague' (2003). Retrieved 5 December 2010 from http://www.imar.ro/~diacon/satyagraha.html.
52. Garfield, Jay L., *Empty Words: Buddhist Philosophy and Cross-Cultural Interpretation* (Oxford, 2002), p. 220.
53. Ardley, Jane, 'Satyagraha in Tibet: toward a Gandhian solution?', *Tibet Journal* 28/4 (2003), pp. 23–38.
54. Rinpoche, Samdhong, 'Satyagraha: truth-insistence'.
55. Rinpoche, Samdhong, 'Satyagraha: truth-insistence'.
56. Ardley, 'Satyagraha in Tibet'.
57. McConnell, Fiona, 'Democracy-in-exile: the 'uniqueness' and limitations of exile Tibetan democracy', *Sociological Bulletin* 58/1 (2009), pp. 115–44.
58. Rinpoche, Samdhong, 'Satyagraha'.
59. Conflict between Tibetans and Indians is rare. The most notorious incident occurred in Dharamsala in April 1994 when an Indian youth was allegedly killed by a Tibetan refugee, sparking a violent riot against the Tibetan community during which the TGiE headquarters and many Tibetan shops and homes were ransacked and looted (*Tibetan Review* 29/7 (1994), p. 18). In 2007, following community tensions after a fracas between an auto-rickshaw driver and newcomer refugee, Tibetans in the area boycotted Indian taxis and shops.
60. Zhou, Sha, 'What is it behind the Dalai Lama's "Plan"', *Beijing Review* February/19–25 (1990), pp. 22–3.
61. Tsundue, Tenzin, 'Tibetan Swaraj', *Tibetan Review* 39/10; Norbu, Jamyang, 'Rangzen!', *Combat Law: the Human Rights and Law Bimonthly* 6/5 (2007), pp. 28–35.
62. Dharamsala, 17 March 2006.
63. Ardley, *The Tibetan Independence Movement*, p. 21; McGranahan, *Arrested Histories.*
64. Schwarz, Ronald, *Circle of Protest: Political Ritual in the Tibetan Uprising* (London, 1994).
65. A detailed 'Lhakar Pledge' was posted on a Tibetan blog in June 2010. It has since been taken down, but an English translation is available here: http://www.highpeakspureearth.com/2011/07/white-wednesday-lhakar-pledge.html.
66. For example, see www.lhakar.org; www.lhakardiaries.com.
67. For example, in his inaugural speech on 8 August 2011: http://tibet.net/about-cta/executive/announcements/inaugural-speech-of-kalon-tripa-dr-lobsang-sangay/.

68. See www.lhakar.org.
69. Dorjee, Tenzin, http://www.globalpost.com/dispatch/worldview/100207/tibet-passive-resistance?page=0,1.
70. Interviews conducted in Dharamsala, September–October 2011.
71. A self-immolation also occurred in 2009 when Tapey, a monk from Kirti monastery in Ngaba, set himself on fire. His current status is not known.
72. Simpson, Peter, 'Tibetan activists adopt self-immolation as political tool', *Voice of America* (25 October 2011). Retrieved 26 October 2011 from http://www.voanews.com/english/news/asia/Tibetan-Activists-Adopt-Self-Immolation-As-Political-Tool-132517228.html.
73. Batty, David, 'China's "ruthless" Tibet policy to blame for monk deaths, says Dalai Lama', *Guardian* (29 October 2011). Retrieved 30 October 2011, from http://www.guardian.co.uk/world/2011/oct/29/dalai-lama-tibet-china-protests.
74. Jan, Yiin-Hua, 'Buddhist self-immolation in medieval China', *History of Religions* 4 (1965), pp. 243–68.
75. In international terms, protest by self-immolation has been notable during the Vietnam War, and the recent case of Tunisian market vendor, Mohamed Bouazizi, whose act in January 2011 is attributed as being a catalyst for the Tunisian revolution and wider 'Arab Spring'.
76. Ardley, *The Tibetan Independence Movement.*
77. Dhondup, Tashi, 'Independence can only be achieved with real sacrifices: an interview with Tsetan Norbu', *Tibetan Review* 33/6 (1998), p. 17. Jane Ardley questions the extent to which TYC adhered to each of Gandhi's strict principals regarding hunger strikes, especially those which state that 'the fast should only be undertaken against those for whom one had reciprocal feelings of love; [and] it should only be embarked upon when the opponents have admitted to unacceptable behaviour' (Ardley, *The Tibetan Independence Movement,* p. 57).
78. On 26 March 2012, at a protest against the presence of Chinese President Hu Jintao at a BRICS Summit in New Delhi, 27-year-old Jamphel Yeshi self-immolated. He died of his burns two days later and was given a martyr's funeral by TYC in Dharamsala.
79. McGranahan, *Arrested Histories*, p. 34.
80. Williams and McConnell, 'Critical geographies of peace', p. 929.
81. For example, Barnett, Clive, 'Deconstructing context: exposing Derrida', *Transactions of the Institute of British Geographers* 24/3 (1999), pp. 277–93.
82. See Megoran, Nick, 'War *and* Peace? An agenda for peace research and practice in geography', *Political Geography* 30/4 (2011), pp. 178–89.
83. McGranahan, *Arrested Histories*, p. 191; Ardley, *The Tibetan Independence Movement.*

# 8

# Transforming 'The Troubles': cultural geographies of peacebuilding in Northern Ireland

*Lia D. Shimada*

## Introduction: the case for cultural geography

On a drizzly night in July 2007, I stood at the edge of a car park in one of Belfast's inner-city enclaves. From the tarmac rose a massive tower, meticulously crafted from wooden crates and draped in Irish flags. Surrounding the structure was a multi-generational crowd waving flags of a different sort: their Union Jacks matched the bunting that had been strung throughout the neighbourhood, from one lamp-post to the next. I watched as a man approached with a small torch of fire. Circling the tower, he lit the base at several different points. Flames soon leapt up the sides, illuminating the height of the structure against the midnight sky. When the first of the Irish flags caught fire, the crowd erupted in cheers. Fireworks whistled overhead, exploding in bright showers while the flames crackled loudly.

This phenomenon, known colloquially as 'Eleventh Night bonfires', occurs annually across Northern Ireland in neighbourhoods loyal to Britain. Not many years previously, this event would have been marked by a very different atmosphere, overtly patrolled – and controlled – by paramilitary gunmen. The significance of the bonfire tradition cannot be underestimated for communities committed to keeping Northern Ireland within the United Kingdom. In these predominantly working-class 'loyalist' communities – so called for their ardent loyalty to Britain and to Northern Ireland's inclusion in the United Kingdom – the bonfires built and burned every July encapsulate the complex triad of territory, culture and identity. Yet as Northern Ireland emerges from 'The Troubles', the Eleventh Night bonfire tradition is, by necessity, transforming as well. Can this paramilitaristic, starkly sectarian tradition offer any promising material for the study of peace? In this chapter, I will discuss these bonfires to explore peacebuilding from a cultural geography perspective.

For societies emerging from violent conflict, political settlement is only one marker of many in the long process of peacebuilding. After the politicians disperse and the news cameras point elsewhere, it is ordinary people who must rebuild their world in extraordinary times. For conflicts arising from competing territorial claims, the challenge is particularly acute. Conflicts about contested places may at their heart be rooted in contested ideas about the identities of place – rigid interpretations of belonging that were invoked, sustained and strengthened during times of trouble. In marked contrast, the advent of peace may open new possibilities for how people imagine these places and their relationships with them. This is no easy task. As Massey observes, 'what is to be the dominant image of any place will be a matter of contestation and will change over time'.[1] The conflict inherent in the transformation of place – both physical and imaginary – poses lingering challenges to the process of peacebuilding. For societies recovering from violent conflict, the advent of peace coincides with new forms of engagement with the wider world, leading to new relationships between place, culture, heritage, identity and belonging. The challenge of building peace is, therefore, one of re-working and reconciling these contested, shifting narratives of place identity.

Cultural geography may not be the obvious starting point for studies of peacebuilding in contested societies. Far more familiar are disciplines of a political bent: political sciences, political geography, sociology and law, to name a few. Yet as a subdiscipline, cultural geography grapples with potent questions: How do transformations of contested places provoke new perceptions of space, scale and belonging? How do these transformations shape the expression, creation and negotiation of human identity in places recovering from violent conflict? Cultural geographers are well placed to address these vital questions. In an overview, Norton[2] succinctly summarizes the importance of people and place to cultural geography: 'Identity is not simply a matter of who we are, but also where we are.'

In this chapter, I explore the scope for geography in general – and cultural geography, in particular – to offer nuanced perspectives on peace. I begin with an overview of peacebuilding practice, focusing on our current understanding of conflict transformation theory, and I position cultural geography as a conceptual framework for interrogating the relationships between place and identity that lie at the heart of conflict over contested territory. I then turn to a case study of Northern Ireland

and its complicated 'post-conflict' aftermath. I draw on the 'Twelfth of July' (the high point of the loyalist cultural calendar) and transformations of the contested Eleventh Night bonfire tradition to examine the challenge of creating meaningful shared spaces in a divided society. To date, despite its significance in defining and creating ideas of place in Northern Ireland, the bonfire tradition has been little researched; this study therefore represents an original perspective on peacebuilding in Northern Ireland. The chapter ends with an interview that I conducted in April 2008 with two senior paramilitary fighters-turned-community activists. Their voices offer insight into the complex transformations at work in Northern Ireland, and illuminate the scope for these transformations to provoke new ways of engaging with culture, identity and belonging in a time – and place – of developing but ambiguous peace.

## Conflict transformation

In the field of peacebuilding, one of the more puzzling elements is the adjective 'post-conflict'. Its inherent assumptions are frequently, and at times dangerously, misleading. According to Harbom *et al.*[3], nearly 40 per cent of peace agreements fail within five years, illustrating the impermanence of conflict termination. Simpson[4] observes: 'The sources of social conflict shift over time, taking on new forms and manifestations. In this sense, there is no such thing as "post-conflict".' As Muggah elaborates, the term 'post-conflict' is a particularly unhelpful designation, as it disguises a vast array of real and perceived threats that face most societies emerging from war.[5] To this end, academic studies of peacebuilding can offer a useful critique of the concept.

Scholarship on peace research has given rise to a large body of literature on handling conflict. In recent years, three main schools of thought have developed, which are generally known as conflict resolution, conflict management and conflict transformation. As Miall notes, these three schools not only articulate varying approaches to conflict intervention, but also reflect different conceptualizations of conflict itself.[6] I take Miall's observation one step further, arguing that they reflect different conceptualizations of peace as well.

Conflict resolution is the traditional, and perhaps most familiar, response to conflicts unable to 'resolve' themselves through violence or by other means. This theory is based in the belief that in communal and identity conflict, people cannot compromise on their fundamental needs.[7] Advocates of conflict resolution argue that it is possible to transcend conflict if parties can be helped to explore, analyse, question and re-frame their positions and interests. This approach emphasizes intervention by third parties to foster new thinking and to forge new relationships. The ultimate goal of conflict resolution is to move conflicting parties from zero-sum, destructive patterns to positive, constructive outcomes.

In contrast with conflict resolution, conflict management theory acknowledges that some conflicts may not have a readily available solution. Shirlow *et al.* suggest that advocates of this approach tend to view violent conflict as the result of differences in values, interests and power within and between communities.[8] According to the conflict management paradigm, resolution is an unrealistic goal for these conflicts. Thus, the best approach is to manage and contain them, generally through interventions to achieve political settlements.

The approaches of conflict resolution and conflict management have been criticized for their respective oversimplification of the conflicts and the actors involved. With conflict resolution, the underlying philosophy suggests that conflict is destructive and that it can be resolved permanently through mediation or other forms of intervention. Such a belief ignores the reality that many conflicts emerge from legitimate injustices or inequalities. While conflict management operates under more realistic assumptions than conflict resolution it, too, can be problematic. By treating violence as the problem, the conflict management approach draws attention from the real issues at the root of violent conflict, even as it suggests – provocatively – that people can be directed and controlled.

Conflict transformation, the third main theoretical school, emerged from this recognition of the inherent complex dynamism of conflict situations. The conflict transformation approach goes beyond the resolution and the containment of issues that fuel violent conflict. In 1997, John Paul Lederach's book *Building Peace: Sustainable Reconciliation in Divided Societies* was published,[9] which peace scholars and practitioners widely recognize as a major milestone in the development of conflict transformation theory. Lederach argues that social conflict is 'by nature lodged in longstanding relationships' that are cyclical and episodic in nature, and that it holds the power to transform the people entrenched in these relationships.[10] If left unchecked, these transformations can spiral the conflict into social destruction. Lederach's conflict transformation approach aims to reduce this potential by helping to transform the relationships, interests and discourses that support the continuation of violent conflict. He proposes a model for understanding the 'dynamic process' of peacebuilding as based on two central concepts. The first concept views conflict as a progression that moves through different stages. The second concept views peacebuilding as a process made up of multiple interdependent roles, functions and activities. Significantly, this approach operates at a number of different levels. It recognizes that enduring peace depends on structural changes that address inequalities and injustices, as well as on individual- and community-level changes to beliefs and perceptions.[11] The conflict transformation approach has been developed subsequently both by theorists and practitioners. Like many theories pressed into practice, it must be continually adjusted in response to the changing nature of the conflicts it addresses.

Conflict transformation may currently be the most widely embraced approach, but it is not without shortcomings, as a number of academics identify.[12] Curiously, the existing scholarship on conflict transformation pays only cursory attention to the transformation of spatial relationships. This is surprising, given the importance of place-derived identities and relationships in conflicts that involve competing territorial claims. In these types of conflict, the land itself can be as determining an actor as are the conflicting parties. As Miall notes, the meaning of a conflict depends largely on the context out of which it arises, with assumptions and attitudes shaped by previous relationships, and driving behaviours based on memories of the past.[13] To a cultural geographer, it is logical that 'place' – as both physical entity and symbolic concept – and the context for peacebuilding are closely entwined. In conflicts that are entrenched in competing territorial claims, people may form relationships across a broad spectrum – from physical to imaginary – with these contested places. Thus, the conflict may be rooted in competing struggles to define this contested terrain. To this end, the spatial dimensions of cultural conflict cannot be underestimated.

Peacebuilding in contested territories involves more than the transformation of relationships between people. Crucially, it calls for the transformation of the fraught, contested relationships between identity and place. Following Graham, I argue that the challenge of peacebuilding involves the creation of shared place-based identities among the conflicting parties.[14] To this end, conflict transformation theories could benefit from a deeper engagement with geography in general, and with cultural geography in particular, to develop more nuanced, comprehensive frameworks for theorizing peace. This chapter focuses on cultural geographies of peacebuilding through a case study of Northern Ireland. I explore their role in reconciling contested notions of place and identity, and in searching for new narratives of belonging on which to build a shared future.

## Northern Ireland: an uncertain peace

Northern Ireland occupies fewer than 5,500 square miles, but the six counties that comprise it are among the most disputed places in the world. Northern Ireland's predominantly Protestant unionists claim this territory for Britain, while the predominantly Catholic national- ists claim it for the Republic of Ireland. The era euphemistically known as 'The Troubles' erupted in 1969, unleashing three decades of turmoil across Northern Ireland and beyond. One of the most striking charac- teristics of the Troubles was the prevalence of paramilitary violence on both sides. While the Irish Republican Army (IRA) fought for a united, 32-county Ireland, the Ulster Volunteer Force (UVF) and the Ulster Defence Association (UDA) fought for loyalty to Britain. The Troubles ushered in an era of conflict that claimed more than 3,000 lives (most of them civilian), entrenched Northern Ireland's patterns of segregation, and left a cultural legacy of violence, suspicion and mutual antagonism.

Over the years, politicians on both sides of the Irish Sea attempted interventions, but it was not until the 1990s that there was sufficient momentum to explore more sustainable solutions. The peace process began with the declaration of the first ceasefire in 1994, and proceeded in fits and starts to the signing of the peace accords in April 1998.[15] The watershed agreement intertwined the pursuit of an equitable and shared society within the framework for political settlements.[16] The agree- ment, however, is far from a perfect solution; many analysts view it with ambivalence.[17] It has been criticized for the contradiction at its heart – an agreement based on two political bodies and mutual respect for both traditions, thus reinforcing two sets of exclusive nationalisms.[18]

The peace process today remains fragile. In many ways, Northern Ireland resides in a twilight zone, caught in its spiral of history and hatred. Its nationalistic fervour for its parent countries is hugely out of step with the more cosmopolitan cultures evolving in both the Republic of Ireland and mainland Britain.[19] Moreover, the decade following the signing of the peace accords witnessed enormous changes to the region's demographic – and, by extension, cultural – landscape. Although com- monly defined by its high-profile conflict between (white) Protestants and (white) Catholics, Northern Ireland is increasingly home to resi- dents who belong to neither of the region's dominant ethno-national traditions. Since the signing of the peace accords, Northern Ireland has garnered the dubious distinction of being labelled the 'race hate capi- tal of Europe',[20] and Belfast 'the most racist city in the world'.[21] These trends point to Northern Ireland's struggle to accommodate other dimensions of diversity. As the power of religious identity declines, the former binary model becomes increasingly outdated.[22] Northern Ireland now faces a crisis of identity as it learns to accommodate a broader spectrum of diversity within the space of its six counties, and within the larger idea of 'Northern Ireland' itself.

At its heart, the struggle over Northern Ireland is a struggle over the contested identities ascribed to and drawn from the land. As Bowman observes, 'For "land" to serve as ground on which to build nationhood, it must be more than a geographical setting.'[23] Instead, it must be a domain of the imagination where people can locate others with whom they see themselves sharing a present situation as well as a future nation. In Northern Ireland, the absence of shared identity is derived from, and reproduces, divisive sectarian conceptualizations of place, such as the so-called 'peace lines' of Belfast. Reid argues that the lack of an overarching narrative of place for Northern Ireland – and for its territorial conflict – has resulted in fragmented, highly localized and strictly bounded senses of place.[24] The absence of a shared identity (re) produces Northern Ireland's divisive, sectarian conceptualizations of physical and imaginative place. These unagreed and contested representations are rooted in the region's fraught historical narratives. For people from Protestant-unionist-loyalist populations, in particular, the challenge is to anchor a valid sense of belonging against the more confident Catholic-nationalist-republican cultural narratives. In contemporary Northern Ireland, culture, identity, heritage and belonging, collide in the complex transformations of longstanding social conflict – and nowhere more so than in transformations of loyalist bonfires.

## Eleventh Night bonfires

At the zenith of the loyalist cultural calendar, the Eleventh Night bonfires celebrate the victory of the Protestant King William III over the Catholic King James II at the Battle of the Boyne in 1690. Academics have written extensively about the Twelfth of July parades that the bonfires herald.[25] I argue that, like the parades, the Eleventh Night bonfires inscribe loyalist cultural ownership over the spaces they define. In recent times, the peace process has provoked massive changes to these traditions. With regard to the bonfires, the changes are particularly poignant. In cities such as Belfast, urban regeneration is claiming many of the sites on which loyalist communities build their bonfires. Moreover, people both within and outside these areas are gaining in confidence to challenge a divisive sectarian tradition that poses widespread risks to the environment and to public health. Today, as the discourse of peace champions the ideal of shared space, loyalists struggle to re-define their tradition and, by extension, the connections they draw between place and identity. When positioned against larger transformations in loyalist culture, the bonfires offer insight into connections between contested cultural identities, new meanings of place, and the re-definition of contemporary loyalism.

Bonfire season begins in the early days of spring. Across loyalist neighbourhoods in Belfast, young people begin to collect their building materials: wooden pallets, rubber tyres, odds and ends of refuse. As the materials amass, other residents (and, at times, complete outsiders) contribute material to the growing pile. For those wishing for cost-free disposal of unwanted furniture and household appliances, bonfire season is a golden opportunity. In neighbourhoods where the bonfire site is well known and highly visible, people may come from miles away with their contributions. From these raw materials arises the bonfire. The advent of wooden pallets, from which contemporary bonfires are largely constructed, allows for greater stability and variation in building design. Bonfires can reach heights of sixty feet or more, dwarfing nearby houses.

The bonfire may be the focal point of the festivities, but it forms only part of the visual landscape. In the days and weeks leading to the Twelfth of July, loyalist communities deck their streets with patriotic bunting. Against this backdrop of red, white and blue, the bonfire may also be draped with flags of a different sort. In some communities, the flags of the Union Jack, Northern Ireland, and loyalist paramilitary organizations may wave briefly from the structure. Out of respect, these are removed before the midnight burning. Universal to nearly all loyalist bonfires, however, is burning of the Tricolour flag of the Irish Republic, alongside other cultural symbols including effigies of the Pope, campaign posters of republican politicians, and vehicle registration plates from south of the border.

On the Eleventh of July, many communities host parties – both impromptu or planned – for local residents. As midnight nears, residents gather at the site. To facilitate ignition, the bonfire is doused liberally with petrol and then set alight. In some places, masked men may fire live rounds of ammunition into the sky, in a display known colloquially as a 'paramilitary show of strength'. The party runs full throttle as local residents celebrate through the night. Many will still be awake come morning, when the members of the flute bands will don their uniforms, assemble for the Twelfth of July parade, and celebrate, once more, the triumph of 'King Billy'.

Bonfires may represent a cornerstone of loyalist tradition, but their negative effects reverberate throughout the region. In the months leading up to July, bonfire sites become *de facto* rubbish dumps, in which rat infestations are common. The wooden pallets that comprise the bulk of most contemporary bonfires are taken, without compensation, from local businesses. Furthermore, and for a variety of reasons (intimidation by paramilitaries, for instance, or loss of clientele) many small businesses feel compelled to close during the days leading up to the Twelfth of July. On Eleventh Night, thick plumes of smoke rise into the sky. Throughout the night, statutory services struggle to contain bonfires that burgeon out of control and threaten nearby homes and buildings. Revellers – some in an alcohol-induced haze – may interpret the firefighters' actions as an attack on their bonfire, leading to attacks on the service itself. Due to their size, the ruins of the bonfires may continue to smoulder for days. When they finally die out, the tarmac on which they rested must be re-paved at the taxpayers' expense. Patriotic flags and bunting are frequently left to moulder on public lamp-posts long after the Twelfth of July.

Arching over everything is the spectre of aggression, intimidation and violence. Despite recent pledges by the two main paramilitary organizations to place their weapons beyond reach, paramilitarism maintains its stranglehold over some loyalist communities. The 'hard men' wield their power from the local pubs or social clubs that serve as unofficial headquarters. As bonfire season approaches, they may demand financial 'donations' from local residents, oversee the building of the structure, and demonstrate their prowess on the night of the Eleventh of July. In the minds of many people, particularly among non-loyalists, bonfires are intimately associated with paramilitarism.

As the peace process moves into its second decade, people across Northern Ireland increasingly challenge the environmental, political and cultural sustainability of the bonfire tradition. The peace process has profoundly transformed the physical and imaginative spaces for bonfires. One of the most visible manifestations is the influx of economic investment in Northern Ireland. The regeneration of Belfast now transforms the urban landscape, as property developers purchase swaths of derelict land and place it beyond the reach of local residents. As a result, vacant lots where bonfires are built are rapidly diminishing in number, with disconcerting effects on the local communities. Curiously, Northern Ireland's planning sector has dedicated little formal dialogue to the subject of bonfires. The omission is striking, given the obvious intersection between Eleventh Night bonfires and planning concerns, particularly in the densely built inner-city areas of Belfast.

The transformations that I have described illustrate how external factors affect the bonfires, yet even more remarkable transformations are taking place within loyalist communities themselves. As public criticism increases, loyalist communities are compelled to re-define the meaning of their tradition in a time of developing peace. In some cities and towns, municipal 'bonfire management programmes' now seek to instil an ethos of good practice within loyalist communities for the benefit of the wider public. These programmes drive many of the tangible transformations they seek to implement: for example, reduction in size; regulation of building materials; and clear lines of communication between bonfire builders and relevant statutory agencies. Yet they are facilitating *in*tangible transformations as well. By creating opportunities for reflection and capacity-building, these programmes encourage participating communities to explore new roles, places and ways of celebrating loyalist heritage and identity.

The Twelfth of July may be the most important date in the loyalist cultural calendar but its adherents increasingly struggle to articulate its contemporary relevance. In many communities, bonfires have become an exercise in structural engineering, unmoored from history and relevant only in the spectacle of their construction. Alcohol has become firmly entrenched in bonfire culture, frequently replacing the Battle of the Boyne as the primary reason for celebration. Loyalism's crisis of cultural identity is particularly apparent in the widespread practice of burning the flag of the Irish Republic. This practice underscores the tendency within loyalism to define itself in opposition to Irish republicanism, rather than framing a positively defined identity of its own.[26] Yet bonfires continue to serve a vital role in loyalist culture. In a time of uncertain identity, Eleventh Night represents the one time of year when a loyalist community may gather together. Moreover, the bonfires connect participants beyond their local sites to celebrations of the wider loyalist community, across space and time. Yet for all that their role in the cultural landscape of loyalism is well established, the triad of identity, culture and territory that bonfires once defined is increasingly open to interpretation. Their transformations can be read as both a product and an agent of the peace process, in turn reflecting and provoking new expressions of loyalist culture – perhaps nowhere more so than in paramilitary controlled communities.

## The changing place of paramilitarism

Somewhere toward the centre of Northern Ireland, a mid-sized town is conducting a bold experiment in bonfire management. The two men with key roles in implementing the programme are community leaders with what might be considered unorthodox backgrounds: they are unapologetic members of Northern Ireland's largest loyalist paramilitary organizations. During the Troubles, two prominent paramilitary bodies emerged for the loyalist cause: the Ulster Volunteer Force (UVF) and the Ulster Defence Association (UDA). At its peak, the UDA had 40,000 members and a large reservoir of support within loyalist communities.[27] Although united in its political aims and its opposition to Irish republicanism, loyalist paramilitarism imploded into feuds between and within the main organizations shortly after the signing of the 1998 peace accords. The repercussions resonate today.[28] The high-profile presence of both Davey and Rob, representatives of the UDA and UVF, respectively, in this town's bonfire management programme speaks to the local council's acknowledgement of tensions that persist within loyalist paramilitarism. I interviewed Davey and Rob in April 2008.[29] Although each bonfire is distinct to the community in which it is built, the narrative that Davey and Rob offer speaks to wider experiences around this loyalist tradition and its contemporary transformations.

Bonfires form part of a cultural landscape in which murals, patriotic colours and other visual markers serve as striking affirmations of territorial identity and ownership. According to Davey, local paramilitary structures may also contribute to this visual dialogue:

> Even through the peace process people were still very territorial and defensive of their territories. You'd have come in and found Ulster Volunteer Force and Ulster Freedom Fighters[30] and Ulster Defence Association flags adorning every lamp-post. You know, and for anybody, even people within the Protestant communities, driving into that sort of went: 'Whoa' ... It was very territorial.

As a high ranking leader, Davey is aware of how symbols can be manipulated to invoke awe and fear, which he captures in his imagined response of a person entering the territory. The flags 'adorning every lamp-post' broadcast the presence of paramilitary organizations within the defined physical space of the estate. In this context, bonfires play their own role of intimidation, both material and symbolic, in the heightened atmosphere of Eleventh Night. Davey describes how, previously, local paramilitaries would emphasize their menacing presence through paramilitary displays of gunfire.

> And on [bonfire night] both fields suddenly went quiet ... The tempo of the music changed, and then you had the masked men coming out

with the balaclavas and the firearms, shooting up into the air. And there was a lot of paramilitary trappings.

There is a performative quality to the spectacle that Davey describes, from the sudden descent of silence to the quickened music that accompanies the 'masked men' and their volleys of gunfire. The 'firearms' evoke not only the armed warfare of the twentieth-century Troubles but also the 1690 battle that gave rise to the bonfire tradition. I read the juxtaposition of these two conflicts as an attempt to legitimate the armed struggle of the Troubles by framing it as an extension of the historic Battle of the Boyne. Moreover, as bonfires are frequently built by, and celebrated within, communities with a strong tradition of sectarian murals, the 'show of strength' re-works in three dimensions some of militant loyalism's most threatening and iconic images, such as armed men with balaclavas. Thus, the performance of the bonfire brings to life the static images that adorn the estate's built environment, further emphasizing the connections between paramilitarism and place. In this way, bonfires and loyalist paramilitary culture co-constitute each other: one emphasizes the power of the other, and in doing so, defines and reinforces a particular type of place-associated loyalist identity.

In recent years, as the peace process spurs broad shifts in public opinion, some loyalists have recognized that the public image of the bonfire tradition must change. In Rob's and Davey's communities, the bonfire programme has given more visionary leaders an opportunity to move away from the stark paramilitarism that characterized their bonfires previously. In our interview, Davey reports that when yet another paramilitary bonfire began on their estate, 'it gave us an avenue to jump ship'. He and Rob shifted their focus to young people, seeking to engage them with the process and the cultural history of bonfire building. Rob took the radical step of re-designing the structure entirely. Rather than following the tower- or beehive-shaped design typically employed in contemporary bonfires, Rob and the young people constructed their bonfire in the shape of a castle. They built a square-shaped frame using large sheets of plywood, with crenellation carved on top. They painted the castle, piled wood inside its four walls and, as usual, decorated the structure with the Irish Tricolour. Despite the sectarian connotations of the Irish flag, the new design represents a significant symbolic break from the more typical paramilitary controlled bonfires on the estate.

New designs aside, where these bonfires differ most dramatically is in their movement away from the culture of violence that characterized their predecessors. In the following extract, Davey, who also supervised the building of another new bonfire on the estate, describes the difference between old and new:

> Initially when you first came down to our bonfire...you hit this wall that had two camouflaged men with machine guns. As bold as you want, red, white and blue letters: UDA, UFF, UYM, Kill All Taigs. The bonfire was absolutely demonic. It was swamped every night of the week by hooded faces...It was like something out of the Wild West. And see now where we are now, we're probably the most timid fire in [the area] Although we still have our fire.

Here, Davey describes a constellation of militant loyalism's iconic imagery: sectarian graffiti, patriotic colours, and 'camouflaged men with machine guns'. The graffiti refer not only to prominent paramilitary branches within the community – the Ulster Defence Association, Ulster Freedom Fighters and Ulster Young Militants – but also contain a direct call to violence: 'Kill All Taigs' is a derogatory anti-Catholic slur frequently employed through visual media in loyalist areas. Although Davey most likely describes a local mural in this excerpt, his description elides with that of the 'demonic' bonfire built in its shadow, with sinister 'hooded faces' tracing the bonfire's progress in the days leading up to Eleventh Night. Through this conflation, the bonfire that Davey describes feeds into, and from, the dense tapestry of identity and place in this loyalist estate. In stark contrast, Davey interprets the bonfire that he now oversees as 'probably the most timid fire in [the area]'. This shift away from a highly masculinized and glorified culture of violence applies not only to the bonfire, but may also describe larger shifts within paramilitary culture itself, as the peace process and public opinion encourage demilitarization. Davey's final comment in this extract – 'Although we still have our fire' – is striking. It emphasizes the centrality of the bonfire itself, in a far simpler form, to a loyalist cultural identity that seeks to move away from paramilitarism.

For Rob and Davey, the challenge now is to define loyalist culture in positive terms, beyond the sectarian and paramilitary framework by which it has come to be known. Davey articulates this task: 'We want to be seen as people that are remembering who we were, and where we came from, to the present day...making it more culturally acceptable.' In so doing, he identifies the importance of locating Protestant culture within the context of its history, from which to re-frame more nuanced forms of loyalist cultural identity that can be sustained in times of peace. There is growing awareness within loyalist communities that the transformation of the bonfire tradition creates valuable opportunities for cultural education. Below, Davey and Rob describe how the bonfires can illuminate for local young people the historic relevance of their tradition:

> *Lia*: How would you say that bonfires are important to your sense of cultural identity?
>
> *Rob*: Our kids aren't ever taught their own culture or their own identity. And we see the bonfires as an opportunity... We bring lambeg drums on to the field, flute bands, different things. And the kids become inquisitive then: 'What's that for?' So it gives us an opportunity to bring our communities together. And through lifting a few pallets or whatever, give them a wee bit of education and, you know, help them understand that it's not... about burning the Tricolour. It's about the kids understanding who they are, because, you know, if these kids are gonna be a part of our future, they have to understand their past.

Alongside the bonfire itself, Rob draws on the material artefacts of the Twelfth of July – 'lambeg drums..., flute bands, different things' – to pique the children's interest in their cultural heritage. The bonfire site becomes a tangible space for learning, where the embodied experience of 'lifting a few pallets' connects the young people powerfully to their history. In this way, Rob traces direct connections between the bonfire tradition and the development of a positively defined cultural identity that is 'not about burning the (Irish) Tricolour'. He suggests that a successful future for loyalist culture depends on the capacity for young people to develop a robust and positively defined cultural identity enriched by collective understanding of loyalist history.

Bonfires are only part of the larger process of re-imagining the place of loyalist culture. Other expressions of paramilitarism, such as flags and murals, still serve as vivid declarations of territorial identity. The peace process may encourage loyalists to reconsider these contested place images, but memories of the Troubles slow the progress. In the sensitive atmosphere of post-ceasefire Northern Ireland, former figures of terror – both loyalist and republican – now work side by side in new political structures, inevitably exacerbating existing tensions. Not surprisingly, the local council's controversial relationship with Rob and Davey invites public criticism. From Davey's perspective, these working relationships – however fraught – are a necessary reality:

> Unless you work with the people that we have to work with, you don't have any success. But there are still councillors in these chambers

who say: 'We're not working with terrorists, full stop'... They shout about these offensive murals, and we've always had the policy: Let's try and get the gunmen off the streets before we worry about cardboard figures and walls... A lot of [the councillors] don't give us the opportunity, [but] unless you're prepared to work with paramilitaries and engage with them and try and help them come out of conflict – through bonfires, through flags, through murals, through whatever process – you're never gonna be successful. You have to speak to them.

This excerpt highlights Davey's understanding of the connections between the process of peacebuilding and the process of re-imagining the meanings attached to place. He identifies the markers of loyalist identity – bonfires, flags, murals – as symbolic and physical material with which loyalist paramilitary organizations must now engage in order to 'come out of conflict'. Earlier in this chapter, I drew on John Paul Lederach's work to argue that a more holistic approach toward conflict transformation should consider the transformation of relationships not only between people in conflict, but between people and the ideas of place that underpin the conflict. As Davey points out in the excerpt above, this is a multi-pronged process, in which success depends on developing relationships with the very people perceived to be entrenched in and fuelling the conflict.

Even beyond the transformation of physical space, the civic bonfire management programme is provoking the bonfire builders to think critically about their tradition in relation to wider scales of impact and, possibly, belonging. Although outsiders to loyalism may view bonfire builders as parochial, provincial in outlook, and selfishly blasé toward the environment, Davey and Rob demonstrate a sophisticated grasp of environmental processes and an awareness of their own impact. In our interview, Rob makes a solid and unambiguous connection between bonfires and the growing threat of climate change: 'Bonfires have a direct effect. There's no doubt about it.' Over the course of the interview, and unprompted by me, he twice refers to their 'carbon footprint'. This concept refers not only to the defined physical space of the site on which a bonfire is built, but also connects loyalist builders and bonfire celebrants to a wider global dialogue about justice and responsibility. To Rob, the future for bonfires is inevitable: 'They're going to change dramatically over the next five to ten years. They have to.'

Former fighters like Rob and Davey are now negotiating new identities that extend beyond the paramilitary framework of their former relationship to loyalism. In the following extract, Davey describes the shift from militancy to political expression of his ideals:

> Like, I make no beef... I am a political representative of the Ulster Defence Association, Ulster Freedom Fighters... I wear who I am and what I am on my sleeve. I was prepared to go to gaol, and worse, for the struggles of this country. We're now in an environment where we want to end that. I don't want to be in gaol and visit my kids through a glass visor. I don't want my kids burying me because I've been murdered at the hands of whoever else. We have to take the struggle on... It's... more than bonfires now.

As Davey points out, bonfires are just the starting point for re-defining loyalism in a changing political environment. The transformation of the bonfire tradition is only a part of the larger transformation of loyalist paramilitarism, and of loyalism itself. The place of paramilitarism in Northern Ireland, in terms of both physical manifestation and symbolic value, must now be renegotiated through the peace process. In communities like Davey's and Rob's, the transformation of the Eleventh Night bonfire tradition offers scope for re-defining loyalist identities in a post-ceasefire – and one day, perhaps, post-paramilitary – Northern Ireland.

## Conclusion

I began this chapter by asking how transformations of the Eleventh Night bonfire tradition could help us to understand 'peace' from a cultural geography perspective. More broadly, I sought to explore how transformations of contested place identities might shift entrenched positions and help to reconcile conflicting notions of allegiance and belonging. Davey and Rob are only two voices of many in the intricate matrix of loyalist cultural identities; they are by no means representative of a monolithic community. Yet their anxieties and achievements resonate with conversations taking shape in the wider context of loyalism and elsewhere in 'post-conflict' Northern Ireland. The arc of their interview traces a marked shift from violently territorial, paramilitary controlled bonfires to more expansive, global expressions of identity and engagement. Will this spell the end of conflict? Not necessarily; not immediately. Emerging here, however, are affinities to place that attempt to define loyalist culture not in territorial terms but rather in terms of heritage, history and pride. In this new found confidence is, perhaps, the basis for identities that are flexible and resilient enough to serve as a springboard for reconciling the longstanding conflict over the idea, and the reality, of Northern Ireland.

The cultural geographies that I have explored in this essay point toward a healthy engagement between ideas of place and theories of conflict transformation. These geographies – by emphasizing the ever shifting dynamics between people, place, culture, identity and belonging – help us to frame 'peace' not as a noun but as a verb. In Northern Ireland, in particular, the concept of a 'peace process' may run the risk of overuse, yet this sense of motion suggests rich scope for the contributions that geographic exploration can offer to peacebuilding, in both theory and practice.

## Acknowledgements

The author would like to acknowledge the assistance of Claire Dwyer and the staff of Groundwork Northern Ireland.

## Notes

1. Massey, Doreen, *Space, Place and Gender* (Cambridge, 1994), p. 12.
2. Norton, William, *Cultural Geography: Environments, Landscapes, Identities, Inequalities*, second edition (Oxford, 2006), pp. 21–2, original emphasis.
3. Harbom, Lotta, Högbladh, Stina and Wallensteen, Peter, 'Armed conflict and peace agreements', *Journal of Peace Research* 43/5 (2006), pp. 617–31.
4. Simpson, Graeme, 'Reconstruction and reconciliation: emerging from transition', *Development in Practice* 7/4 (1997), pp. 475–8, p. 476 cited.
5. Muggah, Robert, 'No magic bullet: a critical perspective on disarmament, demobilization and reintegration (DDR) and weapons reduction in post-conflict contexts', *Round Table* 94/379 (2005), pp. 238–52.
6. Miall, Hugh, 'Conflict transformation: a multi-dimensional task', in *Berghof Handbook for Conflict Transformation* (Berghof Research Centre for Constructive Conflict Management, 2004).
7. Miall, 'Conflict transformation'. See also Dayton, Bruce W. and Kriesberg, Louis, 'Introduction', in B. Dayton and L. Kriesberg (eds), *Conflict Transformation and Peacebuilding: Moving from Violence to Sustainable Peace* (London, 2009).
8. Shirlow, Peter, Graham, Brian, McEvoy, Kieran, Ó hAdhmaill, Félim and Purvis, Dawn, *Politically Motivated Former Prisoner Groups: Community Activism and Conflict Transformation* (Belfast, 2005).
9. Lederach, John P., *Building Peace: Sustainable Reconciliation in Divided Societies* (Washington, 1997).
10. Lederach, *Building Peace*, p. 14.
11. Lederach, John P., *Preparing for Peace: Conflict Transformation Across Cultures* (New York, 1995).

12. Miall, 'Conflict transformation'; Ryan, Stephen, *The Transformation of Violent Inter-communal Conflict* (Aldershot, 2007); Frykman, Maja P., 'Identities in war: embodiments of violence and places of belonging', *Ethnologia Europaea* 27 (1997), pp. 153–62.

13. Miall, 'Conflict transformation', p. 8.

14. Graham, Brian, 'The past in the present: the shaping of identity in loyalist Ulster', *Terrorism and Political Violence* 16/3 (2004), pp. 483–500.

15. The terminology of this agreement is fraught with political connotation. Although the 'Good Friday Agreement' is the common name invoked in the international media, some unionists view it as a term that is biased toward nationalism.

16. Hughes, Joanne and Donnelly, Caitlin, 'Attitudes to community relations in Northern Ireland: signs of optimism in the post cease-fire period?', *Terrorism and Political Violence* 16/3 (2004), pp. 567–92.

17. Gallagher, Tony, 'After the war comes peace? an examination of the impact of the Northern Ireland conflict on young people', *Journal of Social Issues* 60/3 (2004), pp. 629–42.

18. Brown, Kris and MacGinty, Roger, 'Public attitudes toward partisan and neutral symbols in post-agreement Northern Ireland', *Identities – Global Studies in Culture and Power* 10 (2003), pp. 83–108; Anderson, James and Shuttleworth, Ian, 'Sectarian demography, territoriality, and political development in Northern Ireland', *Political Geography* 17/2 (1998), pp. 187–208.

19. Brown and MacGinty, 'Public attitudes'; Shirlow, Peter and Murtagh, Brendan, *Belfast: Segregation, Violence and the City* (London, 2006).

20. BBC, 17 June 2009, 'Racism in Northern Ireland', http://news.bbc.co.uk/1/hi/northern_ ireland/8104978.stm. Retrieved 24 March 2010.

21. McVeigh, Robbie, *The Next Stephen Lawrence? Racist Violence and Criminal Justice in Northern Ireland* (Belfast, 2006), p. 33.

22. Doherty, Paul and Poole, Michael A., 'Religion as an indicator of ethnicity in Northern Ireland – an alternative perspective', *Irish Geography* 35/2 (2002), pp. 75–89.

23. Bowman, Glenn, 'Tales of the lost land: Palestinian identity and the formation of nationalist consciousness', in E. Carter, J. Donald and J. Squires (eds), *Space and Place: Theories of Identity and Location* (London, 1993), p. 81.

24. Reid, Bryonie, 'A profound edge: performative negotiations of Belfast', *Cultural Geographies* 12/4 (2005), pp. 485–506.

25. Jarman, Neil, '*Material Conflicts: Parades and Visual Displays in Northern Ireland*' (Oxford, 1997); Cohen, Shaul, 'Winning while losing: the Apprentice Boys of Derry walk their beat', *Political Geography* 26/8 (2007), pp. 951–67.

26. Graham, Brian, 'No place of the mind: contested Protestant representations of Ulster', *Ecumene* 1/3 (1994), pp. 257–81; Graham, 'The past in the present'.

27. McDonald, Henry and Cusack, Jim, *UDA: Inside the Heart of Loyalist Terror* (London and Dublin, 2004).

28. Gallaher, Carol and Shirlow, Peter, 'The geography of loyalist paramilitary feuding in Belfast', *Space and Polity* 10/2 (2006), pp. 149–69.

29. At the time, I was working as a project officer for a community regeneration organization. In this capacity, I implemented the bonfire management programme in Belfast, working closely with loyalist communities in Northern Ireland's largest city. For professional reasons, I chose to conduct research-related interviews in towns whose bonfire programmes had no formal links with Belfast's.

30. When it served their purpose, members of the UDA would carry out sectarian attacks under its *nom de guerre*, the Ulster Freedom Fighters.

# Part 3

# Practices of coexistence

# 9

# A place of empathy in a fragile contentious landscape: environmental peacebuilding in the eastern Mediterranean

*Stuart Schoenfeld, Asaf Zohar, Ilan Alleson, Osama Suleiman*
*and Galya Sipos-Randor*

On a kibbutz in the Negev desert, close to the Jordanian border, every year since 1996 small groups of Israeli, Palestinian, Jordanian and overseas students – cumulatively numbering by 2011 about 600 – have lived and studied together for one or two semesters at the Arava Institute for Environmental Studies. The Arava Institute has the goal of producing a network of regional environmentalists who are able and willing to work together.

The Arava Institute is an unusual place both in its origin and in its persistence as a peacebuilding initiative. In the period after the PLO–Israeli Oslo Accords (1993), Interim Agreement (1995) and the Jordanian–Israeli Peace Treaty (1994), many dialogue groups, 'people-to-people' programmes and co-operative initiatives began or were reinforced, including a small network of organizations promoting regional environmental co-operation. With the return to armed Palestinian–Israeli hostilities during the second Palestinian Intifada in 2000, most of these groups and initiatives were discontinued.[1] However, several civil society groups that promote environmental co-operation, including the Arava Institute, have persevered.[2]

This chapter pushes the development of a geography of peace by focusing on the Arava Institute as a meeting place in a highly contested landscape. Megoran's exploration of the concept of positive peace as an alternative to 'peace as the absence of war'[3] is apt, as the Arava Institute persists despite the continuing, sometimes violent, conflict. War is not absent, but peacebuilding takes place nonetheless. In addition, Megoran writes – based on his inquiry into the meaning of 'peace' – that 'peace is inseparable from questions of social justice',[4] and this, too, is apt for understanding the institute, its challenges and strategies. In their piece, Williams and McConnell are especially attentive to 'peace as process' and propose 'a more expansive and critical focus around "peace-ful" concepts such as tolerance, friendship, hope, reconciliation, justice, cosmopolitanism, resistance, solidarity, hospitality and empathy'.[5] The institute has, through design and trial-and-error, developed a group culture that cultivates empathy. As students participate in this culture, they go through processes that are aimed at cultivating peaceful interpersonal relationships. These processes are the focus of this chapter.

Earlier work on the Arava Institute has identified structural features that have allowed it to persevere where other peacebuilding projects have failed.[6] Its student body – approximately one-third Jewish Israeli, one-third Arab (Palestinian, Jordanian, Israeli Arab) and one-third overseas students (mostly from the USA) – receive university credit for a full year or semester of environmental studies taught in English. While overseas students pay tuition, Middle East students receive scholarships. After students leave, the institute helps its alumni to network with each other and in their search for work and further education. Through this strategy, the institute does not rely on the idealism of its students but gives them practical educational and professional assistance. The institute has also been flexible, learning from experience and changing. Ongoing research by the authors examines the institute from the perspective of resource mobilization, noting that it has positioned itself as both a social movement organization and a credit granting academic institute, and draws resources from both networks. For example, the institute has income from research projects (academic) and a fundraising (social movement) support group.

Other structural features of the institute provide emotional support for building peaceful relations. Students are somewhat insulated from the surrounding conflict by the isolated setting of Kibbutz Ketura. It is a small group, never more than 45 in any one semester. Students share living space, eat together, spend leisure time with each other, and are hosted by an idealistic communal society.

This chapter, based on interviews with alumni, probes further into the experience of being a student by following the process through which empathy for those from adversarial societies develops at the institute. Literature on environmental peacebuilding and empathy situates this process and intersects with issues of 'the geography of peace'. The interviews indicate the growth of empathic relationships through extended personal contact, shared experiential learning and structured experiences that intentionally evoke conversations over difficult topics. The process analysis in this chapter suggests an approach that could be used in research on similar initiatives.

## Peacebuilding

Peacebuilding is understood and practised in various ways. In some contexts its focus is on post-conflict reconciliation; in others peacebuilders intervene into continuing conflicts. Civil society groups that engage in peacebuilding frequently cite Lederach on theory and practice.[7] In his formulation, peace is not the absence of violent behaviour, but the presence of a just social order and respectful relations between former adversaries. As such, peacebuilding proceeds on two axes. One is vertical: peacebuilders side with the oppressed and work to transform the injustices that sustain conflict into more just social arrangements. The other axis is horizontal: peacebuilders bring together those who are in adversarial relations, so that they can build the human relationships that will transform the conflict. This dual-axis perspective is consistent with Megoran's point above that social justice and peace are inseparable. In a contrasting approach, peacebuilding, following Galtung's distinction between peacemaking, peacekeeping and peacebuilding,[8] has been incorporated into strategies of conflict reduction and conflict resolution. International agencies (for example, the UN and the World Bank) or world powers promote the transition from conflict to co-operation by advocating co-operative projects between adversarial groups, making financial resources available and directly or indirectly promoting personal contact between their members.[9] This perspective is more consistent with what Oliver Richmond calls the 'liberal peace'.[10] All approaches recognize that peacebuilding is emotionally difficult.

Environmental peacebuilding brings adversaries together around common environmental challenges.[11] Much has been written about the eastern Mediterranean as a region of severe and increasing environmental stress.[12] The eastern Mediterranean is poor in water and energy resources, with a rapidly growing population. Drought is severe and becoming more common. The loss of natural areas and widespread pollution have radically degraded rural areas, with a correspondingly diminished quality of life in ever more crowded cities. Species habitats are degraded, with decreasing biodiversity. The Mediterranean and the Red Sea are stressed marine environments. The literature on this regional environmental stress often promotes regional co-operation, which is consistent with the growth in transboundary environmental governance.[13]

Literature on regional environmental challenges, some of it presented at conferences at the Arava Institute or authored by its faculty members, typically focuses on shared problems and benefits of co-operation. There is less attention given to the emotional dimension of environmental peacebuilding. For example, *Water in the Middle East: A Geography of Peace*,[14] consists of expert analyses of water resources and negotiations. Environmental peacebuilding is treated as a rational process, brought to a successful conclusion by cost/benefit negotiations in which all parties get enough of what they want to be satisfied. Antagonistic politics inform the negotiations and make them harder, but in the end the high costs of continued antagonism will lead to an agreed, co-ordinated solution. This is an understandable approach among well educated experts who share a common culture of rational problem solving. When, however, antagonisms persist and intensify, the prospect of successful negotiations and co-ordinated action recedes, suggesting the importance of paying attention to the affective aspects of environmental peacebuilding. The interviews discussed in this chapter show that the experience of study at the Arava Institute is only partly about developing shared knowledge and exploring shared solutions: it is also about transforming adversarial relationships into empathic ones.

## Empathy

A focus on empathy complements the utilitarian aspect of peacebuilding – bringing adversaries together around a common problem and promoting co-operative work that is mutually beneficial[15] – with attention to affective dimensions. The concept of empathy, while subject to debate about its meaning, offers a way to understand the interplay of rationality and affect in these initiatives.

In both its common and scholarly uses, empathy refers to a quality people bring to social interaction. In its common use, empathy refers to some mix of *understanding* – putting oneself in the position of another, *sympathy* – sharing another's feelings or having a similar feeling in response to another's feelings, and *compassion* – feelings of wanting to help in response to another's distress. In academic literature, empathy is sometimes understood primarily as rational, as understanding another without necessarily feeling fellowship or compassion, and sometimes primarily as an emotional response of identifying with, and having compassion for, a fellow human being.

This chapter follows the scholarly work that presents empathy as a combination of understanding and affect.[16] Recent literature on empathy differs, however, in delineating where empathy is located. One perspective approaches empathy as a personality characteristic[17] developed in early childhood,[18] while another locates empathy as an element of cultural evolution.[19]

These differences over origin and location may be integrated by approaching empathy as a quality of *interaction*. People do vary. Individuals come to group activities with different degrees of empathic potential as a consequence of personality characteristics and prior social learning. Groups that cultivate empathy are conscious of the tension between formal and informal normative expectations that guide group activities versus cognitive understandings and behavioural expectations that people bring into the group. Formal design features and informally understood practices cultivate and elicit empathy. The interviews in this chapter speak to learning empathy as a skill, and growth in the capacity for empathic relationships.

Personal and collective narratives are relevant for this exploration of empathy.[20] Stories organize information and make it accessible. They typically contain a mix of information and emotion, a quality they share with empathy. People understand their lives by addressing the question: 'What story am I/are we in?' Stories are teleological, structured around beginnings, middles and ends. Because we are conscious of the teleological structure of narratives, they may assist agency. We can imagine where our story is headed and change our behaviour in order to get to a different ending. With respect to empathy, narratives can promote identification with an in-group in conflict with others, or promote identification with those who are different.

These considerations about narrative influenced our choice of methodology for this study of empathy at the Arava Institute. We supplement what we have learned previously about the structural features that provide emotional support for building peaceful relations by letting alumni tell their stories.

## The interviews

We conducted and transcribed 38 interviews with Arava Institute alumni, some lasting more than an hour. Our interest was in how alumni incorporated their experience at the institute into the narratives of their lives. Rather than enquire abstractly about 'empathy', we asked alumni to narrate the stories of their time at the institute and what it meant to them. Using an inductive approach[21] we coded for themes and identified narratives about the development of empathy. Our sample is neither comprehensive nor representatively random. We cannot give percentages of alumni who became more empathic. We can report that in our sample there are many stories of how empathic relationships developed.

Shared environmental concerns, on which the academic culture is based, and social design features of the institute, set the foundation for both affective and cognitive empathy. Friendly relations promote greater understanding, and both are intensified in a positive feedback loop. The interviews show the following temporal sequence:

- Motivations and preconceptions. People approach a setting in which they encounter those from hostile groups with a mix of hope and apprehension.
- First impressions/getting along. Initial contacts focus on the practical tasks of getting along in a new setting. Students at the institute have personal agendas of acquiring skills and building résumés. They typically do not seek out confrontations that take energy from these goals. Friendships develop and are a basis for more difficult conversations.
- Challenging behaviour. The conflict context of the situation inevitably evokes behaviours that challenge civil, practical getting along.
- Empathy-building strategies and responses. People in the situation respond to these challenges with individual and collective strategies. The organizational culture of the institute is designed to cultivate empathy. Students share in this organizational culture and enact it in their relationships.
- Expressing and sustaining empathy. People are able to articulate that they have become more empathic, both intellectually and emotionally. An alumni organisation maintains relationships

Interview quotations that appear below are illustrative of this process. The transcripts contain many similar quotations. Quotations and comments below are not meant to indicate uniformity of outlook or behaviour, but an analysis of variability is beyond the scope of what is possible in this chapter.

## Motivations and preconceptions

Students come to the Arava Institute both to study environmental issues and for contact with the 'enemy'. Quotations from Palestinian and Israelis students show their apprehension but also their perception that the Institute offers something unique.

I was introduced to…the Arava Institute for Environmental Studies, when I read a brochure at the Islamic University [in Gaza]. It was so weird to see a Jewish organization there. I decided to take that huge step and go eat with enemies, and live with enemies, and share water, food, and education with enemies. I was rejected in my society, because people were calling me a spy, and crazy, traitor, all this weird stuff, and friends just disappeared…because I deal with Israel. Even though I did not deal with Israel, I dealt with the Arava Institute, which is completely different [Palestinian man].

I came with hope and good will about bridging differences, even though I had a rough background from army service. I was in a combat unit, fighting Palestinians, including X [a student] now at the institute. We never met face to face, but knew from stories [Israeli man].

I have been part of/participated on many peacebuilding and co-operation programmes that I thought are not really worthy of my time anymore, because most of them really don't go deep enough to understand the conflict between the Palestinians and Israelis and to come up with co-operation that will benefit both…when I was interviewed by the Arava Institute, I wasn't really sure to do this all over again. I was more interested in the environmental aspect of it [Palestinian woman].

These are only examples of quite diverse motivations and preconceptions. The interviews show that students arrive with some uncertainty about what they are entering into, although they all know from the recruitment and interview process about the institute's objectives. Their expectations are filtered through their previous experiences and agendas that mix pragmatism and idealism.

## First impressions/getting along

Arriving at the institute, students typically do what other students do at residential universities. They settle in, look for friends and start to study.

To be honest with you…in the beginning I didn't care about the environment at all. My interest is to meet new people, and visit a new place.... In the beginning it was for fun, but then I learned a lot of things about the environment, and I learned about things that I wasn't willing to talk about or to deal with before [Jordanian man].

You are like in an aquarium so you develop friendships... friendships developed just by force of contact. You saw these people everyday.... People naturally grouped by affinity. Often that was cultural affinity although other interests brought people together [overseas woman].

I remember sitting up at night with my roommate, who was 7–8 years older than me, but her English was difficult so we read those texts together.... I shared a room with an Israeli woman who is still one of my close friends to this day [overseas woman].

Students from different backgrounds share rooms and suites. The quote below is typical of the amiable curiosity among roommates, and illustrates the use of English as a common, neutral language.

I had an American roommate and the third roommate was a Jordanian. I agree with this idea that you have international roommates in the same room because... the main language would be English. So we just speak English. The second thing would be the culture.... We learn about North American pastimes, Jordanian pastimes, Palestinian pastimes; by that we learn about each other's cultures and learn how each other thinks [Palestinian man].

Shared environmental concerns provide both emotional and cognitive connections between students. Environmentalism and emergent friendships set the stage for the development of empathic relationships when students deal with the continuing conflict.

## Challenging behaviour

The institute began after the Oslo Accords, in the spirit of creating post-conflict co-operation. The quick movement to an agreement anticipated in the mid-1990s did not happen. Hostilities persist, waxing and waning in intensity. Inevitably, Arava students have had to deal with the continuing conflict. The curriculum covers regional environmental issues, environmental policy and environmental ethics. However, because political and environmental issues intersect, difficult political topics surface in classes and student life.

While the institute is committed to peacebuilding, it is in Israel with mostly Israeli faculty. In some interviews, Arab students report frustration and arguments in classes that come from this context. These clashes in the classroom rarely lead to withdrawal from the programme and are taken seriously by instructors, but the comments show that political issues and the emotions around them cannot be kept out of academic discussion.

> We had many arguments in… [the water] course because some people from the Israeli side came who were arguing against the Palestinians, at the same time we were visiting all the Israeli water stations. We didn't visit the Palestinian ones at all. So the knowledge that was given on the Israeli side was more, and richer than what was given on the Palestinian side and the Arab side [Palestinian man].

In subsequent years, the institute reorganized the water trip to go to Israel, the West Bank and Jordan. There are, however, serious issues that are beyond the ability of the institute to change. The following quotation shows a protest when a guest lecturer refuses to engage Palestinian priorities:

> Once there was a guest talking about sustainable development in the West Bank between the Israelis and the Palestinians. Then I raised one of the main issues: that Palestinian people are suffering from the segregation wall. They said that they don't want to talk about the segregation wall. So why did we come! Why did we go to this course? We want to discuss many issues, and we are not going to discuss one of the main environmental issues… between Palestine and Israel! [Palestinian/Jordanian woman].

Emotional challenges in the classroom were not experienced by Arab students only, as the following quote indicates:

> [One] class was a mess. We had a lot of arguments, people walking out crying all the time…. There was just one moment where every Jew in the room felt extremely uncomfortable, no matter what their political background was, it was like a line that no one wanted to cross…. A comment compared the Israeli government to the Nazis. I think everyone in the room just kind of froze; there was a sense in the room of 'just don't go there'…. The facilitators put a stop to the discussion at that point, but there was no taking it back and there was no saying that it didn't make everyone uncomfortable. I know

that whenever you get a group full of Jews together there is a huge proportion of second and third generation holocaust survivors. It wasn't going to go away [overseas woman].

I don't remember any heated political discussions until Israeli Independence Day...suddenly all the Palestinians were wearing black and playing harsh music. We said – what is going on?...I was really naive. I was 19 years old. For me that was a shock, it was like these are my friends and they are so upset and everyone else is so happy, what is going on? [overseas woman].

In the years the unresolved conflict turned into widespread regional hostilities – the outbreak of the Second Intifada in 2000 or the Gaza incursion in 2008–9 – the challenge was particularly strong, but it was always there.

## Empathy-building strategies and responses

The institute was founded in a period where environmental peacebuild-ing could be seen as an aspect of an emerging post-conflict situation. It has adapted to the new situation of unresolved protracted conflict. As in many groups, staff intervene in public disputes between the stu-dents. One student said, 'tempers did flare and people yelled at each other, but the institute got us in groups and we talked about it' [over-seas male].

Indirect but powerful support for developing empathy comes from the institute's practical work. Students gradually develop interpersonal ties to each other and develop deepening empathic relationships, and in addition, the institute established a formal peacebuilding seminar programme. Our research identifies six key empathy-building strate-gies that the institute uses, which will be considered in this section.

The first strategy is to use Arab and Jewish 'Program Associates'. Older, more mature students, similar to university dons or housemas-ters, live in student residences. They are problem solvers, advisors and role models in a setting where academic study and the cultivation of empathy go together.

Secondly, the intimacy of a small group living together for months in an isolated setting – talking over meals, engaging in recreation activities and in small classes – is a major aspect of learning to understand each other and developing sympathy and trust. Empathy increases over time with a positive feedback loop in which closer emotional relationships foster more understanding, which in turn produces more emotional empathy.

> We were not always involved in politics. We were involved in environmental classes, homework and group discussions. If two people had an argument about a political point they would be in the same group in an environmental class and develop a friendship [Palestinian man].

> Plenty of times we used to talk in the evenings, like saying: now explain to me exactly how you see things. It was one on one; it was really about listening to what the other one thinks not what about what you think he thinks [Israeli woman].

Interpersonal trust is a foundation on which difficult conversations can take place and deepen both the cognitive and affective dimensions of empathy. The extended time together seems to matter for developing trust, friendship and a willingness to be empathic.

> At the beginning you feel that everyone is surrounded by his own world. You don't know who you are talking to, you don't know what you're getting, what reactions. After a while, the walls start to break down and then everyone is sleeping in the same bed [Palestinian woman].

> When people stop being politically correct, they know they are at ease, they know they can dare. It doesn't happen in the first semester. When you come back after a three week break [in December], you're happy to see everyone. You did not expect that three weeks before [overseas woman].

Relationships that developed at the institute occasionally led to invitations to visit each other's homes and families and, in at least one case, to be guests at the wedding of an Arava student. One interviewee described a home visit to Jordan:

> In the middle of the first semester, I took like twelve Israelis to my house. To my family it was a shock, but I did it on purpose. I just wanted to show…that you are not talking about an enemy, you are talking about people…. The Israelis came and understood my culture, they kissed my sisters, and helped my sisters. My family said the Israeli girls acted more normal than the American girl. They felt more close, you know [Jordanian man].

Another described a weekend visit to Israel.

> I invited several of the non-Israeli students to stay with us in
> Jerusalem.... We went sightseeing, visited the famous Ben Yehuda
> Midrahov, and even sat in a cafe. Several days or weeks later...a
> suicide attack in Jerusalem hit the same cafe where we were sitting
> just a few days earlier. That was a shocking moment to my Jordanian
> friend.... He could much more easily identify with the Israelis after
> he could relate to the location, the time and the place. He realized
> that had the attack been just a few days before, he could have been
> there too [Israeli man].

The third strategy cultivates empathy through fieldtrips and projects.
Since the institute brings students together in the Middle East, they
could see for themselves the settings in which other students and institute alumni lived.

> My roommate from Oregon – he can't avoid political discussions if
> he lives with a Palestinian. We had a lot of discussions.... He had his
> own ideas on the rights of Israel, the rights of the Jewish state. We
> talked a lot and I argued with him. He did not change until we went
> to Nablus, to Ramallah, around the wall. I think he changed when he
> saw how Israel acts towards Palestinians [Palestinian man].

> Travelling around, looking at the land was great. The water trip was
> great.... The Jordan trip was one of the moments – I was like, wow,
> we do a holy work here. We were at the restaurant and a bunch of
> alumni came to us and it was like everybody started dancing and kiss-
> ing and hugging; it was like wow [overseas woman].

Many students, sometimes with partners, used individual projects as
opportunities to expand their knowledge of the region, sometimes
learning about groups that are more like their own and sometimes
about groups that are quite different. A number of student projects
have explored the situation of Bedouin in Israel's southern arid Negev
region.

Fourthly, and closely connected to this, the projects, fieldtrips and
courses are often connected to institute research projects and environmental innovation. A faculty member does important research on dry
lands agriculture. The research division had a project on the local consequences of the proposed mega-project to link the Red Sea to the Dead
Sea, and has organized conferences with broad regional representation.

The Arava Power Company, which has opened a major solar field on kibbutz land, is closely connected to the institute.

Practical work sometimes becomes activism. Thus, for example, students and staff of the institute participated in the 2008 public protests against relocating the Eilat airport in an ecologically sensitive area, and in 2005 against building an ecologically intrusive superhighway.

Practical work develops students' skills and provides them with a sense of personal empowerment that enables them to go beyond being students and to be environmentalists, sometimes in quiet ways, sometimes as activists.

> The memories that I have are going out at dawn to the wastewater treatment facility as part of the wastewater management course, and checking which animal tracks were there. Just being out in nature. I'd have to clean up the tracks, and make it fresh, but nevertheless it was beautiful [overseas man].

> I was going to be an activist with tools once I left, and I did! It wasn't so much the coursework that helped me, though a lot of the practical stuff helped me, but it was largely the internships. We did a lot of internships or independent projects, and that gave me confidence. And when I went to [university] I was like 'Yeah, I can start a food security group!' I joined every environmental activist group at X University. I knew I could do it because I had already done it at the Arava Institute [overseas woman].

A fifth and crucial strategy involves both staff and students taking responsibility for restoring relations after difficult interactions. Sometimes extended conversations took place after someone was upset, often in a public way. Troubling things happened in class. Emotions varied, including anger and tears. Upsetting events also happened in informal settings. While teachers and staff were involved when students were upset, the students' response to each other mattered most of all for their developing relationships. The following story was independently told in interviews with two overseas students (A, B) from the same year:

> There was a party out on the grass. Someone put on Arab music really loud and there was a request to turn it off, so it was turned off. Twenty minutes later someone else came back and put on a different kind of music. Then an Arab student [threw the tape recorder and broke it with a crash.] (A). X [Arab student] said, 'You don't like us, you don't like our music.' I didn't see X like that before. The depression is too

deep for the Palestinians to ignore. At some point it comes up. [It was] obvious to everyone that we have to talk, there was too much tension in the air.... It was the right thing to do. Some people felt better. Each of us had some new things to think about. (B) There was a dinner and Arab music night organized by the Arab students where they cooked...an Arab meal, which was wonderful, and there was music and dancing. It was a gift to share their culture that way (A).

This incident, remembered slightly differently by the two overseas students, shows both the vulnerability of interpersonal peacebuilding to ruptures and the importance of the students' responses to each other. Students responded with personal reflection, talking to each other and taking steps to repair the threat to their relationships.

A final plank in the institute's cultivation of empathy is the Peacebuilding and Environmental Leadership Seminar (PELS). As it became clear that a period of continuing unresolved conflict was replacing the transition period envisaged by the Oslo Accords, the institute introduced PELS as a structured engagement with the challenge of peacebuilding during a continuing conflict. Attendance at weekly PELS meetings is required despite the fact that it is not a credit course. PELS includes guided discussions, workshops, guest lectures and fieldtrips, all with the aim, as described by the institute's website, of cultivating 'intercultural and interpersonal awareness and understanding', thereby building 'a supportive learning community that emphasizes reflection, self-knowledge, and cultural awareness'.[22] The following quotes are typical of the most common comments on PELS:

...three hours...in the week...you sit down and talk about the 'elephant in the room' that you try to ignore all the time.... When you take part in PELS you realize how students that you live next to and study with don't usually share the ideas that you have, they don't share your beliefs, and you have to, not defend, but at least show your point of view in a way that would get to their minds... when the PELS sessions are over, they will go back to their rooms, maybe go back to their communities in the future and think about what you said, and think about how what you said might be right or might be wrong, and how you can change the ideologies of the other people who have this narrow-minded thinking [Palestinian woman].

We used to get to the point where we are forced to talk about issues that are hard for Jordanians, Palestinians and Israelis to talk about, because in the setting of the programme...we all become friends.

So you might not want to talk about those issues with your friends, unless you are forced to. I think the main idea of the PELS was to force us to talk about the issues. Because, when we used to sit outside, we never talked about these issues. We were only enjoying the bubble that we were in, coexistence, harmony, and peace. But during the PELS sessions we had to talk about the conflict [Jordanian woman].

I found myself expressing myself with political views, being very clear about what I thought.... At the same time, I was listening, too. It's painful. Sometimes it feels like a waste of time because people won't change their minds, but afterward, I think the goal was not to change people's minds but to hear the other. Maybe not to accept it, because it goes against everything you've ever been told it is very hard. But at least you get to listen. People coming from different background, religions, countries, who have been told things, almost brainwashed for years, get to hear where I come from.... I realized how Arab identity is complicated [overseas woman].

Reports on PELS differ due to individual experience and cohort dynamics. Some interviews comment on problematic experiences in PELS sessions.

Israelis would say things that I consider outrageous and I typically would argue with them but when we were with Palestinians I didn't feel like it. Who am I to argue? They should argue... they are here to represent themselves. I can't defend them. They need to defend themselves. It would be wrong for me to step in.... But on the other hand the Palestinians didn't feel empowered enough to present their opinions and fight for what they believe in.... Jews kind of stepped back and let the Palestinians take the floor, and they didn't take the floor because there didn't feel empowered enough and so only the more right-wing Israelis would dominate the discussion and it would look like all Israelis agree with them, while in fact when we were in the small group it was a completely different dynamic [Israeli woman].

I felt really lonely. I didn't get any support from anyone, even my Jordanian friends in the programme at that time. They were staring at me, like they are telling me, 'X be silent.' I didn't like that, because I didn't go to get loved or to be liked from other people, I went there to tell the truth. In the first semester... they used to look at me like I am a terrorist, because of my thoughts. Actually I wasn't defending

Hamas as an organization, as a terrorist movement, I was trying to say that there is no difference between the Israeli Army and what they are doing to the Palestinians; like destroying their houses and killing their children, and what Hamas are doing to the Israelis. For me it is the same ... they told 'X there is a difference, the Israelis are not really killing, the Israelis are trying to defend their rights, they are trying to defend themselves', and so I was, 'OK Hamas is doing the same.'...One American student...told me 'X, you were very brave to raise these issues, you are the only one that is interested in this programme in the way you want to talk about peace.' This is peace, I didn't come to tell you 'take the land,' and 'it is for you'. We are all Palestinians, and I was angry all the time because they were telling us that we are Jordanian students. At the same time we are not, because all of us were originally Palestinians. My parents were raised in Palestine, and one day we are supposed to be there [in Palestine] [Jordanian-Palestinian woman].

PELS is one element of a multi-dimensional environmental peacebuilding programme. For many students it is an important, useful experience while others look back on it less favourably. Sometimes, what started in PELS in a way that was uncomfortable could be continued elsewhere.

I really appreciated the compassionate listening.[23] What I like the most is that it brings people together. It is...a chance for people to...see and hear each other in different ways....There is often continued conversation, and sometimes it's about really harsh things. Last semester...X was coming very much from a perspective of social justice and Palestinian rights, and another student was Israeli and served in the army. They...[had] these discussions back and forth after PELS sessions that were really...really emotional, and really good for both of them [Overseas woman].

Sometimes we continued the discussions, but when we continued the discussions that were opened in the PELS sessions, we continued in a way that we accept each other's opinions [Jordanian woman].

## Expressing and sustaining empathy

There was virtually universal agreement amongst alumni whom we interviewed that the experience of studying at the Arava Institute helped students to understand each other's point of view. For example:

Now I know what Israelis think about the conflict. Before I only knew what the government or the media think [Jordanian woman].

If you don't agree with somebody, to know how to put what you think is a fact aside and just try to listen....Everybody carries pain, and everybody's pain is legitimate, maybe you can work through that but first you have to understand where people come from [Israeli woman].

...to be a student at the Arava Institute...made me have a different perspective....I came to the point where I understand that everybody is right and there is nobody that is wrong. But you have different perspectives, different point of views....I can understand how Israelis think and understand how the Jews think. I can understand how the radical Muslims think. Without judging, but still I have my own points of view [Jordanian man].

Some of the students, Israelis and American Jews and some of the Arabs, were having a fight...the talk led to talking about the prophet Mohammad and the cartoons of the prophet Mohammad. They asked why I was so pissed off about it and then I started to explain why, as a Muslim, I was pissed off....It made me realize that from my background, I just know that those cartoons are bad, but from their background it's something normal. It is free speech. So I try to explain to them why, as a Muslim, I was mad. One student told me, 'Wow, you are mad like this, now I can understand why all the Muslims were mad...because I saw you, you who is so open, and you are pissed off, so I can understand' [Jordanian man].

The interviews contain many strong positive statements about the emotional impact of the institute. One Israeli said that the institute 'is like a lighthouse in a dark and roaring sea' and another said that after being at the institute, 'Nobody can take away my belief in peace.'

I was friends with Arabs and Jews. I did not feel segregated. I did not take part in [extended political] discussions because I don't like to. I think we hear enough about that in the media. We just became friends. We went to their houses. After the year I had Palestinian friends, I had Jordanian friends. They are people like the rest of us.

That was a very awakening experience. Before – my parents are Israelis and my family is from here – they were enemy, they were the others, and now, after that year, they are my friends [Israeli man].

The people I met changed my life. I have the privilege of... affecting their lives too. I think that the most important thing about the institute is the small things you do, just explaining your daily life and how you, like how do you survive; whether you're a Palestinian or Israeli or Jordanian, that really humanize the conflict that is happening between us and makes you want to do some change, some actual changes in your community [Palestinian woman].

... We go in with so much hatred for each other, and we leave, feeling sorry and feeling sad that we're not going to see each other every day [Palestinian man].

It is important to note that the institute does not see its task as completed by working with cohorts of students over four or eight months to develop more empathy towards each other. A key argument of this book is that peace is not an endpoint but a fragile process that is contextual.[24] In recognition of this, the institute fostered the creation of the Arava Alumni Peace and Environment Network (AAPEN). Although the interviews did not cover participation, AAPEN needs to be mentioned as part of the institute's evolving strategy. Founded in 2005 and run by alumni with staff support, AAPEN assists alumni networking. Its annual meetings – one hundred Middle Eastern alumni attended the meeting in Aqaba, Jordan in 2010 – make visible projects that alumni are involved with and allow them to share personal time. The institute's alumni director uses a variety of strategies – a Facebook page, small grants for alumni projects, networking – to maintain relationships after the intense residential experience. Peace is a process that can be quickly reversed, and thus needs continued attention. Future research to study the long-term impact of the institute's work and the alumni network will help understand its effects outside the context of the residential experience.

## Conclusion

Environmental education at the Arava Institute cultivates relationships. In a part of the world where other issues take priority over the severity of environmental challenges, the institute teaches about environmental problems and responses from a regional perspective and nurtures a net-work of alumni who share its outlook. The institute recruits in Israel, the Palestinian territories, Jordan and outside the region. Over four or eight months, and afterwards through the alumni network, the insti-tute works on relationships. Students live in mixed residences, share leisure time, work together in classes and on projects, take fieldtrips and participate in seminars that raise difficult political issues.

The interviews conducted for this chapter show the develop-ment of empathy through this process. Students come wanting to get something personal from the experience, not wanting to argue and be placed in difficult situations. While shared environmental challenges present an initial point of departure for personal and collective jour-neys, it is impossible to avoid the larger context of the continuing con-flict. Emotionally charged differences come out, sometimes in classes and during leisure time, but they are also intentionally evoked in the Peacebuilding and Environmental Leadership Seminar series (PELS). Challenging behaviours and the direct challenges of PELS interact with the gradual development of trust, understanding and friendship. Young people living together, each knowing in a personal way about the toll that conflict in the region exacts, develop the skills of listening to each other, explaining to each other, understanding each other and having sympathy for each other.

This study speaks to our understanding of empathy as a quality of interaction that can develop through social processes. At the institute, the rational and affective dimensions of empathy interact. The rational and affective act as a feedback loop, with emotional connections the first stage in the process. The greater the affective connection, the more openness to understanding there is. The more there is understanding, the greater the affective connection. Even though those who come to the institute are self-selected, and arguably more open to engaging with others than most people, they do not necessarily come empathic to people who represent opposing sides or viewpoints in the Arab-Israeli conflicts, or empathic in general. The interviews express apprecia-tion for the way in which the institute has fostered personal growth in empathy.

This study of the institute highlights the importance of mutuality – opening up to each other. Empathy would not grow if it were one sided. Mutuality begins with the gradual growth of trust that comes from such experiences as having roommates or project partners who are from adversarial groups. These personal relationships are carried into larger group processes, inhibiting rigid alliance formation along lines of group identity and expanding group willingness to be open to each other.

The institute's culture cultivates a way of being with each other in which it is possible to disagree, and disagree emotionally, yet still understand each other, work together, care about each other and be part of each other's lives. Students participate in this culture and actively shape it. It is a culture with its own internal tensions. On the one hand, this culture of empathy is not peace, and it is certainly hard to sustain this culture in a conflict zone. The institute and its alumni have been tested and challenged, and will be again. Periods of heightened violence, pain inflicted by governments or members of one group on the other, and enforced separation by legal means or social pressure all challenge a culture of empathy and promote polarization. On the other hand, this culture of empathy is grounded in awareness of severe, intensifying environmental stress in the eastern Mediterranean and the potential importance of a shared response. Shared environmentalism helps explain how the institute is different from groups that existed only for dialogue, that were consequently largely unsuccessful at cultivating empathy and thus were more vulnerable to collapse with the onset of the violence of the Second Intifada.

The literature on empathy cited above, and other similar sources, argue as well that empathy is grounded in human nature. Human nature has within it a selfish side, based on our personal needs, the pleasure we get from meeting them, the pain we feel when our needs go unmet, and competition for meeting needs. Human nature equally has an empathic, altruistic side, based on our need for reciprocal help, our need to receive and give affection, awareness of our embeddedness in the deep biological networks of children, parents, relatives and species, and our collective search for understanding and creating meaning in life. We find understanding of this potential for empathic relationships in Kant and other moral philosophers, in the existence of the 'Golden Rule' in many cultures, in the sociology of relationships, in the psychologies of human development, happiness and meaning, in the studies of everyday peaceful relations that Williams and McConnell describe, and in many cultures in the articulation of 'peace' along the lines described by Megoran.[25]

Shared or potentially shared environmental management, and the cultivation of a shared environmentalist culture, may be foci from which a 'geography of peace' can develop. Literature on environmental peacebuilding often comments on the goal of empathy. The view that properly managed shared space creates shared empathic relationships is common in proposals for peace parks on contested borders[26] and for shared management of water systems and other natural resources. Rifkin takes this view to the highest level of generality, arguing that the combination of contemporary communications media and growing awareness of a global environmental crisis is leading to an empathic biospheric consciousness.[27] These observations suggest the usefulness of research on the development of empathy when examining specific environmental peacebuilding initiatives.

Attending to the development of empathy complements another potential linkage of place to peace – work that links environmental security to human security.[28] This literature addresses the material dimension of peace by moving the concept of 'security' out of the domain of warfare into the domains of ecological balance and human welfare. Providing for ecological sustainability and human needs is foundational for the practical work of peacebuilding, as Simon Dalby argues in his contribution to this book. Empathy is similarly foundational to the emotional and process dimensions that link peacebuilding to human security.

Specific findings from this study suggest ways to develop the research agenda on environmental peacebuilding and empathy. The mix of strategies used by the Arava Institute to foster empathy may be found in other settings or replicable in other initiatives. The interviews indicate that the joint experience of border crossing – both spatially and socially (being face to face while going from place to place) – is an especially powerful contributor to empathy between members of adversarial groups. It may be significant for other environmental peacebuilding efforts that the Arava Institute brings people together in their own region and takes cross-border fieldtrips. Likewise, the future orientation of the institute, with its focus on shared solutions to serious common problems, is foundational to its emotional work. This study shows the importance of cultivating a culture of empathy when doing peacebuilding, and how the linkages between peacebuilding and empathy are experienced. It thus suggests an approach that could be fruitful in exploring the work of other, similar initiatives.

## Notes

1. Herzog, Shira and Hai, Avivit, *The Power of Possibility* (Berlin, 2005); Abu Zayyad, Ziad and Schenker, Hillel (eds), 'People-to-people: what went wrong and how to fix it?', *Palestine–Israel Journal of Politics, Economics, and Culture* 12/4 and 13/1 (2006). Retrieved 27 October 2011 from http://www.pij.org/current.php?id=40
2. Schoenfeld, Stuart, 'Environment and human security in the eastern Mediterranean: regional environmentalism in the reframing of Palestinian–Israeli–Jordanian relations', in P. H. Liotta, D. Mouat, J. Lancaster, B. Kepner and D. Smith (eds), *Achieving Environmental Security: Ecosystem Services and Human Welfare* (Amsterdam, 2010); Schoenfeld, Stuart, 'Nature knows no boundaries: notes toward a future history of regional environmentalism', in D. E. Orenstein, A. Tal and C. Miller (eds), *Between Ruin and Restoration: An Environmental History of Israel* (Pittsburgh, 2013); Schoenfeld, Stuart

and Rubin, Jonathan, 'Contrasting regional environmentalisms in the eastern Mediterranean: a social constructionist perspective', *L'Espace politique* 14 (2011). Retrieved 1 August 2011 from http://espacepolitique.revues.org/index1939; Harari, Nicole and Roseman, Jesse, *Environmental Peacebuilding Theory and Practice: A Case Study of the Good Water Neighbors Project and In Depth Analysis of the Wadi Fukin/Tzur Hadassah Communities* (Amman, Bethlehem and Tel Aviv, 2008)

3.  Megoran, Nick, 'War *and* peace? An agenda for peace research and practice in geography', *Political Geography* 30/4 (2011), pp. 178–89.
4.  Megoran: 'War *and* peace?', p. 182.
5.  Williams, Philippa and McConnell, Fiona, 'Critical geographies of peace', *Antipode* 43/4 (2011), pp. 927–31.
6.  Alleson, Ilan and Schoenfeld, Stuart, 'Environmental justice and peacebuilding in the Middle East', *Peace Review*, 19/3 (2007), pp. 371–9; Zohar, Asaf, Alleson, Ilan and Schoenfeld, Stuart, 'Environmental peacebuilding strategies in the Middle East: the case of the Arava Institute for Environmental Studies', *Peace and Conflict Review* 5/1 (2010). Retrieved 3 March 2011 (no page numbers on online version).
7.  Lederach, John P., *Preparing for Peace: Conflict Transformation Across Cultures* (Syracuse, 1995).
8.  Galtung, Johan, 'Three approaches to peace: peacekeeping, peacemaking and peacebuilding', in Johan Galtung, *Peace, War and Defense – Essays in Peace Research*, Volume II (Copenhagen, 1975b), pp. 282–304.
9.  Boutros-Ghali, Boutros, *An Agenda for Peace: Preventive Diplomacy, Peacemaking and Peacekeeping*, Document A/47/277 – S/241111, 17 June 1992 (New York, 1992). Retrieved 24 March 2011 from http://www.un.org/Docs/SG/agpeace.html
10. See introduction to this volume.
11. Carius, Alexander, *Environmental Peacebuilding: Cooperation as an Instrument of Crisis Prevention and Peacebuilding: Conditions for Success and Constraints* (Bonn, 2006); Conca, Ken and Wallace, Jennifer, 'Environment and peacebuilding in war-torn societies: lessons from the UN Environment Programme's experience with postconflict assessment', *Global Governance* 15/4 (2009), pp. 485–504; Halle, Silja (ed.), *From Conflict to Peacebuilding: The Role of Natural Resources and Environment* (Nairobi, 2009).
12. For sources, see Schoenfeld and Rubin: 'Contrasting regional environmentalisms in the eastern Mediterranean'.
13. Balsiger, Jorge and van der Veer, Stacy, 'Environmental governance and environmental problems', in R. A. Denemark (ed.), *International Studies Encyclopedia* 9 (Hoboken, 2010).
14. Amery, Hussein A. and Wolf, Aaron (eds), *Water in the Middle East: A Geography of Peace* (Austin, 2000).
15. Kelman, Herbert C., 'Interactive problem solving: changing political culture in the pursuit of conflict resolution', *Peace and Conflict: Journal of Peace Psychology*, 16/4 (2010), pp. 389–413.
16. Morrell, Michael E., *Empathy and Democracy: Feeling, Thinking, and Deliberation* (University Park, PA, 2010).
17. Baron-Cohen, Simon, *The Science of Evil: On Empathy and the Origins of Cruelty* (New York, 2011).
18. Goleman, Daniel, *Emotional Intelligence* (New York, 2006).
19. Rifkin, Jeremy, *The Empathic Civilization: The Race to Global Consciousness in a World in Crisis* (New York, 2009).

20. McAdams, Dan P., Josselson, Ruthellen, Lieblich, Amia (eds), *Identity and Story: Creating Self in Narrative* (Washington, DC, 2006).
21. Strauss, Anselm and Corbin, Juliet, *Basics of Qualitative Research: Grounded Theory Procedures and Techniques* (Newbury Park, 1990).
22. Taken from the institute's website, www.arava.org Retrieved 7 November 2011.
23. See Green, Leah, 'A short history of the compassionate listening project'. Retrieved 31 March 2011 from http://www.compassionatelistening.org/about/history
24. See chapter 1 of this volume.
25. Megoran, 'War *and* peace?'; Williams and McConnell, 'Critical geographies of peace'.
26. Ali, Saleem (ed.), *Peace Parks* (Boston, 2007).
27. Rifkin, *Empathic Civilization*.
28. Brauch, Hans Günter, Oswald Spring, Úrsula, Grin, John, Mesjasz, Czeslaw, Kameri-Mbote, Patricia, Chadha Behera, Navnita, Chourou, Béchir, and Krummenacher Heinz (eds), *Facing Global Environmental Change: Environmental, Human, Energy, Food, Health and Water Security Concepts* (Heidelberg, 2009); Liotta, Peter H., Mouat, David, Lancaster, Judith, Kepner, Bill and Smith, David (eds), *Achieving Environmental Security: Ecosystem Services and Human Welfare* (Amsterdam, 2010).

# 10

# Everyday peace, agency and legitimacy in north India

*Philippa Williams*

On Tuesday, 7 March 2006, just one week before the Hindu festival of Holi, the Indian city of Varanasi was the target of two terrorist attacks. The first bomb exploded in one of the city's most popular Hindu temples, the Sankat Mochan temple, as evening prayer was due to commence. Sixteen worshippers were killed immediately, and a further five subsequently died in hospital.[1] Two more people died fifteen minutes later in two further bomb blasts at the Varanasi Cantonment Railway Station, one near the enquiry office and another on platform 1 from which the express train was about to depart for New Delhi. In addition to the twenty-three people killed in the attacks, more than a hundred others were injured.[2] In the aftermath of the bomb blasts the city was gripped by an atmosphere of anticipated tension, which diffused across the state of Uttar Pradesh (UP) and New Delhi. Given India's precarious history concerning Hindu–Muslim relations, there were well-founded concerns that the attacks, which were widely assumed to be the work of Islamist activists, would precipitate retaliatory actions by right-wing Hindu groups.[3] The terrorist attacks had created a moment that was responded to in different ways by an array of actors in the days immediately following the blasts, including political leaders at the state and national level, the police administration, religious authorities, the Hindi and English media and city residents from all walks of life. The underlying question on everyone's minds was: Would the terrorist attacks instigate further violence, or would everyday peace be maintained?

Two to three days after the bomb blasts, and contrary to the fears and expectations of many, it was apparent that everyday peace would persist. It is within this context that my chapter discusses the events that influenced the active reproduction of inter-community peaceful relations. It might seem incongruous to emphasize the importance of understanding peace in the light of terrorist attacks on the city. On the contrary, that this incident of terrorism, arguably designed to destabilize everyday peace between Hindu and Muslim communities, did not result in inter-community violence, provides us with a valuable insight into the city's social world. The exogenous shock of the terrorist attacks effectively lifted the lid on everyday Hindu–Muslim relations in Varanasi.

By turning attention to everyday peace through this particular functional moment I attempt to make peace visible as a process. More specifically, I contend that to understand the (re)production of peace we must take into account the (differential) role of agency and the specific cultural political economies within which they are inspired, interpreted, and ultimately gain legitimacy, or not. The chapter draws on insights generated through qualitative fieldwork conducted during the days and weeks immediately after the attacks, as well as discussions with key informants over the next four years. The reconstruction of events is therefore told through the perspectives of residents, in an attempt to understand the meaning of peace within a situated context. The chapter proceeds first by introducing the Indian context, before outlining different theoretical approaches to the chapter's interlocking concerns of peace, agency and legitimacy. Second, I elucidate further upon the empirical findings concerning the interacting role of agency and narrative in the aftermath of the bomb blasts. In the third section I pay special attention to how the actions of local religious personalities were situated, and explore how legitimacy was forged, notably through the everyday economic transactions of the city's silk sari industry. The fourth part reflects upon the relationship between the reproduction of peace and the politics of citizenship. In concluding the chapter I open up discussion for thinking about the process of maintaining peace as transformative.

## Theorizing geographies of everyday peace and agency

The argument that geography has, to date, failed to examine adequately the meaning and realities of peace has been widely articulated.[4] The point I wish to build upon here is that whilst peace as a process and a practice is an inherently complex one, informed by a range of intersecting sites and scales, bodies and narratives, the role of agency deserves particular attention. Not least, because it is agency that may help to explain the intimate and often overlapping relationship between violence and nonviolence, war and peace. As Sara Koopman has recently asserted, there are many different kinds of peace(s) operating across different planes, as well as different ways of thinking about peace.[5] I focus here on 'everyday peace' in order to draw attention to the situated ways in which tensions are mediated and managed by various actors so that 'peace' as an ongoing process is sustained. In thinking about 'everyday peace', this chapter conceptualizes 'peace' as a variegated terrain which is constituted through, and informs, shifting cultural political economies. Whilst 'negative' conceptions of peace suggest that peace is a condition without, or after, politics I assert that peace as a process is in itself political, and implicated in the articulation and reproduction of power and inequality/difference.[6]

In order to situate agency in the context of everyday peace, I bring into dialogue three bodies of literature. First, I outline the contours of inter-disciplinary research on Hindu–Muslim relations in India. Second, I look to contemporary developments in critical international relations (IR) thinking which challenge the hegemony of peacebuilding as a top-down agenda, by calling for a shift towards incorporating 'the local' and the everyday as well as agency into conceptions of peace. Finally, I show how feminist geopolitical approaches not only attend to the local and subaltern perspectives, but also seek to foreground the ways in which connections and solidarities form across lines of apparent difference.

The aftermath of the terrorist attacks offers an interesting moment in which to examine how differences between Hindus and Muslims informed both associations and antipathy between these groups. Underpinning the atmosphere of anticipated inter-community tension, which shaped Varanasi life after the terrorist attacks, is a history of inter-community difference within postcolonial India. The partition of the Indian subcontinent in 1947 led to the creation of the secular, multicultural nation of India, with a sizeable majority Hindu population, and the 'Muslim state' of Pakistan. The act of partition was realized through months of intense material and rhetorical violence that took place across the Indian subcontinent, as India's Muslims and Pakistan's Hindus moved to be on the 'right' side of the border, and through this process the perception of religious difference became reified.[7] Ironically, more Muslims remained in India than settled in Pakistan, but as the largest religious minority they have experienced practices of discrimination within economic, educational and political life as well as physical violence since Indian independence.[8] Such realities have undermined their potential to fully realize their formal citizenship rights.[9] With the rise of popular Hindu nationalism during the mid-1980s to early 2000s, Hindu–Muslim 'riots' have taken place with increased intensity and frequency, more often in parts of urban north India.[10] Considerable academic labour has been devoted to the task of deconstructing India's apparent propensity to violence, and the conditions and causalities underpinning such events. The debate has been typically characterized by positions that conceptualize 'ethnic' violence as the normative narrative of inter-community relations, as an inevitable product of capitalist modernity and as the failed rationale of Indian secularism.[11] However, more recently, scholars have shifted their gaze away from such large-scale ideologies towards accounts that seek to uncover relational dynamics within civil society and political arenas. This work has begun to open up space for thinking about peace as a process that is constituted within and reproduced through the everyday, and is shaped by individual agencies and local contexts.[12]

In his analysis of the active components in the 'production of riots', Brass emphasizes the possibility that riots may be willed actions, concerted productions of thinking acting people.'[13] By studying the occurrence of riots, Brass necessarily focuses on the destructive capacity of agency. Indeed, scholars have highlighted the insidious activities of Hindu religious actors in encouraging anti-Muslim violence in the Gujarat riots in 2002.[14] However, it would be myopic to perceive religious actors as only capable of waging violence against the other.[15] To understand the dynamic production of peace, the performance of potentially destructive *and* constructive agencies must, therefore, be examined. Of course, agents do not operate in a vacuum: rather, their actions are enabled and constrained by the cultural political economies within which they are situated.[16] The question concerning which actors have the capacity to make a difference is also an important one. Stephen Wilkinson places the emphasis on India's politicians. He contends that national and state governments do possess the *ability* to prevent ethnic violence from occurring, but whether the *will* exists is a different matter, which depends on the electoral and party political landscape.[17] The potential for maintaining peace is contingent on political necessity, and in particular the capricious agency of politicians. As Wilkinson claims, even the staunchest anti-minority politicians have been known to reverse previous policy positions, lessen their anti-minority rhetoric, and even make trips to symbolic sites and shrines of the groups they formerly railed against, in order to generate party political support.[18]

Pursuing another line of argument, Ashutosh Varshney argues that the capacity for peace actually depends on the composition of civil society, rather than on governmental actions. What really matters are 'pre-existing local networks of civic engagement between the two communities'.[19] Strong institutional ties can act as a mechanism to prevent ethnic *conflict*, which is inevitable, from spiralling into ethnic *violence*, which is not. Conversely, in cities where such ties are limited, any provocation or misunderstanding has the potential to generate widespread disturbances. Whilst Varshney's thesis usefully advances understandings concerning the persistence of peace in some places and not others contingent on the make-up of local civil society, he fails to take into account how civil society may be characterized by structural inequalities which enable or inhibit the actions of individuals.

Scholarship in IR has also reflected a shift in perspective towards thinking more critically about the production of peace.[20] Whilst the peace studies arm of IR has long engaged with questions of peacemaking and peacebuilding, such scholarship has tended to focus on post-conflict settings and top-down agendas for securing peace, most recently that of 'liberal peace'. Oliver Richmond has been instrumental in leading the challenge against such normative narratives.[21] He contends that attention should be directed towards the everyday in order to fully comprehend and incorporate the role of situated agencies and local conceptions of peace within peacebuilding programmes. Richmond proposes the notion of 'hybrid' peace agendas, which integrate both 'bottom-up' and 'top-down' approaches.[22] In his research on peacebuilding in Tajikistan, John Heathershaw highlights the circulation of multiple narratives in the (re)production of peace which find expression across different scales. He distinguishes between the international rhetoric of 'peacebuilding', the elite notion of *mirostroitelstvo* (Russian: peacebuilding) and the popular *tinji* (Tajik: wellness/peacefulness) and suggests that different actors differentially draw upon these narratives in their everyday and institutional work towards maintaining peace.[23] However, by focusing on the narratives rather than the actors involved, little is actually revealed about what local agency looks like, and how the actions of some may acquire the legitimacy actively to maintain peace, whilst the actions of others may not. To put it another way: why do some actors act with peaceful intentions within some times and places, and not others?

In order to attend to questions of 'the local' and agency in the context of maintaining everyday peace, feminist geopolitical research proves particularly instructive. Such scholarship destabilizes the primacy afforded to geopolitical action and discourse, and foregrounds how the geopolitical is not only made manifest at the level of the body, household and community, but is also produced through the everyday and from the margins. To understand everyday peace, I find it productive to draw on two epistemologies which characterize feminist geopolitics and, above all, overcome the shortfalls in current approaches to conceptualizing peaceful relations in India. First, feminist geopolitics grounds politics in practice and in place, in a way that makes the experiences of the disenfranchised more visible.[24] Such exposure necessarily attends to matters of subaltern agency,[25] which may be situated within particular histories of violence and nonviolence.[26] These contextualized accounts are therefore important for understanding how agency may be differentially articulated and interpreted rather than simply enacted.[27] Second, as well as uncovering the politics of difference, feminist geopolitics has examined the connections and the conditions under which alliances are formed across scales.[28] Underlying these approaches is a concern that 'the political is not just about differences – either between people or between perspectives; it is also about the webs of power and social relationships that are the basis of connections'.[29] The knowledge that sometimes the presence of differences may underscore the formation of solidarities and connections will thus inform the interpretation of empirical realities concerning peaceful relations and practices outlined in the rest of this chapter.

## Making peace and agency visible

In this section, I examine the various activities and events that unfolded in the aftermath of the bomb blasts, paying special attention to how local people perceived the role of different actors in the explanations for the maintenance of peace.

The charismatic and widely respected Home Minister of the Congress-led United Progressive Alliance (UPA), Sonia Gandhi, visited Varanasi in the early hours of the morning following the attacks, thereby demonstrating a decisive move by the central government to attempt to prevent violence escalating in Varanasi or beyond. Besides demonstrating solidarity with victims of the blasts and their families, the central government strongly condemned the terrorist attacks and called for the maintenance of peace in the city. The political climate in Uttar Pradesh at the time undoubtedly contributed towards the UPA's swift action. The government had been recently accused of appeasing the Muslim community over their public objection to the publication of cartoons in Denmark depicting the Prophet Mohammad. In addition, protests by Muslim organizations against the visit of the US President had further exacerbated tensions. In this context, the Congress-led UPA was particularly sensitive to the possibility of a Hindu backlash and so immediately acted to minimize the potential space in which agents might capitalize on the situation and polarize communities along religious lines. The subsequent reactions by state level party political leaders reinforced the moderate message of the centre by also universally condemning the blasts and appealing for restraint and calm.

Politicians and local government may have been conspicuous actors following the terrorist attacks; however, the role of 'law and order' occupies an important place in the narrative of events by virtue of its initially low profile. Neither the Senior Superintendent of Police (SSP) nor the Deputy Magistrate (DM) was present in Varanasi at the time of the attacks. Some reports cite that the police arrived twenty minutes after the first bomb exploded at Sankat Mochan temple.[30] Under these circumstances, it was necessary for the temple administration, and arguably the public, to introduce their own strategies to manage the period after the attack. Following the attacks, police presence was heightened in the city, with security reinforced by the Provincial Armed Constabulary (PAC) forces at designated 'trouble spots' near Hindu and Muslim community boundaries. By 10 March 2006, there were no incidents of further violence reported anywhere in the district. Whilst the police were absent in co-ordinating the response immediately after the attacks, it is apparent that the high profile of the police and PAC in the following days, and their prompt reaction at the sign of trouble – for instance, in quickly dispersing a protest against the UP chief minister's visit with a police *lathi* (stick) charge – contributed to preventing the outbreak of further violence in Varanasi.

I return to explore Wilkinson's argument that a government's electoral interests will inform the nature of police action during a period of potential violence. The UP electorate is divided between four main parties.[31] Therefore, because of the narrow margin required to win the UP parliamentary seat, we might presume that the UP government needed to protect the Muslim minority and thereby secure its future popularity amongst this group. However, to what extent electoral calculations can be attributed to the prevention of violence is debatable, given that within the same state and the same electoral timeframe inter-religious violence was not prevented in Mau, Aligarh and Meerut in the months preceding Varanasi's bomb blasts.

This fact suggests the presence of other agencies operating outside the purview of government institutions that had an interest in preserving peace in Varanasi and possessed the legitimacy to act effectively. Although the Hindu nationalist and main national opposition party, the Bharatiya Janata Party (BJP), joined state parties in calling for calm, it did not hesitate to blame Pakistan and, by association, India's Muslim community. The intention of the party's leaders was to maximize the potential political profit gained by mobilizing supporters around the terrorist attacks. BJP chiefs announced the launch of twin 'national integration *yatras* [journeys]'.[32] Protests were conducted across the city, opposing the terrorist attacks and the failure of the state government to avert them. A BJP leader attempted to stage a *dharna* [peaceful sit-in protest] in the temple. Notably, these initiatives to politicize the Hindu community along religious lines failed to capture the public imagination and to inspire renewed support for the Hindu right-wing party.

If the BJP initiatives were designed to inculcate tensions between Hindus and Muslims for political gain, as they have successfully done in the past, why did such actions fail in this particular context?[33] Riots are produced by precipitating events, such as the killing of a politician, the theft of a religious idol, or an attack on a religious place of worship. 'One reaction then leads to another, generating a chain, which if not immediately contained will lead to a major conflagration.'[34] In this case, the terrorist attacks in Varanasi did precipitate reactions by the BJP and its supporters, stimulating the production of a first link in the chain. But subsequent links failed to materialize. Why sufficient momentum could not be generated to enact a second link in the chain demands several explanations. First, the BJP was struggling to unite its members following its defeat in the 2004 Lok Sabha elections. The political fatigue and infighting of party members, in association with a lack of clarity in its political direction, simply failed to inspire its electoral base. Even the announcement of the twin *rath yatras* was characterized by discord amongst party members disputing the timing and appropriateness of the strategy.[35]

Second, Brass suggests that when

> too deliberate an effort to create the conditions for a riot by an identifiable political party or organisation such as the BJP from which they stand to benefit becomes too 'transparent'…people do not want to be manipulated.[36]

This attitude was conveyed by my respondents. Not only were the actions of the BJP transparent, but there was a sense of fatigue towards their style of political mobilization. Moreover, that the BJP was trying to use terrorist attacks for their political capital was widely regarded to be inappropriate. In the first instance, people wanted to see *real* empathy from the politicians and *real* help for the victims and their families; instead, they were incensed by the blatant political opportunism demonstrated. The style of the terrorist attacks meant the perpetrators were not visible members of the local community. Although not confirmed at the time, they were widely believed to have been conducted by Islamic fundamentalists from outside India. One milkman told me:

> We think terrorists are to blame. We can't blame any special caste, because terrorists have no caste, we can't blame Muslim or Hindu or Christian. I only know that terrorists are responsible. Terrorism itself is a religion.

The clear differentiation made by Hindus I interviewed between terrorists and Muslims informs the other half of the explanation for why the BJP failed to inspire support around this issue. Central to their mobilization campaign is the threat of the Muslim 'other'; however, in this instance the 'other' was a terrorist, perceived as distinct from the local Muslim community. Both Hindus and Muslims were the possible targets of the attack at the Cantonment Railway Station, and both communities were similarly angered and saddened by the blasts. Concurrently, blame was not directed towards the local Muslim community. However, as discussed below, despite such testimonies Muslim informants did feel the weight of suspicion.

In this context, actions and narratives by city residents conveyed the belief that state agencies and formal political parties were best kept at a distance from everyday civil society, especially where there was potential for events to become politicized. When I explored the impact of the state on the lives of my respondents, they demonstrated an element of wizened cynicism towards the response of local and national government actors. It was evident that both the Hindu and Muslim communities in Varanasi did not rely on the local government and administration for guidance and support during this tense period, but instead looked to their own local communities. A printing press owner remarked how the 'administration and politicians didn't do anything [to maintain the peace]...it was the people who demonstrated their morality and humility not the politicians'. This opinion was corroborated by a local Hindu doctor, who explained: 'The community led the way and showed its strength, not the political leaders.'

This sense of distrust evidently extends beyond the contemporary state government to encompass feelings of frustration and scepticism towards the actions of politicians in general. Political parties have repeatedly failed to provide basic utilities in Varanasi, creating a very disappointed electorate. The common sentiment is that politicians act purely in their own interests to win votes, while the people are left to fend for themselves. In association with this disillusionment was a palpable desire for politics to be kept separate from everyday community relations. Interference by politicians and the police was believed to exacerbate tensions, and sometimes even to stimulate trouble, as a young Muslim weaver informed me:

If the administration wants to, they can create a riot like in 1992.... Then a nervous atmosphere was created and so there was a riot. But when it's left to the people, we don't want to riot, we never want to fight with each other.

In the days and weeks after the attacks two religious leaders in particular continuously came to the foreground of accounts as being instrumental in maintaining peace. These were the Chief Priest of the Sankat Mochan temple, or *mahant* as he is known, and a prominent young Muslim cleric who was the Mufti-e-Banaras and whom I refer to as the *mufti*.

## The importance of local actors, networks and legitimacy

The emphasis placed on the importance of actors operating 'outside' the state strikes a chord with research by Varshney on civil society and the production of peace.[37] However, where Varshney's argument emphasizes the value of inter-community ties in facilitating peace, my argument goes further. I suggest that it is not just the structure of civil society but also the actions of particular agents within it – which are both enabled and constrained by the particular cultural political economy – that are particularly crucial in explaining the preservation of everyday peace. Pre-existing inter-community ties of engagement alone may not have produced peace in the face of efforts by the BJP to exploit the situation for political gain. Rather, the strong leadership, underpinned by the *mahant's* religiously inclusive, secular approach was critical in this instance, especially given the apparent absence of police assistance directly after the attacks. The *mahant* and his colleagues led the response initiative. They were conscious that *aarti* (evening ritual prayer) should resume as soon as possible, thereby projecting the idea that life can and must continue as normal, not only within the temple but also within the city. The local and national media projected the temple's official message, which was one of peace, not anger or blame. These decisions were informed by an acute awareness that the nature of activities taking place at the temple could impact on the psyche of the wider Hindu community. Had the attack been construed as an assault on the whole Hindu community, this incident could easily have created the potential for a violent backlash against the city's Muslim residents.

The 'secular' agency of the *mahant* implicitly and explicitly countervailed attempts by the BJP to politicize the incident. On two notable occasions, he refused to acquiesce to the demands of a BJP leader. First, on the matter of staging the *dharna*, and second, following the visit by a Muslim lyricist to the temple, the BJP leader's insistence that the temple should be 'cleansed' with holy water from the nearby River Ganges. The *mahant's* firm rejection was a conscious decision to ensure that Hindu worship should not be confused with radical Hindu politics, as he made quite clear:

> We are all practising Hindus; we are not radical Hindus and so the temple is for worship... the radical Hindus, or radical Hindu parties,

are exploiting the sentiments and are not helping the process.... And if there is any practical problem with religious institutions, any problem created by the society today, they are not going to come to our rescue or help. They will suck the blood and go. That is what I feel.[38]

Whilst the constructive agency of the *mahant* certainly played an important role in minimizing potential violence and communicating a message of routine calm, it was the partnership he formed with the *mufti* that was most widely attributed to shaping the course of peace in the city.[39] The *mufti* and *mahant* were introduced by one of the *mahant's* sons in the days following the attacks to discuss how they could form a united public face in order to allay the possibility of a backlash by the Hindu right. In the days immediately after the attacks, the religious leaders gave interviews together on news programmes, voiced their collective sympathies in local newspapers and were photographed together in countless national and local publications. In a nation that is sensitive to its religious political differences, the image of a Hindu priest and Muslim cleric speaking on the same platform with one message is a very powerful one.

In a photograph that appeared in *Outlook*, a nation-wide current affairs magazine, the two men are sat on plastic chairs on the terrace outside the *mahant's* house. The *mufti* is to the left wearing a skull cap and keffiyeh, and the *mahant* is dressed in white kurta-pajamas. Both men look relaxed and to be enjoying each other's company. The strategic bringing together of bodies marked by their corporeal differences, in order to create spaces of peace, evokes some parallels with Koopman's research on peace accompaniment in Columbia.[40] There, she shows how less vulnerable US citizens move alongside more vulnerable Colombian peace activists to enable situated protection from armed groups. Here, however, it is imagined spaces for peace as inter-community solidarity, which gain legitimacy and circulate within the city and the Indian nation more generally.

What is interesting to ask here is why these two religious actors were able to capture the imaginations of city residents in appealing for continued inter-religious peace. Why did they become the subject of positive local attention and media coverage in a way that state and national level politicians did not? What granted them the legitimacy to act as effective peace brokers in this particular scenario?

The physical alignment of the *mufti* and *mahant* was reinforced by their common rhetoric. Both men appealed to shared imaginaries of 'Hindu–Muslim *bhaiachara* or brotherhood, which they rooted in the city's cultural and economic environments through reference to vernacular narratives of peace. The notion of *Ganga-jamuna Sankriti/tehzeeb* was widely evoked, and refers to the confluence of the River Ganges and River Jamuna in the region: the former is associated with Hindu rituals and the latter with Muslim connotations. More broadly this narrative referred to a history of cultural collaboration between Muslims and Hindus with regards to their artistic, literary and musical production in the region. Another narrative analogized their interwoven economic relationships to the tightly interlocked warp and weft threads that constitute silk fabric, the *tana-bana*. Muslim weavers and Hindu businessmen would routinely remark upon their inter-community relations, saying 'we are like *tana-bana*', a notion which extended beyond the industry itself to the wider city milieu.

Vernacular expressions of peaceful dynamics form an important part of this story, not least because they lent the *mufti* and *mahant* collective imaginations to appeal to, but they also placed the responsibility, and the possibility, for maintaining peace within the hands of ordinary city residents. The presence of everyday and associational civic engagements in Varanasi was a critical enabling factor. The silk sari industry is one of the city's largest employers and depends upon inter-community working relations. Muslims have typically comprised the majority of artisan weavers and labourers in the industry, whilst Hindus largely control the markets. The associational networks both created through, and critical for the success of, the silk sari industry provided the economic and social impetus for maintaining Hindu–Muslim peace. But they also constituted everyday spaces of Hindu–Muslim intimacy and provided the organizational relations and concurrent channels of communication through which tensions could be mediated. It is within this context that the *mufti* and *mahant* had access to, and were able to effectively appeal to, vernacular imaginaries of peace. Conversely, governmental actors on the whole were not regarded as legitimate 'peace keepers'. Instead, their actions were met with scepticism and they were seen as detached from, and unsympathetic to, the real concerns of Varanasi life, whether during periods of tension or not.


## Peace and the political: unequal citizens

As the previous section suggests, it is important not to view peace as a romantic condition in which equality and justice are realized by all. With this in mind, in the final section I reflect upon the uneven politics of maintaining everyday peace. As the largest religious minority within a majority Hindu nation, India's Muslims have been (rather paradoxically) central subjects in the project of nation building and (re)defining India's imagined and physical borders with the neighbouring 'Muslim' states of Pakistan and, to a lesser extent, Bangladesh. The provocative 'Muslim question' – 'Can a Muslim be an Indian?' – continues to gain traction in some sections of Indian society and the media, and Muslims experience pervasive discrimination within economic, educational and political spheres of everyday and institutional life.[41] In contemporary India, geopolitical narratives that came into circulation following the War on Terror have inflected local and national discourses that prominently construct Muslims as either 'terrorists' or 'victims'. In this context the notion of the Muslim as an equal Indian citizen is denied natural currency, and instead has to be repeatedly reaffirmed by Muslim individuals.

Given that the terrorist attacks were regarded as the work of Islamist activist groups, Varanasi's Muslims found themselves on the defensive, even despite the general sentiment voiced by Hindu informants that local Muslims were not to blame. Key Muslim informants imparted a sense of the expectations placed upon them and their community institutions to speak out against the attacks, or risk becoming aligned with a 'Muslim terrorist' agenda. Having been previously accused by the local media of harbouring Islamist terrorists, some of the *madrasas* (Islamic educational institutions) in the city took action to ensure transparency and greater communication within the wider city population. A former journalist and social activist took the initiative to co-ordinate the thinking of *madrasas* in Varanasi, which until then had acted much more autonomously. The 'Constitution of the Coordination Committee of Madrasas' was set up, and introduced stringent admission criteria and codes of conduct for its students, to prevent the admission of anti-national elements into Islamic institutions. In addition, regular classes aimed at developing patriotism amongst the students were introduced into the syllabus. On 10 April 2006 an inter-community faith workshop was held at Jamia Ismalia Madrasa to which Hindu, Sikh, Muslim and Christian leaders were invited to share a platform to discuss their shared understandings of peace and brotherhood.

Meanwhile, female activist academics made a formal enquiry to the *mufti* of Varanasi about the role of terrorism in Islam. In response he issued the first *fatwa* against terrorism in Islam, emphasizing the message that ordinary Indian Muslims were not aligned with the motivations and actions of Islamist terrorist groups. Muslim community leaders were also vocal in their calls for businesses across the Muslim *mohallas* (neighbourhoods) to participate in an immediate *bandh* (closure), which continued throughout 8 March 2006 in an effort to maintain and visibly demonstrate solidarity in the city. A weaver from Lalapura described how 'The *mufti* gave the call—he said you must all participate in the *bandh*. *Tan man dhan, lekar saamne aayein* [put all your effort into it].' Others, like the president of the Almeen Society of India, personally visited Muslim localities, urging people to co-operate in the *bandh* and maintain communal harmony.[42] These measures were variously aimed at reaffirming to the wider Varanasi public a sense of Muslim patriotism and a commitment to maintaining peaceful inter-community life. Thus, whilst it was apparent that Hindu groups and individuals beyond the immediate Sankat Mochan temple community were actively maintaining peaceful city relations, it was evident that the city's Muslims really bore the weight of responsibility concerning the maintenance of peace. Not only were Muslim terrorist groups blamed for the attack, but the city's Muslim inhabitants had the most to lose.[43]

Muslims in Varanasi have typically been hardest hit during periods of rioting in India, so during what was generally recognized as a phase of decline in the silk handloom business Muslim weavers and businessmen were particularly eager to ensure that violence did not result.[44] Increasing market competition from China following the 1996 Indian economic liberalization policies has progressively undercut the city's silk market. This, coupled with a growth in the power loom sector in Surat and Bangalore, and the changing demands of the market, has increasingly crippled the Varanasi weaver.[45] The situation has led to high unemployment and economic insecurity amongst the city's Muslim residents. Without undermining what was undoubtedly an expression of sympathy for the victims of the blasts, actions by the *mufti* and key individuals within the Muslim community should also be interpreted as conscientious strategies to demonstrate their community's solidarity and commitment to the nationalist project, and to appeal to the wider Hindu community that everyday peace could be maintained.

This clearly illustrates one of the main contentions both of this chapter and indeed the entire book: that the reproduction of peace is political. On the face of it, the actions taken by the *mahant* and the *mufti*, and the narratives of peace they drew upon, appeared to reflect wider practices of solidarity and tolerance between the city's Hindu and Muslim populations. However, I argue that such actions and rhetoric necessarily concealed patterns of inequality and relative vulnerability between their respective communities. The responsibility for maintaining peace rested largely with Muslim weavers and businessmen, who actively engaged in activities designed to deflect the potential finger of blame and to preserve good inter-community relations. I suggest that such actions represented forms of resilience, and also a degree of acceptance rather than resistance towards the uneven politics that characterize their experiences of Indian citizenship.

## Conclusions: peace and generative possibilities

This chapter has examined a range of responses that were articulated in the aftermath of the 2006 bomb blasts in Varanasi, north India, in an attempt to capture what peace as a process looks like. More specifically, I have highlighted the influential role that different agencies played in enabling the maintenance of everyday peace, and how agency is inevitably shaped and informed by the cultural political economy within which it is situated. In this scenario, I suggest that the actions and strategic partnership of the two key actors – the Hindu *mahant* and the Muslim *mufti* – were of paramount important in realizing the continuation of everyday peace in Varanasi. Their public relationship, bolstered by their common narratives of vernacular peace, helped to reinforce actual and imagined spaces of inter-community peace within the city.

However, I caution against the risk of romanticizing 'everyday peace' as a condition of blissful inter-community harmony and tolerance, enabling equal citizenship and justice for all. I suggest that precisely because the city's Muslim minority experienced patterns of increasing economic marginalization and pervasive discrimination within India's broader cultural political economy, the need to secure ongoing peace proved to be especially vital during this particular period. Moreover, the actions taken by different Muslim individuals and groups to disassociate themselves and the community from the perpetrators of the attacks functioned to reinscribe rather than contest their marginal citizenship status.

I wish to finish with a more positive observation: that the reproduction of peace may also, in some circumstances, represent a generative process: one that may create new possibilities and give rise to new formations. A month after the bomb blasts, Hindu and Muslim tension had once again arisen following a dispute between the two communities over the installation of a *Shiva linga* (religious statue) in a temple adjacent to a mosque in Hartirath, one of Varanasi's neighbourhoods. The local administration called on the *mahant* and the *mufti* to assist in mediating the tension.[46] The recognition by the police that these particular religious leaders had the potential to broker the peace is an interesting and important statement in the aftermath of the terrorist attacks. Indeed, when I talked with the *mufti* in the Madrasa Yatimkhana Mazharul-Uloom in 2011, five years after the terrorist attacks, it was apparent just how instrumental this period had been in shaping his public profile amongst the administration, politicians and Varanasi residents from all religious backgrounds. Local Muslim opinion may be divided about the *mufti's* religious politics, but all recognized that he now served an important role in representing the 'Muslim community' at the city-wide level and in protecting their collective interests during moments of perceived tension. The active work to maintain peace in the aftermath of the attacks had therefore given risen to new inter-community partnerships and lent a new legitimacy to certain personalities. However, whether such partnerships will continue to be cordial and whether such actors will always work towards peace remains to be seen, as agencies can be both constructive and destructive.

## Acknowledgements

The research for this chapter was enabled thanks to an ESRC doctoral fellowship. I am very grateful to Hemant Sarna, Pintu Tripathi and Pinku Pandey for their assistance with this research, and to the respondents and key informants with whom I spent time in Varanasi between 2006 and 2008. My thanks also to Bhaskar Vira for his constructive criticism on earlier versions, and to Fiona McConnell and Nick Megoran for their careful editing and suggestions.

## Notes

1. Kumar Singh, Binay, 'Blasts kill 16 in Varanasi, red alert sounded across India', *Times of India,* 8 March 2006. Retrieved 8 March 2006 from http://timesofindia. indiatimes.com/india/Blasts-kill-16-in-Varanasi-red-alert-sounded-across-India/ articleshow/1442293.cms.
2. Pradhan, Sharat, 'Ancient Varanasi keeps its peace, proves its mettle', *Combating Communalism* 7/114. Retrieved 18 March 2006 from http://www.sabrang.com/cc/ archive/2006/mar06/varanasi/media1.html.
3. Some media outlets suggest that a little known group called Lashkar-e Kahar/Qahab claimed responsibility for the attacks. For instance, see Bhatt, Sheela and Ahmad, Mukhtar, 'Little known group owns up to Varanasi blasts'. Rediff.com. 9 April 2006. Retrieved 2 April 2006 from http://ia.rediff.com/news/2006/mar/09varanasi.htm.
4. See the introduction to this volume.
5. Koopman, Sara, 'Let's take peace to pieces', *Political Geography* 30/4 (2011), pp. 193–4.
6. For a more expansive version of this argument see Williams: 'Reproducing everyday peace in north India: process, politics, and power', *Annals of the Association of American Geographers* (2013) 103/1, pp. 230–250.
7. For accounts of Partition violence see Khan, Yasmin, *The Great Partition: The Making of India and Pakistan* (New Haven, 2007); Pandey, Gyanendra, *Remembering Partition: Violence, Nationalism and History in India* (Cambridge, 2001).

8.  See Hasan, Mushirul, *Legacy of a Divided Nation: India's Muslims since Independence* (New Delhi, 2001).

9.  See Williams, Philippa 'An absent presence: experiences of the "welfare state" in an Indian Muslim mohalla', *Contemporary South Asia* 19/3 (2011), pp. 263–80.

10. For example, on the riots in Ayodhya (1991–2) see van der Veer, Peter, *Religious Nationalism: Hindus and Muslims in India* (Berkeley, 1994); in Mumbai (1993) see Hansen, Thomas Blom, *The Saffron Wave: Democracy and Hindu Nationalism in Modern India.* (Princeton, NJ, 1999) and *Wages of Violence: Naming and Identity in Postcolonial Bombay* (Princeton, NJ, 2001); and on the Gujarat riots (2002) see Varadarajan, Siddharth, *Gujarat: The Making of a Tragedy* (New Delhi, 2002).

11. For example, Nandy, Ashis, with Trivedy, Shika, Mayaram, Shail and Yagnik, Achyut, *Creating a Nationality: The Ramjanmabhumi Movement and Fear of the Self* (Delhi, 1995); Engineer, Ashgar Ali, *Lifting the Veil: Communal Violence and Communal Harmony in Contemporary India* (Bombay, 1995); Tambiah, Stanley, *Leveling Crowds: Ethnonationalist Conflicts and Collective Violence in South Asia* (Berkeley, 1995); Kakar, Sudhir, *The Colours of Violence: Cultural Identities* (Chicago, 1996).

12. For example, Varshney, Ashutosh, *Ethnic Conflict and Civic Life: Hindus and Muslims in India* (New Delhi, 2002); Brass, Paul, *The Production of Hindu–Muslim Violence in Contemporary India* (New Delhi, 2003); Wilkinson, Stephen I., *Votes and Violence: Electoral Competition and Communal Riots in India* (Cambridge, 2004).

13. Brass, *The Production of Hindu–Muslim Violence in Contemporary India*, p. 20.

14. Varadarajan, *Gujarat.*

15. Appleby, R. Scott, *The Ambivalence of the Sacred: Religion, Violence, and Reconciliation* (Oxford, 2000).

16. Radcliffe, Sarah, 'Latin American indigenous geographies of fear: living in the shadow of racism, lack of development, and anti-terror measures', *Annals Association of American Geographers* 97/2 (2007), pp. 385–97.

17. Wilkinson, *Votes and Violence.*

18. Wilkinson, *Votes and Violence*, p. 238.

19. Varshney, *Ethnic Conflict and Civic Life*, p. 9, emphasis in original.

20. For example, Richmond, Oliver, *The Transformation of Peace* (Basingstoke, 2005); Heathershaw, John, 'Tajikistan's virtual politics of Peace', *Europe–Asia Studies* 61/7 (2009), pp. 1315–36.

21. Richmond, *The Transformation of Peace.*

22. Richmond, Oliver, 'Becoming liberal, unbecoming liberalism: liberal–local hybridity via the everyday as a response to the paradoxes of liberal peacebuilding', *Journal of Intervention and Statebuilding* 3/3 (2009), pp. 324–34.

23. Heathershaw, John, 'Peacebuilding as practice: discourses from post-conflict Tajikistan', *International Peacekeeping* 14/2 (2008), pp. 219–23.

24. Koopman, 'Alter-geopolitics: other securities are happening', *Geoforum* 42/3 (2011), pp. 274–84.

25. Sharp, Joanne, 'Subaltern geopolitics: introduction', *Geoforum* 42/3 (2011), pp. 271–3.

26. Dowler, Lorraine and Sharp, Joanne, 'A feminist geopolitics?' *Space and Polity* 5/3 (2001), pp. 165–76; Abu-Lughod, Lila, 'The romance of resistance: tracing transformations of power through Bedouin women', *American Ethnologist* 17/1 (2008), pp. 41–55.

27. See Katz, Cindi, *Growing up Global: Economic Restructuring and Children's Everyday Lives* (Minneapolis, 2004).

28. Katz, *Growing up Global*; Koopman, Sara, 'Imperialism within: can the master's tools bring down empire?' *ACME* 7/2 (2008), pp. 283–307.

29. Staeheli, Lynn and Kofman, Eleanore, 'Mapping gender, making politics: feminist perspectives on political geography', in L. Staeheli, E. Kofman and L. Peake (eds), *Mapping Women, Making Politics: Towards Feminist Political Geographies* (London and New York, 2004), p. 6.

30. Roy, P. K., 'Terror in Temple Town', *Organiser*, 19 March 2006. Retrieved 16 October 2012 from http://organiser.org/archives/historic/dynamic/modulescf3e.html?name=Content&pa=showpage&pid=122&page=2.

31. Wilkinson, *Votes and Violence*.

32. Chatterjee, Mohua, 'Poll-bound UP to be centre of BJP yatras', *Times of India*, 10 March 2006. Retrieved 11 March 2006 from http://timesofindia.indiatimes.com/india/Poll-bound-UP-to-be-centre-of-BJP-yatras/articleshow/1444831.cms?.

33. In 1992 the BJP's *rath yatra* (chariot journey) proved to be a powerful instrument in mobilizing the electorate around the issue of the Babri mosque.

34. Brass, Paul, *Theft of an Idol. Text and Context in the Representation of Collective Violence* (Princeton, 1997), p. 257.

35. Mukerji, D., 'Popularity test ride: Advani's yatra has few supporters in the BJP', *Week*, 16 April 2006.

36. Brass, *Theft of an Idol*, p. 258.

37. Varshney, *Ethnic Conflict and Civic Life*.

38. Interview with Professor Veer Bhadra Mishra, Mahant of Sanket Mochan temple on 5 May 2006.

39. See also Gupta, Smita, 'The Benarasi weave: separated by religion but united by the spirit of Kashi this duo holds the peace in the holy town', *Outlook*, 27 March 2006. Retrieved 6 June 2006 from http://www.outlookindia.com/article.aspx?230673.

40. Koopman, 'Alter-geopolitics'.

41. See Pandey, Gyanendra, 'In defense of the fragment: writing about Hindu–Muslim riots', *India Today*, 37 (1992), pp. 27–55 and Sachar, Rajinder, 'Social, economic and educational status of the Muslim community of India', *Prime Minister's High Level Committee*, Government of India (New Delhi, 2006).

42. Pradhan, Sharat, 'Ancient Varanasi keeps its peace, proves its mettle'.

43. In the aftermath of the Gujarat riots in 2002, Heitmeyer also observed that the city's Muslims bore the responsibility to maintain peaceful inter-community relations. Heitmeyer, Carolyn, '"There is peace here": managing communal relations in a town in central Gujarat', *Journal of South Asian Development* 4/1 (2009), pp. 103–20.

44. During the riot in 1991, rich Muslims in Varanasi suffered the most (Engineer, *Lifting the Veil*, p. 205). See the study by Showeb which concludes that communal riots disturb the economic stability of the weavers' community in Varanasi: Showeb, Mohammad, *Silk Handloom Industry of Varanasi: A Study of Socio-economic Problems of Weavers* (Varanasi, 1994).

45. *The Economist*, 'Looming extinction', 8 January 2009. Retrieved on 11 January 2009 from http://www.economist.com/world/asia/displaystory.cfm?story_id=12906512.

46. *The Hindu*, 'Tension over installation of idol in Varanasi', *The Hindu*, 20 April 2006. Retrieved on 17 October 2012 from http://www.thehindu.com/todays-paper/tp-national/tension-over-installation-of-idol-in-varanasi/article3149897.ece?css=print.

# Migration and peace: the transnational activities of Bukharan Jews

*Nick Megoran*

In the spring of 1997 I was living in an ethnically Uzbek village on the outskirts of the Kyrgyzstani city of Osh, preparing to begin field research on the materialization of an international boundary in Central Asia's Ferghana Valley.[1] It was here that I became aware for the first time of the connections between Uzbekistan's leading singer, Sherali Juraev, and the Uzbekistani Jewish émigré community in Israel. I sat eating and drinking with a group of young men watching a bootlegged copy of a performance he gave at a wedding party in Israel. The wedding guests – Bukharan (Central Asian) Jews – were conspicuously displaying their wealth by showering him with money, to the studied interest of the Uzbeks watching the video with me. As anti-Semitic sentiment is not uncommon in the region, I was intrigued at my Muslim Uzbek friends being so enthralled by a Jewish wedding in Israel. This chapter explains how it was that Sherali Juraev (who is Muslim) came to perform at that wedding, and suggests that the agenda for a geography of peace can be widened by exploring how human mobility can promote better understanding between human groups where there have been histories of tension, mistrust and disdain.

I will illustrate this by considering one of the traditional staples of geographical enquiry – migration. Migration is a topic that has moved increasingly to the forefront of political geography, with the greater securitization of border controls and movements post-September 2001. States frequently understand migration as a source of social tension and a threat to national security, and even political geographers who contest this operate on a terrain of debate that is effectively set by those who see migration as a problem. Therefore it is important to ask how migration can also be productive of more peaceful and mutually enriching human coexistence.

The particular form of migration that is the focus of this chapter is transnationalism. Transnationalism is characterized by ongoing movement between two or more sites. Following a brief discussion of this literature, the chapter will look at how the transnational activities of the Uzbekistani–Israeli Bukharan Jewish billionaire, Lev Leviev, facilitated the visits of Sherali Juraev to Israel, and how these visits contributed towards the development of Juraev's sense of his musical vocation as one of promoting understanding and sympathy between human groups whose inter-relations are marked by hostility or mistrust. The material is based on an extended interview with Juraev in 2004, fleshed out with ethnographic research on Bukharan Jews in the Uzbekistani cities of Tashkent in Bukhara during two field research trips in the same year. This chapter builds on recent work that emphasizes the agency of elite actors in producing geographical imaginations,[2] and in acting to defuse and de-escalate potentially lethal tensions.[3]

## Geography, peace and migration

There is an emerging interest within geography in general, and political geography in particular, on peace. This marks itself out from the oppositional stance of 1990s critical geopolitics to classical and neo-classical geopolitics, and the copious geographical studies of war that have been produced since 2001. Derek Gregory's 2009 plenary lecture at the Royal Geographical Society – Institute of British Geographers' annual conference is a case in point: although entitled 'War and peace', it was almost solely about war, with little to say on peace.[4] Emerging geographies of peace rather spotlight how conflicts are avoided or de-escalated, and how everyday coexistence belies accounts of social relations in particular places as indelibly hostile and fractious.[5]

In this chapter, I extend these discussions to consider a topic that has thus far received little investigation within the emerging geographies of peace literature – migration. As a political geographer, I surveyed (with Fiona McConnell) a decade of the two leading subdisciplinary journals, *Political Geography* and *Geopolitics*, from 2000 until 2009. We noted when and how migration was handled, either in passing or as the focus of articles. Despite a reasonable number of articles, and one special issue on migration in each journal during this period, the dominant theme of most articles was how the discursive presentation or regulation of migration and other mobilities reinforced difference,[6] entrenched class privilege[7] in new forms of neoliberalism,[8] or underwrote oppressive state control of territory in a way that was hostile to outsiders[9] and often as part of a broader, militarized geopolitical agenda.[10]

Certainly, writers were critical of these processes – and rightly so, in my opinion. Geographers have a responsibility to understand and challenge the ways in which geographical controls of movement are used to define political communities and thereby protect the privileges of some at the economic or cultural expense of others. However, it is striking that whether for or against the politicization and securitization of migration controls, the terrain of debate is effectively set by those who see migration as a problem.

A rare exception is Lynn Staeheli's 2008 short essay in *Geopolitics*, 'Migration, civilisational thinking, and the possibility of democracy'.[11] Staeheli posits the idea of immigrants as 'super citizens' who can help host communities in the West to reflect on the positive and negative qualities of actually existing democracies, if we are willing to listen to their stories and experiences. In this approach, Staeheli can be placed within a long tradition of thinkers and activists who invoke migration as positively beneficial for human society. For example, the economist Nigel Harris argues that the freedom to move within and between countries is a necessary counterpart of the 'right to work', and a properly liberal approach to poverty reduction and wealth creation is to abolish migration controls.[12] From a different perspective, that of multiculturalism, activist Teresa Hayter argues that consigning migration controls 'to the dustbin of history' could 'make the world a more harmonious and peaceful and less racist place, and make possible cooperation and democracy and greater mutual understanding worldwide'.[13]

I argue that in order to draw the geographical study of (international) migration into recent debates within the discipline about 'peace', it would be productive to consider how movement can benefit both sending and receiving communities and promote greater understanding and mutual acceptance between migrants and host societies. Staeheli's focus is thus an important correction to the geographical focus on critiquing the securitization of boundaries. However, that it is a short think-piece, only underlines the lack of research attention to the transformative possibilities of migration.

One geographical article that refuses to remain in the terrain set by actors hostile to migration is Jonathan Darling's study of Sheffield's asylum politics (see the following chapter).[14] He considers how a broad-based activist network had Sheffield declared a 'city of sanctuary' for refugees, and sought to weave a politics of hospitality into the fabric of the city. This network tried to re-cast the image of Sheffield to one as a welcoming place, and to educate the local population about the contributions refugees had made to UK national life. Darling suggests that this can be understood as relational politics: distance, ethics, responsibility, and how the arrival of refugees can be seen as a positive opportunity to re-make destination places and communities. I suggest that more research of this kind is necessary to develop a broad political geographical contribution to peace, and to resist the discussion of migration in terms set down by those who are scared by or hostile to it, even if only in opposing this agenda.

## Transnationalism

This chapter travels along the direction pointed by Darling's work, but is located within debates about one particular form of migration: 'transnationalism'. Although the term continues to generate substantial definitional debate, as Faist puts it: whenever we talk about transnationalism 'we usually refer to sustained ties of persons, networks, and organizations across the borders across multiple nation-states, ranging from little to highly institutionalized forms'.[15] Older models of migration assumed that migrants would largely assimilate, or that they would form 'diasporas' that maintained links with co-ethnics elsewhere but were themselves largely stationery. Transnationalism literature highlights the numerous ways in which linkages are more intense, and 'generally underscores the fact that large numbers of people now live in social worlds that are stretched between, or located in, physical places and communities in two or more nation-states'.[16]

A major topic of interest to scholars of transnationalism, drawing on and sometimes merging with the tradition of diaspora studies,[17] is that of the effects of transnationalism on identity. As Vertovec observes, identity 'has long been one of the slipperiest concepts in the social scientist's lexicon', but it is nonetheless useful in being suggestive of ways in which people conceive of themselves and are characterized by others.[18] For instance, in an insightful study, Vasile shows how transnational processes linking Tunisia with France transformed the identities of those moving and their families, effecting understandings of religion, class and gender.[19] Vasile's work, like that of Kong's study of transnational Singaporean migrants,[20] is an example of how geography's more explicitly spatialized analysis is able to connect processes at different scales.[21]

These texts assume that the self-understandings and cultural practices of transnational migrants themselves will be transformed by their migratory experiences; but they rarely consider whether transnationalism will have a concomitant effect on the other communities with whom they come into contact. Using the example of Lev Leviev and

Sherali Juraev, the remainder of this chapter will demonstrate that this can be the case, and that such effects can promote better understanding between groups whose inter-relationships are often marked by hostility or mistrust.

## Bukharan Jewry: historical background

Bukharan Jews are a Judaeo-Persian speaking diaspora who use Sephardic rites in worship.[22] When Jews reached Central Asia is a moot point. Shterenshis speculates that they might first have come with the armies of Alexander,[23] whilst Datkhayev suggests that the basis of the present community was laid in the ninth and tenth centuries.[24] Gitelman holds that whilst Jews appeared in Central Asia in ancient times, contemporary Bukharan Jews date to a fourteenth-century in-migration.[25] It is likely that Bukharan Jews became connected more closely to the Sephardic stream of world Jewry in the eighteenth century.[26] Whatever their provenance, the longstanding existence of Bukharan Jewish communities in what is present-day Uzbekistan and neighbouring states, and their concentration in the city of Bukhara itself, is in some ways a remarkable fact. This is especially the case given the disappearance of so many non-Muslim communities in the region, such as the Christian Assyrians,[27] following the Muslim conquest of the region by Arab armies in the seventh and eight centuries.[28]

Jews have played prominent roles as transnational actors in the post-Soviet period. Gidwitz reckons that 'several thousand' Soviet or post-Soviet era Jewish émigrés from the USSR have become transnationals, which she defines as maintaining residences in one of the successor states as well as in Israel or a Western country. She argues that '[T]heir knowledge of the ex-USSR, combined with skills and experience in countries of migration, have facilitated their entry into international trade involving their former homeland... they remain a presence in post-Soviet foreign trade'.[29]

There are two main reasons why Bukharan Jews have been able to emerge as important transnational actors. The first is the pre-existing diaspora of Bukharans in Israel, whose modern links to the land of Palestine date to the late nineteenth century. The impact that Zionism had on Bukharan Jews in that period is disputed. Dymshits argues that it was minimal,[30] whereas Elazar claims that it took root easily after its introduction from 1860 by Ashkenazi businessmen and soldiers.[31] Whatever the case may be, between 1880 and 1914 some 1,500 Bukharans (an estimated one-eighth of their total population), emigrated to Palestine. They settled a Bukharan neighbourhood in Jerusalem, established a religious school, and created a literary version of their language and a publishing infrastructure. This meant that links intensified between Bukharans and Sephardis, as young men went from Central Asia to study in Sephardic *yeshivas*.[32]

These connections were ruptured with the formation of the Soviet Union. The story of the Soviet Union's shifting attitude to Jews, and later to the state of Israel, is complex. Tsarist Russia was marked by an anti-Semitism that meant Jews in Central Asia were subject to varying restrictions on where they could or could not live.[33] The Bolshevik conquest in 1920 led many wealthy Jews to flee Bukhara to Afghanistan, and thence on to Turkey, Britain, the USA and elsewhere. The early Soviet period saw the regime reject Tsarist anti-Semitism, enabling a flowering of Jewish culture with publications, theatres, museums and schools.[34] This came to an end with Stalin's purges of 1938, when Jewish schools throughout the Union were closed and contact with Jews outside the USSR was criminalized. The USSR quickly recognized the state of Israel in 1948, and an Israeli embassy was opened the same year. Ties were broken by Stalin one month before his death in 1953, then re-opened the same year, and broken again by the Soviet authorities in June 1967 due to the Six Day War.[35] Gitelman claims that between the early 1970s and the 1980s 15,000 Jews had left Central Asia for Israel, which he puts down to rising tensions with Muslims who increasingly associated them with Israel post-1967.[36] The 1971 Soviet–American détente facilitated this exodus, as immigration became part of international agendas in US-USSR relations. However, the freedom to emigrate was curtailed with the advent of the Second Cold War and the breakdown of US–Soviet relations following Soviet intervention in Afghanistan in 1980. However, the Soviet economic crisis of the 1980s, and the increased ability to emigrate ushered in with Gorbachev's policy of *glasnost*, precipitated a large exodus of Bukharan Jews to Israel and thence the USA. Thus in the period of Russian rule of Central Asia a substantial Bukharan diaspora established itself in Palestine.

The second factor enabling Bukharan Jews to establish themselves as transnational actors has been the policies of President Islam Karimov's government of Uzbekistan since the independence of the republic in 1991. Shterenshis claims that the end of the Soviet Union has led to the virtual disappearance of anti-Semitism from Uzbekistan. He observes that Israel was the third country, after the USSR and Turkey, to recognize the independence of Uzbekistan, and good diplomatic and economic ties have been fostered by Islam Karimov. For example, Karimov

allowed the re-opening of a Jewish school in Bukhara, supported finan-
cially by Israel.[37] Although Shterenshis correctly identifies the sympathetic position of the Uzbek government to Jews, his conclusion is
arguably too sanguine in that it concentrates only on state policy and
does not take account of more widespread anti-Israeli and anti-Jewish
prejudice. For example, in 2004 the Israeli embassy in Tashkent was
bombed by unknown assailants. Less spectacularly, I have frequently
encountered anti-Semitic views in Uzbekistan, including 'blood libel'
accusations that Uzbekistan's Jews kill Muslim children to use their
blood in secret rituals. Dymshits claims that as Uzbekistan moved to
sovereignty, a 'pogrom' against Jews in the Uzbekistani city of Andijon –
Sherali Juraev's native town – acted as a major catalyst for increased
Bukharan Jewish emigration.[38] It may thus be fair to say that while anti-
Semitism has historically been evident amongst some sections of the
Uzbek population, the government of the country has adopted a pro-
Jewish and pro-Israel stance, pursuing good relations and close eco-
nomic ties with Israel and protecting its own Jewish population.

Therefore the late Tsarist and Soviet-era development of a Bukharan
diaspora in Israel/Palestine, and the liberal position of the Uzbekistani
government towards Jews and Israel, has created the conditions for the
development by Bukharan Jews of transnational links between Israel
and Uzbekistan. For example, in 2004, when conducting ethnographic
research in Bukhara, I spoke to two local Jewish businessmen with
close links to Israel, who were building *kosher* hotels to cater for Jewish
tourism to the city.

The most prominent of these Bukharan Jewish transnational actors
is Lev Leviev, one of Israel's richest citizens, whose family emigrated
from Tashkent when he was a teenager. *Forbes* lists him as the world's
278th richest man, a billionaire who 'cuts and polishes more diamonds
than anyone else in the world'.[39] His investments also include toll
roads, swimsuit manufacturers, the leisure industry, property, chemicals
and sport.

He has used his fortune to fund many post-Soviet Jewish organizations and institutions. Through his organization Ob Avner, set up in
1993, he provides financial support to community rabbis, and to day
schools and youth clubs throughout the former USSR and particularly
in Uzbekistan.[40] He is a supporter of the Chabad-Lubavitch, a stream
of orthodox Jewry that emphasizes, amongst other things, conver-
sion to a devout Jewish lifestyle. Both his business and religious dealings have been controversial, from his mining investments in Angola
to his attempts to open Israel's first private prison, a move that was
blocked by the Israeli High Court of Justice.[41] He is also committed to

the building of settlements in occupied Palestinian territory. For example, in 2005 his Africa-Israel company completed a controversial $230-million 5,800 apartment project for the Haredi sector in Modi'in Illit in the West Bank.[42] Such activities have sparked many protests, including a successful campaign in Britain (where he maintains a home) to prevent the UK government from renting its Tel Aviv property from his company.[43] Nonetheless Leviev was constantly referred to with admiration by Jews in Bukhara and Tashkent with whom I spoke during my research and his transnational activities will play a significant role in this chapter. And it was Leviev who was responsible for first bringing Sherali Juraev to Israel, as the next section explains.

## Sherali Juraev

Sherali Juraev, known simply to the country as 'Sherali', is arguably Uzbekistan's best known singer in the Uzbek classical tradition and a significant figure in the cultural life of the republic.[44] His social importance is not simply a product of the fame and respect that he has earned, but is also due to the controversial political roles that he has at times developed. His scepticism of the Soviet system brought him into disfavour before 1991.[45] After independence his espousal of a putative classical Uzbek musical tradition meant that he was feted by politicians. Adams observes that his eloquent performance of a patriotic song by poet Abdulla Oripov, calling on Uzbeks to be aware of the greatness of their historical legacy, 'stole the show' at a 1996 state-sponsored concert of patriotic music as part of the government's building of an ideology of national identity.[46] He even accompanied Uzbekistan's President Karimov on a trip to Mecca, although this relationship was not sustained over time.

As indicated above, I first became aware of his contact with Uzbekistan's Jews after watching a bootlegged copy of a concert he gave in Israel that was being watched in a rural home in 1997. Somewhere between the years 2002 and 2004 (the cassette is undated), he released a commercially produced video entitled *O'zbegim* ('My Uzbek [people]'), of another concert performance in Israel. The blurb on the back of the video jacket begins:

> Beautiful songs and music which bring peace and pleasure to the soul do not discriminate on the basis of nationality. People in every corner of the world will love to listen to them. Out of His love, beauty, purity, mercy and wisdom our gracious God created the parents of

humanity, Adam and Eve. Therefore we all have the same origin and share the same kin... Sherali Juraev's music draws nations, peoples, and ethnic groups together.[47]

When I first read this, I immediately dismissed it as the type of meaningless 'Friendship of the Peoples' Soviet discourse. This Brezhnev-era slogan imagined the Soviet Union as bringing its multiple nations together in harmony to build socialism.[48] 'Friendship of the peoples'-type language has remained fashionable in certain successor states, such as Uzbekistan and Kyrgyzstan, to promote the idea of minorities living happily within the new national polity.[49] Yet such slogans often conceal(ed) rampant nationalism and the systematic disadvantage of ethnic minorities. Thus Tohfaxan, a Bukharan Jewish musician regarded as one the greatest *sazandas* (female wedding singers) of her time, quit newly independent Uzbekistan for the USA, citing the injustice of a system that differentiated between an Uzbek and a Jew when it came to awarding recognition.[50] In her study of Soviet evacuees to Uzbekistan during the Second World War, Manley shows that although Jews were formally warmly welcomed under the 'Friendship of the Peoples' banner, '[e]xpressions of anti-Semitism, manifest across the country, underscore just how precarious the Friendship of the Peoples really was'.[51]

Nonetheless, in spite of initially dismissing this, I was fascinated that Israel's Uzbekistani diaspora had brought a Muslim singer to Israel at a time of fraught Arab–Jewish relations (the Second Intifada). This led to me to contact the singer at his home in Uzbekistan's capital city Tashkent and to seek an interview. The material for the remainder of this chapter is drawn from an extended (three hour) interview with Sherali Juraev. As such, it is limited in that the claims in the material are uncorroborated with other potential actors, such as his Jewish hosts in Israel, the company that produced the videos of his concerts for sale, or the Uzbek government officials responsible for regulating the popular music industry and the political content of its productions.[52] Without ignoring this shortcoming, the interview nonetheless is valuable insofar as it offers an insight into an important Uzbekistani cultural leader's self-presentation and first-person narrative of negotiating inter-ethnic and inter-religious relations, and of how the dynamic coexistence of 'everyday peace' is produced. In being open about many extraordinary incidents in his personal spiritual journey, he told me that these were stories he had not vouchsafed to many people before. I think that my positionality as an Uzbek-speaker broadly sympathetic to, and sharing, his theistic worldview facilitated this openness to some extent.

Following an introduction by an Uzbek scholar of musicology, on Thursday 4 November 2004 I was invited to Sherali's home for *iftar*, the evening meal breaking the Ramadan fast. The guests assembled for a splendid feast were composed of many notables from Tashkent society, including a senior figure from the local Islamic clerisy who was dressed in very fine robes. Probably because it was known that I was interested in Sherali's Israel visits, the conversation turned towards Judaism and the relationship between Islam and other religions. Sherali recounted that some Jews had visited his home to invite him to Israel, but would not eat the food that he had especially prepared because they regarded it as ceremonially unclean. The senior cleric took this as evidence of how believers of other religions, especially Jews, were mistaken in their beliefs and practices, which were inferior to those of Islam. Displaying no little arrogance, he held forth on these themes.

After the cleric and the other guests had left, Sherali invited me and his son to sit next to him at the high table vacated by more important guests. We talked for many hours about music, politics, religion, Jews, Israel and his life and work, and he played a small number of songs for me as we discussed his work. The kitschiness of the bootlegged and commercially released videos that I had seen had led me to assume, sceptically, that they were simply commercial enterprises with meaningless Soviet-style slogans added to the video jacket, words that were undermined by the tone and contents of the dinner discussion that I had witnessed. I could not have been more wrong: Sherali's transnational engagement with Jews and Israel has been deeply spiritual and radically transformative of his understanding of Muslim–Jewish relations.

Sherali explained how he first came to visit Israel for a wedding in the mid-1990s (I did not record the date, but he confirmed that this visit was the one captured in the video that I had seen in 1997). He explained that some Bukharan Jews, whom he thinks he might have seen in passing in the street, approached his friends to ask him if he would do a concert in Israel. He was interested because he had wanted to see the holy places there, and was particularly keen to pray in the Al-Aqsa mosque. Soon after this invitation, he had a dream of a beautiful great building with water pipes and rocks in one corner, standing in place of his own home in Andijon. A white mulberry tree was growing alongside it, and he pulled off a bunch of mulberries and held them in his palm. They gave out light (*nur*), which he likened to that which streamed from the face of the Prophet Moses after he had been given the revelation [of the Ten Commandments] by God. A good-looking young man in the dream said to him, 'This is our home', and Sherali became aware that it was both his own home and that of this young man.

After this he went to Israel to play at the wedding. The building that he had seen in his dream turned out in fact to have been the Al-Aqsa mosque! Furthermore, he met the young man whom he had seen in the dream, a certain Abrom Tolmasov, a Bukharan Jew and musician who played alongside him at the wedding. While he was there, Tolmasov invited him to perform at another diaspora wedding, which he did. He was struck by how the Bukharan Jews living in Israel knew his music, and he told me that they paid more respect to his music than Uzbeks did.

It was during Sherali's second visit that the commercially released video was made. Sherali explained the background to this visit. In around 2002, his then 14-year-old son (the one present during our conversation) was out cycling when two women driving past in a car sprinkled water out of the car door in front of Sherali's home. This, Sherali claimed, was black magic, leading to the death of anyone who would step on it. The son returned and stood on the water, and immediately became very ill, with his liver displaying symptoms that resembled a form of hepatitis. The doctors were unable to assist and as his condition deteriorated someone advised him that his only hope for undoing this magic was to go to Jerusalem. Then he saw two Jewish boys in a dream, who said to him, 'Come, it would be wonderful if you could come to our home.' The next day the phone rang and someone called Slavic (who would compère the concert released as the commercial video) invited him to come to Jerusalem. Sherali said that he agreed immediately, somewhat to the surprise of Slavic!

It transpired that the concert was sponsored by none other than Lev Leviev, the transnational Bukharan-Jewish businessman introduced above. Sherali explained to me that he thought the concert was organized (with no charge for admittance) by Leviev to bolster his own position amongst Israel's émigré Bukharan Jewish community, by acting as their patron. This took place over two events. The first was the concert that was recorded for the video; the second a restaurant performance that evening, which was not released as a film.

After giving the first concert, Sherali reported, he went back to his hotel room and fell asleep. He dreamt that he saw the mountains around Jerusalem covered with praying people, although he was not sure to which religion they adhered. A large man in white, the size of ten people, praying alongside him, turned to him and said, his hands still in prayer, 'I will pray for you three times, everyone will be well: now go!' Sherali woke up and went to give the second performance, in the restaurant, which was a more religious affair with no dancing. He told a non-Uzbekistani Jew, via a Russian translator, that his son was ill. The Jew asked Sherali if they could pray for him. Sherali described being deeply moved by the sight of up to what he estimated were a thousand religious Jews all standing and praying together that his son would be healed.

In a dream following this, he saw a man just like the one whom he had spoken with at the restaurant. The man approached Sherali and said to him, 'God is pleased with you and will bless you. There is only one condition – when you see a Jewish boy, you must make him glad.' Sherali spoke of other moving moments, such as when he and the Jews affirmed together that 'God is one', and that Christians, Jews and Muslims were all praying in the same place [Jerusalem]. When he returned to Uzbekistan, his son made a full recovery, and some of the Jews whom he had met came to visit him on his birthday.

I asked Sherali what effect these events had had upon him. He said it was a very profound one:

> I believe in one God, who sent the prophets, made us all, and made the world as a place of testing for all of us. We are all one, *aka-uka* [like brothers]. I see everyone as a relative, regardless of who it is, whether I like them or not.

He spoke further that his views of Jews had changed, and that he no longer shared the prejudices of the Uzbek clergy that had been exhibited earlier in the evening. He confirmed that the words on the back of the video sleeve were written by himself, and that he meant them profoundly. He continued that his experiences in Israel had led him to pen them, and said that when he gives concerts now he urges people to foster good intercommunal relations, and speaks highly of the Jews. My initial scepticism was thus misplaced. He spoke at length about other spiritual experiences in his life, including an out-of-body experience upon reading the Qur'an for the first time in the 1980s, and a dream about Jesus Christ that led him to name his daughter Maryam in honour of His mother.

In an insightful article on Islam in Uzbekistan, Rasanayagam investigates folk or everyday forms of Uzbek Islam that emphasize phenomena such as experiences of illness and healing, and visions, that may be tolerated by clerics but were being squeezed out by more 'scripturalist' interpretations of Islam. He conceives these practices as being constitutive of a certain form of Uzbek identity.[53] Whilst Sherali's experience likewise led him to contest official clerical interpretations, the result of a train of events set in motion by these practices in his biography led not to shoring up the borders of a particular notion of Uzbekness but rather to a spiritual engagement with other religions. They led to a re-examination of his own prejudices regarding Jews and an attempt to pass on the lessons that he has learnt to his listeners.

The coming together of an understanding of faith rooted in local forms of Islam with the diasporic organizational strategy of a wealthy Uzbekistani–Israeli Jewish transnational businessman transformed the self-understanding of one of Uzbekistan's most influential Muslim cultural figures through an unlikely spiritual intimacy. In their study of Bosnian and Eritrean refugees in Europe, Al-Ali *et al.* found that musical concerts were important in cementing transnational networks.[54] This study argues something further – not only does it cement such networks, but paradoxically it can be transformative of identities, not only of the transnational agents but of other groups alongside whom they move and who become affected in unexpected ways.

## Conclusion

In his book *Geopolitics and Empire: The Legacy of Halford Mackinder*, Gerry Kearns criticizes the geopolitical tradition for conceiving of international relations as being the connections between states, rather than people. Kearns suggests, instead, that we might

> invoke a moral economy of migration that recognizes some of the ways that global interrelations tie us in diverse ways as consumers, citizens, and producers to people in distant places.

The 'incompatibility principle' seems to be invoked to prevent sharing of resources or 'any other benefits that may come from in-migration', he bemoans.[55] A geography that is committed to peace should aim to uncover and foreground the pacific contributions of migration, showing how it can promote better understanding between human groups where there have been histories of tension, mistrust and disdain.

In this chapter, I demonstrate how that can be done through an exploration of how Uzbek singer Sherali Juraev's attitude to the Jewish minority in his country was transformed through a series of significant spiritual episodes in his life that took place in Israel. These led him to seek to question and contest the prejudices in his own society, and refined his sense of musical vocation as one of promoting understanding and sympathy between people who are different. Geographies of migration, whether through transnational movements or temporary relocation for work or refuge, can be productive of more peaceful and mutually enriching human coexistence. Methodologically, as

Kuus[56] clearly advocates, and as Adams illustrates insightfully in the Uzbekistan context,[57] elite interviews can be invaluable in illuminating how geopolitical visions are produced.

It would, however, be naive and irresponsible to romanticize this account by disembedding it from its political and economic contexts. Spatiality is crucial to both the Israeli occupation of Palestinian land and to its ideological justification.[58] Sherali Juraev's visit to Israel was funded as a political move by a billionaire with no recent ancestral links to Israel, yet who was able to emigrate purely on account of his Jewishness, and who upon migrating has supported the settler movement's ideologically driven seizure and occupation of Palestinian land. In contrast, Palestinians with historic links to the same land, yet who were forcibly expelled by Israel in 1948, are prevented from returning, in contravention of UN Resolution 194 mandating their return. This illustrates some of the major conceptual arguments of this volume. 'Peace' should be understood as embedded within power relations, as peace *for* one group of people may not be good news for another. The specific meanings and invocations of 'peace' need therefore to be interrogated anew in each context. Peace is not to be understood primarily as an idealized endpoint, but as a precarious and problematic process.

Nonetheless, and paradoxically, at the same time the transnational activities of a conservative Bukharan Jewish émigré to Israel have contributed to how one of Uzbekistan's most significant Muslim figures has transformed his attitude to inter-ethnic relations. In a context where anti-Semitic prejudice is a reasonably common and frequently unchallenged form of racism, Sherali Juraev's desire and efforts publicly to counter it do matter. Peace happens in surprising places. A geography that seeks to play a contribution towards moving to a more peaceful world should pay more attention to uncovering these hidden stories of migration's potential to challenge – and even transform – negative assumptions about, and attitudes towards, people who are different.

## Acknowledgements

The author would like to thank Fiona McConnell for assistance in identifying relevant journal articles for this study, and for everyone in Bukhara who assisted my research. In particular, I am grateful to Sherali Juraev for his generosity in sharing his time and vouchsafing his significant spiritual experiences. Thank you Fiona and Philippa for your editing of this chapter.

# Notes

1. Megoran, Nick, 'Rethinking the study of international boundaries: a biography of the Kyrgyzstan–Uzbekistan boundary', *Annals of the Association of American Geographers* 102/2 (2012), pp. 464–81.

2. Kuus, Merje, 'Professionals of geopolitics: agency in international politics', *Geography Compass* 2/6 (2008), pp. 2062–79; Müller, Martin, 'Situating identities: enacting and studying Europe at a Russian elite university', *Millennium: Journal of International Studies* 37/1 (2008), pp. 3–25.

3. Williams, Philippa, 'Hindu–Muslim brotherhood: exploring the dynamics of communal relations in Varanasi, north India', *Journal of South Asian Development* 2/2 (2007), pp. 153–76.

4. Gregory, Derek, 'War and peace', *Transactions of the Institute of British Geographers* 35/2 (2010), pp. 154–86.

5. The introduction to this volume maps out some of the terrains of recent debate. See also Williams, Philippa and McConnell, Fiona, 'Critical geographies of peace', *Antipode* 43/4 (2011), pp. 927–31; Megoran, Nick, 'War *and* peace? An agenda for peace research and practice in geography', *Political Geography* 30/4 (2011), pp. 178–89; Inwood, Joshua and Tyner, James A., 'Geography's pro-peace agenda: an unfinished project', *ACME* 10/3 (2011), pp. 442–57.

6. Giordano, Benito, 'Italian regionalism or "Padanian" nationalism – the political project of the Lega Nord in Italian politics', *Political Geography* 19/4 (2000), pp. 445–71.

7. Sparke, Matthew, 'A neoliberal nexus: economy, security and the biopolitics of citizenship on the border', *Political Geography* 25/2 (2006), pp. 151–80.

8. Coleman, Matt, 'US statecraft and the US – Mexico border as security/economy nexus', *Political Geography* 24/2 (2004), pp. 185–209.

9. Mountz, Alison, 'Embodying the nation-state: Canada's response to human smuggling', *Political Geography* 23/3 (2004), pp. 323–45.

10. Amoore, Lousie, 'Biometric borders: governing mobilities in the war on terror', *Political Geography* 25/3 (2006), pp. 336–51; Ackleson, Jason, 'Constructing security on the US–Mexico border', *Political Geography* 24/2 (2004), pp. 165–84.

11. Staeheli, Lynn, 'Migration, civilisational thinking, and the possibility of democracy', *Geopolitics* 13/4 (2008), pp. 479–52.

12. Harris, Nigel, *Thinking the Unthinkable: The Immigration Myth Exposed* (London, 2002).

13. Hayter, Teresa, *Open Borders: The Case Against Immigration Controls* (London, 2000), p. 172.

14. Darling, Jonathan, 'A city of sanctuary: the relational re-imagining of Sheffield's asylum politics', *Transactions of the Institute of British Geographers*, 35/1 (2010a), pp. 125–40.

15. Faist, Thomas, 'Transnationalization in international migration: implications for the study of citizenship and culture', *Ethnic and Racial Studies* 23/2 (2000), pp. 189–222.

16. Vertovec, Steven, 'Transnationalism and identity', *Journal of Ethnic and Migration Studies* 27/4 (2001), pp. 573–82.

17. King, Charles and Melvin, Neil (eds), *Nations Abroad: Diaspora Politics and International Relations in the Former Soviet Union* (Oxford, 1998); Cohen, Robert, *Global Diasporas* (London, 1997).

18. Vertovec, 'Transnationalism and identity', p. 578.

19. Vasile, Elizabeth, 'Re-turning home: transnational movements and the transformation of landscape and culture', *Antipode* 29/2 (1997), pp. 177–96.

20. Kong, Lily, 'Globalisation and Singaporean transmigration: re-imagining and negotiating', *Political Geography* 18/5 (1999), pp. 563–89.

21. McEwan, Cheryl, 'Transnationalism', in J. Duncan, N. Johnson, and R. Schein (eds), *A Companion to Cultural Geography* (Oxford, 2004), pp. 499–512; Mitchell, Katharyne, 'Transnational discourse: bringing geography back in', *Antipode* 29/2 (1997), pp. 101–14.

22. Broadly speaking, world Jewry is divided into two liturgical streams. Ashkenazi Jews have roots in northern and western Europe, and Sephardic Jews in the Mediterranean world.

23. Shterenshis, Michael, *Tamerlane and the Jews* (London, 2002), p.17.

24. Datkhayev, Yu, *The Bukharan Jews: A Short Chronicle*, second edition (New York, 1995).

25. Gitelman, Zvi, *A Century of Ambivalence: The Jews of Russia and the Soviet Union, 1881 to the Present*, second edition (Bloomington, IN, 2001).

26. Cooper, Alanna, 'Reconsidering the tale of Rabbi Yosef Maman and the Bukharan Jewish diaspora', *Jewish Social Studies* 10/2 (2004), pp. 80–115.

27. Naby, Eden, 'The Assyrian diaspora: cultural survival in the absence of state structure', in T. Atabaki and S. Mehendale (eds), *Central Asia and the Caucasus: Transnationalism and Diaspora* (London, 2005), pp. 214–30.

28. Golden, Peter, *Central Asia in World History* (Oxford, 2011), pp. 50–62.

29. Gidwitz, Betsy, *Post-Soviet Jewry: The Critical Issues* (Jerusalem, 1999), pp. 60–1.

30. Dymshits, Valery, 'The eastern Jewish communities of the former USSR', in (no editor) *Facing West: Oriental Jews of Central Asia and the Caucasus* (Zwolle, no date), pp. 12–13.

31. Elazar, Daniel, *People and Polity: The Organizational Dynamics of World Jewry* (Detroit, 1989), p. 393.

32. Dymshits, 'The eastern Jewish communities of the former USSR', pp. 12–13.

33. Poujol, Catherine, 'Approaches to the history of Bukharan Jews' settlement in the Ferghana Valley, 1867–1917', *Central Asian Survey* 12/4 (1993), pp. 549–56.

34. Dymshits, 'The eastern Jewish communities of the former USSR', p. 21.

35. Gidwitz, *Post-Soviet Jewry*, p. 48.

36. Gitelman, *A Century of Ambivalence*, p. 209.

37. Shterenshis, *Tamerlane and the Jews*, pp. 109–10.

38. Dymshits, 'The eastern Jewish communities of the former USSR', p. 27.

39. Forbes.com (undated) 'Lev Leviev', www.forbes.com.

40. Gidwitz, *Post-Soviet Jewry*, p. 19.

41. Zarchin, Tomer, 'International legal precedent: no private prisons in Israel', *Haaretz*, 20 November/2009. Retrieved January 2012 from www.haaretz.com

42. Zohar, Gill, 'Bukharan quarter landmarks saved by Lev Levayev', *Arutz Sheva 7*, www.israelnationalnews.com, 1 July 2007. Retrieved January 2012.

43. Hayeem, Abe, 'Boycott this Israeli settlement builder', *Guardian* 'Comment is free' 28 April 2011. Retrieved January 2012 from www.guardian.co.uk/commentisfree/2009/apr/28/israel-boycott-leviev.

44. Sultanova, Razia, 'Music and identity in Central Asia: Introduction', *Ethnomusicology Forum* 14/2 (2005), pp. 131–42.

45. Interview, Sherali Juraev, Tashkent, 4 November 2004.

46. Adams, Laura, *The Spectacular State: Culture and National Identity in Uzbekistan* (London, 2010), p. 101.
47. Author's translation from Uzbek.
48. Shaw, Charles, 'Friendship under lock and key: the Soviet Central Asian border, 1918–34', *Central Asian Survey* 30/3–4 (2011), pp. 331–48.
49. For the Kyrgyzstan example, see Murzakulova, Asel and Schoeberlein, John, 'The invention of legitimacy: struggles in Kyrgyzstan to craft an effective nation-state ideology', in S. Cummings (ed.), *Symbolism and Power in Central Asia: Politics of the Spectacular* (London, 2010), pp. 144–63.
50. Cited in Sengupta, Anita, *Heartlands of Eurasia: The Geopolitics of Political Space* (Plymouth, 2009), p. 118.
51. Manley, Rebecca, *To The Tashkent Station: Evacuation and Survival in the Soviet Union at War* (London, 2009), p. 233.
52. Klenke, Kerstin (2001), '*Eurasian grooves:* popular music, identity, and politics in Uzbekistan', Ethnomusicological Research Seminar, Goldsmiths College, London.
53. Rasanayagam, Johan, 'Healing with spirits and the formation of Muslim self-hood in post-Soviet Uzbekistan', *Journal of the Royal Anthropological Society (N.S.)* 12/2 (2006), pp. 377–93.
54. Al-Ali, Nadje, Black, Richard and Koser, Khalid, 'Refugees and transnationalism: the experience of Bosnians and Eritreans in Europe', *Journal of Ethnic and Migration Studies* 27/4 (2001), p. 625.
55. Kearns, Gerry, *Geopolitics and Empire: The Legacy of Halford Mackinder* (Oxford, 2009), pp. 615–34.
56. Kuus, 'Professionals of geopolitics'.
57. Adams, *The Spectacular State*.
58. Weizman, Eyal, *Hollow Land: Israel's Architecture of Occupation* (London, 2007); White, Ben, *Israeli Apartheid: A Beginner's Guide* (London, 2009).

# 12

# Welcome to Sheffield: the less-than-violent geographies of urban asylum

*Jonathan Darling*

'Although the "facts" of violence can be assembled, tallied, and categorized, the cultural scope and emotional weight of violence can never be entirely captured through empirical analysis' (Simon Springer).[1]

Recent work on the spatial politics of asylum has seen a renewed interest in exploring a series of broadly 'positive' modes of engagement with asylum seekers in the UK, Canada and the USA, centred around practices, ideals and social movements of sanctuary and hospitality.[2] These developments all reflect particular conceptions of citizenship, migrant rights and social justice, yet they also reflect particular notions of interaction and engagement as means to 'welcome' others. It is to these dimensions of asylum that this chapter is addressed in exploring the potentials and limits of seemingly convivial encounters within a politics of everyday asylum. As Williams and McConnell suggest, practices of hospitality, conviviality and friendship might form part of an expanded appreciation of the spatial practice and performance of peace, and it is to this expanded sense of what peace may mean that this chapter contributes.[3] Peace is here figured not simply in terms of the absence of conflict, but as a more nuanced, embodied and affectively imbued series of relations to violence, both past and present, physical, emotional and symbolic.

Focusing upon how accounts of asylum practice, procedure and representation come to condition and contain acts of everyday engagement, the chapter considers relations of violence and nonviolence as constituted through interrelations between sites of prosaic enactment, national policy shifts and localized urban imaginaries. The folding together of these scales, processes and representations is, in part, what constitutes moments of violence and nonviolence.[4] This account thus seeks to recognize the impossibility of untangling relations of violent and nonviolent actions, spaces and times, and instead interrogates the ways in which moments of prosaic negotiation become invested with meaning and importance.

This chapter draws upon a series of interviews with asylum seekers conducted during an eleven-month period of fieldwork in Sheffield, UK (2006–7), to consider the ways in which they spoke about, experienced and narrated the city. This research involved the interviews with asylum seekers, councillors, charity workers and support organizations that form this chapter, a series of diary interviews with six asylum seekers, and a ten-month period of participant observation of an asylum drop-in centre in the city. Sheffield is a city of 555, 500 people, located in South Yorkshire.[5] In March 2011, Sheffield was home to 400 asylum seekers, making it the largest recipient of asylum seekers in the Yorkshire and Humber dispersal zone.[6] Since 1999 the UK has followed a policy of dispersing asylum seekers across the country whilst they await decisions on their asylum claims. In this process Sheffield has been a key dispersal site, accommodating between 1700 and 400 individuals at any one time across the last decade. It was this key position within the politics of dispersal, together with the city's championing of a 'progressive' approach to asylum provision that led this research to focus on the city.[7] (Sheffield was the first UK city to join the Gateway Protection Programme Scheme, a UNHCR refugee resettlement initiative and the UK's first 'City of Sanctuary'.) In approaching Sheffield, this chapter argues that we must take seriously the interwoven nature of moments of apparent peaceful coexistence and modalities of everyday violence, and that if there is any way in which we can think about peace for those seeking asylum, then it is precisely in the ways in which it is *sensed* within everyday life as moments of temporary transformation and subjective belonging.

The chapter proceeds as follows. First, I consider briefly the ways in which we might think of asylum as a violent geography. This relies upon a reading of violence which is not simply about physical force but which is extended to encompass the imposition of power through the 'normal state of things'.[8] With these discussions in mind, the chapter examines narratives of Sheffield offered by those seeking asylum. These highlight banal moments of 'welcome', which were taken to extend beyond the moment in hand and came to pattern an account of the city as a whole. The chapter then moves to highlight the limits of such positive encounters, focusing upon situated relations that carry with them diverse repertoires of violence *and* possibility. In this manner, I suggest that the experience of everyday asylum is one of practices which can only ever be understood contextually and which can never be fully absolved of their violent potential. It is to recent discussions of peace and its spatial practice that I turn first.

## Asylum, peace and objective violence

What, then, might we mean by peace? In a series of recent discussions centring upon the concept's role within political geography, a number of scholars have advanced work that views peace as an object of geographical concern and has sought to extend and expand the ways in which peace is understood as geographically constituted.[9] These discussions, though varied in their articulations of peace and nonviolent action, all focus upon expanding a critical account of peace and a practical agenda *for* peace, beyond its negative constitution as the absence of violence. Indeed, Williams and McConnell crystallize such debate when highlighting the importance of conceptualizing peace as more than simply 'a point of reference, an empty "other" defined by an absence of violence', preferring a broader account of peace which is both spatially differentiated and open to the 'spectrum of violence and non-violence'.[10] Similarly, Koopman notes that whilst we often frame political geographies in terms of a binary of war and peace – and more often war *or* peace – the two are both co-constitutive and always co-present.[11] Such discussions have thus called for a recognition of the ways in which forms of violence *and* peace are often 'situated within the same situations and places',[12] forming a complex geography of differential and differentiated peace, violence and conflict.

In these formulations, peace is articulated as a social process attached to notions of social justice, co-operation and well being. Megoran argues that 'peace is inseparable from questions of social justice' and distinguishes two central forms of peace.[13] For Megoran, drawing on Galtung, 'negative peace' refers to the prevention of armed conflict but may in itself be a repressive maintenance of a status quo; whilst a 'positive peace' refers to a far broader series of just, social relations in which conflict is not only prevented but where a wider process of social transformation is set in motion.[14] It is this latter, more emancipatory conception of peace that Megoran seeks to further through a call for geographical practice actively to promote peaceful geographical imaginaries. The distinction established by Megoran is important when considering the limits of peace as it is currently thought in relation to asylum, for, as Ross suggests, a concern with distinguishing 'negative' and 'positive' frames of peace must lead us to 'look at the violence and the injustices of what passes as the putative peace'.[15] Exploring in detail the violence inherent within an idea of peace for asylum seekers highlights the impurity of any conception of peaceful action and, as such, raises questions for the kinds of response to asylum that are advocated around ideals of sanctuary and hospitality.[16] The starting point for such enquiry is thus in examining the varied modalities of violence that mark the experience and politics of asylum itself.

In exploring the contours of violence, Žižek highlights a distinction between forms of 'subjective' and 'objective' violence within everyday life.[17] For Žižek there are two forms of 'objective' violence: first, 'symbolic violence', which is embedded in language and forms of cultural domination,[18] and second, 'systemic violence', which relates to the 'often catastrophic consequences of the smooth functioning of our economic and political systems'.[19] In contrast to these 'invisible' forms of violence, 'subjective' violence is that violence 'performed by a clearly identifiable agent' and encompasses 'acts of crime and terror, civil unrest, [and] international conflict'.[20] For Žižek, the ways in which we perceive and understand such modalities of violence are interwoven, thus:

> The catch is that subjective and objective violence cannot be perceived from the same standpoint: subjective violence is experienced as such against the background of a non-violent zero level. It is seen as a perturbation of the 'normal', peaceful state of things. However, objective violence is precisely the violence inherent to this 'normal' state of things. Objective violence is invisible since it sustains the very zero-level standard against which we perceive something as subjectively violent.[21]

It is this account of a nonviolent or peaceful 'normal' state of things that a critical geography of peace might seek to problematize. For, in many accounts of peaceful relations, it is often the 'subjective' violence of clearly defined acts of terror and war which take centre stage. However, a consideration of this wider category of 'objective' forms of violence, and the ways in which such modalities of domination might help to sustain and order a 'putative peace', undermines any clear-cut assertions over what 'peace' encompasses and where we might witness its emergence.

Returning to the lives of those seeking asylum in the UK, we can see the resonances of this form of thinking in a number of ways. At first glance we might suggest that many of those seeking asylum do indeed find some level of peace in the UK. For many awaiting decisions within the asylum system, the subjective violence of war, abuse and harassment is absent following the often hazardous journey to claim refuge in the UK. However, this account of peace is undermined if we consider the objective forms of violence that accompany this process. In the UK, asylum has long been coded as an issue of *domopolitics,* a matter of sovereign authority, selection and categorization, such that individuals are presented as a threat to the nation cast as a home and, as such, must be contained and controlled until a decision on their suitability to enter the homely space of the nation is reached.[22] Domopolitics dictates a specific way of thinking about, and acting upon, the lives and bodies of those caught at the border. It presents those seeking asylum as figures of national distinction and selection, and reproduces a vision of the homely nation and the homely citizen as assuming a 'right to decide' over the suitability and 'worthiness' of others.[23] The implications of such a hierarchical account of asylum are far-reaching, from the legitimation of media discourses which present asylum seekers as 'needy' victims of humanitarian concern or as suspicious 'scroungers' seeking to subvert 'our' hospitality,[24] through to the demand to make the lives of those contained within domopolitics as discomforting as possible through enforced mobility, detention and increasingly restrictive welfare provision.[25] Here 'symbolic' and 'systemic' modalities of violence fuse together, as the 'normal' state of things – the orderly governing of national space, welfare provision and regimes of citizenship – is reliant upon the symbolic liminality of those not yet deemed worthy of a place within the nation.

I draw on these strands of thought to explore the experiences of asylum seekers in the city of Sheffield, in order to illustrate how we might think of peace, violence and convivial contact as inherently situational, contextual and individual practices within the city. To do this, the chapter develops a critical reading of the ways in which the affectivities of everyday encounters in the city helped to forge and sustain an image of the welcoming city in the minds of some of Sheffield's asylum seekers.

## Encountering welcome

Throughout the fieldwork discussed earlier, a dominant narrative that was presented about the city from those asylum seekers dispersed there was that of Sheffield as a welcoming place. Sheffield was seen to display a 'friendly' ethos, a mood within public space which made many asylum seekers feel comfortable, secure and to a certain extent, 'at home'. It is this generalized affective atmosphere, its production, resonance and distillation into specific moments of encounter, that I want to focus on before considering how these moments interact with ideas of peace and violence. Such a narrative can be viewed in the account of Jacob, a charity worker for a Sheffield asylum NGO and refugee:[26]

London is dog eat dog, but in Sheffield actually people were welcoming. It's very interesting, like when you get into a bus somebody will say hi to you and when they go they will say bye, and to me that is more than I had seen before...Sheffield is more receptive compared to other places.

Jacob's account views Sheffield as a 'receptive' city, relationally constructed in contrast to other cities viewed as less welcoming. What such a view gestures towards is the intangible nature of what makes Sheffield 'welcoming'. Asylum seekers had difficulty pinning down exactly what achieved this urban sensibility. Partially, it was the help and support offered through local charitable organizations and drop-in centres, but it was also performed through the general 'mood' of the city. This mood, for many, was distilled through a series of moments in which communication and kindness came to the fore. Thus, as Amin and Thrift argue, 'encounter, and the reaction to it, is a formative element in the urban world. So places...are best thought of not so much as enduring sites but as *moments of encounter*'.[27] Viewing the city through such moments of encounter provides one means through which the city was constructed as a welcoming space by specific individuals and at specific times. To explore this further, I want to turn to two moments of encounter discussed by asylum seekers in the city, the first of which comes from an interview with Rubi. Rubi had lived in Sheffield for two years at the time of our interview, and was still awaiting a decision on her asylum status, having been dispersed to the city following arrival from Libya. We discussed her first days in the city:[28]

*Jonathan*: So these first people you met and spoke to in Sheffield... what were they like?

*Rubi*: It was my first day in Sheffield and the first thing that has happened to me make me feel comfort, or that I am going to be, you know, alright in this country. Even those people I met on the first day, like I ask them and they give me directions, and the bus driver I never can forgot him. I didn't know about the money for the bus and just I took the money and realised it was £20 but I didn't know how much that was, but I give it to him and he understand and he say you're alright and didn't take any money, he gave me the trip for free and dropped me in the town and he showed me the place, and how I should go to the shops, and said when I finish I should go to that place to get the bus back home. So that made me feel it's all right and give me a big smile and you know the first impression I get of the people is they are nice, they are helpful and this has made me carry on from then.

In a similar vein Ilya, an asylum seeker from Russia who had spent nearly three years in the city, highlights his first experience of Sheffield as a positive one:

I have a solicitor in Sheffield and I couldn't find the address of where to get a bus, and I meet a guy, a stranger, I asked for the bus stop and so he did a u-turn and he walked me to a bus stop about three hundred metres and he made sure this bus was going there, and he asked the driver to check. I was amazed and a bit embarrassed, but it's like he gave me a very human impression and a very good impression.

For Rubi and Ilya these encounters, through which strangers displayed a sense of care and concern, reflected a general attitude and ethos of Sheffield. For those like Rubi who were dispersed to the city with little knowledge of English the simple act of 'getting by' on a daily basis, of finding a bus stop, finding the shops, of counting the appropriate amount of money and of tracing a route back home again, proved anything but simple. The public spaces of the city took on a challenging dimension for asylum seekers trying to navigate them, and for some a sense of urban isolation, discomfort and uncertainty was built upon the well documented uncertainties of awaiting the decisions of the asylum process.[29] In such a context, moments of interaction and engagement come to matter all the more, precisely because they are unexpected and unpredictable.

Whilst such encounters may appear insignificant and unremarkable, the accounts of Rubi and Ilya suggest that, for them, the responsive dispositions displayed by these individuals took on a significant affective value. Indeed, another asylum seeker, Faheem, argued that the context of past experiences in the city, together with an individual's position relative to the regulatory mechanisms of domopolitics, are key factors in determining how one views the city. He suggested that 'if you have a bad experience in the past then you will never feel that you are in your home at all, being suffered in the past and being still suffered'. The interplay between past encounters and events and the context of the present shown in these accounts is indicative of the ways in which the city was constructed as a welcoming place for some. A common thread here was to focus upon the welcoming nature of the population and how 'small acts' such as the smiles and communication of Sheffield's residents impacted individual's views of the city. This theme also emerged in an interview with Sercan, an asylum seeker from Iran who had been in Sheffield for five months at the time of our interview:

> *Jonathan*: So do everyday things make a difference?
> *Sercan*: Yes, in everyday acts you find people you know, more and more helpful and even now we know that if you need it, if you need some help, then you can get it here.
> *Jonathan*: Do those things add up to provide a sense of the city?
> *Sercan*: Until now yes, I found the other people more hospitable, but you know a while ago I go to Broomhill to go to a GP's and all the other people there were English and they start looking at me and to say what is this person doing here because there are no foreigners in that place. But even so I was waiting for a bus after I finished and one old man come and he make a joke with me about the weather and so he was very welcoming you know, maybe he found me strange to be here but even so he didn't mind.

Sheffield was constructed for Sercan as a hospitable place, partially at least, through his encounters with people on the street, with the man at the bus stop, the smile from the stranger and in such 'everyday acts'. While welcome was never complete – a sense of foreignness still gripped him in the waiting room, for example – the performative reiteration of gestures of friendliness, from smiles to directions and jokes among strangers, allowed many asylum seekers to feel, if not 'at home', then at least more comfortable in the present. The 'everyday acts' that Sercan discusses here are important as markers of an affective comfort – albeit brief.

These accounts, then, suggest that the construction of Sheffield as a welcoming city is a complex one, and one which is often highly individual, personal and situational, relying upon the interaction of multiple performances, narratives, encounters and histories. However, we can begin to trace here how encounters in public space act to draw together these strands of welcoming, solidify them into moments of caring presence and connect an affective encounter to an individual's sense of the city and of their potential future within it.

## The less-than-violent act

So far I have argued that by examining the accounts of asylum seekers in Sheffield we can note the ways in which particular positive encounters come to prominence in dictating and directing the ways in which individuals view the city. From such accounts we might suggest that if an idea of peace for asylum seekers is to take meaning, it might do so through the responsiveness of interpersonal encounters and engagements which open the possibility of alternative futures. However, I want to complicate this account somewhat by suggesting that what such acts represent is not an account of peace in the everyday, or of peaceful interaction,[30] but rather an account of the 'less-than-violent'. Focusing on the less-than-violent nature of such acts shifts our attention away from a concern with peace as the absence of violence and examines instead the situated practice of relations which occur *across* and *within* ever-present modalities of violence. A concern with the less-than-violent is thus animated around critically interrogating any simple opposition of violence and nonviolence, whilst also seeking to destabilize accounts of peace and violence as singular, fixed or complete. Rather, to explore the less-than-violent encounters of everyday life is to focus upon the multiple relations that bind moments of peace and violence together in the very performing of relations.

A concern with the less-than-violent therefore draws upon a range of work within critical geography that focuses upon the complicity of our everyday lives with systems of domination, violence and distant harm, to consider the 'contextually derived positions' that perform relations of peace and violence.[31] Crucially though, a focus on the less-than-violent does more than simply critically interrogate relations of violence in order to promote peace. Rather, the less-than-violent marks a critical reading of the persistence of violence in apparently peaceful relations of care and conviviality; it also highlights the critical potential and transformative purchase that may lie within such relations. The less-than-violent is that which lies in the ambiguous and contested space between the violent and the peaceful, at once both a critical interrogation of violence and a hopeful orientation to the potentiality of peace. These ambiguous moments may thus establish altered ways of relating across the intersection of peace and violence, moments and gestures that hold the possibility of performing established positions of authority and privilege differently. As such, the less-than-violent act may offer a bridging point, a site of translation from subjective and objective violence to points of engagement which challenge and contest such violence. As current discussions of the varied geographies of peace and violence suggest, such a process of translation and critique is far from easy and its complexity, contradictions and contestations are what I hope to articulate in the remainder of this chapter through an account of how less-than-violent acts in Sheffield make small, but significant, differences to the lives of those seeking asylum in the city. A politics of such less-than-violent moments would thus be one which was incremental in nature and critical in tone, one centred upon employing the potential for change in relations of violence that these moments open up, whilst not romanticizing the promise of peace as an endpoint devoid of violence. In thinking about the less-than-violent act empirically, then, we might note that whilst each of the accounts provided by Rubi, Ilya and Sercan on Sheffield is markedly different, each one points to a response which might be seen to fall into a category of care in some way. From the warmth of a shared joke to the consideration of offering directions, these responses might be seen to mark a civility centred upon respect for others. However, whilst such moments of prosaic care might be argued to be central elements of peaceful coexistence with difference, they might also be seen as inherently conservative markers of a putative peace.[32] These acts of care are often positive gestures in terms of their effects on individuals, but they also rarely question or challenge the forms of objective violence that position asylum seekers within a social hierarchy as those in need of such care.[33] The responsivity of the street is about engagement, but centrally not about social justice, equality or the political rights of those marginalized within domopolitics. To locate such responses within a framework of the peaceful or the nonviolent would thus be to overlook the politics inherent in assuming a privileged position within a hierarchy of care.[34] In such a context, the less-than-violent act is one wherein modes of subjective violence are suspended and actively opposed through relations of care, but the objective violence of prosaic domination is often left unchallenged and unaddressed. Such acts are convivial moments with important affective outcomes, but they cannot be decoupled from the modes of dominance that arrange some individuals as capable of acts of compassion and hospitality. The less-than-violent act is thus inherently a product and a *device* of the 'normal' state of things.

The less-than-violent acts of everyday asylum noted so far, occur within the objective violence of domopolitics, yet they also offer moments of respite amid the exclusions of asylum dispersals and welfare restrictions.[35] Considering the nature of such acts highlights the situational character of how different modalities of violence are understood. Thus, as Žižek writes,

[V]iolence is not a direct property of some acts, but is distributed between acts and their contexts ... The same act can count as violent or non-violent, depending on its context; sometimes, a polite smile can be more violent than a brutal outburst.[36]

Žižek thus highlights the difficulty of predicting the way in which an act will be understood or interpreted in everyday life. It is this unpredictable quality that a concern with less-than-violent acts brings to the fore, as these are acts which oscillate between interpretations of violence and nonviolence and categories of subjective and objective violence. The less-than-violent act is therefore one whose position within the negotiations of everyday life is still to be determined, whose intent, meaning and 'moral outcome' is open to the vagaries of context. As such, these acts hold potential, but also are understood through personalized histories and moral judgments, such that here:

> Morality is not...a purely cognitive process. It has strong affective components. It is quite clear that all kinds of situations are freighted with affective inputs and consequences that are central to their moral outcomes which come from affective histories that arise from complex histories of being victims and of victimization that produce a sense of fairness and concern that will build into a consensus in some situations and not in others.[37]

In this manner, those less-than-violent acts of urban asylum detailed thus far might be interpreted as moments of moral or ethical potential. These acts may be seen as responses which offer the opportunity for a 'receptive generosity' to be expressed towards those seeking asylum. Such a generosity is one which serves to question the preconceptions of the 'giver' and to challenge critically the power relations imbued in normalized relations of giving and receiving.[38] The expression of 'receptive generosity' is about opening relations such that assumed accounts of position and privilege are contested in the act of relating to others. Indeed, here Massumi argues that the 'ethical value of an action is what it brings out *in* the situation, *for* its transformation, how it breaks sociality open',[39] and it is this opening which is important, for this emerges in the situation of responding to others and it challenges the way such situations might be approached in the future, altering perceptions, dispositions and sensibilities.[40] Thus while Rubi, Ilya and Sercan all reflected upon those less-than-violent acts they encountered, these acts influenced and opened their accounts of the city in different ways, making them more comfortable or more hopeful than they previously had been. The potential of these less-than-violent encounters in allowing individuals to engage with the city differently and to envision a position within the city that is not so heavily mired in the exclusions of domopolitics, is therefore a minor yet crucial mode of transformation.

Transformation of this form does not directly address the injustices of asylum marginality, but it does reflect a personal micropolitics of shifting outlooks, hopes and resiliencies, which at the very least may momentarily offset the affective discomforts of domopolitics. The relational interaction of various scales and sites of political imagination is thus critical here, not only to how everyday acts are understood – as influenced by national framings of asylum policy and representation – but also, as to how these acts may offer points of potential transformation within the relational construction of the city for certain individuals. Through these moments, the ways in which the city is tied into wider networks of asylum dispersal and exclusion can be opened to challenge, as those seeking asylum witness the possibility of a city that interacts with such exclusionary politics differently. The interjection of the asylum system as a device for sorting, classifying and ordering individuals is notable here: from the impact of a Home Office rejection letter on the atmosphere of a drop-in centre, to the discretionary denial of National Health Service care for *some* asylum seekers and not others, demarcations of exclusion and marginality pattern these engagements with the city *through* domopolitics.[41] With the affective discomforts of such a politics in mind, I want to consider a second set of affective resonances in the city.

## The limits of the less-than-violent

Here I want to focus not on the subjective violence of harassment, abuse and attack, although these are very real and well documented dangers for asylum seekers in the UK,[42] but rather on a far more nuanced category of urban aversion and suspicion that has a set of resonances for the lives of those seeking asylum. Pile argues that today if 'cities are characterised by any one mood, then maybe it is indifference',[43] and this affective response was certainly clear in accounts of Sheffield's response to asylum. Mark, the director of a local refugee charity, exemplified this sensibility when discussing how asylum seekers view the city:

*Jonathan:* Drawing on your experiences how do you think asylum seekers and refugees react to Sheffield?

*Mark:* I think that's varied really. I think that despite all the problems that people face, I think people do find – for want of a better word – a friendly place. I think there's the same racism here and intolerance around these issues but I think as Sheffield has become somewhat more of a multicultural city, I think it's just a more general friendliness in people finding their way around, so you may have more public hostility, but people talk about the difference between public hostility and private friendliness really.

Mark presents a complex reading of Sheffield's response to asylum, one broadly positive, yet at the same time significantly conditioned. Mark's distinction between 'public hostility' and 'private friendliness' reflects the uneven and unpredictable nature of relying upon everyday encounters as the marker of urban sensibilities. What we see here is a reticent daily negotiation of the heterogeneity which might be seen as an essential constituent of urban life.[44] What such negotiation suggests is a 'getting by' which is at times open and responsive as shown in the accounts already discussed but which can also be disinterested, indifferent and at times evasive. The terrain of urban everyday encounters is thus an unreliable one, which is dependent upon the sensibilities of individuals, the context of their actions and the location of such practices. There is no guarantee that encounters in the everyday spaces of urban life, from the park and the street to spaces of public transport, will produce responses or reactions that are positive or welcoming.[45] Rather, as Mark suggests, reactions may be friendly at one moment and hostile at the next, as responses are structured around a limit that enables individuals to 'get by' in daily life. This 'getting by' and its sense of a 'generalized' but fragile 'friendliness' might thus be thought of as a marker of a broadly positive, but still problematic, putative peace. For here a general mood of 'friendliness' is maintained without moving beyond a relative indifference to the wider forms of violence, repression and domination that maintain this apparently peaceful state of affairs.

Here, the distinction between 'public hostility' and 'private friendliness' is instructive, for it suggests that it is the objective violence of a perceptual system of domopolitics, through which citizens are *distanced from* and *elevated above* the claims of those seeking asylum, which maintains and naturalizes the right of the citizen to be either hostile *or* friendly. Here, that relational gesture of re-thinking the city's position within the context of wider networks of asylum politics and of how such a position may be transformed, is left undone.[46] A hierarchy of belonging for those with the rights of the citizen is maintained, but in doing so, so too is a scalar politics of dispersal and domopolitical sorting, through which the city is positioned as a container of difference to be dictated to, rather than a site of political contestation which 'speaks back' to the violences of domopolitics.

The second response to highlight here is that of suspicion. For whilst indifference marked the domopolitical positioning of citizens as those with a right to both hostility and hospitality, the relational connections of the city illustrate how the diverse geopolitics of other spaces, times and narratives, fuse into the present and bring a fear of subjective violence to bear. Such connections became clear following a terrorist attack on Glasgow airport in June 2007, the impacts of which I discussed with Sercan:

> *Sercan*: ... after what happened in Glasgow I was walking in the street and people were looking at me as if I was going to bomb them, but we should not forget that not all people are terrorists, just if I have black hair it does not mean I am a terrorist.
>
> *Jonathan*: So what do you think the repercussions of those attacks are likely to be?
>
> *Sercan*: In Sheffield you know people start to look in a strange way at us, but they're trying not to show it. They are still polite with you, they are not trying to hurt you, but you can see the fear in their eyes.
>
> *Jonathan*: What do you think that is a fear of?
>
> *Sercan*: Fear that everybody that has black hair will try to kill us one day, maybe not today but one day, especially if you are carrying a bag they fear that you are carrying a bomb, and it's an uncomfortable feeling.

The terror attack on Glasgow airport in June 2007 appeared to act as a catalyst for the emergence of fear and suspicion which were directed towards those asylum seekers who walked the streets of Sheffield and 'looked different'. In Sercan's account his dark hair and rucksack combined with a series of media and anecdotal narratives to create what Swanton terms the 'becoming terrorist', a racial assemblage which fixes bodies viewed as 'out of place'.[47] At a point where a murderous transgression is feared, previously unspoken assertions of national belonging are starkly exposed, as questions of allegiance and integrity are asked in the blink of a suspicious eye. Within such a glance, indifference is transformed into misanthropy, aggression and fear. Such action brings to the surface a series of implicit urges towards what Haldrup *et al.* term 'practical orientalism', an orientalism '(re)produced and negotiated in banal, bodily and sensuous practices'.[48] Thus, through 'numerous small acts, comments, telling of anecdotes, corporeal attitudes and so on, borders between "them" and "us" are redrawn, reproduced and enacted'.[49] This 'practical orientalism' is another form of that spatial management described by Hage as a means to order the 'homely' nation as a space of domopolitics.[50] The glances which Sercan mentions serve not only to make him uncomfortable, but also serve to question his right to space, his right to be *there*, at that moment, just possibly threatening 'our' lives. Here, again, the complexities of relations between violence, spatiality, the city and cultural markers of belonging, undermine any simple reading of everyday life for those seeking asylum as either nonviolent or peaceful and call for a far more situational approach to understanding how moments of aversion, fear and hostility lie side by side with gestures of hospitality and care.

Gestures of indifference, suspicion and fear are thus not subjectively violent, but they are symptoms of wider processes of objective violence in which those seeking asylum are positioned as suspicious and questionable presences to be kept at a distance from affective and material belonging.[51] This form of violence is dependent upon a series of ingrained and continually re-made perceptions of asylum, nation, citizenship and position, such that narratives of the 'scrounger' and the 'illegal immigrant' circulate, resonate and legitimate responses of indifference, aggression and hostility. Furthermore, as the suspicions that arose following the terror attack of June 2007 highlight, any account of a peaceful present is susceptible to inversion by the relational impacts of violence elsewhere. This is especially the case for those seeking asylum, whose very presence is in many ways tied to the subjective violence of other places and other times. Violence, in this context, must be no longer thought of as a practice confined to specific sites but rather 'as an unfolding process, arising from broader geographical phenomena and temporal patterns'.[52]

Viewed from such a relational lens, the everyday relations of a less-than-violent present in Sheffield are always open to the interruption of violence beyond the city and the ways in which this violence may re-work sensibilities towards others within the city, often calling forth a reassertion of positions of belonging. What such fragility suggests is precisely the problematic and uncertain nature of any putative peace. For, whilst those acts of care depicted by Rubi and others went some way to creating comfort in the present, this was a comfort structured around a position of profound discomfort. Crucially, these less-than-violent moments of relationality were not opposed to the objective violence of domopolitics: rather, they were moments of sociality *within* such a 'normal' state of things. They may have offered moments in which the relational imaginary of the city as a space of asylum could be transformed around notions of care and responsibility;[53] however, these moments were always vulnerable to the interruption and reassertion of domopolitics as an exclusionary logic of provision. These less-than-violent moments thus emerge from the relational complexities of interwoven scales and narratives of asylum, folding together the city and the nation, the prosaic interaction and the policy document, and the lives of those positioned within regimes of domopolitical authority and governance.[54]


## Conclusion

Peace, as I have attempted to argue, is a highly contextual and often highly personal state of being and one connected to notions of belonging and security. As Koopman suggests, peace exists within war and war within peace, and I would argue that moments of violence are always present in our assumptions of peace, not least because many of those assumptions are reliant upon violence for their maintenance. In this chapter, I have sought to explore some of these assumptions and foundations in the case of those seeking asylum. Just as peace is 'not a static thing, nor an endpoint, but a socio-spatial relation that is always made and made again',[55] so too is it highly individual, contextual and fragile. There is perhaps too great a tendency to think of peace and nonviolence in pure terms, as clear and unquestionably positive states of being, yet the experiences of those asylum seekers noted here casts such a reading in doubt, for they highlight the ways in which any 'peaceful' present is always maintained through certain positions, orderings and modes of governance and control. Work emerging around the varied geographies of peace has begun the task of questioning such presumptions and sought to produce nuanced readings of the spatial specificities and contradictions of peace, violence and conflict. In this chapter, I have sought to contribute to such an analytical task through exploring the relations of peace and violence that constitute everyday asylum. However, the chapter has also proposed the need to move carefully when discussing the 'spectrum of violence and non-violence'[56] that is often argued to constitute such 'geographies of peace'. For, examining the relations of peace and violence that form contemporary experiences of urban asylum, suggests a need to interrogate critically the grounds for peaceful acts or encounters, to explore their assumptions and unspoken normativities. To do so I have described a series of less-than-violent everyday acts to reflect not simply the complex interplay of visions of peace, violence and nonviolence in the everyday, but also to begin the process of thinking about the critical opportunities and transformative potentials opened within a space of translation between peace and violence. To take seriously the complexities of such everyday accounts of peace and relations of care therefore demands that we take

seriously the limits of such less-than-violent relations and the assumptions they shed light upon, whilst also exploring the possibilities these
relations expose for performing everyday politics differently.

Taking seriously the everyday nature of peace as a relational accom-
plishment might thus lead us to thinking through the politics of peace
in distinct ways. I conclude with two suggestions for how such thought
may progress. First, all of these practices of less-than-violent intent
take sustained work to become embodied in the everyday interactions
of urban life. Whilst a wide-ranging literature has considered the sociality of the urban,[57] the complex interplay between moments of hostility
and those of hospitality is only recently coming into view. What such
work highlights, though, is that considerations of judgment, affect,
memory and the emotional resonances of place, are central not only
to decisions on how to respond to others but also to how we interpret
the demands, needs and desires of others in everyday life. The 'everyday' is thus not simply a background state of prosaic conviviality: it is
an actively practised series of relations which carry with them certain
forms of violence, expectation, force, harm and possibility. The challenge of thinking through a geography of peace is both to enhance
the possibility of such relations becoming positive and transformative
moments through which the city is seen anew, and actively to work at
training our own dispositions to encounter. Such dispositional labour
must, critically, remain sensitive to the nature of the violence that we
may, perhaps unwittingly and unconsciously, perpetuate, perform and,
all too often, implicitly benefit from.

Second, this kind of ethico-political sensitivity and sensibility might
appear insignificant when compared with the 'bigger' scales of peace,
war and conflict that dominate geopolitics.[58] However, it is within this
politics of small achievements that some of these wider narratives and
modalities of objective violence might be, albeit fleetingly, tempered.
This is especially the case if, as I have argued here, we envisage the politics of place as one of relational interconnections through which different narratives, scales and sites continually frame the present, thus
challenging any straightforward notion of scalar primacy or privilege.[59]
To take seriously a geography of the less-than-violent moments that
sustain everyday conviviality demands a critical account of how past
encounters, relational connections to others, places and times and personal and emotive histories interact. These less-than-violent moments
are inevitably positioned within that wider spectrum of objective violence and domopolitical marginality that positions the bodies of asylum seekers as liminal presences. However, it is only through engaging
with their interaction and the sometimes unsettling implications of

complicity that such interaction involves, that we might view a geography which is both realistic about the violence it embodies and is committed to a critically responsive outlook to difference.[60] While the challenges of the objective violence of domopolitics remain, an effective political response will demand both large and small acts of resistance, citizenship and imagination.

## Acknowledgements

An earlier version of this chapter was presented at the RGS–IBG Annual Conference 2011 in the session 'Geographies of Everyday Peace'. My thanks to the session organizers and audience for their comments. Thanks to Fiona McConnell, Nick Megoran and Philippa Williams for their invitation to write about nonviolence, for their editorial guidance and the constructive conversations had on these themes over recent years. Thanks to all those asylum seekers and refugees who gave their time and insight for this research. Finally, thanks to Helen Wilson for her comments on earlier drafts of this chapter and for her always receptive support and generosity.

## Notes

1. Springer, Simon, 'Violence sits in places? Cultural practice, neoliberal rationalism, and virulent imaginative geographies', *Political Geography* 30/2 (2011), pp. 90–8.
2. See Darling, Jonathan, 'Becoming bare life: asylum, hospitality and the politics of encampment', *Environment and Planning D: Society and Space* 27/4 (2009), pp. 649–65; Darling, Jonathan, 'Just being there…ethics, experimentation and the cultivation of care', in B. Anderson and P. Harrison (eds), *Taking-Place: Non-Representational Theories and Geography* (Farnham, 2010b), pp. 241–60; Lippert, Randy, *Sanctuary, Sovereignty and Sacrifice: Canadian Sanctuary Incidents, Power and Law* (Vancouver, 2005); Lippert, Randy, 'Sanctuary discourse, powers and legal narratives', *Studies in Law, Politics and Society* 38 (2006), pp. 71–104; Ridgley, Jennifer, 'Cities of refuge: immigration enforcement, police, and the insurgent genealogies of citizenship in US sanctuary cities', *Urban Geography* 29 (2008), pp. 53–77; Squire, Vicki, 'From community cohesion to mobile solidarities: the *City of Sanctuary* network and the *Strangers into Citizens* campaign', *Political Studies* 59 (2011), pp. 290–307.
3. Williams, Philippa and McConnell, Fiona, 'Critical geographies of peace', *Antipode* 43/4 (2011), pp. 927–31.
4. See Amin, Ash, 'Regions unbound: towards a new politics of place', *Geografiska Annaler*, 86B/1 (2004), pp. 33–44; Allen, John, and Cochrane, Allan, 'Beyond the territorial fix: regional assemblages, politics and power', *Regional Studies*, 41/9 (2007), pp. 1161–75.

5. Office of National Statistics, *Population Estimates for UK, England and Wales, Scotland and Northern Ireland, Mid-2010*, (2011). Retrieved 10 April 2012 from http://www.ons.gov.uk/ons/publications/re-reference-tables.html?edition=tcm%3A77–231847

6. Home Office, *Control of Immigration: Quarterly Statistical Summary, United Kingdom, Quarter 1 2011*. Retrieved 9 February 2012 from http://www.homeoffice.gov.uk/publications/science-research-statistics/research-statistics/immigration-asylum-research/control-immigration-q1–2011-t/?view=Standard&pubID=891312

7. City of Sanctuary is a social movement designed to promote a 'culture of welcome and hospitality' in British towns and cities. The movement began in Sheffield in 2005 and focuses upon establishing cultural events in order to facilitate contact between asylum seekers and the wider urban population.

8. Bourdieu, Pierre, *Language and Symbolic Power* (Cambridge, 1991); Žižek, Slavoj, *Violence: Six Sideways Reflections* (London, 2008).

9. Megoran, Nick, 'Towards a geography of peace: pacific geopolitics and evangelical Christian Crusade apologies', *Transactions of the Institute of British Geographers* 35/3 (2010), pp. 382–98; Megoran, Nick, 'War *and* peace? An agenda for peace research and practice in geography', *Political Geography* 30/4 (2011), pp. 178–89; Williams and McConnell: 'Critical geographies of peace'; Koopman, Sara, 'Let's take peace to pieces', *Political Geography* 30/4 (2011b), pp. 193–4; Ross, Amy, 'Geographies of war and the putative peace', *Political Geography* 30/4 (2011), pp. 197–9.

10. Williams and McConnell, 'Critical geographies of peace', pp. 928, 930.

11. Koopman, 'Let's take peace to pieces'.

12. Grundy-Warr, Carl, 'Pacific geographies and the politics of Buddhist peace activism', *Political Geography* 30/4 (2011), pp. 190–2.

13. Megoran, 'War *and* peace', p. 182.

14. Megoran, 'War *and* peace', p. 179; Galtung, Johan, 'What is peace research?', *Journal of Peace Research* 1/1 (1964), pp. 1–4.

15. Ross, 'Geographies of war and the putative peace', p. 198.

16. See Darling, Jonathan and Squire, Vicki, 'Everyday enactments of sanctuary: the UK *City of Sanctuary* movement', in R. Lippert and S. Rehaag (eds), *Sanctuary Practices in International Perspective* (London, 2012).

17. Žižek, *Violence*.

18. Bourdieu, *Language and Symbolic Power*.

19. Žižek, *Violence*, p. 1.

20. Žižek, *Violence*, p. 1.

21. Žižek, *Violence*, p. 2.

22. Walters, William, 'Secure borders, safe haven, domopolitics', *Citizenship Studies* 8/3 (2004), pp. 237–60; Ingram, Alan, 'Domopolitics and disease: HIV/AIDS, immigration, and asylum in the UK', *Environment and Planning D: Society and Space* 26/5 (2008), pp. 875–94; Darling, Jonathan, 'Domopolitics, governmentality and the regulation of asylum accommodation', *Political Geography* 30/5 (2011a), pp. 263–71.

23. Hage, Ghassen, *White Nation: Fantasies of White Supremacy in a Multicultural Society* (Annandale, 1998); Sales, Rosemary, 'The deserving and the undeserving? Refugees, asylum seekers and welfare in Britain', *Critical Social Policy* 22/3 (2002), pp. 456–78.

24. Derrida, Jacques, *On Cosmopolitanism and Forgiveness* (London, 2001); Squire, Vicki, *The Exclusionary Politics of Asylum* (Basingstoke, 2009).

25. Gill, Nicholas, 'Governmental mobility: the power effects of the movement of detained asylum seekers around Britain's detention estate', *Political Geography* 28/3 (2009), pp. 186–96; Tyler, Imogen, '"Welcome to Britain": the cultural politics of asylum', *European Journal of Cultural Studies* 9/2 (2006), pp. 185–202; Zetter, Roger and Pearl, Martyn, 'Sheltering on the margins: social housing provision and the impact of restrictionism on asylum seekers and refugees in the UK', *Policy Studies* 20/4 (1999), pp. 235–54.

26. All names presented throughout this chapter are pseudonyms in order to protect the identity of research participants.

27. Amin, Ash and Thrift, Nigel, *Cities: Reimagining the Urban* (Cambridge, 2002), p. 30, original emphasis.

28. This interview transcript is a verbatim account of our discussion and as such the occasionally awkward nature of the narrative reflects the challenges of communicating in English experienced by a number of Sheffield's asylum seekers as the research was unfortunately unable to offer translators for the interview process.

29. Squire, *The Exclusionary Politics of Asylum*.

30. See Ring, Laura, *Zenana: Everyday Peace in a Karachi Apartment Building* (Bloomington, IN, 2007); Williams, Philippa, 'Reproducing everyday peace in north India: process, politics, and power', *Annals of the Association of American Geographers* (2013) 103/1, pp. 230–250.

31. Hyndman, Jennifer, 'The question of "the political" in critical geopolitics: querying the "child soldier" in the "war on terror"', *Political Geography* 29 (2010), pp. 247–55; Koopman, Sara, 'Imperialism within: can the master's tools bring down the empire?', *ACME* 7/2 (2008), pp. 283–307.

32. Sennett, Richard, *Respect in a World of Inequality* (London, 2003); Ross, 'War and the putative peace'.

33. Darling, Jonathan, 'Giving space: care, generosity and belonging in a UK asylum drop-in centre', *Geoforum* 42/4 (2011b), pp. 408–17.

34. Beasley, Christine and Bacchi, Carol L., 'The political limits of "care" in re-imagining interconnection/community and an ethical future', *Australian Feminist Studies* 20/46 (2005), pp. 49–64; Darling, 'Giving space'.

35. Darling and Squire, 'Everyday enactments of sanctuary'.

36. Žižek, *Violence*, p. 180.

37. Thrift, Nigel, 'But malice aforethought: cities and the natural history of hatred', *Transactions of the Institute of British Geographers* 30/2 (2005), pp. 133–50.

38. Coles, Romand, *Rethinking Generosity: Critical Theory and the Politics of Caritas* (London, 1997).

39. Massumi, Brian, 'Navigating movements' in M. Zournazi (ed.), *Hope: New Philosophies for Change* (London, 2002), pp. 210–42.

40. See Wilson, Helen F., 'Passing propinquities in the multicultural city: the everyday encounters of bus passengering', *Environment and Planning A* 43/3 (2011), pp. 634–49.

41. See Darling, 'Giving space'; Darling, 'Domopolitics'.

42. See Kundnani, Arun, *The End of Tolerance: Racism in 21st Century Britain* (London, 2007).

43. Pile, Steve, 'Memory and the city', in J. Campbell and J. Harbord (eds), *Temporalities, Autobiography and Everyday Life* (Manchester, 2002), pp. 111–27.

44. Donald, James, *Imagining the Modern City* (London, 1999).

45. See Wilson, 'Passing propinquities in the multicultural city'.

46. See Darling, Jonathan, 'A city of sanctuary: the relational re-imagining of Sheffield's asylum politics', *Transactions of the Institute of British Geographers* 35/1 (2010a), pp. 125–40.

47. Swanton, Daniel, 'Sorting bodies: race, affect and everyday multiculture in a mill town in northern England', *Environment and Planning A* 42/10 (2010), pp. 2332–50.

48. Haldrup, Michael, Koefoed, Lasse and Simonsen, Kirsten, 'Practical orientalism – bodies, everyday life and the construction of otherness', *Geografiska Annaler* 88B/2 (2006), pp. 173–84.

49. Haldrup *et al.*, 'Practical orientalism', p. 183.

50. See Hage, *White Nation*.

51. Fortier, Anne-Marie, 'Proximity by design? Affective citizenship and the management of unease', *Citizenship Studies* 14 (2010), pp. 17–30; Tyler, Imogen, 'Designed to fail: a biopolitics of British citizenship', *Citizenship Studies* 14 (2010), pp. 61–74.

52. Springer, 'Violence sits in places', p. 91.

53. Darling, 'A city of sanctuary'.

54. See Darling, 'Domopolitics'; Gill, 'Governmental mobility'.

55. Koopman, 'Let's take peace to pieces', p. 194.

56. Williams and McConnell, 'Critical geographies of peace', p. 930.

57. See Amin, Ash, 'Re-thinking the urban social', *City* 11/1 (2007), pp. 100–14; Amin, Ash, 'Collective culture and urban public space', *City* 12/1 (2008), pp. 5–24; Tonkiss, Fran, *Space, the City and Social Theory* (Cambridge, 2005).

58. See Flint, Colin R., (ed.), *The Geography of War and Peace: From Death Camps to Diplomats* (Oxford, 2005); Gregory, Derek, 'War and peace', *Transactions of the Institute of British Geographers* 35/2 (2010), pp. 154–86.

59. Marston, Sallie A., Jones III, John Paul and Woodward, Keith, 'Human geography without scale', *Transactions of the Institute of British Geographers*, 30/4 (2005), pp. 416–32.

60. Connolly, William, *Why I Am not a Secularist* (Minneapolis, 1999).

# 13

# Geographies of peace, geographies for peace

*Nick Megoran, Philippa Williams and Fiona McConnell*

## Arms and the place

Jonathan Schell begins his acclaimed book on the achievements and prospects for nonviolence, *The Unconquerable World*, by starkly juxtaposing the maxims of two first-century near-contemporaries: the Roman poet Virgil and the Jewish prophet Jesus of Nazareth. Virgil celebrated imperial Rome, hymning 'arms, and the man', a eulogy of the weapons and resolve of the patriotic male warrior. Jesus, when being arrested and subsequently executed by those very Roman soldiers for fomenting rebellion against the Empire, told his followers not to fight them but to, 'Put up your sword. For they that live by the sword shall die by the sword.'[1] Schell contends that these two maxims represent two alternative traditions – the war system and co-operative power/nonviolence – that have coexisted down the centuries.[2] His book traces what he believes is the recent acceleration in the eclipse of the former by the latter.

This juxtaposition is, of course, an oversimplification for, as Schell's narrative acknowledges, the positions he identifies can be seen as poles of a continuum rather than as an irresolvable opposition. Nonetheless it points to a phenomenon that David Cortright observes in his history of the peace movement and the ideas that sustain it.[3] Since the creation of the first formal peace societies in the UK and the USA, at the end of the Napoleonic Wars, there has been a palpable (if partial) shift across many cultures from eulogizing the warrior to celebrating the peacemaker. This change is multifaceted. Structurally, it is represented by the emergence of international treaties and co-operation, pan-state organizations and unions, mass participation anti-war organizations, changing forms and structures of national and international law, and grassroots activism. Significant developments range from the resolution of territorial disputes by plebiscites in the aftermath of the First World War and the signing of the United Nations Charter, to the generation of small-scale grassroots developments such as protective accompaniment and community mediation. Culturally it is indicated by phenomena as diverse as the establishment of peace museums, prizes, fellowships and institutes. Notable episodes include religiously informed mass nonviolent movements for political change in British India and segregationist USA, war resistance in 1930s Western Europe, and 'anti-politics' in the 1980s Soviet bloc. Landmark movements include conscientious objection, nuclear freeze, and anti-war mobilizations over the Vietnam and Iraq wars. Ideologically, it is informed by religious, philosophical, liberal, moral, feminist, socialist, democratic nationalist and other thinkers and reformers from around the world. At the same time, an unprecedented degree of scholarly analysis and reflection on the meanings and causes of peace and violence has been developed.[4]

Many of these phenomena have precedents, but what is new is that they have become increasingly prevalent and mainstream. This does not mean that the end of war is nigh and that we stand on the dawn of some millennial age of peace. Increasingly sophisticated theorization of violence has shown it to be more pervasive, multifaceted and dynamic than previous definitions of 'war' would allow. Progress in one area can be paralleled by regression in another, and sudden catastrophes and crises can arrest, erase or reverse apparent progress. Nonetheless the legitimacy of 'the war system' and other forms of violence is being challenged as never before: violence is increasingly seen as a problem to be solved, rather than an acceptable extension of politics or an inevitable facet of social life. Likewise, militarism – the embeddedness of war cultures and symbols in everyday life – is increasingly regarded as a phenomenon to be identified and problematized, rather than as an unremarkable, taken-for-granted aspect of daily life. We identify ourselves as committed to the broad peace movement thus outlined, and seek to harness the power of geographical inquiry to its service. As we set out in the introduction to this book, we have been concerned that geographers have lagged behind cognate disciplines when it comes to problematizing and exploring peace. We need to devote the same analytical energy and empirical rigour to researching peace as we have done to studying violence. This volume is primarily intended to move this forwards and to reposition geography as one of the 'arts of peace'.[5] It also has the secondary aim of commending to scholars working on peace in other disciplines the utility of geographical analysis.

## What is peace?

In common uses of the term, the word 'peace' often seems to necessitate little further clarification. Rather, it assumes a universal quality across time and place that means it is '...sentimentally idealized as either simply not-war, or that all is good'.[6] Rejecting such assumptions, the contributors to this volume have each sought to problematize peace. Collectively, they have destabilized and exposed the political work of peace as practice, process and discourse. Engaging with the concept and practice of peace in different contexts, they show that peace is experienced and interpreted in multiple ways through time and space, and that a straightforward definition is elusive and always contested. Underpinning the contributions to this volume are questions about how we research peace, what methodologies we employ, what questions we ask and how we might theorize peace.

The aim of understanding peace in more expansive and multi-dimensional terms – conceptually, theoretically and empirically – is at the heart of this book. We have shown that not only are there different geographies of peace but that geography offers the possibility of capturing the complex reality of peace(s) both through the discipline's plural yet integrated approach and the foregrounding of concepts of space, place and scale.[7] As we noted in the introductory chapter, our intention has been to foster 'geographies of peace' as a broad umbrella rather than a narrow dogma. To that end, the preceding chapters have approached peace from a wide range of subdisciplinary fields, from geopolitics and political geography, to social and cultural geography, environmental and development geographies.

We believe that approaching the question of what peace is from an integrated geographical perspective offers important insights. We wish to foreground here three particular themes that have emerged throughout this book and that illuminate how a geographical approach exposes ways in which peace is experienced, constructed, interpreted and contested in different spatial, temporal and cultural contexts. First, in thinking critically about peace, our contributors have variously engaged with the complex relationship between violence and nonviolence. As Donaldson's chapter sets out, state-based approaches often presume that the difference between 'war' and 'peace' hangs on a razor's edge. Together, we have argued that peace is not simply an end product that is reached 'after' war and the elimination of the enemy. Indeed, in 'post-conflict' situations, the event of war may be just one in a series of episodes where violence is made manifest in both dramatic and banal ways. Daley, Darling, Donaldson and Laliberte have argued from different contexts that even after formal arbitration, violence may continue to find expression through everyday acts of subjugation, coercion, oppression and subordination. As Daley's and Laliberte's chapters demonstrate, interventions by international organizations made in the name of peace more often compromise the capacity of individuals and groups to carve out space for peaceful geographies and just societies. Indeed, Darling goes as far as to caution that the concept of 'less-than-violent' offers a more honest framing of reality. It seems the challenge here is to recognize both the limits and realities of peaceful geographies, and the extent to which structural and symbolic violence also plays a role within ostensibly peaceful places. It is also important to appreciate that the very idea of peace can be variously interpreted, and that the dominance of one particular narrative may in itself constitute an act of violence *vis-à-vis* other peaceful imaginaries. For instance, many anti-war agendas often focus on solutions rooted in Western liberal thinking and thus preclude larger discussions about *alternatives* to our present condition.[8] This has the material effect of creating a situation in which a largely 'peaceful' society continues to produce uneven development and inequality. Indeed, as Inwood and Tyner have argued, peace as the opposite of war does not necessarily entail a 'just' or 'benign' society.[9]

In problematizing the intricately intertwined relationship between violence and nonviolence it can be difficult to know what we might recognize as peace. Sometimes it is against a backdrop of ongoing (international) antagonism, as Schoenfeld *et al.* set out so clearly in the context of Israel–Palestine relations. At other times, as Shimada and Williams demonstrate from starkly different contexts, it is in the memory of violent encounters or threats to everyday urban peace that notions of peace become crystallized. In other settings nonviolent ideas and practices are instrumental in forging community identities and political strategies, as Laliberte and McConnell demonstrate with the cases of a human rights organization in northern Uganda and exile Tibetan politics respectively. Yet, as Darling illustrates, 'peace' can also be subtle in its appearance and needs to be sensed through the 'normal' state of things.

The second broad theme to emerge from this book is the role of situated agency in the production and reproduction of peace, as foregrounded in most of the chapters. The actors presented here cut across a range of scales to include international organizations, state agencies, non-state institutions, national and local religious leaders, independent philanthropists, migrants, refugees, former paramilitaries and non-elites. Operating within and across a range of sites, such actors do things (both deliberately and inadvertently) in ways that cultivate and/or support peaceful practices. Interpreting the articulation of agencies within specific contexts aids our understanding of the complex and shifting dynamic between violence and nonviolence.

As the chapters in this volume make apparent, creating and sustaining peace demands considerable labour, which may not always result in the anticipated outcome. This is aptly demonstrated in Donaldson's contribution, where he outlines how the demarcation of territorial boundaries designed to minimize conflict can actually spark new political and social antagonisms. As Shimada, Williams and McConnell show, where the production and reproduction of peace is contingent on the agency of groups and individuals, agents of peace might also have been or may later become agents of violence within other times and places.

Underpinning these questions regarding agency and peace, as well as the relationship between violence and nonviolence, is the third cross-cutting theme: that of power. Every contribution demonstrates that peace narratives, processes and strategies are shot through with power relations. The imaginary of peace is so powerful precisely because it is constructed as universal. Yet the diversity of ways in which different actors articulate the idea of peace for political ends across time and place highlights its malleability. 'Peace' affords considerable political capital for different actors and can be used as a political strategy (as McConnell's description of exile Tibetan politics attests) and to protect the legitimacy, influence and position of states, organizations, individuals, and social groups. For example, as Laliberte shows, successfully reconfiguring violent social relations for more equitable and peaceful practices can inadvertently reproduce local patriarchal power structures. Dalby and Donaldson demonstrate that the drawing up and enforcement of international boundaries and security in the name of peace are exercises of state power that may be productive of other types of violence. The pursuit of 'peace' does not necessarily embody the realization of equality and justice. Hegemonic discourses of peace may obscure other possible ways of being peaceful. As Oliver Richmond puts it, any critical academic study of peace must ask 'who creates and promotes [peace], for what interests, and who is [it] for?'[10] Such an unveiling of the power relations within which peace is embedded, paves the way for a more candid appreciation of both the possibilities and limitations of peace, and poses the important question of the extent to which peace is transformative in different political, social and cultural contexts. This is not to undermine the value of peace, but rather to foreground how it can be politicized.

## Why geography?

In highlighting these three themes which cross cut the chapters in this volume – the intertwining of violence and nonviolence, the role of agency, and the power relations which underpin peace – we have sought to place the study of peace more firmly on the agenda of human geographers. However, concerns with process, agency and power are in the purview of social sciences as a whole. It is important not to lose sight of what is distinctly geographical about the approaches to peace set out in this volume.

We suggest that these three themes in the chapters point to a twofold geographical contribution to the study of peace: concerns and concepts. First, by revisiting traditional geographical *concerns* (including migration, borders, geopolitics, and nature–human interaction) and asking how they can be productive of peace, our authors make original contributions to the study of peace. Second, the contributions to this volume demonstrate the utility of working with the key geographical *concepts* of place, space and scale. Peace looks different in different places at different scales. Because places are distinct, so ideas and practices of peace – be they versions of the liberal peace or ideas such as *satyagraha* – change as they move location through both space and time. Although no disciplinary monopoly over these concerns and concepts is claimed, we argue that by foregrounding them we can identify a useful and distinct geographical contribution to the study of making, sustaining and unmaking peace.

## Why peace?

Geographies of peace thus attend to the complexities and contradictions of peace and to the necessity of understanding peace in the plural. The risk of such an endeavour is, of course, that the concept of peace is stretched so far as to become meaningless. If 'peace' encompasses topics as diverse as development, the politics of asylum, inter-communal relations, transnationalism, post-conflict reconstruction, grassroots movements, human rights, boundary delimitiations and global geopolitics, then what *isn't* peace? If 'peace' is so contested a term, one requiring so many caveats and qualifiers and which signifies so much to people from so many different (and sometimes opposing) positions, does it not become an empty term? As Koopman has noted, a result of analysing a plethora of 'peaceful concepts' is that 'the term peace can be vague, broad, amorphous and mythical'.[11] Do these objections not fatally undermine this project?

First, and to begin to respond to this, we note that many of the concepts that are so important to social life in the modern world are contested: justice, love, religion, rights and democracy, for example. Because something is broadranging and contested does not undermine its utility or importance as a theme for consideration. Like 'peace', 'violence' is also a contested term: but we ignore both at our risk. By continually and critically revisiting the term 'peace', by interrogating its meanings and interpretations and showing how they 'work' in contexts of unequal power relations, as this volume does, we hope to obviate the danger of 'peace' becoming an empty or a taken-for-granted term.

Second, working with the concept of 'peace' allows us to do things that we could not do otherwise. On the one hand, exploring different interpretations of peace and thinking critically about the concept of peace brings to the fore both practical and discursive alternatives to the dominant narratives of violence, conflict and hostility. It also opens up questions and research avenues that otherwise might not directly be considered. As such, it provides valuable points of intersection by bringing a range of themes (such as boundaries, geopolitics, migration, development, environmentalism, post-conflict situations) and debates (including tolerance, empathy, hospitality, friendship and rights) into dialogue. Related to this, engaging with ideas of peace connects geographers to interdisciplinary debates with anthropologists, international relations theorists, theologians and others. These are debates to which we, as geographers, with our spatial focus, can make original and engaging contributions as we also learn from others. As we hope that this volume demonstrates, place and space matter for peace.

Third, we believe that there is a disciplinary responsibility to study peace. Histories of the discipline have shown how geographers have either provided direct support for militarism and other forms of violence, or created intellectual architectures that made violence appear inevitable and even necessary.[12] There is thus, we contend, a moral obligation to revisit critically the ways in which geographers have provided justifications for violence, by explicating how 'militarist mappings of global space' construct contexts that justify violence. This is important, not least because it is mistaken to assume that the links between geography and violence have ceased.[13] However, the issue is not simply that it is enough to stop explicitly supporting violence by critiquing it. To be against violence is not necessarily the same as being for peace: as we have argued throughout, certain concepts and ways of doing peace entail their own forms of violence. It seems thus logical that we should contribute to transformation, to the movement along the spectrum between violence and peace.

Finally, therefore, we identify the endeavour of building a geography of peace as a modest contribution to what Cortright calls the 'movements and ideas for peace'.[14] This movement – involving a huge range of thinkers, activists, politicians, and diplomats who might disagree on many aspects – has nonetheless been productive of a major shift in world culture that we regard as a shift in the right direction. Conflict may well be an inevitable component of human existence for the time being: that question is beyond the remit of geographers. The issue is whether conflict is addressed violently or not, and how it can be resolved, not just without throwing punches and bombs but with greater justice. That is a question that geographers can undoubtedly help answer: and because they can, they should.

## For peace

The implication of our argument is that geography should be 'for peace'. This is hardly an original contention. In 1885 Kropotkin wrote that geography ought to be a means of 'dissipating' the 'wars... national self-conceit... of national jealousies and hatreds' manipulated by warmongers.[15] One of the most enduring definitions of geography is that it is the study of the earth as the home of humanity. In 1973 Bunge wrote:

> Geographers must labor to make sure that the earth's surface truly becomes the home of man, that mankind comes to some peace, some rest, some harmony, and ultimate unity with nature. The ultimate contribution of geography is not merely to describe the earth's surface as the home of man, but to help make the definition come true.[16]

Bunge's work, particularly his superb 1988 *Nuclear War Atlas*,[17] was part of a reaction by geographers against the Cold War arms race that was an important precedent to today's emerging geography of peace. However, as we argued in the introduction, most of the work on 'geographies of war and peace' has heavily accented the war dimension. A geography that is for peace must not just say that it is, but must devote equal energy to exploring and analysing 'peace'.

We want a geography that is as ambitious in developing an agenda for peace as it has been at investigating the geographical correlates of violence. To do this it must address a range of questions. For example, how have some creative approaches to sharing and limiting sovereignty mitigated or transformed territorial disputes that once seemed intractable? How have some communities been able to deal with religious, racial, cultural, and class conflict better than others? What spatial factors have facilitated the success or precipitated the failure of some peace movements or diplomatic negotiations relative to others? How is it that the same religious or atheistic worldviews have been productive of violence in some places, but co-operation in others? How have antagonistic geopolitical scripts been overcome or rewritten? Why does gender (in)equality and sexual-based violence differ from place to place? Why do some nonviolent campaigns for social justice work and others fail? How and why are the statistical correlates of war changing over space and time? What can be learned from the historical geography of institutions such as the United Nations or movements such as the Peace Pledge Union and the global anti-war protests in 2001–2003? Likewise, the history of peace in the discipline is still waiting to be rewritten.

At the same time, we contend that this emerging geography of peace needs to be *critical*. It must not simply ask about 'peace', but ask what *kind* of peace and *for whom* that peace is created. Who benefits from this particular peace settlement, and who loses? What unjust social relations have been preserved by the powerful as they managed to head off an urban riot or armed rebellion in the name of peace? How do male peacekeeping forces create new forms of violence against trafficked women in the brothels that follow the blue helmets? What violence has been done to sexual and ethnic minorities and to women by peace and justice movements that suppress differences and maintain oppressive power structures in the name of culture and the greater cause? What oppression has been allowed to persist when an anti-war movement successfully prevents a military intervention against an autocrat committing heinous crimes against his own population? What façades have been maintained by the theatre of a formal peace process? How do very different actors mean very different things when they talk about peace, and what is the effect of this in negotiation and policy implementation?

A geography that is for peace should, we have argued, see itself as part of the peace movement as broadly defined. This entails a responsibility to work with those who work on peace, whether they be non-elites, grassroots activists, employees of international organizations, or politicians and policy-makers. Obviously, as peace is so contested a term, geographers will disagree about with whom we should collaborate: there is room for difference. We should ask ourselves: how can we learn from, and feed back to, the communities we work with? How can we make useful and informative contributions to public debate? And how can we support each other in doing this collaboratively?

However, praxis is not simply about engagement or collaboration: it also entails asking how we can do the profession of academic geography more peaceably. As Inwood and Tyner contend: 'Efforts at education are central for constructing a pro-peace agenda.'[18] How can the material that we teach inculcate a pro-peace understanding whilst being rigorously committed to presenting the whole perspective of viable opinions? How can our pedagogical approaches facilitate critical thinking? How can fieldwork on peace-related topics be transformative? And how can we work with schools to support the teaching of peace there? More generally, what would a more peaceable practice of professional geography look like? In ungainly pushes for promotion and limited resources, and in macho performances in attacking the views of others or defending one's own arguments, geography departments, journals and conferences can become spaces of aggression and intimidation. And what should we do about the military presence on campus through funding, recruitment, investment and war memorials to students and alumni killed-in-action?

It may be the case that academics have a habit of overestimating their own importance. Nonetheless we believe that researching, writing, teaching and engagement matter. They matter because ideas matter. Ideas do not just stay in libraries. Returning to Schell's invocation of Virgil at the beginning of this chapter: if it is true that warriors need arms, then it is also the case that ideas have legs. For example, consider four of the most visible achievements of the modern peace movement: the International Court of Justice in resolving boundary disputes without war; the US civil rights movements in terminating formal segregation without bloody revolution; and the Gandhian and Soviet-bloc mass movements that ended empires without armed insurrection. Study each of these and you will find that men and women thought, prayed, argued, read, debated, meditated, studied, worshipped, dreamed, taught and wrote – usually as part of a movement, and often with many false starts – before they achieved the success that earned them lasting respect as peacemakers. Institutions and practices that have made important (if imperfect) contributions to resolving, averting or de-escalating violent conflict began with the theories, suggestions, proposals, schemes – that is, the ideas – of thinkers, politicians and activists. Most ideas that are born do not get beyond the crawling stage (and we should probably be grateful for that) but some do. For good or ill, ideas have legs.

That is why we think it is worth researching, writing and teaching about peace, and thinking hard about how we do that peaceably. Since Virgil and earlier, monarchs, poets and publics have lauded the warrior. Especially in recent times, states have devoted vast resources to training people how to fight, to developing the weapons technology to assist them, and to studying the science of how to win wars. By contrast, the resources that human societies have committed throughout history to understanding how to be peacemakers are paltry. Much has been achieved on a relative budgetary shoestring since the founding of the first peace societies two centuries ago.[19] But still our theoretical and empirical understanding of how peace can be created and sustained, and our conceptual grasp of what peace is, remains relatively underdeveloped. We believe that this volume shows that geographers can genuinely make a useful contribution to remedying this. We believe that there is a place for geographies of peace.

## Notes

1. Bible, Matthew 26: 52.
2. Schell, Jonathan, *The Unconquerable World: Power, Nonviolence and the Will of the People* (New York, 2003), pp. 1–2.
3. Cortright, David, *Peace: A History of Movements and Ideas* (Cambridge, 2008).
4. Pinker, Stephen, *The Better Angels of our Nature: Why Violence has Declined* (London, 2011).
5. Gregory, Derek, 'War and peace', *Transactions of the Institute of British Geographers* 35/2 (2010), pp. 154–86.
6. Koopman, Sara, 'Let's take peace to pieces', *Political Geography* 30/4 (2011), pp. 193–4, p. 193.
7. For a discussion of 'engaged pluralism' in the context of economic geography see Barnes, Trevor J. and Sheppard, Eric, '"Nothing includes everything": towards engaged pluralism in Anglophone economic geography', *Progress in Human Geography* 34/2 (2010), pp. 125–42.
8. Vavrynen, Tarja, 'Gender and UN peace operations: the confines of modernity', *International Peacekeeping* 11/1 (2004), p. 133.
9. Inwood, Joshua and Tyner, James, 'Geography's pro-peace agenda: an unfinished project', *ACME* 10/3 (2011), pp. 442–57, p. 447.
10. Richmond, Oliver, *Peace in International Relations* (London, 2008), p. 16.
11. Koopman, 'Let's take peace to pieces', p. 194.
12. Polelle, Mark, *Raising Cartographic Consciousness: The Social and Foreign Policy Visions of Geopolitics in the Twentieth Century* (Oxford: 1999); Kearns, Gerry, *Geopolitics and Empire: The Legacy of Halford Mackinder* (Oxford, 2009).
13. Dalby, Simon, 'Recontextualizing violence, power and nature: the next twenty years of critical geopolitics?', *Political Geography* 29/5 (2010), pp. 280–88.
14. Cortright, *Peace*, p. 21.
15. Kropotkin, Peter, 'What geography ought to be', *The Nineteenth Century*, 19 December (1885), p. 1956.
16. Bunge, William, 'The geography of human survival', *Annals of the Association of American Geographers* 63/3 (1973), pp. 275–95.
17. Bunge, William, *The Nuclear War Atlas* (Oxford, 1988).
18. Inwood, J. and Tyner, J. A., 'Geography's pro-peace agenda'.
19. According to David Cortright, the first peace societies were the New York Peace Society (1815) and the British Society for the Promotion of Permanent and Universal Peace (1816), (Cortright, *Peace*, Chapter, 'The first peace societies').

# Bibliography

Abu-Lughod, Janet (1991) 'Going beyond global babble', in A. King (ed.), *Culture, Globalization and the World-System* (London: Macmillan).

Abu-Lughod, Lila (2008 [1990]), 'The romance of resistance: tracing transformations of power through Bedouin women', *American Ethnologist* 17/1, pp. 41–55.

Abu Zayyad, Ziad and Schenker, Hillel (eds), 'People-to-people: what went wrong and how to fix it?', *Palestine–Israel Journal of Politics, Economics, and Culture* 12/4 and 13/1 (2006). Retrieved 27 October 2011 from http://www.pij.org/current.php?id=40.

Acholi Religious Leaders Peace Initiative (2001), *Let My People Go: The Forgotten Plight of the People in the Displaced Camps in Acholi* (Gulu: Acholi Religious Leaders Peace Initiative).

Ackleson, Jason (2004), 'Constructing security on the US-Mexico border', *Political Geography* 24/2, pp. 165–84.

Adami, Vittorio (1927), *National Frontiers in Relation to International Law*, trans. T. T. Behrens (London: Oxford University Press/Humphrey Milford).

Adams, Laura (2010), *The Spectacular State: Culture and National Identity in Uzbekistan* (London: Duke University Press).

Adams, Vincanne (1998), 'Suffering the winds of Lhasa: politicised bodies, human rights, cultural difference and humanism in Tibet', *Medical Anthropology Quarterly* 12/1, pp. 74–102.

African Rights (1995), *Not So Innocent: When Women Become Killers* (London: African Rights).

Agba, A. M. O., Akpanudoedehe, J.J., and Ushie, E.M. (2010), 'Socio-economic and cultural impacts of resettlement on Bakassi people of Cross River State, Nigeria', *CS Canada, Studies in Sociology of Science* 1/2, pp. 50–62.

Agnew, John (1994), 'The territorial trap: geographical assumptions of international relations theory', *Review of International Political Economy* 1/1, pp. 53–80.

—— (2000), 'Commentary: Classics in human geography revisited: Sack, R., "Human Territoriality"', *Progress in Human Geography* 24/1, pp. 91–9.

—— (2009a), *Globalization and Sovereignty* (Lanham MD: Rowman and Littlefield).

—— (2009b), 'Killing for cause? Geographies of war and peace', *Annals of the Association of American Geographers* 99/5, pp. 1054–9.

Akçalı, Emel and Antonsich, Marco (2009), '"Nature knows no boundaries": a critical reading of UNDP environmental peacemaking in Cyprus', *Annals of the Association of American Geographers* 99/5, pp. 940–7.

Al-Ali, Nadje, Black, Richard and Koser, Khalid (2001), 'Refugees and transnationalism: the experience of Bosnians and Eritreans in Europe', *Journal of Ethnic and Migration Studies* 27/4, pp. 615–34.

Alatout, Samer (2009), 'Walls as technologies of government: the double construction of geographies of peace and conflict in Israeli politics, 2002-present', *Annals of the Association of American Geographers* 99/5, pp. 956–68.

Alexander's Gas and Oil Connections (2008) 'Overview of Latin American oil exports to the USA', www.gasandoil.com/news/n_america/3cd816c5a3d1696189f fb00a4a4b10f7. Retrieved 17 October 2011.

Allen, John, and Cochrane, Allan (2007), 'Beyond the territorial fix: regional assemblages, politics and power', *Regional Studies* 41/9, pp. 1161–75.

Alleson, Ilan and Schoenfeld, Stuart (2007), 'Environmental justice and peacebuilding in the Middle East', *Peace Review* 19/3, pp. 371–9.

Amadiume, Ifi (1997), *Reinventing Africa: Matriarchy, Religion, and Culture* (London: Zed Books).

Amin, Ash (2004), 'Regions unbound: towards a new politics of place', *Geografiska Annaler* 86B/1, pp. 33–44.

—— (2007), 'Re-thinking the urban social', *City* 11/1, pp. 100–14.

—— (2008), 'Collective culture and urban public space', *City* 12/1, pp. 5–24.

Amin, Ash, and Thrift, Nigel (2002), *Cities: Reimagining the Urban* (Cambridge: Polity).

Amoore, Louise (2006), 'Biometric borders: governing mobilities in the war on terror', *Political Geography* 25/3, pp. 336–51.

Anderson, James and Shuttleworth, Ian (1998), 'Sectarian demography, territoriality, and political development in Northern Ireland', *Political Geography* 17/2, pp. 187–208.

Annan, Jeannie, and Moriah Brier (2010), 'The risk of return: intimate partner violence in northern Uganda's armed conflict', *Social Science & Medicine* 70/1, pp. 152–9.

Appleby, R. Scott (2000), *The Ambivalence of the Sacred: Religion, Violence, and Reconciliation* (Oxford: Oxford University Press).

Arango, Diana and Romoser, Annalise (2011), *Closer to Home: A Critical Analysis of Colombia's Proposed Land Law* (Baltimore, MD and Bogotá, Colombia, US Office on Colombia: Lutheran World Relief and IndePaz), www.usofficeoncolombia.org. Retrieved 26 February 2011.

Ardley, Jane (2002), *The Tibetan Independence Movement: Political, Religious and Gandhian Perspectives* (London: RoutledgeCurzon).

—— (2003), 'Satyagraha in Tibet: toward a Gandhian solution?', *The Tibet Journal* 28/4, pp. 23–38.

Arpi, Claude (2005), *India and her Neighbourhood: A French Observer's Views* (New Delhi: Har-Anand).

Asad, Talal (2003), *Formations of the Secular: Christianity, Islam, Modernity* (Stanford, CA: Stanford University Press).

Asiwaju, Anthony I. (ed.) (2007), *Peaceful Resolution of African Boundary Conflicts: The Bakassi Peninsula Settlement* (Imeko Ogun State-Nigeria: African Regional Institute).

Atwood, Wallace (1935), 'The increasing significance of geographic conditions in the growth of nation-states', *Annals of the Association of American Geographers* 25/1, pp. 1–16.

Austerre, Séverine (2009), 'Hobbes and the Congo: frames, local violence and international intervention', *International Organization* (63/Spring), pp. 248–80.

Ayala, Edgardo (2011), 'El Salvador: forgotten people of the border pact', *Inter Press Service/Global Information Network*, 29 March 2011.

Bailey, Frederick, G. (1996), *The Civility of Indifference: On Domesticating Ethnicity* (Ithaca, NY: Cornell University Press).

Ballvé, Teo (2012), 'Everyday state formation: territory, decentralization, and the Narco land-grab in Colombia', *Environment and Planning D: Society and Space*. 30/4, pp. 603–22.

Barnes, Trevor J. and Sheppard, Eric (2010), '"Nothing includes everything": towards engaged pluralism in Anglophone economic geography', *Progress in Human Geography* 34/2, pp. 193–214.

Barnett, Clive (1999), 'Deconstructing context: exposing Derrida', *Transactions of the Institute of British Geographers* 24/3, pp. 277–93.

Baron-Cohen, Simon (2011), *The Science of Evil: On Empathy and the Origins of Cruelty* (New York: Basic Books).

Batty, David (2011), 'China's "ruthless" Tibet policy to blame for monk deaths, says Dalai Lama', *Guardian*, 29 October 2011. Retrieved 30 October 2011, from http://www.guardian.co.uk/world/2011/oct/29/dalai-lama-tibet-china-protests

BBC (2009), 'Racism in Northern Ireland', *BBC News*, 29 October 2011. Retrieved 24 March 2010 from http://news.bbc.co.uk/1/hi/northern_ ireland/8104978.stm

BBC Monitoring (2009), 'Kenyan youth destroy railway line over island row with Uganda', *BBC Monitoring Africa*, 25 April 2009.

Beasley, Christine and Bacchi, Carol L. (2005), 'The political limits of "care" in re-imagining interconnection/community and an ethical future', *Australian Feminist Studies* 20/46, pp. 49–64.

Ben-Porat, Guy (2005), 'Grounds for peace: territoriality and conflict resolution' *Geopolitics* 10/1, pp. 147–66.

Bergquist, Charles, Peñaranda, Ricardo and Sánchez, Gonzalo (2001), *Violence in Colombia, 1990–2000: Waging War and Negotiating Peace* (Lanham, MD: Rowman & Littlefield).

Bichsel, Christine (2009), *Conflict Transformation in Central Asia: Irrigation Disputes in the Ferghana Valley* (London: Routledge).

Biger, Gideon (ed.) (1995), *The Encyclopaedia of International Boundaries* (New York: Facts on File).

Blanchard, Erica M. (2003), 'Gender, international relations, and the development of feminist security theory', *Signs: Journal of Women in Culture and Society* 28/4, pp. 1289–1312.

Blumen, Orna and Halevi, Sharon (2009), 'Staging peace through a gendered demonstration: Women in Black in Haifa, Israel', *Annals of the Association of American Geographers* 99/5, pp. 977–85.

Bonta, Bruce D. (1996), 'Conflict resolution among peaceful societies: the culture of peacefulness', *Journal of Peace Research* 33/4, pp. 403–20.

Borer, Tristan Anne (2009), 'Gendered war and gendered peace: truth commissions and post-conflict violence: lessons from South Africa', *Violence Against Women* 15, pp. 1169–93.

Boulding, Kenneth E. (1999), 'Nonviolence and power in the twentieth century', in S. Zunes, L. R. Kurtz and S. B. Asher (eds), *Nonviolent Social Movements: A Geographical Perspective* (Oxford: Blackwell), pp. 11–17.

Bourdieu, Pierre (1991), *Language and Symbolic Power* (Cambridge: Polity).

Boutros-Ghali, Boutros (1992), *An Agenda for Peace: Preventive Diplomacy, Peacemaking and Peace-keeping*, Document A/47/277 – S/241111, 17 June 1992. (New York: Department of Public Information, United Nations). Retrieved March 24, 2011 from http://www.un.org/Docs/SG/agpeace.html

—— (1995), *An Agenda for Peace*, second edition (New York: United Nations).

Bouvier, Virginia Marie (2009), *Colombia: Building Peace in a Time of War* (Washington, DC: United States Institute of Peace).

Bowman, Glenn (1993), 'Tales of the lost land: Palestinian identity and the formation of nationalist consciousness', in E. Carter, J. Donald and J. Squires (eds), *Space and Place: Theories of Identity and Location* (London: Lawrence & Wishart), pp. 73–99.

Brass, Paul (2003), *The Production of Hindu-Muslim Violence in Contemporary India* (New Delhi: Oxford University Press).

Brauch, Hans Günter, Oswald Spring, Úrsula, Grin, John, Mesjasz, Czeslaw, Kameri-Mbote, Patricia , Chadha Behera, Navnita, Chourou, Béchir, and Krummenacher Heinz (eds) (2009), *Facing Global Environmental Change: Environmental, Human, Energy, Food, Health and Water Security Concepts* (Heidelberg: Springer).

Briggs, Jean L. (1994), '"Why don't you kill your baby brother?" The dynamics of peace in Canadian Inuit camps', in L. E. Sponsel and T. Gregor (eds), *The Anthropology of Peace and Nonviolence* (Boulder, CO: Lynne Rienner), pp. 155–81.

Brigham, Albert P. (1919), 'Principles in the determination of boundaries', *Geographical Review* 7/4, pp. 201–19.

Brown, Kris and MacGinty, Roger (2003), 'Public attitudes toward partisan and neutral symbols in post-agreement Northern Ireland', *Identities: Global Studies in Culture and Power* 10/1, pp. 83–108.

Brownlie, Ian (1979), *African Boundaries: A Legal and Diplomatic Encyclopaedia* (London: C. Hurst).

Brunhes, Jean and Vallaux, Camille (1921), *La géographie de l'histoire: Géographie de la paix et de la guerre sur terre et sur mer* (Paris: Alcan).

Brunn, Stanley, and Munski, Douglas (1999), 'The international peace garden: a case study in locational harmony', *Boundary and Security Bulletin* 7, pp. 67–74.

Brunn, Stanley, Nooruddin, Vaseema and Sims, Kimberly (2006), 'Place, culture, and peace: treaty cities and national culture in mediating contemporary international disputes', *Geojournal* 39/4, pp. 331–43.

Bull, Hedley (1977), *The Anarchical Society: A Study of Order in World Politics* (New York: Columbia University Press).

Bunge, William (1973), 'The geography of human survival', *Annals of the Association of American Geographers* 63/3, pp. 275–95.

—— (1988), *The Nuclear War Atlas* (Oxford: Blackwell).

Burke, Enid de Silva, Klot, Jennifer and Bunting, Ikaweba (2001), *Engendering Peace: Reflections on the Burundi Peace Process* (Nairobi: UNIFEM United Nations Development Fund for Women).

Butler, Judith (1993), *Bodies That Matter: On the Discursive Limits of Sex*, 1st edition (London: Routledge).

Campbell, Susanna, Chandler, David and Sabaratnam, Meera (eds), *The Liberal Peace? The Problems and Practices of Peacebuilding* (London: Zed Books).

Carius, Alexander (2006), *Environmental Peacebuilding: Cooperation as an Instrument of Crisis Prevention and Peacebuilding: Conditions for Success and Constraints* (German Federal Ministry for Economic Cooperation and Development).

Castaneda, Sebastian (2009), 'Land: Colombia's natural resource curse', *Colombia Reports*, 2009 colombiareports.com/opinion/117-cantonese-arepas/6609-land-colombias-natural-resource-curse.html. Retrieved 20 December 2011.

Chatterjee, Mohua (2006), 'Poll-bound UP to be centre of BJP yatras', *Times of India*, 10 March 2006. Retrieved 11 March 2006 from, http://timesofindia.indiatimes.com/india/Poll-bound-UP-to-be-centre-of-BJP-yatras/articleshow/1444831.cms.

Chatterjee, P. (2004), *The Politics of the Governed: Reflections on Popular Politics in Most of the World* (New York: Columbia University Press).

CIP, Center for International Policy, LAWG – EF, the Latin America Working Group Education Fund, and WOLA, the Washington Office on Latin America (No date), 'Just the facts: a civilian's guide to US defense and security assistance to Latin America and the Caribbean', justf.org. Retrieved 11 October 2010.

Clark, Howard (ed.) (2009), *People Power: Unarmed Resistance and Global Solidarity* (London: Pluto Press).

Clausewitz, Carl von (1968), *On War* (Harmondsworth: Penguin) (Original *Vom Kriege*, 1832).

Clayton, Jonathan and Bone, James (2004), 'Sex scandal in Congo threatens to engulf UN's peacekeepers', *The Times*, London.

Coaffee, Jon and Murakami Wood, David (2008), 'Terrorism and surveillance', in T. Hall, P. Hubbard and J. R. Short (eds), *The Sage Companion to the City* (London: Sage), pp. 352–72.

CODHES (No date), 'CODHES: Consultoría Para Los Derechos Humanos y El Desplazamiento', www.codhes.org. Retrieved 8 February 2011.

Cohen, Robert (1997), *Global Diasporas* (London: UCL Press).

Cohen, Shaul (2007), 'Winning while losing: the apprentice boys of Derry walk their beat', *Political Geography* 26/8, pp. 951–67.

Coleman, Matthew (2007), 'A geopolitics of engagement: neoliberalism, the war on terrorism, and the reconfiguration of US immigration enforcement', *Geopolitics* 12/4, pp. 607–34.

Coles, Romand (1997), *Rethinking Generosity: Critical Theory and the Politics of Caritas* (London: Cornell University Press).

Collier, Paul and Hoeffler, Anke (2004), 'Greed and grievance in civil war', *Oxford Economic Papers* 56, pp. 563–95.

Conca, Ken and Wallace, Jennifer (2009), 'Environment and peacebuilding in war-torn societies: lessons from the UN environment programme's experience with postconflict assessment', *Global Governance* 1/4, pp. 185–205.

Confortini, Catia C. (2006), 'Galtung, violence, and gender: the case for a peace studies/feminist alliance', *Peace & Change* 31/3, pp. 333–67.

Connolly, William (1999). *Why I am not a Secularist* (Minneapolis, University of Minnesota Press).

Cooper, Alanna (2004), 'Reconsidering the tale of Rabbi Yosef Maman and the Bukharan Jewish diaspora', *Jewish Social Studies* 10/2, pp. 80–115.

Cornwall, Andrea and Nyamu-Musembi, Celestine (2004), 'Putting the "rights-based approach" to development into perspective', *Third World Quarterly* 25/8, pp. 1415–37.

Cortright, David (2008), *Peace: A History of Movements and Ideas* (Cambridge: Cambridge University Press).

Coulibaly, Issa (2010), 'Démarcation des frontières africaines post-conflit: L'expérience de la démarcation de la frontière Mali–Burkina', in J. Donaldson (ed.), *Boundary Delimitation and Demarcation: An African Union Border Programme Practical Handbook* (Addis Ababa: African Union/GIZ limited print report).

Council, UN Security (2004), 'Regarding the events that occurred at Gatumba – letter from the Secretary General to the President of the UN Security Council' (UN Security Council).

Cowen, Deborah and Gilbert, Emily (eds) (2008), *War, Citizenship, Territory* (New York: Routledge).

Crampton, Jeremy (2006), 'The cartographic calculation of space: race mapping and the Balkans at the Paris Peace Conference of 1919', *Social and Cultural Geography* 7/5, pp. 731–52.

Crawford, N. (2000), 'The passion of world politics: propositions on emotion and emotional relationships', *International Security* 24(4), pp. 116–56.

Crowder, Michael (1987), 'Whose dream was it anyway? Twenty-five years of African independence', *African Affairs* 86/342, pp. 7–24.

Curzon, George N. (1908), *Frontiers: The Romanes Lectures 1907* (Oxford: Clarendon Press).

Dalai Lama (18 February 2011), *Ancient Wisdom, Modern Thought*. Retrieved 30 October 2011 from http://www.dalailama.com/webcasts/post/170-ancient-wisdom-modern-thought.

Dalby, Simon (1991), 'Critical geopolitics: discourse, difference and dissent', *Environment and Planning D: Society and Space* 9/3, pp. 261–83.

—— (1994), 'Gender and critical geopolitics: reading security discourse in the new world disorder', *Environment and Planning D: Society and Space* 12, pp. 595–612.

—— (2008), 'Warrior geopolitics: *Gladiator, Black Hawk Down* and the *Kingdom of Heaven*', *Political Geography* 27/4, pp. 439–55.

—— (2009a), 'Geopolitics, the revolution in military affairs and the Bush doctrine', *International Politics* 46/2–3, pp. 234–52.

—— (2009b), *Security and Environmental Change* (Cambridge: Polity).

—— (2010), 'Recontextualising violence, power and nature: the next twenty years of critical geopolitics?', *Political Geography* 29/5, pp. 280–8.

—— (2011a), 'Geographies of the international system: globalisation, empire and the anthropocene', in P. Aalto, S. Moisio and V. Harle (eds), *International Studies: Interdisciplinary Approaches* (Basingstoke: Palgrave Macmillan), pp. 125–48.

—— (2011b), 'Critical geopolitics and the control of arms in the twenty-first century', *Contemporary Security Policy* 32/1, pp. 40–56.

—— (2013), 'Realism and geopolitics in the anthropocene', in K. Dodds, M. Kuus and J. Sharp (eds), *Companion to Critical Geopolitics* (Aldershot: Ashgate), pp. 33–48.

Daley, Patricia O. (2008), *Gender and Genocide in Burundi: The Search for Spaces of Peace in the Great Lakes Region of Africa* (Oxford: James Currey).

Dallaire, Romeo (2004), *Shake Hands with the Devil: The Failure of Humanity in Rwanda* (London: Arrow Books).

DANE (no date), 'DANE – Departamento Administrativo Nacional De Estadistica', www.dane.gov.co/daneweb_V09/#twoj_fragment1-4. Retrieved 3 July 2011.

Daniel, Tim (2002), 'After judgment day', in C. Schofield, D. Newman, A. Drysdale and J. A. Brown (eds), *The Razor's Edge: International Boundaries and Political Geography* (London: Kluwer Law International), pp. 269–86.

Darling, Jonathan (2009), 'Becoming bare life: asylum, hospitality and the politics of encampment', *Environment and Planning D: Society and Space* 27/4, pp. 649–65.

—— (2010a), 'A city of sanctuary: the relational re-imagining of Sheffield's asylum politics', *Transactions of the Institute of British Geographers* 35/1, pp. 125–40.

—— (2010b), 'Just being there…ethics, experimentation and the cultivation of care', in B. Anderson and P. Harrison (eds), *Taking-Place: Non-Representational Theories and Geography* (Farnham: Ashgate), pp. 241–60.

—— (2011a), 'Domopolitics, governmentality and the regulation of asylum accommodation', *Political Geography* 30/5, pp. 263–71.

—— (2011b), 'Giving space: care, generosity and belonging in a UK asylum drop-in centre', *Geoforum* 42/4, pp. 408–17.

Darling, Jonathan, and Squire, Vicki, (2012), 'Everyday enactments of sanctuary: the UK *City of Sanctuary* movement', in R. Lippert and S. Rehaag (eds), *Sanctuary Practices in International Perspective* (London: Routledge), pp. 191–204.

Das, Veena (2007), *Life and Words: Violence and the Descent into the Ordinary* (Berkeley,CA: California University Press).

Datkhayev, Yu (1995), *The Bukharan Jews: A Short Chronicle*, 2nd edition (New York: Autograph).

Dayton, Bruce W. and Kriesberg, Louis (2009), 'Introduction', in B. Dayton and L. Kriesberg (eds), *Conflict Transformation and Peacebuilding: Moving from Violence to Sustainable Peace* (London: Routledge), pp. 1–12.

Deibert, Ronald J. and Rohozinski, Rafal (2010), 'Risking security: policies and paradoxes of cyberspace security', *International Political Sociology* 4/1, pp. 15–32.

Delaney, David (2005), *Territory: A Short Introduction* (Oxford: Wiley).

de la Pradelle, Paul G. (1928), *La Frontière: Étude De Droit International* (Paris: Editions Internationales).

Derrida, Jacques (2001), *On Cosmopolitanism and Forgiveness* (London: Routledge).

Dhondup, Tashi (1998), 'Independence can only be achieved with real sacrifices: an interview with Tsetan Norbu', *Tibetan Review* 33.

DIIR (2010), *Middle Way Policy and All Recent Related Documents* (Dharamsala: CTA).

Dillon, M. and Reid, J. (2009), *The Liberal Way of War: Killing to Make Life Live* (London: Routledge).

Dinar, Shlomi (ed.) (2011), *Beyond Resource Wars: Scarcity, Environmental Degradation, and International Cooperation* (Cambridge, MA: MIT Press).

Diop, Bineta (2002), 'Engendering the peace process in Africa: women at the negotiating table', *Refugee Survey Quarterly* 21 (special issue), pp. 142–54.

Diop, Cheikh Anta (1987), *Precolonial Black Africa: A Comparative Study of the Political and Social Systems of Europe and Black Africa, from Antiquity to the Formation of Modern States* (London: Lawrence Hill Books).

——(1989), *The Cultural Unity of Black Africa: The Domains of Matriarchy & Patriarchy in Classical Antiquity* (London: Karnak House).

Dittmer, Jason (2010) *Popular Culture, Geopolitics and Identity* (Lanham, MD: Rowman and Littlefield).

Dodds, Klaus and Ingram, Alan (eds) (2009), *Spaces of Security and Insecurity: Geographies of the War on Terror* (Aldershot: Ashgate).

Doherty, Paul and Poole, Michael A. (2002), 'Religion as an indicator of ethnicity in Northern Ireland – an alternative perspective', *Irish Geography* 35/2, pp. 75–89.

Dolan, Chris (2009), *Social Torture: the Case of northern Uganda, 1986–2006* (New York: Berghahn).

Donald, James (1999), *Imagining the Modern City* (London: Athlone Press).

Donaldson, John and Williams, Alison (2008), 'Delimitation and demarcation: analysing the legacy of Stephen B. Jones' Boundary-Making', *Geopolitics* 13/4, pp. 676–701.

Dorjee, Tenzin (2010), 'Opinion: Tibetans make Gandhi proud', *Global Post*, 10 February 2010, Retrieved 22 November 2011 from: http://www.globalpost.com/dispatch/worldview/100207/tibet-passive-resistance?page=0,1

Dowler, Lorraine and Sharp, Joanne (2001), 'A feminist geopolitics?', *Space and Polity* 5/3, pp.165–76.

Duffield, Mark (2001), *Global Governance and the New Wars: The Merging of Development and Security* (London: Zed Books).

——(2007), *Development, Security and Unending War* (Cambridge: Polity).

Dunham, Mikel (2004), *Buddha's Warriors: The Story of the CIA-backed Tibetan Freedom Fighters, the Chinese Invasion, and the Ultimate Fall of Tibet'* (Los Angeles: J.P. Tarcher).

Durán, Mauricio García (2006), *Movimiento Por La Paz En Colombia, 1978–2003* (Bogotá: Colombia, Centro de Investigacion y Educacion Popular, Cinep).

—— (2009), 'Colombia – nonviolent movement for peace and international solidarity', in H. Clark (ed.), *People Power: Unarmed Resistance and Global Solidarity* (London: Pluto Press), pp. 64–75.

Dymshits, Valery (No date), 'The eastern Jewish communities of the former USSR', in Valery Dymshits and Tatjana Emelyanenko, *Facing West: Oriental Jews of Central Asia and the Caucasus* (Zwolle: Waanders Publishers), pp. 7–31.

Edney, Matthew (1997), *Mapping an Empire: The Geographical Construction of British India 1765–1843* (Chicago, IL and London: University of Chicago Press).

Elazar, Daniel (1989), *People and Polity: The Organizational Dynamics of World Jewry* (Detroit: Wayne University Press).

El-Bushra, Judy and Sahl, M. G. Ibrahim (2005), 'Cycles of violence: gender relations and armed conflict', ACORD.

Elden, S. (2009), *Terror and Territory: The Spatial Extent of Sovereignty* (Minneapolis, MI: University of Minnesota Press).

Engineer, Ashgar Ali (1995), *Lifting the Veil: Communal Violence and Communal Harmony in Contemporary India* (Bombay, Hyderabad: Sangam Books).

Enloe, Cynthia (2000), *Maneuvers: The International Politics of Militarizing Women's Lives* (Berkeley, CA: University of California Press).

—— (2002), 'Demilitarization – or more of the same? Feminist questions to ask in the postwar moment', in C. Cockburn and D. Zarkov (eds), *The Post-war Moment: Militaries, Masculinities and International Peacekeeping* (London: Lawrence and Wishart), pp. 22–32.

Eriksen, Stein S. (2009), 'The liberal peace is neither: peacebuilding, statebuilding and the reproduction of conflict in the Democratic Republic of Congo', *International Peacekeeping* 16/5, pp. 652–66.

Eriksson-Baaz, Maria and Stern, Maria (2010), *The Complexity of Violence – A Critical Analysis of Sexual Violence in the DRC* (Uppsala: North Africa Institute).

Faist, Thomas (2000), 'Transnationalization in international migration: implications for the study of citizenship and culture', *Ethnic and Racial Studies* 23/2, pp. 189–222.

Falah, Ghazi-Walid (2005), 'The geopolitics of "enclavisation" and the demise of a two-state solution to the Israeli–Palestinian conflict, *Third World Quarterly* 26/8, pp. 1341–72.

Fall, Juliet (2010), 'Artificial states? On the enduring geographical myth of natural borders', *Political Geography* 29, pp. 140–7.

Ferguson, James (1990), *The Anti-politics Machine: 'Development,' Depoliticization and Bureaucratic Power in Lesotho* (Cambridge: Cambridge University Press).

Ferguson, Niall (2006), *The War of the World: Twentieth Century Conflict and the Descent of the West* (New York: Penguin).

Fisk, Robert (2006), *The Great War for Civilisation: The Conquest of the Middle East* (London: Harper Perennial).

Flint, Colin R. (ed.) (2005), *The Geography of War and Peace: From Death Camps to Diplomats* (Oxford: Oxford University Press).

Flint, Colin, Diehl, Paul, Scheffran, Juergen, Vasquez, John and Chi, Sang-hyun (2009), 'Conceptualising conflictspace: toward a geography of relational power and embeddedness in the analysis of interstate conflict', *Annals of the Association of American Geographers* 99/5, pp. 827–35.

Flint, Colin and Kirsch, Scott (2011), 'Conclusion', in S. Kirsch and C. Flint (eds), *Reconstructing Conflict: Integrating War and Post-War Geographies* (Farnham: Ashgate).

Fluri, Jennifer (2009), '"Foreign passports only": geographies of (post)conflict work in Kabul, Afghanistan', *Annals of the Association of American Geographers* 99/5, pp. 986–94.

—— (2011), 'Bodies, bombs and barricades: geographies of conflict and civilian (in)security', *Transactions of the Institute of British Geographers* 36/2 (April), pp. 280–96.

Forbes.com (undated), *Lev Leviev*. Retrieved January 2012 from www.forbes.com

Fortier, Anne-Marie (2010), 'Proximity by design? Affective citizenship and the management of unease', *Citizenship Studies* 14/1, pp. 17–30.

Foucault, Michel (2003), *'Society Must Be Defended': Lectures at the Collège De France, 1975–1976* (New York: Picador).

Fry, Douglas (1994), 'Maintaining society tranquility: internal and external loci of aggression control', in L. E. Sponsel and T. Gregor (eds), *The Anthropology of Peace and Nonviolence* (Bouldler, CO: Lynne Rienner Publishers), pp 133–54.

Frykman, Maja P. (1997), 'Identities in war: embodiments of violence and places of belonging', *Ethnologia Europaea* 27, pp. 153–62.

Gallagher, Tony (2004), 'After the war comes peace?An examination of the impact of the Northern Ireland conflict on young people', *Journal of Social Issues* 60/3, pp. 629–42.

Gallaher, Carol and Shirlow, Peter (2006), 'The geography of loyalist paramilitary feuding in Belfast', *Space and Polity* 10/2, pp. 149–69.

Galtung, Johan (1964), 'What is peace research?', *Journal of Peace Research* 1/1, pp. 1–4.

—— (1969), 'Violence, peace, and peace research', *Journal of Peace Research* 6/3, pp. 167–91.

—— (1971), 'A structural theory of imperialism', *Journal of Peace Research* 8/2, pp. 81–117.

—— (1975a), *Peace, War and Defence: Essays in Peace Research,* vol.2 (Copenhagen: Christian Ejlers)

—— (1975b), 'Three approaches to peace: peacekeeping, peacemaking and peace-building', in Christian Ejlers (ed.), *Peace, War and Defense: Essays in Peace Research* (Copenhagen: Christian Ejlers), vol. 2, pp. 282–304.

—— (1989), 'Principles of nonviolent action: the Great Chain of Nonviolence hypothesis', in J. Galtung, *Nonviolence and Israel/Palestine* (Honolulu, HI: University of Hawaii Institute for Peace), pp. 13–34.

—— (1996), *Peace by Peaceful Means: Peace, Conflict, Development and Civilization* (Oslo and London: International Peace Research Institute Oslo and Sage Publications).

Garfield, Jay L. (2002), *Empty Words: Buddhist Philosophy and Cross-cultural Interpretation* (Oxford: Oxford University Press).

Gibbing, Sheri Lynn (2011), 'No angry women at the United Nations: political dreams and the cultural politics of United Nations Security Council Resolution 1325', *International Feminist Journal of Politics* 13/4, pp. 522–38.

Gibson-Graham, J. K. (2008), 'Diverse economies: performative practices for "other worlds"', *Progress in Human Geography* 32/5, pp. 613–32.

Giddens, Anthony (1984), *The Constitution of Society: Outline of the Theory of Structuration* (Cambridge: Cambridge University Press).

Gidwitz, Betsy (1999), *Post-Soviet Jewry: The Critical Issues* (Jerusalem: Jerusalem Centre for Public Affairs).

Gilady, Lilach and Russett, Bruce (2002), 'Peacemaking and conflict resolution', in W. Carlsnaes, T. Risse and B. A. Simmons (eds), *Handbook of International Relations* (London: Sage).

Giles. (2004), *Sites of Violence: Gender and Conflict Zones* (Berkeley: University of California Press).

Gill, Nicholas (2009), 'Governmental mobility: the power effects of the movement of detained asylum seekers around Britain's detention estate', *Political Geography* 28/3, pp. 186–96.

Gilmour, Ann, (2011), 'Bolivia to take Chile to court over sea access', *IHS Global Insight Ltd*, 24 March 2011.

Giordano, Benito (2000), 'Italian regionalism or "Padanian" nationalism – the political project of the Lega Nord in Italian politics', *Political Geography* 19/4, pp. 445–71.

Gitelman, Zvi (1998, 2001), *A Century of Ambivalence: The Jews of Russia and the Soviet Union, 1881 to the Present,* 2nd edition (Bloomington, IN: Indiana University Press).

Golden, Peter (2011), *Central Asia in World History* (Oxford: Oxford University Press).

Goleman, Daniel (2006), *Emotional Intelligence* (New York: Random House Digital).

González, Fernán, Bolívar, Ingrid Johanna, and Vázquez, Teófilo (2003), *Violencia Política En Colombia: De La Nación Fragmentada a La Construcción Del Estado* (Bogotá, Colombia: CINEP, Centro de Investigación y Educación Popular).

Government of Uganda (1995), *Constitution of the Republic of Uganda*, Article 20/1.

Graham, Brian (1994), 'No place of the mind: contested Protestant representations of Ulster', *Ecumene* 1/3, pp. 257–81.

—— (2004), 'The past in the present: the shaping of identity in Loyalist Ulster', *Terrorism and Political Violence* 16/3, pp. 483–500.

Graham, Brian and Nash, Catherine (2006), 'A shared future: territoriality, pluralism and public policy in Northern Ireland', *Political Geography* 25/3, pp. 253–78.

Graham, Brian and Shirlow, Peter (2002), 'The Battle of the Somme in Ulster memory and identity', *Political Geography* 21/7, pp. 881–904.

Graham, Stephen (2010), *Cities Under Siege: The New Military Urbanism* (London: Verso).

Gramsci, Antonio (1971), *Prison Notebooks* (Bodmin and Kings Lynn: Lawrence and Wishart).

Grandin, Greg (2007), *Empire's Workshop: Latin America, the United States, and the Rise of the New Imperialism* (New York: Holt Paperbacks).

Green, Leah (2010), 'A short history of the compassionate listening project'. Retrieved 31 March 2011 from http://www.compassionatelistening.org/about/history

Gregory, Derek (1994), *Geographical Imaginations* (Oxford: Blackwell).

—— (2004), *The Colonial Present: Afghanistan, Palestine, Iraq* (Oxford: Blackwell).

—— (2006), 'The Black Flag: Guantanamo Bay and the space of exception', *Geografiska Annaler B* 88(4), pp. 405–27.

—— (2010), 'War and peace', *Transactions of the Institute of British Geographers* 35, pp. 154–86.

Gregory, D. and Pred, A. (eds) (2007), *Violent Geographies: Fear, Terror, and Political Violence* (New York: Routledge).

Grundy-Warr, Carl (2011), 'Commentary: pacific geographies and the politics of Buddhist peace activism', *Political Geography* 30/4, pp. 190–2.

Gupta, Smita (2006), 'The Benarasi weave: separated by religion but united by the spirit of Kashi this duo holds the peace in the holy town', *Outlook*, 27 March 2006.

Gutiérrez, Gustavo (1988 ([1973]), *A Theology of Liberation: History, Politics and Salvation* (London: SCM Press).

Hage, Ghassen (1998), *White Nation: Fantasies of White Supremacy in a Multicultural Society* (Annandale: Pluto Press).

Haldrup, Michael, Koefoed, Lasse and Simonsen, Kirsten (2006), 'Practical orientalism – bodies, everyday life and the construction of otherness', *Geografiska Annaler* 88B/2, pp. 173–84.

Halle, Silja (ed.) (2009), *From Conflict to Peacebuilding: The Role of Natural Resources and Environment* (Nairobi: United Nations Environment Programme).

Hannah, Matthew (2006), 'Torture and the ticking Bomb: the war on terrorism as a geographical imagination of power/knowledge', *Annals of the Association of American Geographers* 96/3, pp. 622–40.

Hansen, Emmanuel (ed.) (1987), *Africa: Perspectives on Peace and Development* (London: United Nations University and Zed Books).

Hansen, Thomas Blom (1999), *The Saffron Wave: Democracy and Hindu Nationalism in Modern India* (Princeton, NJ: Princeton University Press).

—— (2001), *Wages of Violence: Naming and Identity in Postcolonial Bombay* (Princeton, NJ and Oxford: Princeton University Press).

Harari, Nicole and Roseman, Jesse (2008), *Environmental Peacebuilding Theory and Practice: A Case Study of the Good Water Neighbors Project and In Depth Analysis of the Wadi Fukin/Tzur Hadassah Communities* (Amman, Bethlehem and Tel Aviv: EcoPeace/Friends of the Earth Middle East).

Haraway, Donna (1992), 'The promises of monsters', in L. Grossberg, C. Nelson and P. Treichler (eds), *Cultural Studies* (London: Routledge), pp. 295–337.

Harbom, Lotta, Högbladh, Stina and Wallensteen, Peter (2006), 'Armed conflict and peace agreements', *Journal of Peace Research* 43/5, pp. 617–31.

Harris, Nigel (2002), *Thinking the Unthinkable: The Immigration Myth Exposed*. (London: I.B.Tauris).

Harvey, David (2003), *The New Imperialism* (Oxford: Oxford University Press).

—— (2006), 'Space as a keyword', in D. Gregory and N. Castree (eds), *David Harvey: A Critical Reader* (Oxford: Wiley-Blackwell, 2006), pp. 270–98.

Hasan, Mushurul (2001), *Legacy of a Divided Nation: India's Muslims since Independence* (New Delhi: Oxford University Press).

Hayeem, Abe (2009), 'Boycott this Israeli settlement builder', *Guardian* 'Comment is free', 28 April 2009, Retrieved 22 October 2011 from http://www.guardian.co.uk/commentisfree/2009/apr/28/israel-boycott-leviev

Hayter, Teresa (2000), *Open Borders: The Case Against Immigration Controls* (London: Pluto).

Heathershaw, John (2008), 'Seeing like the international community: how peacebuilding failed (and survived) in Tajikistan', *Journal of Intervention and Statebuilding* 2/3, pp. 329–351.

—— (2009), 'Tajikistan's virtual politics of peace', *Europe-Asia Studies* 61/7, pp. 1315–36.

Heitmeyer, Carolyn (2009), '"There is peace here": managing communal relations in a town in central Gujarat', *Journal of South Asian Development* 4/1, pp. 103–20.

Henderson, Victoria L. (2009), 'Citizenship in the line of fire: protective accompaniment, proxy citizenship, and pathways for transnational solidarity in Guatemala', *Annals of the Association of American Geographers* 99/5, pp. 969–76.

Henrikson, Alan K. (2005), 'The geography of diplomacy', in C. Flint (ed.), *The Geography of War and Peace: From Death Camps to Diplomats* (Oxford: Oxford University Press).

Herb, Guntram H. (2005), 'The geography of peace movements', in C. Flint (ed.), *The Geography of War and Peace: From Death Camps to Diplomats* (Oxford: Oxford University Press), pp. 347–68.

Herbst, Jeffrey (2004), *States and Power in Africa* (Princeton, NJ: Princeton University Press).

Hertslett, Edward (1891), *Map of Europe by Treaty* (London: HM Stationery Office).

Hess, Julia M. (2009), *Immigrant Ambassadors: Citizenship and Belonging in the Tibetan Diaspora* (Stanford: Stanford University Press).

Hewitt, Kenneth (1983), 'Place annihilation: area bombing and the fate of urban places', *Annals of the Association of American Geographers* 73/2, pp. 257–84.

Higate, Paul and Henry, Marsha (2009), *Insecure Spaces: Peacekeeping in Liberia, Kosovo and Haiti* (London: Zed Books).

High Peaks Pure Earth (2011), 'White Wednesday: the "Lhakar pledge"', *High Peaks Pure Earth*, 4 July 2011. Retrieved 22 November 2011 from http://highpeakspureearth.com/2011/white-wednesday-the-lhakar-pledge/

Hill Collins, Patricia (1999), *Black Feminist Thought: Knowledge, Consciousness and the Politics of Empowerment* (New York and London: Routledge).

Hills, E. H. (1906), 'The geography of international frontiers', *Geographical Journal* 28/2.

Hochschild, Adam (1998), *King Leopold's Ghost: A Story of Greed, Terror and Heroism in Colonial Africa* (London: Macmillan).

Holdich, Thomas (1916), *Political Frontiers and Boundary Making* (London: Macmillan and Co.).

Holsti, Kalevi (1991), *Peace and War: Armed Conflicts and International Order, 1648–1989* (Cambridge: Cambridge University Press).

Home Office (2011), *Control of Immigration: Quarterly Statistical Summary, United Kingdom, Quarter 1 2011*. Retrieved 9 February 2012 from http://www.homeoffice.gov.uk/publications/science-research-statistics/research-statistics/immigration-asylum-research/control-immigration-q1-2011-t/?view=Standard&pubID=891312

Horrabin, Frank (1943), *An Outline of Political Geography* (Tillicoultry: NCLC)

Huber, Toni (1997), 'Green Tibetans: a brief social history', in F. J. Korom (ed.), *Tibetan Culture in the Diaspora. Papers presented at a panel of the 7th International Seminar of Tibetan Studies, Fraz, 1995* (Vienna: Verlag der Österreichischen Akademie der Wissenschaften), pp. 103–19.

Hudson, Heidi (2009), 'Peacebuilding through a gender lens and challenges of implementation in Rwanda and Cote d'Ivoire', *Security Studies* 18/2, pp. 287–318.

Hudson, Manley (1957), 'The succession of the International Court of Justice to the Permanent Court of International Justice', *American Journal of International Law* 53/3, pp. 569–73.

Hughes, Joanne and Donnelly, Caitlin (2004), 'Attitudes to community relations in Northern Ireland: signs of optimism in the post cease-fire period?', *Terrorism and Political Violence* 16/3, pp. 567–92.

Human Security Report Project (2011), *Human Security Report 2009/2010: The Causes of Peace and the Shrinking Costs of War* (Oxford: Oxford University Press).

Hylton, Forrest (2006), *Evil Hour in Colombia* (London and New York: Verso).

Hyndman, Jennifer (2003), 'Beyond either/or: a feminist analysis of September 11th', *ACME*, pp. 1–13.

Inayatullah, Naeem and Blaney, D. L. (1995), 'Realizing sovereignty', *Review of International Studies* 21, pp. 3–20.

Informe Nacional De Desarrollo Humano (2011), *Colombia Rural, Razones Por La Esperanza* (UNDP Colombia, 2011), http://pnudcolombia.org/indh2011/. Retrieved 20 December 2011

Ingelaere, Bert (2009), '"Does the truth pass across the fire without burning?" Locating the short circuit in Rwanda's Gacaca courts', *Journal of Modern African Studies* 47/4, pp. 507–28.

Ingram, Alan (2008), 'Domopolitics and disease: HIV/AIDS, immigration, and asylum in the UK', *Environment and Planning D: Society and Space* 26/5, pp. 875–94.

Ingram, Alan and Dodds, Klaus (eds) (2009), *Spaces of Security and Insecurity* (Aldershot: Ashgate).

Institute of Development Studies (2005), Special Edition: 'Developing Rights' *IDS Bulletin* 36/1.

Internal Displacement Monitoring Centre (2008), *Focus Shifts to Securing Durable Solutions for IDPs: A Profile of the Internal Displacement Situation* (Geneva: Internal Displacement Monitoring Centre).

International Boundaries Research Unit (2001), 'Concern mounts over Ethiopia dam project while border tensions with Kenya are addressed', *Boundary News*, 16 August 2011.

International Crisis Group (2004), 'Maintaining momentum in the Congo: the Ituri problem', *Africa Report* 84 (Nairobi and Brussels: ICG).

Inwood, Joshua and Tyner, James A. (2011), 'Geography's pro-peace agenda: an unfinished project', *ACME* 10/3, pp. 442–57.

Isacson, Adam, and Rojas Rodriguez, Jorge (2009), 'Origins, evolution and lessons of the Colombian peace movement', in V. Bouvier (ed.), *Colombia: Building Peace in a Time of War* (Washington, DC: United States Institute of Peace), pp. 19–38.

Jacquin-Berdal, Dominique and Plaut, Martin (eds) (2004), *Unfinished Business: Eritrea and Ethiopia at War* (Trenton, NJ: Red Sea Press).

Jan, Yiin-Hua (1965), 'Buddhist self-immolation in medieval China', *History of Religions* 4, pp. 243–68.

Jarman, Neil (1997), *Material Conflicts: Parades and Visual Displays in Northern Ireland* (Oxford: Berg).

Jeffrey, Alex (2007), 'The politics of "democratization": lessons from Bosnia and Iraq', *Review of International Political Economy* 14/3, pp. 444–66.

Jerryson, Michael and Juergensmeyer, Mark (eds) (2010), *Buddhist Warfare* (Oxford: Oxford University Press).

Jones, Reece (2011), 'Border security: 9/11 and the enclosure of civilisation', *Geographical Journal* 177/3, pp. 213–17.

Jones, Stephen B. (1959), 'Boundary concepts in the setting of place and time', *Annals of the Association of American Geographers* 49/3–1, pp. 241–55.

—— (1945), *Boundary-Making: A Handbook for Statesmen, Treaty Editors and Boundary Commissioners* (Washington, DC: Carnegie Endowment for International Peace).

Justice for Colombia (no date), 'About Colombia', www.justiceforcolombia.org/about-colombia. Retrieved 21 October 2010.

Jutila, Matti, Pehkonen, Samu and Väyrynen, Tarja (2008), 'Resuscitating a discipline: an agenda for critical peace research', *Millennium: Journal of International Studies,* 36/3, pp. 623–40.

Kaikobad, Kaiyan (2007), *Interpretation and Revision of International Boundary Decisions* (Cambridge: Cambridge University Press).

Kakar, Sudhir (1996), *The Colors of Violence: Cultural Identities, Religion and Conflict* (Chicago, IL: Chicago University Press).

Kaldor, Mary (2006), *New and Old Wars: Organized Violence in a Global Era* (Cambridge: Polity).

——— (2007), *Human Security: Reflections on Globalization and Intervention* (Cambridge: Polity).

Katz, Cindi (2004), *Growing up Global: Economic Restructuring and Children's Everyday Lives* (Minneapolis, MI: Universtiy of Minnesota Press).

Kearns, Gerry (2009), *Geopolitics and Empire: The Legacy of Halford Mackinder* (Oxford: Oxford University Press).

——— (2011), 'Progressive historiography', in "Reading Gerry Kearns' *Geopolitics and Empire: The Legacy of Halford Mackinder*' *Political Geography*" 30/1, pp. 55–7.

Keenan, Jeremy (2004), 'Terror in the Sahara: the implications of US imperialism for north and west Africa', *Review of African Political Economy* 31/101, pp. 475–96.

Kelman, Herbert C. (2010), 'Interactive problem solving: changing political culture in the pursuit of conflict resolution', *Peace and Conflict: Journal of Peace Psychology* 16/4, pp. 389–413.

Khan, Yasmin (2007), *The Great Partition: The Making of India and Pakistan* (New Haven, CT: Yale University Press).

King, Charles and Melvin, Neil (eds) (1998), *Nations Abroad: Diaspora Politics and International Relations in the Former Soviet Union* (Oxford: Westview).

King, Martin Luther (Jr) (1991), *A Testament of Hope: The Essential Writings and Speeches of Martin Luther King, Jr* (San Francisco, CA: Harper).

Kirsch, Scott and Flint, Colin (eds) (2011), *Reconstructing Conflict: Integrating War and Post-War Geographies* (Farnham: Ashgate).

Klenke, Kerstin (2001), Ethnomusicological Research Seminar, Goldsmiths College, London.

Kliot, Nurit and Waterman, Stanley (eds) (1991), *The Political Geography of Conflict and Peace* (London: Belhaven Press).

Knaus, John K. (2000), *Orphans of the Cold War: America and the Tibetan Struggle for Survival* (New York: Public Affairs).

Knight, W. Andy (2003), 'Evaluating recent trends in peacebuilding research', *International Relations of the Asia-Pacific* 3, pp. 241–64.

Kobayashi, Audrey (2009), 'Geographies of peace and armed conflict: introduction', *Annals of the Association of American Geographers* 99/5, pp. 819–26.

Kofman, Eleonore (1984), 'Information and nuclear issues: the role of the academic', *Area* 16/2, p. 166.

Kolås, Ashild (1996), 'Tibetan nationalism: the politics of religion', *Journal of Peace Research* 33/1, pp. 51–66.

Kong, Lily (1999), 'Globalisation and Singaporean transmigration: re-imagining and negotiating', *Political Geography* 18/5, pp. 563–89.

Koopman, Sara (2011a), 'Alter-geopolitics: other securities are happening', *Geoforum* 42/3, pp. 274–84.

——— (2011b), 'Let's take peace to pieces', *Political Geography*, 30/4, pp. 193–4.

——— (2012), Making Space for Peace: International Protective Accompaniment in Colombia, 2007–2009, unpublished dissertation (Vancouver, BC: University of British Columbia).

—— (no date), 'Decolonizing solidarity', decolonizingsolidarity.blogspot.ca. Retrieved 9 April 2012.

Korf, Benedikt (2011), 'Resources, violence and the telluric geographies of small wars', *Progress in Human Geography* 35/6, pp. 733–56.

Kristof, Ladis (1959), 'The nature of frontiers and boundaries', *Annals of the Association of American Geographers* 49/3–1, pp. 269–82.

Kropotkin, Peter (1885), 'What geography ought to be', *The Nineteenth Century* 18, pp. 1940–56.

Kumar Singh, Binay (2006), 'Blasts kill 16 in Varanasi, red alert sounded across India', *Times of India,* 8 March 2006. Retrieved 27 October 2012 from http:// timesofindia.indiatimes.com/india/Blasts-kill-16-in-Varanasi-red-alert-sounded-across-India/articleshow/1442293.cms

Kundnani, Arun (2007), *The End of Tolerance: Racism in 21ˢᵗ Century Britain* (London: Pluto Press).

Kurlansky, Mark (2007), *Non-violence: The History of a Dangerous Idea* (London: Vintage).

Kurtz, Lester (ed.) (2008), *Encyclopaedia of Violence, Peace and Conflict,* vols 1–3, 2nd edition (London: Academic Press).

Kuus, Merje (2008), 'Professionals of geopolitics: agency in international politics', *Geography Compass* 2/6, pp. 2062–79.

Lacoste, Yves (1976), *La géographie, ça sert d'abord, à faire la guerre* (Paris: Maspéro).

—— (1977), 'The geography of warfare. An illustration of geographical warfare: Bombing of the dikes on the Red River, North Vietnam', in R. Peet (ed.), *Radical Geography* (London: Methuen).

Lafitte, Gabriel (1999), 'Tibetan futures: imagining collective destinies', *Futures* 31/2, pp. 155–69.

Le Billion, Philippe (2008), 'Corrupting peace? Peacebuilding and post-conflict corruption', *International Peacekeeping* 15/3, pp. 344–61.

Le Billon, Philippe, and Cervantes, Alejandro (2009), 'Oil prices, scarcity, and geographies of war', *Annals of the Association of American Geographers* 99/5, pp. 836–44.

Lederach, John P. (1995), *Preparing for Peace: Conflict Transformation Across Cultures* (New York: Syracuse University Press).

—— (1997), *Building Peace: Sustainable Reconciliation in Divided Societies* (Washington: United States Institute of Peace Press).

Lefebvre, Henri (1991), *The Production of Space*, trans. by D. Nicholson-Smith (Oxford: Blackwell).

LeGrand, Catherine (2003), 'The Colombian crisis in historical perspective', *Canadian Journal of Latin American and Caribbean Studies* 28/5, pp. 165–209.

—— (2009), 'The roots and evolution of conflict in Colombia', presented at the conference Colombia, the Conflicts and Beyond, 19 April, Simon Fraser University, Vancouver, Canada.

Lemarchand, Rene (2009), *The Dynamics of Violence in Central Africa* (Philadelphia: University of Pennsylvania Press).

Ling, L. H. M. (2000), 'Global passions withing global interests: race, gender and culture within our postcolonial order', in R. Palan (ed.), *Global Political Economy* (London: Routledge), pp. 242–55.

Lippert, Randy (2005), *Sanctuary, Sovereignty and Sacrifice: Canadian Sanctuary Incidents, Power and Law* (Vancouver, BC: University of British Columbia Press).

—— (2006), 'Sanctuary discourse, powers and legal narratives', *Studies in Law, Politics and Society* 38, pp. 71–104.

Lorde, Audre (2007), *Sister Outsider: Essays and Speeches* (Darlinghurst, New South Wales: Crossing Press).

Loyd, Jenna M. (2009), '"A microscopic insurgent": militarization, health and critical geographies of violence', *Annals of the Association of American Geographers* 99/5, pp. 863–73.

—— (2011), '"Peace is our only shelter": questioning domesticities of militarization and white privilege', *Antipode* 43/3 (June), pp. 845–73.

McAdams, Dan P., Josselson, Ruthellen and Lieblich, Amia (eds) (2006), *Identity and Story: Creating Self in Narrative* (Washington, DC: American Psychological Association).

McConnell, Fiona (2009), 'Democracy-in-exile: the "uniqueness" and limitations of exile Tibetan democracy', *Sociological Bulletin* 58/1, pp. 115–44.

—— (2013), 'The geopolitics of Buddhist reincarnation: contested futures of Tibetan leadership', *Area* 45/2, pp. 162–69.

MacDonald, David (2010), 'Ubuntu bashing: the marketisation of "African values" in South Africa', *Review of African Political Economy* 37/124, pp. 139–52.

McDonald, Henry and Cusack, Jim (2004), *UDA: Inside the Heart of Loyalist Terror* (London and Dublin: Penguin).

McEwan, Cheryl (2004), 'Transnationalism', in J. Duncan, N. Johnson and R. Schein (eds), *A Companion to Cultural Geography* (Oxford: Blackwell), pp. 499–512.

McEwen, Alec (1971), *International Boundaries of East Africa* (Oxford: Clarendon Press).

McGranahan, Carole (2010), *Arrested Histories: Tibet, the CIA and Memories of a Forgotten War* (Durham, NC: Duke University Press).

McMahon, A. Henry (1897), 'The southern borderlands of Afghanistan', *Geographical Journal* 9/4, pp. 393–415.

McVeigh, Robbie (2006), *The Next Stephen Lawrence? Racist Violence and Criminal Justice in Northern Ireland* (Belfast: Northern Ireland Council for Ethnic Minorities).

Magnusson, Jan (2002), 'A myth of Tibet: reverse orientalism and soft power', in P. C. Klieger, (ed.), *Tibet, Self, and the Tibetan Diaspora: Voices of Difference* (Leiden: Brill), pp. 195–212.

Mahmood, S. (2005), *Politics of Piety* (Princeton, NJ: Princeton University Press).

Mahony, Liam, and Eguren, Enrique (1997), *Unarmed Bodyguards: International Accompaniment for the Protection of Human Rights* (West Hartford, CN: Kumarian Press).

Mamadouh, Virginie (2005), 'Geography and war, geographers and peace', in C. Flint (ed.), *The Geography of War and Peace: From Death Camps to Diplomats* (Oxford: Oxford University Press), pp. 26–60.

Mamdani, M. (1995), 'Democratic theory and democratic struggles', in E. Chole and J. Ibrahim (eds), *Democratisation Processes in Africa: Problems and Prospects* (Dakar: Codesria Book Series).

Manley, Rebecca (2009), *To the Tashkent Station: Evacuation and Survival in the Soviet Union at War* (London: Cornell University Press).

Marston, Sallie A., Jones III, John Paul and Woodward, Keith (2005), 'Human geography without scale', *Transactions of the Institute of British Geographers* 30/4, pp. 416–32.

Martin, Brian and Varney, Wendy (2003), 'Nonviolence and Communication', *Journal of Peace Research* 40/2, pp. 213–32.

Massey, Doreen (1994), *Space, Place and Gender* (Cambridge: Polity).

Mearsheimer, John J. (2001), *The Tragedy of Great Power Politics* (New York: Norton).

Megoran, Nick (2003), 'Review essay: International boundaries and geopolitics: two different lectures, two different worlds?', *Political Geography* 22/7, pp. 789–96.

—— (2009), 'Neoclassical geopolitics', *Political Geography* 30, pp. 1–3.

—— (2010), 'Towards a geography of peace: pacific geopolitics and evangelical Christian Crusade apologies', *Transactions of the Institute of British Geographers* 35/3, pp. 382–98.

—— (2011), 'War *and* peace? An agenda for peace research and practice in geography', *Political Geography* 30/4, pp. 178–89.

—— (2012), 'Rethinking the study of international boundaries: a biography of the Kyrgyzstan-Uzbekistan boundary', *Annals of the Association of American Geographers* 102/2, pp. 464–81.

—— (2013), 'Violence and peace', in K. Dodds, M. Kuus and J. Sharp (eds), *The Ashgate Companion to Critical Geopolitics* (Farnham: Ashgate, pp. 189–207).

Mehler, Andreas (2009), 'Peace and power sharing in Africa: not so obvious a relationship', *African Affairs* 108/432, pp. 453–73.

Melvern, Linda. R. (2000), *A People Betrayed: The Role of the West in Rwanda's Genocide* (London: Zed Books).

Merrills, J.G. (1991), *International Dispute Settlement*, 2nd edition (Cambridge: Grotius Publications).

Messerschmidt, James W. (1993), *Masculinities and Crime: Critique and Reconceptualization of Theory* (Lanham, MD: Rowman and Littlefield).

Miall, Hugh (2004), 'Conflict transformation: a multi-dimensional task', in *Berghof Handbook for Conflict Transformation* (Berghof Research Centre for Constructive Conflict Management).

Miller, Byron (2000), *Geography and Social Movements: Comparing Antinuclear Activisim in the Boston Area* (Minneapolis, MI: University of Minnesota Press).

Mills, Martin (2009), 'This circle of kings: modern Tibetan visions of world peace', in P. Wynn Kirby (ed.), *Boundless Worlds: An Anthropological Approach to Movement* (Oxford: Berghan), pp. 95–114.

Minghi, Julian (1991), 'From conflict to harmony in border landscapes', in J. Minghi and D. Lumley (eds), *The Geography of Border Landscapes* (London: Routledge), pp. 15–30.

Minghi, Julian and Lumley, Dennis (1991), 'Introduction: the border landscape concept', in J. Minghi and D. Lumley (eds), *The Geography of Border Landscapes* (London: Routledge), pp. 1–14.

Mitchell, Don and Smith, Neill (1991), 'Comment: the courtesy of political geography', *Political Geography Quarterly* 10, pp. 338–41.

Mitchell, Katharyne (1997), 'Transnational discourse: bringing geography back in', *Antipode* 29/2, pp. 101–14.

Molomo, Mpho G. (2009), 'Building a culture of peace in Africa: towards a trajectory of using traditional knowledge systems', *Journal of Peacebuilding and Development* 4/3, pp. 57–69.

Morrell, Michael E. (2010), *Empathy and Democracy: Feeling, Thinking, and Deliberation* (University Park, PA: Pennsylvania State University Press).

Morrissey, John (2011), 'Liberal lawfare and biopolitics: US juridical warfare in the war on terror', *Geopolitics* 16/2, pp. 280–305.

Mountz, Alison (2004), 'Embodying the nation-state: Canada's response to human smuggling', *Political Geography* 23/323, pp. 323–45.

Muggah, Robert (2005), 'No magic bullet: a critical perspective on disarmament, demobilization and reintegration (DDR) and weapons reduction in post-conflict contexts', *Round Table* 94/379, pp. 238–52.

Mukerji, D. (2006), 'Popularity test ride: Advani's yatra has few supporters in the BJP', *Week*, 16 April 2006.

Müller, Martin (2008), 'Situating identities: enacting and studying Europe at a Russian elite university', *Millennium: Journal of International Studies* 37/1, pp. 3–25.

Murillo, Mario (2003), *Colombia and the United States: War, Unrest, and Destabilization* (New York: Seven Stories Press).

Murithi, Tim (2009), 'An African perspective on peace building: ubuntu lessons in reconciliation', *International Review of Education* 55, pp. 221–33.

Murzakulova, Asel and Schoeberlein, John (2010), 'The invention of legitimacy: struggles in Kyrgyzstan to craft an effective nation-state ideology', in S. Cummings (ed.), *Symbolism and Power in Central Asia: Politics of the Spectacular* (London: Routledge), pp. 144–63.

Naby, Eden (2005), 'The Assyrian diaspora: cultural survival in the absence of state structure', in T. Atabaki and S. Mehendale (eds), *Central Asia and the Caucasus: Transnationalism and Diaspora* (London: Routledge), pp. 214–30.

Nagar, Richa, and Lock Swarr, Amanda (2005), 'Organizing from the margins: grappling with "empowerment" in India and South Africa', in L. Nelson and J. Seager (eds), *A Companion to Feminist Geography* (Oxford: Blackwell Publishing), pp. 291–304.

Nandy, Ashis with Trivedy, Shikha, Mayaram, Shail and Yagnik, Achyut (1995), *Creating a Nationality: the Ramjanmabhumi Movement and Fear of the Self* (Delhi, Bombay, Calcutta, Madras: Oxford University Press).

Neocosmos, M. (2006), 'Can human rights culture enable emancipation? Clearing the theoretical ground for the renewal of a critical sociology', *South African Review of Sociology* 37/2, pp. 356–79.

Newman, David (2002), 'The geopolitics of peacemaking in Israel–Palestine', *Political Geography* 21/8, pp. 629–46.

—— (2005a), 'From the international to the local in the study and representation of boundaries: theoretical and methodological comments', in H. Nicol and I. Townsend-Gault (eds), *Holding the Line: Border in a Globalized World* (Vancouver, BC: University of British Colombia Press), pp. 400–13.

—— (2005b), 'Conflict at the interface: the impact of boundaries and borders on contemporary ethnonational conflict', in C. Flint (ed.), *The Geographies of War and Peace: From Death Camps to Diplomats* (Oxford: Oxford University Press), pp. 321–46.

Newman, David and Paasi Anssi (1998), 'Fences and neighbours in the postmodern world: boundary narratives in political geography', *Progress in Human Geography* 22/2, pp. 186–207.

Nicley, Erinn P. (2009), 'Book review: out of the grassroots and into a geo-political economy of post-conflict reconstruction', *Political Geography* 28/8, pp. 508–10.

Norbu, Jamyang (1997), 'Non-violence and non-action: some Gandhian truths about the Tibetan peace movement', *Tibetan Review* 32/9, pp. 151–60.

—— (2007), 'Rangzen!', *Combat Law: the Human Rights and Law Bimonthly* 6/5, September–October 2007, pp. 28–35.

Norton, William (2006), *Cultural Geography: Environments, Landscapes, Identities, Inequalities*, 2nd edition (Oxford and New York: Oxford University Press).

Nowrojee, Binaifer (2005), *Your Justice is Too Slow: Will the ICCTR Fail Rwanda's Rape Victims?* (Geneva: United Nations Research Institute for Social Development Occasional Papers).

Nye, Joseph S. (2004), *Soft Power: The Means to Success in World Politics* (New York: Public Affairs).

Office of National Statistics (2011), *Population Estimates for UK, England and Wales, Scotland and Northern Ireland, Mid-2010*. Retrieved 10 April 2012 from http://www.ons.gov.uk/ons/publications/re-reference-tables.html?edition=tcm%3A77-231847

Olita, Reuben (2009a), 'International Court to decide on Migingo', *New Vision (Kampala)/All Africa Global Media*, 20 April 2009.

—— (2009b), 'Kenyan youth block railway', *New Vision (Kampala/All Africa Global Media*, 27 April 2009.

Olonisakin, Funmi and Okech, Awino (2011), *Women and Security Governance in Africa* (Cape Town, Dakar, Nairobi and Oxford: Pambazuka Press).

O'Loughlin, John (2005), 'The political geography of conflict: civil wars in the hegemonic shadow', in C. Flint (ed.), *The Geography of War and Peace* (Oxford: Oxford University Press), pp. 85–112.

O'Loughlin, John and Raleigh, Clionadh (2008), 'Spatial analysis of civil war violence', in K. Cox, M. Low and J. Robinson (eds), *A Handbook of Political Geography* (London: Sage), pp. 493–508.

O'Loughlin, John and van der Wusten, Herman (1986), 'Geography, war and peace: notes for a contribution to a revived political geography', *Progress in Human Geography* 10/3, pp. 484–510.

Oluoch, Fred (2010), 'Burundi's "smallest" military budget highest as fraction of GDP in region', in *The East African* (Nairobi).

Osei-Hwedie, Bertha Z. and Abu-Nimer, Mohammed (2009), 'Editorial: enhancing the positive contributions of African culture', *Peacebuilding and Development* 4/3, pp. 1–5.

Oslender, Ulrich (2007), 'Violence in development: the logic of forced displacement on Colombia's Pacific coast', *Development in Practice* 17/6, pp. 752–64.

—— (2008), 'Another history of violence: the production of "geographies of terror" in Colombia's Pacific Coast Region', *Latin American Perspectives* 35/5, pp. 77–102.

Ó Tuathail, Gearóid (1996), *Critical Geopolitics* (London: Routledge).

—— (2010), 'Localizing geopolitics: disaggregating violence and return in conflict regions', *Political Geography* 29/5, pp. 256–65.

Ó Tuathail, Gearóid and Dahlman, Carl (2011), *Bosnia Remade: Ethnic Cleansing and its Reversal* (New York: Oxford University Press).

Pain, Rachel and Smith, S. (eds) (2008), *Fear: Critical Geopolitics and Everyday Life* (Aldershot: Ashgate).

Palestine–Israel Journal of Politics, Economics, and Culture (2006), 'People-to-people: what went wrong and how to fix it?' Special double-issue of journal *Palestine–Israel Journal of Politics, Economics, and Culture*, 12(4) and 13(1), no editor identified.

Pandey, Gyanendra (2001), *Remembering Partition: Violence, Nationalism and History in India* (Cambridge: Cambridge University Press).

Parel, Anthony J. (1997), *Gandhi: Hind Swaraj and Other Writings* (Cambridge: Cambridge University Press).

Paris, Roland (1997), 'Peacebuilding and the limits of liberal internationalism', *International Security* 22/2, pp. 54–89.

Peace Talks (2010), radio programme, 'Peaceful strategies for protecting human rights defenders'.

Pepper, David and Jenkins, Alan (eds), (1985), *The Geography of Peace and War* (New York: Basil Blackwell).

Phillips, Kevin (1999), *The Cousins' Wars* (New York: Basic Books).

Pickles, John (2004), *A History of Spaces: Cartographic Reason, Mapping and the Geo-coded World* (London: Routledge).

Pile, Steve (2002), 'Memory and the city', in J. Campbell and J. Harbord (eds), *Temporalities, Autobiography and Everyday Life* (Manchester: Manchester University Press), pp. 111–27.

Pinker, Steven (2011), *The Better Angels of our Nature: Why Violence has Declined* (New York: Viking).

Podhoretz, Norman (2007), *World War IV: The Long Struggle Against Islamofascism* (New York: Doubleday).

Polelle, Mark (1999), *Raising Carthographic Consciousness: The Social and Foreign Policy Visions of Geopolitics in the Twentieth Century* (Oxford: Lexington).

Poujol, Catherine (1993), 'Approaches to the history of Bukharan Jews' settlement in the Ferghana Valley, 1867–1917', *Central Asian Survey* 12/4, pp. 549–56.

Pradhan, Sharat (2006), 'Ancient Varanasi keeps its peace, proves its mettle', *Combating Communalism* 12/114.

Pratt, Nicola and Richter-Devore, Sophie (2011), 'Critically examining UNSCR 1325 on women, peace and security', *International Feminist Journal of Politics* 13/4, pp. 489–503.

Prescott, John, R. V. (1975a), *Map of Mainland Asia by Treaty* (Carlton, Victoria: Melbourne University Press).

—— (1975b), *Political Frontiers and Boundaries* (London: Allen & Unwin).

Prescott, Victor and Triggs, Gillian D. (2008), *International Frontiers and Boundaries: Law, Politics and Geography* (Leiden: Martinus Nijhoff).

Puechguirbal, Nadine (2003), 'Women and war in the Democratic Republic of Congo', *Signs: Journal of Women in Culture and Society* 28/4, pp. 1271–81.

Ramose, Mogobe B. (2002), 'The philosophy of ubuntu and ubuntu as a philosophy', in P. H. Coetzee and A. P. J. Roux (eds), *Philosophy from Africa*, 2nd edition (Cape Town: Oxford University Press).

Rasanayagam, Johan (2006), 'Healing with spirits and the formation of Muslim selfhood in post-Soviet Uzbekistan', *Journal of the Royal Anthropological Society (NS)* 12/2, pp. 377–93.

Reeves, J. S. (1921), 'Treaty of Rapallo', *American Journal of International Law* 15/2, pp. 252–5.

Reid, Bryonie (2005), 'A profound edge: performative negotiations of Belfast', *Cultural Geographies* 12/4, pp. 485–506.

Reid, Herbert and Yanarella, Ernest (1976), 'Toward a critical theory of peace research in the United States: the search for an "intelligible core"', *Journal of Peace Research* 13/4, pp. 315–41.

Réseau des Femmes pour un Développement Associatif (RFDA), Réseau des Femmes pour la Défense des Droits et la Paix (RFDDP) and International Alert (IA) (2005), *Women's Bodies as a Battleground: Sexual Violence Against Women and Girls During the War in the Democratic Republic of Congo, South Kivu (1996–2003)* (London: International Alert).

Richani, Nazih (2002), *Systems of Violence: The Political Economy of War and Peace in Colombia* (Albany, NY: State University of New York Press).

Richardson, Hugh E. (1978), 'The Sino-Tibetan Treaty inscription of AD 821/23 at Lhasa', *JRAS* 3, pp. 153–4.

Richmond, Oliver (2008), *Peace in International Relations* (Abingdon: Routledge).

Richmond, Oliver P. (2009), 'Becoming liberal, unbecoming liberalism: liberal–local hybridity via the everyday as a response to the paradoxes of liberal peacebuilding', *Journal of Intervention and Statebuilding* 3/3, pp. 324–44.

—— (2010a), 'Resistance and the post-liberal peace', *Millennium: Journal of International Studies* 38/3, p. 665–92.

—— (2010b), 'A genealogy of peace and conflict theory', in O. Richmond (ed.), *Peacebuilding: Critical Developments and Approaches* (Basingstoke: Palgrave Macmillan).

—— (2011), *A Post-Liberal Peace* (London: Routledge).

Richmond, Oliver and Mitchell, Audra (eds) (2011), *Hybrid Forms of Peace: From Everyday Agency to Post-Liberalism* (Basingstoke: Palgrave Macmillan).

Ridgley, Jennifer (2008), 'Cities of refuge: immigration enforcement, police, and the insurgent genealogies of citizenship in US sanctuary cities', *Urban Geography* 29/1, pp. 53–77.

Rifkin, Jeremy (2009), *The Empathic Civilization: the Race to Global Consciousness in a World in Crisis* (New York: J.P. Tarcher/Penguin).

Ring, Laura (2007), *Zenana: Everyday Peace in a Karachi Apartment Building* (Bloomington, IN: Indiana University Press).

Rinpoche, Samdhong (1995), 'Satyagraha: truth-insistence', *World Tibet News*. Retrieved 4 April 2007, from http://tibet.ca/en/newsroom/wtn/archive/old?y=1995&m=8&p=11_1

—— (2002), 'Speech on Hind Swaraj, DIIR, Dharamsala, 19 August 2002'. Retrieved 4 April 2007, from http://www.friendsoftibet.org/sofar/himachal/20020819-hind_swaraj-rinpoche_talk.html

—— (2003), 'Satyagraha: Speech delivered at 4th International Conference of Tibet Support Groups, Prague, 2003'. Retrieved 5 December 2010, from http://www.imar.ro/-diacon/satyagraha.html

Ripper, Velcrow (1999), *In the Company of Fear* (video).

Rose, Gillian (1999), 'Performing space', in D. Massey, J. Allen and P. Sarre (eds), *Human Geography Today* (Cambridge: Polity Press), pp. 247–59.

Ross, Amy (2011), 'Geographies of war and the putative peace', *Political Geography* 30/4, pp. 197–9.

Ross, Fiona (2003), *Bearing Witness: Women and the Truth and Reconciliation Commission in South Africa* (London: Pluto Press).

Roy, P. K. (2006), 'Terror in Temple Town', *Organiser*, 19 March 2006. Retrieved 16 October 2012 from http://organiser.org/archives/historic/dynamic/modulescf3e.html?name=Content&pa=showpage&pid=122&page=2

Ryan, Stephen (2007), *The Transformation of Violent Intercommunal Conflict* (Aldershot: Ashgate).

Sachar, Rajinder (2006), *Sachar Committee Report on Social, Economic and Educational Status of the Muslim Community of India* (New Delhi).

Sahlins, Peter (1990), 'Natural frontiers revisited: France's boundaries since the seventeenth century', *American Historical Review* 95/5, pp. 1423–51.

Sales, Rosemary (2002), 'The deserving and the undeserving? Refugees, asylum seekers and welfare in Britain', *Critical Social Policy* 22/3, pp. 456–78.

Sameh, Catherine (2011), 'Discourses of equality, rights and Islam in the One Million Signatures Campaign in Iran', in D. Collins, S. Falcon, S. Lodhia and M. Talcott (eds), *New Directions in Feminism and Human Rights* (London: Routledge), pp. 152–71.

Samuel, Geoffrey (1982), 'Tibet as a stateless society and some Islamic parallels', *Journal of Asian Studies* 41/2, pp. 215–29.

—— (1993), *Civilized Shamans: Buddhism in Tibetan Societies* (Washington DC: Smithsonian Institute Press).

Sangay, Lobsang (2011), Inaugural speech of Kalon Tripa Dr. Lobsang Sangay, 8 August 2011, *Central Tibetan Administration*. Retrieved 22 November 2011 from http://tibet.net/about-cta/executive/announcements/inaugural-speech-of-kalon-tripa-dr-lobsang-sangay/

Schell, Jonathan (2003), *The Unconquerable World: Power, Nonviolence and the Will of the People* (New York: Metropolitan Books).

Scheper-Hughes, Nancy (1992), *Death without Weeping: The Violence of Everyday Life in Brazil* (Berkeley, CA: University of California Press).

Schoenfeld, Stuart (2010), 'Environment and human security in the Eastern Mediterranean: regional environmentalism in the reframing of Palestinian-Israeli-Jordanian relations', in P. H. Liotta, D. Mouat, J. Lancaster, B. Kepner and D. Smith (eds), *Achieving Environmental Security: Ecosystem Services and Human Welfare* (Amsterdam: IOS Press), pp. 113–31.

—— (2013) 'Nature knows no boundaries: notes toward a future history of regional environmentalism', in D. E. Orenstein, A. Tal and C. Miller (eds), *Between Ruin and Restoration: An Environmental History of Israel* (Pittsburgh, University of Pittsburgh Press), pp. 334–56

Schoenfeld, Stuart and Jonathan Rubin (2011), 'Contrasting regional environmentalisms in the Eastern Mediterranean: a social constructionist perspective,' *L'Espace politique* 14. Retrieved 1 August 2011, from http://espacepolitique.revues.org/index1939

Schwarz, Ronald (1994), *Circle of Protest: Political Ritual in the Tibetan Uprising* (London: Hurst).

Sengupta, Anita (2009), *Heartlands of Eurasia: The Geopolitics of Political Space* (Plymouth: Lexington).

Sennett, Richard (2003), *Respect in a World of Inequality* (London: Norton).

Shakabpa, Tsepon W. D. (1967), *Tibet: A Political History* (New Haven, CT: Yale University Press).

—— (2010), *One Hundred Thousand Moons: An Advanced Political History of Tibet*, vol.1 (Leiden: Brill).

Sharp, Joanne (2011), 'Subaltern geopolitics: Introduction', *Geoforum* 42/3, pp. 271–3.

Shaw, Charles (2011), 'Friendship under lock and key: the Soviet Central Asian border, 1918–34', *Central Asian Survey* 30/3–4, pp. 331–48.

Shaw, Malcolm (1986), *Title to Territory in Africa: International Legal Issues* (Oxford: Oxford University Press).

Shirlow, Peter, Graham, Brian, McEvoy, Kieran, O'hAdhmaill, Félim and Purvis, Dawn (2005), *Politically Motivated Former Prisoner Groups: Community Activism and Conflict Transformation* (Belfast: Community Relations Council).

Shirlow, Peter and Murtagh, Brendan (2006), *Belfast: Segregation, Violence and the City* (London: Pluto).

Shiromany, A. A. (ed.) (1998), *The Political Philosophy of HH the XIV Dalai Lama: Selected Speeches and Writings* (New Delhi: TPPRC).

Shivji, Issa (1989), *The Concept of Human Rights in Africa* (London: Codesria Book Series).

Showeb, Mohammed (1994), *Silk Handloom Industry of Varanasi: A Study of Socio-Economic Problems of Weavers* (Varanasi, Ganga: Kaveri Publishing House).

Shterenshis, Michael (2002), *Tamerlane and the Jews* (London: RoutledgeCurzon).

Siddiqui, Ataullah (1991), 'Muslims of Tibet', *Tibet Journal* 16/4, pp. 71–85.

Simić, Olivera (2010), 'Does the presence of women really matter? Towards combating male sexual violence in peacekeeping operations', *International Peacekeeping* 17/2, pp. 188–99.

Simpson, Graeme (1997), 'Reconstruction and reconciliation: emerging from transition', *Development in Practice* 7/4, pp. 475–8.

Simpson, Peter (2011), 'Tibetan activists adopt self-immolation as political tool', *Voice of America*. 25 October 2011. Retrieved 26 October 2011 from http://www.voanews.com/english/news/asia/Tibetan-Activists-Adopt-Self-Immolation-As-Political-Tool-132517228.html

Singer, P.W. (2009), *Wired for War: The Robotics Revolution and Conflict in the Twenty 21ˢᵗ Century* (New York: Penguin).

Smith, Neil (2003), *American Empire: Roosevelt's Geographer and the Prelude to Globalization* (Berkley, CA: University of California Press).

Smith, Neil and Cowen, Deborah (2011), 'Martial law on the streets of Toronto: G20 security and state violence', *Journal of Human Geography* 3/3, pp. 29–46.

Soja, Edward (1980), 'The socio-spatial dialectic', *Annals of the Association of American Geographers* 70/2, pp. 207–25.

—— (1985), 'The spatiality of social life: towards a transformative re-theorisation', in D. Gregory and J. Urry (eds), *Social Relations and Spatial Structures* (New York: St Martin's Press), pp. 90–127.

Sparke, Matthew (2006), 'A neoliberal nexus: economy, security and the biopolitics of citizenship on the border', *Political Geography* 25/2, pp. 151–80.

Sperling, Elliot (2001), '"Orientalism" and aspects of violence in the Tibetan tradition', in T. Dodin and H. Räther (eds), *Imagining Tibet: Perceptions, Projections, and Fantasies* (Somerville, MA: Wisdom), pp. 315–29.

Sponsel, Leslie E. and Gregor, Thomas (eds) (1994), *The Anthropology of Peace and Nonviolence*. (Boulder, CO: Lynne Rienner).

SPRING (2010), *Unpacking the "P" in PRDP*, Conflict and Recovery Briefing (Gulu: USAID).

Springer, Simon (2011), 'Violence sits in places? Cultural practice, neoliberal rationalism, and virulent imaginative geographies', *Political Geography* 30/2, pp. 90–8.

Spykman, Nicholas (1942), 'Frontiers, security, and international organization', *Geographical Review* 32/3, pp. 436–47.

Squire, Vicki (2009), *The Exclusionary Politics of Asylum* (Basingstoke: Palgrave Macmillan).

—— (2011), 'From community cohesion to mobile solidarities: the *City of Sanctuary* network and the *Strangers into Citizens* campaign', *Political Studies* 59/2, pp. 290–307.

Staeheli, Lynn (2008), 'Migration, civilisational thinking, and the possibility of democracy', *Geopolitics* 13/4, pp. 749–52.

Steans, Jill (1998), *Gender and International Relations: An Introduction* (New Brunswick, NJ: Rutgers University Press).

Stephenson, Carolyn (2008), 'Peace Studies', in L. Kurtz (ed.), *Encyclopedia of Violence, Peace and Democracy*, 2nd edition (London: Academic Press), pp. 1534–48.

Stoddard, Heather (1994), 'Tibetan publications and national identity', in R. Barnett (ed.), *Resistance and Reform in Tibet* (Bloomington, IN: Indiana University Press), pp. 121–56.

Stokke, Kristian (2009), 'Crafting liberal peace? International peace promotion and the contextual politics of peace in Sri Lanka', *Annals of the Association of American Geographers* 99/5, pp. 932–9.

Strauss, Anselm and Corbin, Juliet M. (1990), *Basics of Qualitative Research: Grounded Theory Procedures and Techniques* (Newbury Park: Sage).

Sultanova, Razia (2005), 'Music and identity in Central Asia: introduction', *Ethnomusicology Forum*, 14/2, pp. 131–42.

Swanton, Daniel (2010), 'Sorting bodies: race, affect and everyday multiculture in a mill town in northern England', *Environment and Planning A* 42/10, pp. 2332–50.

Tambiah, Stanley (1996), *Leveling Crowds: Ethnonationalist Conflicts and Collective Violence in South Asia* (Berkeley, CA: University of California Press).

Tate, Winifred (2007), *Counting the Dead: The Culture and Politics of Human Rights Activism in Colombia* (Berkeley, CA: University of California Press).

*The Economist* (2009), 'Looming extinction', 8 January 2009. Retrieved 11 January 2009 from http://www.economist.com/world/asia/displaystory.cfm?story_id=12906512

*The Hindu* (2012), 'Tension over installation of idol in Varanasi', *The Hindu*, 20 April 2006. Retrieved 17 October 2012 from http://www.thehindu.com/todays-paper/tp-national/tension-over-installation-of-idol-in-varanasi/article3149897.ece?css=print

*The Pioneer* (1996), 'Do and die: Prof. S. Rinpoche proposes a programme for launching Tibetan satyagraha', *The Pioneer*, 26 November 1996. Retrieved 30 March 2010 from http://w3.iac.net/-moonweb/Tibetan/News/TibetNews1.html

Thomson, Susan (2011), 'The darker side of transitional justice: the power dynamics behind Rwanda's Gacaca courts', *African Affairs* 81, pp. 373–90.

Thrift, Nigel (2000), 'It's the little things', in K. Dodds and D. Atkinson (eds), *Geopolitical Traditions: A Century of Geopolitical Thought* (London: Routledge), pp. 380–7.

—— (2005), 'But malice aforethought: cities and the natural history of hatred', *Transactions of the Institute of British Geographers* 30/2, pp. 133–50.

Tibetan Government-in-Exile (1992), *Guidelines for Future Tibet's Polity and Basic Features of its Constitution*, draft translation (Dharamsala: Central Tibetan Administration).

*Tibetan Review* (1994), 'Trouble in Dharamsala, *Hindustan Times*, New Delhi 26.4.1994', *Tibetan Review* 29/6, p. 20.

Tonkiss, Fran (2005), *Space, the City and Social Theory* (Cambridge: Polity).

Toure, Ai and Sani Isa (2010), 'Post conflict demarcation of African boundaries: the Cameroon-Nigeria experience', in J. Donaldson (ed.), *Boundary Delimitation and Demarcation: An African Union Border Programme Practical Handbook* (Addis Ababa: African Union/GIZ limited print report).

Tsundue, Tenzin (2004), 'Tibetan Swaraj', *Tibetan Review* 39/10, pp. 21.

Tuchman, Barbara (1962), *The Guns of August* (New York: Random House).

Tull, David M. and Mehler, Andreas (2005), 'The hidden cost of power-sharing: reproducing insurgent violence in Africa', *African Affairs* 104/416, pp. 375–98.

Tyler, Imogen (2006), '"Welcome to Britain": the cultural politics of asylum', *European Journal of Cultural Studies* 9/2, pp. 185–202.

—— (2010), 'Designed to fail: a biopolitics of British citizenship', *Citizenship Studies* 14/1, pp. 61–74.

van Acker, F. (2004), 'Uganda and the Lord's Resistance Army: the new order no one ordered', *African Affairs* 103/412 (July), pp. 335–57.

van Creveld, Martin (1991), *The Transformation of War* (New York: Free Press).

van der Veer, Peter (1994), *Religious Nationalism: Hindus and Muslims in India* (Berkeley, CA: University of California Press).

van der Wusten, Herman (2002), 'Viewpoint: new law in fresh courts', *Progress in Human Geography* 26/2, pp. 151–3.

van der Wusten, Herman and O'Loughlin, John (1986), 'Claiming new territory for a stable peace: how geography can contribute', *Professional Geography* 38/1, pp. 18–28.

van der Wusten, Herman and van Korstanje, H. (1991), 'Diplomatic networks and stable peace', in N. Kliot and S. Waterman (eds), *The Political Geography of Conflict and Peace* (London: Belhaven Press).

van Houtum, Henk, Kramsch, O. and Zierhofer, W. (eds), (2005), *B/ordering Space* (Aldershot: Ashgate).

Varadarajan, Siddharth (2002), *Gujarat: The Making of a Tragedy* (New Delhi: Penguin Books India).

Varshney, Ashutosh (2002), *Ethnic Conflict and Civic Life: Hindus and Muslims in India* (New Delhi: Oxford University Press).

Vasile, Elizabeth (1997), 'Re-turning home: transnational movements and the transformation of landscape and culture', *Antipode* 29/2, pp. 177–96.

Vasquez, John A. and Henehan, Marie T. (2011), *Territory, War and Peace* (London: Routledge).

Vaughan-Williams, Nick (2009), *Border Politics: The Limits of Sovereign Power* (Edinburgh: Edinburgh University Press).

Vavrynen, Tarja (2004), 'Gender and UN peace operations: the confines of modernity', *International Peacekeeping* 11/1, pp. 125–42.

Vertovec, Steven (2001), 'Transnationalism and identity', *Journal of Ethnic and Migration Studies*, 27/4, pp. 573–82.

Vervisch, Thomas (2011), 'The solidarity chain: post-conflict reconstruction and social capital building on three Burundian hillsides', *Journal of Eastern African Studies* 5/1, pp. 24–41.

Walker, Michael (2008), 'Oil and US policy toward Colombia', *Colombia Journal*, colombiajournal.org/oil-and-us-policy-toward-colombia.htm. Retrieved 17 October 2011.

Walker, Robert B. J. (2010), *After the Globe, Before the World* (London: Routledge).

Walsh, Heather (2011), 'Gold eclipses cocaine as rebels tap Colombian mining wealth', *San Francisco Chronicle*, 14 October 2011.

Walters, William (2004), 'Secure borders, safe haven, domopolitics', *Citizenship Studies* 8/3, pp. 237–60.

Waltz, Kenneth E. (1988), 'The origins of war in neorealist theory', *Journal of Interdisciplinary History* 18/4, pp. 615–28.

WangYaNan (2011), 'Kenya says to take disputed islands to Hague', *Xinhua News Agency*, 31 May 2011.

Weil, Prosper (1989), *The Law of Maritime Delimitation: Reflections* (Cambridge: Grotius).

Weizman, Eyal (2007), *Hollow Land: Israel's Architecture of Occupation* (London: Verso).

White, Ben (2009), *Israeli Aparthied: A Beginner's Guide* (London: Pluto Press).

Whitmore, Todd, (2010), 'Genocide or just another "Casualty of War"?', *Practical Matters*, http://www.practicalmattersjournal.org/issue/3/analyzing-matters/genocide -or-just-another-casualty-of-war.

Wilhelm-Solomon, Matthew (2011), Displacing AIDS: Therapeutic Transitions in Northern Uganda, DPhil thesis in Department for International Development. Oxford: University of Oxford.

Wilkinson, Steven I. (2004), *Votes and Violence: Electoral Competition and Communal Riots in India* (Cambridge: Cambridge University Press).

Williams, Philippa (2007), 'Hindu–Muslim brotherhood: exploring the dynamics of communal relations in Varanasi, north India', *Journal of South Asian Development* 2/2, pp. 153–76.

—— (2011), 'An absent presence: experiences of the 'welfare state' in an Indian Muslim mohalla', *Contemporary South Asia*, 19/3, pp. 263–80.

—— (2013), 'Reproducing everyday peace in north India: process, politics, and power', *Annals of the Association of American Geographers* 103/1, pp. 230–50.

Williams, Philippa and McConnell, Fiona (2011), 'Critical geographies of peace', *Antipode* 43/4, pp. 927–31.

Wilson, Helen F. (2011), 'Passing propinquities in the multicultural city: the everyday encounters of bus passengering', *Environment and Planning A* 43/3, pp. 634–49.

Wilson, Woodrow (1919), *The State: Elements of Historical and Practical Politics* (London: D.C. Heath).

Wood, Deni (1992), *The Power of Maps* (New York: Guilford Press).

World Health Organization (2005), *Health and Mortality Survey Among Internally Displaced Persons* (Geneva: WHO).

Yuval-Davis, Nira (1997), *Gender and Nation* (London: Sage).

Zacher, M. (2001), 'The international territorial order: boundaries, the use of force and normative change', *International Organization* 55, pp. 215–50.

Zarchin, Tomer (2009), 'International legal precedent: no private prisons in Israel', *Haaretz* 20/11/2009. Retrieved January 2012 from www.haaretz.com .

Zetter, Roger and Pearl, Martyn (1999), 'Sheltering on the margins: social housing provision and the impact of restrictionism on asylum seekers and refugees in the UK', *Policy Studies* 20/4, pp. 235–54.

Zhou, Sha (1990), 'What is it behind the Dalai Lama's "Plan"', *Beijing Review*, February 19–25, pp. 22–3.

Žižek, Slavoj (2008), *Violence: Six Sideways Reflections* (London: Verso).

Zohar, Asaf, Alleson, Ilan and Schoenfeld, Stuart (2010), 'Environmental peace-building strategies in the Middle East: the case of the Arava Institute for Environmental Studies', *Peace and Conflict Review* 5/1, pp. 1–14.

Zohar, Gill (2007), 'Bukharan Quarter landmarks saved by Lev Levayev', *Arutz Sheva* 7, 1/7/2007. Retrieved January 2012 from www.israelnationalnews.com .

## Legislation, international agreements and decisions of international courts/tribunals

*Agreement between the Republic of Cameroon and the Federal Republic of Nigeria concerning the Modalities of Withdrawal and Transfer of Authority in the Bakassi Peninsula*, 12 June 2006.

*Arbitration Agreement between the Government of the Republic of Slovenia and the Government of the Republic of Croatia*, 4 November 2009.

'Decreto 95–99, 11 June 1999' *La Gaceta: Diario Oficial de la Republica de Honduras* Num. 28.905 (1999).

Flores, Francisco, Speech to the Nation delivered by the President of the Republic of El Salvador, 10 September 2002. Forwarded to the Organization of American States (OAS), 11 September 2002. http://www.oas.org/sap/peacefund/honduras-andelsalvador/ (16 November 2011).

International Court of Justice, 'Costa Rica institutes proceedings against Nicaragua and requests to indicate provisional measures', Press Release No. 2010/38, 19 November 2010.

International Court of Justice, 'Nicaragua institutes proceedings against Costa Rica with regard to "violations of Nicaraguan sovereignty and major environmental damages to its territory"' Press Release No. 2011/40, 22 December 2011.

International Court of Justice, 'Cambodia files an Application requesting interpretation of the Judgment rendered by the Court on 15 June 1962 in the case concerning the Temple of Preah Vihear (Cambodia *v.* Thailand) and also asks for the urgent indication of provisional measures', Press Release No. 2011/14, 2 May 2011.

International Court of Justice, 'Frontier dispute (Burkina Faso/Mali) Judgment of 22 December 1986' *ICJ Reports* (1986), pp. 554–651.

International Court of Justice, 'Case concerning the Temple of Preah Vihear (Cambodia v. Thailand), judgment of 15 June 1962', *ICJ Reports* (1962).

International Court of Justice, 'Land and Maritime Boundary between Cameroon and Nigeria (Cameroon v. Nigeria with Equatorial Guinea intervening, Judgment of 10 October 2002', *ICJ Reports* (2002).

International Court of Justice, 'Frontier dispute (Burkina Faso/Mali), judgment of 22 December 1986', *ICJ Reports* (1986).

International Court of Justice, 'Land, island and maritime frontier dispute (El Salvador/Honduras: Nicaragua intervening), judgment of 11 September 1992', *General List* No. 75.

# Index